ADVANCE PRAISE FOR *INVENTING IMAGINARY WORLDS*

"Showing the great value of having dual gifts when trying to understand great creativity, Michele Root-Bernstein, an artist and a creativity scholar, opens up a whole new area of creativity study, which we may have suspected but now have a rich, detailed, and compelling case for its importance. This work will be a standard in the field for years to come." —**David Henry Feldman**, Ph.D., professor and chair, Eliot-Pearson Department of Child Development, Tufts University

"*Inventing Imaginary Worlds* captures some of the most interesting research available on the topic of creative cognition. Root-Bernstein's descriptions of polymaths and imaginary worlds are engaging, and the practical implications numerous. Root-Bernstein is, for example, quite clear about the role of play in learning, and the impact of school and computers. You will finish reading this book and understand that make believe is indeed a form of 'creative capital.'" —**Mark Runco**, Ph.D., Torrance Professor of Creativity Studies, University of Georgia, Athens; editor, Creativity Research Journal

"Michele Root-Berstein's book is wonderful in two ways. It takes you into the private, imaginary worlds of childhood and it relates playful childhood invention to adult creativity. This is fun and it is also important—just like the secret places it explores." —**Desmond Morris**, author of *The Naked Ape*; zoologist; visual artist

"I was delighted when I heard that Michele Root-Bernstein had written a book on imaginary worlds for two reasons. First, I believe that her book with Robert Root-Bernstein, *Sparks of Genius: The Thirteen Thinking Tools of the World's Most Creative People* is a wonderful resource and guide for people seeking to increase creative thinking. I know her work to be intellectually honest yet accessible. Second, I believe that the topic of imaginary worlds has not been well researched and documented, so I was excited to think that a respected researcher was writing about this phenomenon. I was not disappointed. *Inventing Imaginary Worlds* is engaging, authentic, and innovative. It is an important work that anyone interested in creativity, imagination, and the development of creative children should read and refer to regularly." —**Bonnie Cramond**, Ph.D., director, Torrance Center for Creativity & Talent Development; professor, Department of Educational Psychology, The University of Georgia

"More important than great cities in history seem the great places of our imaginations—the invented worlds where we spend years enacting rich, pretend lives; lives sporting fantastical creatures, improbable feats, and complex relationships in need of attention. Ten years ago, the Root-Bernsteins exposed the influential creative and artistic pasts of great scientists. In *Inventing Imaginary Worlds*, Michele Root-Bernstein performs even more magical surgery—extracting the stories of artists, writers, scientists, youth, and even MacArthur Fellows who reco··· ··· ·····
nary and formative worlds. We're talking of Ejuxria (
(Alice Rivlin), and the Kingdom of King Squirrel (Ni

D1208268

Back (Mozart). Root-Bernstein makes a sweeping and entertaining case that identity formation is, at heart, a creative process." —**James S. Catterall**, professor emeritus, University of California at Los Angeles; director, Centers for Research on Creativity, Los Angeles/London U.K.

"This book provides a beautifully written and comprehensive account of one of the most impressive feats of childhood imagination—the spontaneous creation of entire fictional worlds. Michele Root-Bernstein covers historical examples, the ground-breaking research of Robert Silvey and his colleagues, her own empirical studies, and her naturalistic observations of her children. The literature on imaginary worlds is meticulously researched, carefully interpreted, and presented in all its fascinating detail. This is the authoritative volume on the subject and will be essential reading for anyone interested in the development of imagination." —**Marjorie Taylor**, professor of psychology, University of Oregon; author of *Imaginary Companions and the Children Who Create Them*; editor of *The Oxford Handbook of the Development of Imagination*.

Inventing Imaginary Worlds

From Childhood Play to Adult Creativity Across the Arts and Sciences

Michele Root-Bernstein

ROWMAN & LITTLEFIELD EDUCATION

A division of
ROWMAN & LITTLEFIELD PUBLISHERS, INC.
Lanham • Boulder • New York • Toronto • Plymouth, UK

Published by Rowman & Littlefield Education
A division of Rowman & Littlefield Publishers, Inc.
A wholly owned subsidary of The Rowman & Littlefield Publishing Group, Inc.
4501 Forbes Boulevard, Suite 200, Lanham, Maryland 20706
www.rowman.com

10 Thornbury Road, Plymouth PL6 7PP, United Kingdom

British Library Cataloguing in Publication Information Available

Library of Congress Cataloging-in-Publication Data

Root-Bernstein, Michele, 1953-
  Inventing imaginary worlds : from childhood play to adult creativity across the arts and sciences / Michele Root-Bernstein.
     pages cm
  Includes bibliographical references and index.
  ISBN 978-1-4758-0978-7 (cloth : alk. paper) — ISBN 978-1-4758-0979-4 (pbk. : alk. paper) — ISBN 978-1-4758-0980-0 (electronic) 1. Play. 2. Imagination. 3. Creative ability. 4. Creative ability in science. I. Title.
  LB1137.R63 2014
  153.3—dc23
                                                                          2014009630

∞™ The paper used in this publication meets the minimum requirements of American National Standard for Information Sciences—Permanence of Paper for Printed Library Materials, ANSI/NISO Z39.48-1992.

Printed in the United States of America

POETRY CREDITS

ILLUSTRATION CREDITS

Contents

List of Figures

Acknowledgments

A book such as this has many muses. I am indebted to the many MacArthur Fellows and other professionals who responded to my queries and to those who also agreed to further interviews. I owe much to the professors at Michigan State University who allowed me to query their students and to the dozen or so parents who graciously permitted me to interview their children. I thank, too, the innumerable colleagues, friends, family members, acquaintances, and strangers who took interest in my work over the years and thus helped keep the project going. Lastly, I owe more than I can express to my husband for his unflagging support and to my two children, now all grown up, who set me on the path.

Introduction

The Story of Worldplay

Most of us, I suppose, have a secret country.

—C. S. Lewis, novelist

Once upon a time, three sisters and a brother living on the bleak moors of Victorian England played in a make-believe "Glass Town" and wrote up their adventures in tiny handmade books. At the turn of the century, in America, another young girl played by herself in a secret country nestled in the designs of a Persian rug, and a young boy produced a daily news bulletin for a fictional realm called "Exlose." A generation later, another young boy imagined a secret and pacifist country, a "Concordia" complete with constitution and laws and political problems. Yet another drew up a map for "Edfaloba," an imaginary place part Maine island part Martian colony that he shared with a sibling and two friends.

When these children grew up, they carried something of their play with them. Drawing on their experience as world makers, the three sisters wrote novels that placed them in literary halls of fame. Well out of the limelight, the young girl at play on the Persian rug became an artist and memoirist. The boy who reported on imaginary affairs studied child psychology. A few decades later, the boy enamored with constitutions and peace became a well-known actor who paid tribute to his childhood play in film and took up honorary statesmanship on behalf of the United Nations Children's Fund. And the boy who was handy with maps grew up to be a well-regarded artist.

All this is the story of worldplay.

What is worldplay? Let me offer a brief definition, one that will guide us through this book:

world·play \ˈwərld·plā \ *noun*
1. the invention of an imaginary world, sometimes called a paracosm;
2. in childhood and youth, an outcome of the normally developing imagination, often associated with play in secret, found, and constructed places;
3. self-generated make-believe, tending to the sustained mental modeling of a hypothetical place or system;

4. in the arts, a plausible pretense; in the sciences and social sciences, a possible world;
5. a touchstone experience, a creative strategy

As such, worldplay belongs to the many individuals we shall meet within these pages—to a young Charlotte Brontë at play on the moors, to the adult Peter Ustinov at work in theater, in film, and on the political stage. More, it belongs to us all. For if what novelist C. S. Lewis supposed is true (and I suspect it is), in one way or another all of us have known some secret country.

Perhaps as a child you spent hours and hours inventing a special world, a land of fairies slipping from here to there or a labyrinth of trains whistling through an original countryside. Maybe you, like me, have cared for a child who draws family trees for imaginary friends or keeps statistics for an imaginary baseball league. Or you immerse yourself, as so many adults do, in the play of theater, movies, art, or music. You read history or play simulation games on the computer.

It may even be as a musician, novelist, lawyer, or biologist that some part of your work calls for the assumption of a plausible scenario, the supposition of a "separate reality," or the invention of a "possible world, or a piece of a possible world." In the private country of the mind, you create visions of the way things were and the way they might be. You enter into imagined realms and shape an alternative space and time. To one degree or another, we all do. Although hardly aware of what to call it, we engage in worldplay.

Now imagine we don't know how. Imagine we get no active practice immersing ourselves in imaginary worlds, whether those made up by others or those we make up ourselves. Forgetting how to play as children, we forget how to play as adults. We forgo make-believe and all else that takes imagination—novels, movies, music, art, computer games, history, science. Is such an unimaginative world possible? Perhaps more than we might think.

Over the last several decades, changes in lifestyle, child rearing, and education have, in fact, pushed aside pretend play in favor of commercial entertainments and test-driven learning. Since the 1970s, children have lost twelve hours of free time per week, which translates to 50 percent less time in unstructured outdoor activity and 25 percent less time in play overall. Should this cause us concern? Bet on it. Richard Louv and others have argued that lack of outdoor play in green spaces can lead to "nature deficit disorder." Lack of free play in countries of the mind just as easily results in "imagination deficit disorder."

The truth is, children who cannot play do not develop the impulse control, the negotiating skills, the problem-solving tools, or the collaborative capabilities necessary to succeed in modern society. Children who do not make believe get little practice developing curiosity, "what if" thinking, flexibility of response, or empathy, respect and tolerance for others. Lacking play experience, they fall behind in emotional, social, and intellectual growth. They are shortchanged in life readiness—and in creative readiness, as well. "Curiosity, imagination and creativity are like muscles," says one child psychologist, "if you don't use them, you lose them."

At the same time, these same skills go missing in our schools. Numerous works of advocacy and pedagogical initiative attempt to address the problem, from Costa and Kallick's *Habits of Mind Across the Curriculum* (2009) to the Partnership for 21st Century Skills's online Framework for 21st Century Learning. All agree that solutions to the complex problems of the future, whether scientific, technological, political, or social, will require curiosity, originality, and inventiveness; capability in problem articulation, problem solving, and idea generation; tolerance for risk taking and ambiguity; and comfort with the notion of "no right answer."

What remains unsaid and unexplored is that many of these skills and behaviors are first exercised in childhood play. By shrinking time and support now for a whole range of make-believe, from dress-up to fort building to world making, we may well be shrinking our future pool of creative adults. As educator Deborah Meier has put it, the marginalization of pretend play "cheat[s] our children and our society in a far more critical way than we're inclined to understand." Consequently, she has argued, "our national genius for inventiveness may be at stake."

Play matters. How children play matters, too. The book you hold in your hands explores the *why* and the *how* through the magnifying lens of worldplay. What do children gain from inventing imaginary worlds, in terms of imaginative stimulation, self-directed learning, or the development of creative potential? What does society gain, as they become adults? Can or should worldplay be encouraged at home and in school as a means of fostering future innovation in the arts and sciences, the humanities and technologies? In an increasingly wired and collaborative age, does privately constructed worldplay even have a future?

As I address these questions and fill in the contours of imaginary world invention across the lifespan, my purpose is to convince you that this complex form of make-believe has great personal and social value—and for the following reasons.

First, worldplay calls for imagination. The common dictionary definition of that term refers to the act or process of forming a conscious idea or mental image of something *never before wholly perceived,* a feat achieved by stitching together a crazy quilt of sense images, memories, and speculations. Inventing imaginary worlds, children and youth explore their very own never-before-wholly-perceived alternatives to reality—whether those involve toy lands or countries on Mars.

Second, that imaginative exploration can also be creative, involving the composition of languages and codes, the writing of stories and histories, the drawing of pictures and maps, the building of model towns, or the fabrication of make-believe games. In conception and construction, imaginary worlds call forth the mind's power to join the unknown to known experience and bring something new and meaningful into existence. In sustained make-believe, children and youth develop imaginative skills and creative behaviors that add up to a rich inner life.

Third, early experiences with complex make-believe can have lifelong consequences. Creators of all kinds have thrived on the experiences of youth, likening elements of adult genius to the purposeful cultivation of childlike play. For well-known writers, artists, and scientists, and for numerous unrecognized individuals as well, childhood play in imaginary worlds has powered adult strategies for imagining, modeling, and creating effective re-visions of reality.

To make the case, this book examines the worldplay experience from various points of view: the historical, the psychological, the literary, the sociological, and even the zoological. Anecdotal histories are tied to scholarship on play, imagination, and creativity, drawing out the art as well as the science of world invention. And because to build understanding of the worldplay impulse is to construct another sort of possible world, this book also records something of my research journey.

There are personal as well as professional reasons for that journey. In addition to my work in creativity studies over the last twenty years, I have had the privilege of observing the invention of an imaginary world at close hand as a parent. From the age of nine to nineteen, my daughter returned again and again to a particularly consistent game of make-believe. Playful ways of speaking, writing, and counting, playful stories, drawings, and songs all nestled together in one enduring "secret country." What she gained from the pretense and what I learned from her along the way have provided the intimate perspective that helps shape the organization of this book.

Part I traces how my parental immersion in worldplay led me to a larger history of the phenomenon and to formal study of childhood worldplay in contemporary groups of people.

Part II explores imaginary world invention as a complex form of make-believe play, as a manifestation of child-centered giftedness, and as a learning laboratory for creative growth and development.

Part III examines the maturation of worldplay as a lifelong creative strategy, with implications for professional work and the synthesis of vocation and avocation.

And finally, Part IV investigates the implications that worldplay may hold for education, for attitudes towards computer play, for the parental nurture of imaginary world invention, and ultimately, for the future of cultural innovation.

Like my journey, there are multiple pathways through this book. Parents and other caretakers may want to start with an introduction to the hidden worlds of childhood (chapter 1) and their origins in placing-making play (chapter 4), then consider how computer games can simulate (chapter 11) and how adults can stimulate (chapter 12) a self-generated worldplay. Educators may wish to follow first pages with an exploration of how the invention of imaginary worlds can serve as a "learning laboratory" promoting creative giftedness (chapters 5 and 6) and then take a look at how worldplay may be harnessed to classroom objectives (chapter 10).

Inventors of imagined worlds may like to begin with the company they keep (chapters 2 and 3), then move on to transitions from early to mature worldplay (chapter 7) and the creative strategies that place that worldplay at the heart of work in many professions (chapters 8 and 9). For those readers generally interested in imaginary worlds or the development of imagination and creativity throughout the lifespan, I recommend the whole itinerary.

No matter the path, I'll try to tell the many-faceted story of worldplay. I'll explore its history, survey its countries, describe its peoples, investigate its imaginative cultures, and weigh its benefits. The invention of imaginary worlds serves as a compass for locating the complex interchange between play, imagination, and creativity as these capacities develop lifelong. Consider this book, if you will, as a map to the hidden treasure in make-believe play for our children, ourselves, and our society.

Part I

DISCOVERING WORLDPLAY
WHERE IT GROWS

## Chapter One

Hidden Worlds of Play:
A Journey Through the Land of Kar

crayon map
my son shows me the way
to Neverland

—John McManus, poet

I first learned about the imaginary worlds of play from my daughter. Most parents remember baby's first smile. Many will never forget the toddler's first steps. I recall in vivid detail my first child's first forays into pretend play. Sometime between the ages of one-and-a-half and two, Meredith took to arranging her rocking horse just so on the living room floor, a bucket of blocks beneath its nose, the wooden rabbit close by. A stuffed bear and a yarn-haired dolly sat in a miniature camp chair a few feet opposite the horse, perched above a pile of books. Even as she began to walk and talk, my daughter began to make believe.

Much of that very early play—and of the play she soon shared with her younger brother, Brian—is engraved in my memory. I can still see the silent adventures of Dog in the Top Hat and One-Eyed Squirrel, two plastic wind-up toys whose springs had sprung. Something in the way Meredith jiggled them up and down had me convinced that they were talking, though the three-year-old would never say what about.

I remember, too, the dress-up play called "Alec and Arinna," which required a cape for my toddler son, a scarf for my daughter, now four years old, and two stick horses. A pretend house stood on the patio and wild horses ran free in the pretend mountains at the back of our very level yard.

I reminisce, as well, about the many games with rules (hotly contested!) that the two absorbed themselves in when six and seven and eight years old. The most memorable of these was "Footsie Olympics," a sports competition for golf-ball sized pom-poms decked out with plastic eyes, antennae, and one big flat foot. The kids flipped, knocked, and joggled their teams through a series of events. "We're only fuzz and feet," went the Footsie motto, "but we can still compete!"

All this play felt familiar to me as a parent. I recognized the solitary make-believe with toys, the dramatic and absorbing sibling play with props and costumes, and the high seriousness of made-up games, having experienced much the same when I my-self was a child. But then, over the course of weeks, months perhaps, I became aware of a new and unexpected turn in my daughter's imaginative activity, something be-yond my own experience. In her ninth year Meredith began to invent a pretend place called "Kar."

I had heard of children making up imaginary companions, of course. But this was different; this was a whole world, a parallel place or *paracosm*, mapped out bit by bit, day after day. Meredith's tenacious memory for every aspect of the game surprised me, as did the sheer joy and exuberance with which she generated a variety of play materials. She loved the game, and I grew to love it, too—for the windows it opened onto her mind and heart, certainly, but also onto the wonders of imagination in gen-eral.

Like Dog in a Top Hat, Alec and Arinna, or Footsie Olympics, only more so, Kar awakened in me an intense curiosity for the mechanisms of make-believe. Where did this complex pretense come from? What motivated the return again and again to the same play place? Come to think of it, did other children invent their own countries? If so, why had I never heard about them before?

I soon learned that very little attention has been paid to child-constructed imaginary worlds, perhaps due to the reluctance among practitioners young or old to reveal much about them. As the otherwise garrulous Peter Ustinov remarked, "Immediately you begin to share secrets of this kind, you begin to entertain, and the utility of such a place, and its reality, are destroyed." Yet, stretching over the past two hundred years and more, we *do* have records, however sketchy, of "neverlands" long lost: "All-mood," "The Lodge," "The Dicks," "Nancy and Plum," "Bath Bian Street," "Tsoly-anu," "Fourlands," "Alagaësia," "Kirsy-Lirsy Land," "Abixia," "Rontuia," and more.

Several outings to the library later, I was on my way to acquiring a growing col-lection of imaginary worlds, marvelous and diverse—and a growing list of reasons why worldplay, as I was soon to call it, might just be the most important neglected phenomenon of childhood.

"I MADE IT UP WHEN I WAS A LITTLE KID"

In 1806 one Benjamin Heath Malkin published *A Father's Memoirs of His Child*—not, as he said, to parade the erudition of an intellectual prodigy, but to showcase the boy's imaginative promise, something quite different. True, son Thomas had been a very fast study, teaching himself to read and write by the age of two, imbibing classi-cal languages with his mother's milk. He was also the inventor, in his father's words, of "a visionary country, called Allestone."

As king of that imaginary country, Thomas recorded its history, drew its map, described its social institutions, and wrote its stories. He invented a language for Allestone, using Latin as a model, though in sound and rhythm it was the product of "whim." He tried his hand, too, at composing comic operas and "imaginary music" by noting something of his melodies in the treble and bass clefs.

Malkin senior described this music, as well as histories and stories of Allestone, in order to trace how the boy "enlisted every circumstance into his service," how he recast what he learned of reality into fanciful story or song, how he copied the style and manner of operas, dictionaries, and geographers' maps. In play Thomas displayed powers "resembling so nearly in their early promise, whatever has delighted and improved mankind in the works of mature genius."

At about the same time, in nearly the same locale, another small boy named Hartley Coleridge set about spinning the "extraordinary daydreams," in which, according to his brother, Derwent, he passed a "visionary boyhood." Son of the Romantic poet Samuel Taylor Coleridge, Hartley was a hyperactive little force of nature wrapped up in the wonder of his own vivid thoughts—and in worldplay. Sometime in early childhood, he had found a small spring burbling up through the earth near his home. On the banks of this "Jug-force" he envisioned a peopled world. By the time he was eight, Jug-force had cut loose from its physical confines to become the island continent of "Ejuxria."

Over many years, Derwent recalled, Hartley elaborated many nations on that island, "each with its separate history, civil, ecclesiastical, and literary, its forms of religion and government, and specific national character." As Hartley's confidant, the younger Derwent often found himself "beguiled" by the latest dispatch from Ejuxrian shores. Indeed, that imaginary world seemed as utterly "real" as it was "free and poetical." Hartley himself later recalled, "I was a great story-teller. . . . What I heard or read, I worked up into a tale of my own." The make-believe was, in his estimation, an imitative kind of art, yet embellished with "great circumstantiality of description" and originality.

Except for a kingdom of children invented by little Wolfgang Amadeus Mozart and his sister Nannerl, Thomas's Allestone and Hartley's Ejuxria are among the earliest childhood worlds on record. In the next one hundred to two hundred years, however, public mentions of worldplay blossomed.

Undoubtedly, the best known of these is the imaginary "Glass Town" invented by the four siblings, Charlotte, Branwell, Emily, and Anne Brontë. But other writers, known and unknown, also played in worlds of their own making. As a child, the well-known novelist Anthony Trollope spun hours of make-believe into a "castle in the air"; the less well-known translators Catherine and Susanna Winkworth ruled twin fairy kingdoms; the obscure Una Hunt, artist and memoirist, dreamed up a world in her mother's rug.

Individuals destined for careers outside the literary life also made up worlds in childhood. Long before he became a visual artist, Fairfield Porter mapped the Martian-Maine island realm of "Edfaloba" (see figure 1.1). Ustinov sketched out the constitution of his pacificist "Concordia" well in advance of his work as actor, director, and writer. The geologist Nathaniel Shaler, the lawyer Austin Tappan Wright, the neurologist Oliver Sacks, and zoologist-artist Desmond Morris all made up realms of the mind in youth, too.

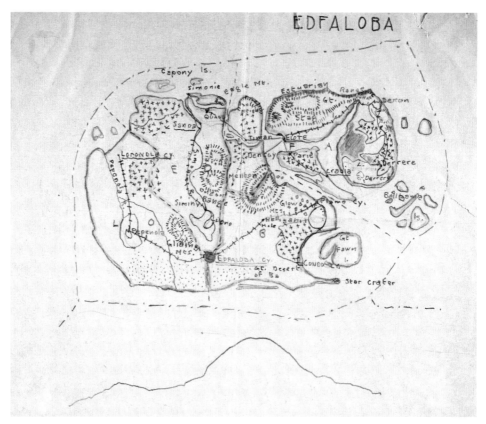

Fig. 1.1. The Martian world of Edfaloba. Drawing by Fairfield Porter, age 11. Edfaloba is super-imposed upon the map of Great Spruce Head Island in Penobscot Bay, Maine, where Porter's family summered.

In some of these instances little more remains than the gist of the game. Kenneth Grahame, author of *The Wind in the Willows*, invented an imaginary "City" as a boy. Maurice Baring, man of letters and high society, made up a "gibberish language" with his younger brother Hugo that bloomed into "Spankaboo," a make-believe continent of countries, towns, and hundreds of characters. C. J. Jung, pioneer psychologist of the unconscious mind, imagined himself ruler of a medieval castle with a mysterious taproot conducting a "certain inconceivable something" to a dungeon lab. Physicist David Lee worked up an imaginary railroad. Mozart and his sister shared a secret language and addressed one another as "King" and "Queen."

In other instances somewhat more information has survived the wreck of memory and time. According to Elizabeth Forster-Nietzsche, she and her brother Friedrich invented an imaginary world for certain "tiny china figures of men and animals, lead soldiers [and] a little porcelain squirrel about an inch and a half high." Young Friedrich wrote poems and plays and composed music on King Squirrel's behalf and even produced a gallery of art for that diminutive monarch. The pictures he painted were proportionate to their royal patron and housed in a building of toy bricks constructed, so remembered his sister, "in a beautiful classic style."

In yet other instances it is the actual stuff of worldplay that remains, often because its later importance to adults motivated efforts to preserve the evidence. Just as Benjamin Malkin reprinted maps and histories of Allestone, Helen Follett catalogued the poems and stories left behind by her daughter Barbara, a literary wunderkind whose imaginary "Farksolia" shaped her first novel at age thirteen.

Of course, the biggest cache of worldplay artifacts undoubtedly belongs to the Brontë siblings. Many of their tiny hand-sewn books can be examined in library archives, as can their voluminous juvenile manuscripts. So, too, can the original drawings and handwritten stories of the Oxford don and literary critic, C. S. Lewis, author of the perennially best-selling *Chronicles of Narnia*.

Situated in a "secret country" reached through an old wardrobe, the Narnia stories ring true in no small part because Lewis had had a lot of practice making up imaginary worlds as a child. In the early years of the twentieth century, C. S. (known as Jacks) and his brother W. H., or Warnie, played for hours on end in make-believe lands. Warnie, the elder by three years, invented a world of trains and steamships he called "India." Jacks invented a world of dressed-up animals and medieval knights called "Animal-Land" (see figures 1.2 and 1.3).

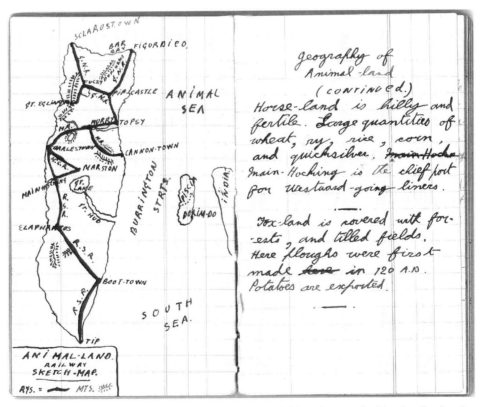

Fig. 1.2. Animal-Land, map by C.S. Lewis, drawn in childhood. Note the bit of India showing on the right of the map.

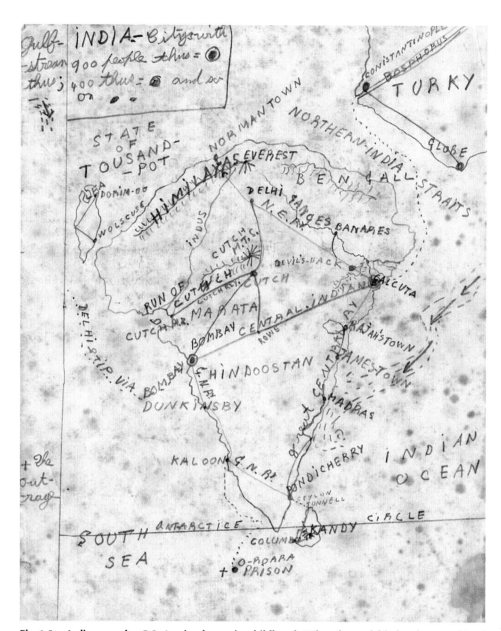

Fig 1.3. India, map by C.S. Lewis, drawn in childhood. When he and his brother combined Animal-Land and India into Boxen, Jacks spent much time coordinating histories as well as geographies of the two make-believe countries.

After Warnie left for preparatory school, Jacks combined the two play-worlds into "Boxen," producing a lot of drawings, maps, histories, and intertwined stories that involved a growing cast of characters, including the dapper dressed frog, Lord Big (see figure 1.4). The game petered out when he reached his mid-teens, but Boxen still lives for us all because the adult C. S. found in it much that anticipated his professional career. "In mapping and chronicling Animal-Land," he believed, "I was training myself to be a novelist."

Sorting through old Boxen materials in the late 1920s, Lewis made a list of extant documents and established a chronology of events, compiling these in what he called the *Encyclopedia Boxoniana.* Published after his death, the Boxen maps, stories, and histories limned the formative experience that had prepared him to create Narnia. Presumably, Boxen play had also helped prepare his brother, who wrote popular histories with great flair.

Others, too, found in childhood worldplay the origins of adult creative endeavor—and not just in the literary arts. The visual artist and sculptor Claes Oldenburg, known for his brash, outsized sculptures of everyday objects, once provocatively remarked, "Everything I do is completely original—I made it up when I was a little kid." In a very real sense, he had. In the 1930s, from the age of seven and for many years thereafter, young Claes immersed himself in the invention of an imaginary world called "Neubern," an island somewhere indiscernible in the expanse between Africa and South America.

Filling many a scrapbook with maps, drawings, diagrams, plans, and specifications, Oldenburg learned at an early age to think of himself as a creator with a vision. As a mature artist that vision led him to reconceive everyday objects in whimsical materials, fiddling playfully with size and shape in such a way that the ordinary becomes extraordinary. The result has been a kind of adult worldplay, an art that is, in his own words, "a parallel reality according to the rules of (my) fantasy."

The science-trained philosopher and writer Stanislaw Lem, author of the novel *Solaris,* also gave credit to childhood worldplay for laying the foundations of his mature work. Gripped, around the age of twelve, by "the passion for inventing things," young Stanislaw drew up specifications for perpetual motion machines and blueprints for bikes propelled by handlebars. He also constructed passports and other bureaucratic licenses, using silver thread from his school badge to sew small sheets of paper into booklets and dipping coins in India ink to stamp their covers. There were no characters to this play, no plot, no place. Nevertheless, Lem later wrote, "A shape began to emerge from nothingness, a Building, a Castle unbelievably High, with a Center of Mystery never named."

Lem's inventing game and his castle game were separate, yet in each, the adult believed, the work of imaginative invention "was also play and also a creative act . . . and needed no reason or goal outside itself." There were, however, lasting results. He joked that his early devotion to blank passports in the 1920s anticipated the anti-novel of the later twentieth century, particularly his own. His "pseudomachines" similarly served as palimpsest for his science-based futurology, which was especially concerned with the man-machine interface. In content and conception the imaginary play of childhood had propelled him to the twin thresholds of art and of science.

Fig. 1.4. Lord Big, ruler of Boxen and, as dressed frog, a chimeric blend of familiar animal and authority figure. Drawing by C.S. Lewis, in childhood.

The relevance for lifelong creativity that Lewis, Oldenburg, and Lem found in childhood worldplay was a revelation to me. Many individuals seek mature inspiration in memories of early wonder and expression, but this was something more, a direct channeling of the child's creative spirit and powers. Moreover, that same impulse appeared to manifest itself among others, too—poets, artists, and musicians, historians, psychologists, and biologists—in a wide array of adult endeavors. By implication, whatever behaviors the child exercised in worldplay must be of general value to the individual, capable of development in more than one direction.

Against this backdrop, I began to realize that as witness to my daughter's play, I had the unique opportunity to consider firsthand how the invention of make-believe worlds might shape imaginative and creative growth. What I learned from Lem or Lewis, from Hartley Coleridge or Barbara Follett might guide me in discerning salient features in my daughter's play. What I learned from my daughter might similarly shed light on the silences in worldplay records that no longer breathed with immediate life. I could, after all, ask her questions, as any parent might, *while she played*.

And I did. I paid attention to her construction of Kar Land. I watched for inspirations and influences, and for the materials and circumstances that motivated play. I kept alert for budding capacities, creative processes, insights, and discoveries. Observing the lived experience of one child, I looked to recover its benefit for many.

"HOW THE WORLD BEGAN"

With many an adventure, we find ourselves well in before we know it has begun. Thinking back on the origins of Kar, I realized that my daughter's make-believe world first surfaced as a language game. Like many another child, Meredith found spelling highly disagreeable. As a kind of retort, an attempt to rationalize spoken and written communication, the fourth-grader played around with codes and alphabets and the phonetic rendering of sounds. The result was a pictorial language based on nouns that did away with alphabets and spelling altogether—at least initially (see figure 1.5).

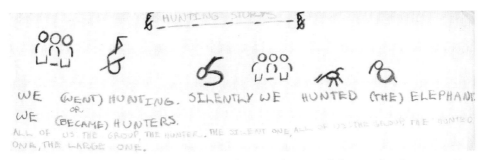

Fig. 1.5. The first Kar story, with English translation and names of pictographs, circa 1991. Meredith, age 8 or 9. "All of us: the group. The hunter. The silent one. All of us: the group. The hunted one. The large one." Colloquially rendered as: "We (went) hunting (or: We (became) hunters). Silently we hunted (the) elephant."

Soon enough, however, Meredith began assigning spoken sounds to her pictographs and writing them out (see figure 1.6).

Each spoken word was to be rendered with three letters. This meant any one word could have only one, two, or three syllables (as in oob, obo, or oao). These three elements—pictograph, spoken word, and three-letter spelling—were the plain linguistic facts beyond which my daughter did not want to go. In order for the game to be fun, it had to have rules, and simple ones at that.

Meredith's rule making proved to be a characteristic shared with other inventors of imaginary worlds. Young Fairfield Porter and his companions pretended that "everything in Edfaloba runs by sunlight." The poet W. H. Auden made a point of stocking his "private sacred world" of mines and moors with bona fide machines only. "A secondary [imaginary] world," he wrote in retrospect, "must be as much a world of law as the primary. One may be free to decide what these laws shall be, but laws there must be." Trollope kept his wool-gathering within a set of narrative rules and unities: "Nothing impossible was ever introduced."

Alongside the rule making, there also emerged a kind of spontaneous serendipity, a logic of circumstance. The immediate impetus for imaginary world invention, for instance, took many forms. Hartley Coleridge responded to a special place in nature, Stanislaw Lem to an accumulation of hand-crafted passports and seals. In Meredith's case, an invented language supposed someone or something to write about and for. She settled on a primitive tribe living in an open savannah (later an island), hunt-

Fig. 1.6. Kar pronunciation and three-letter spelling, circa 1992. Meredith, age 9. The manuscript reads, in part: "Bay Fom See Het Bay" ("Today I see the sun.")

ing and gathering their food and making everything by hand. These became the Kar people. Almost at once, she began providing them fairy tales by rendering the ones she knew best into the Kar language and landscape.

When she was almost ten years old, for example, she penned the Kar version of the three little pigs and the big bad wolf. "Today a mouse, a bird and a bear go to make a house. The mouse makes her house from corn. The bird makes her house from trees. And the bear makes his house from earth." One can guess the rest. Some elements of the fairy tale (protagonists and plot) were *copied*, duplicated almost exactly; some (setting and characterization) were *imitated* or transposed with significant variation. Like a young C. S. Lewis, Meredith recreated for herself the process by which stories come into being, developing narrative imagination along with basic literary skill.

Imitation as transposition was, in fact, a constant element threaded through my daughter's worldplay—just as it had been for Friedrich Nietzsche and the art gallery of King Squirrel or Claes Oldenburg and the material artifacts of Neubern. In 1994, when she was eleven and a half years old and had been writing Kar stories for some two or three years, she made her first Kar drawing and quickly followed it with others (see figure 1.7).

These pictures were based on replicas of cave paintings and Egyptian wall art she found in books. Like their models, Kar drawings largely depicted a natural world in which figures see and are seen from a single angle.

More to the point, nearly all the drawings featured some amount of text that illustrated or anticipated a Kar story. In essence, my daughter began transposing from within the Kar universe, as well as from without. The first Kar drawing depicts "Moi Covcul," "Person Makes-All," in his various manifestations as antelope, fish, frog,

Fig. 1.7. The first Kar drawing, dated May 8, 1994. Meredith, age 11.

and bird. Around the age of fourteen, Meredith fully described their activities in "How the World Began," a story that was as much about the origins of imaginary worldplay as it was about Kar origins:

> Once there was nothing except a person who could be any animal. One day he turned into a bird and flew far into the blackness. He returned with a bit of mud. When it fell from his beak it turned into the ground of the land. Then he became an antelope. He ran and ran into the darkness, and returned with three seeds in his mouth. As they fell from his mouth, they landed in the ground and sprouted into trees, bushes and grasses. Then he turned into a fish. He swam far into the darkness. He got some water and brought it back. He spread it around, making many rivers and the sea. Then the person became a frog. He hopped quickly through the darkness. He returned to the earth with a bit of air. It covered up the land.

In coming years Meredith wrote many more stories and drew many more pictures built on and around "How the World Began." Kar thrived on consistency of vision, just as Malkin's Allestone and Lewis's Animal-Land had done. What's more, this make-believe pastime, stretching over a decade, became its own constructive effort. Over and over the play progressed through the stages of problem preparation, incubation, insight, evaluation, and elaboration typically found in theoretical models of creative process. Practitioners sometimes offer alternative schematics, such as the creative spiral cycling back and forth through idea, action, feedback, and review. Traces of all these elements were to be found in my daughter's juvenilia.

Time and again, Meredith prepared for worldplay by setting herself a problem: How, for instance, did the Kar actually come to write their stories? To my knowledge, she never explicitly articulated the question as such, but curiosity for the origins of language and literature incubated in the back of her mind as she gathered information and ideas about the earliest legends, the earliest writing, the earliest books and so forth. (She was particularly enamored with Eyewitness Books™ and other heavily illustrated material on these subjects.)

At some point around the age of twelve, the imagined development of spoken and written language coalesced for her with the imagined emergence of simple writing implements and an imagined economy that valued narrative goods. On the strength of such insight, she took action, elaborating a history of the "time . . . called the word explosion," in which "at a market, a person can get a fine blanket or a pot for a story, or more for a book." Two years later, after a latent period of feedback, review, and evaluation, she strengthened and elaborated her initial insight by drawing and detailing the writing desk of the professional Kar scribe.

Meredith's worldplay was shot through with yet another well-recognized ingredient of creative thinking, the comparison and synthesis of two or more unlike things. As the mathematician and poet Jacob Bronowski famously expressed it, the discoveries of science and of art "are explorations—more, are explosions, of a hidden likeness." The same holds true for the insights generated in worldplay. Documents of play in imaginary worlds bear evidence of early metaphor making and analogizing. C. S. Lewis, like many a child, combined the animal and the human in Lord Big. Una Hunt conflated bold designs in her mother's rug with woods, rivers, and seas. Stanislaw

Lem blended burned-out transistor tubes and spools of thread into impossible machinery.

In Meredith's case, the marriage of word and image revealed her personal discovery that visual iconography is like narrative myth is like the very foundations of an imagined world view. Unconsciously, perhaps, but surely, she produced a synthesis of arts and understandings that became Kar through and through.

The combined processes of imitating, transposing, and blending, of preparing, incubating, and elaborating had one additional creative dimension. They were also a personal construction of knowledge. From the age of twelve onward, Meredith had been busy translating into the world of Kar nearly everything that piqued her interest about the real world. In order to draw the Kar people, she had had to design for them indigenous clothing. That accomplished, she set upon organizing and cataloging dress, hair, and other adornments. She moved on to Kar housing and Kar food and then to Kar livelihoods, holidays, and politics, writing up, in English, illustrated pages in the manner of her beloved Eyewitness Books.

These documents bore strong similarity to the Boxen materials preserved by C. S. Lewis, the notebooks full of charts and drawings recalled by Claes Oldenburg, the pseudomachines mocked up by Stanislaw Lem—only now, thanks to Meredith, I could discern the creative process that lay behind these constructs. Worldplay, I realized, was the child's way to make personal sense of human culture—of literature, art, social studies, math, and science—and to *learn about* by *making believe*.

Many aspects of my daughter's imaginary world invention had direct links to what she learned in school. This was not too surprising—Thomas Malkin used his Latin learning to elaborate his imaginary language; Barbara Follett co-opted vocabulary and plots from the literature on which she was schooled to write her Farksolian stories.

What did surprise, in Meredith's case, was where the outside influence sometimes took her. Just about the time her fourth grade teacher insisted she memorize the multiplication tables, for instance, she began making up a Kar arithmetic, which resulted in an alternative means of multiplying, dividing, and recording the results. Her arithmetical understanding was all the deeper for the free-choice invention of her own symbol system.

In imaginary play, Meredith wore the many hats of linguist, poet, visual artist, musician, anthropologist, historian, and mathematician. Moreover, she learned to wear several hats at a time, to see the ramifications that one area of life might have on another.

Consider that, from the start, her world invention had had one overarching rule, which was that *everything be real-seeming*. Many other worldplaying children shared that same concern. Informed by his brother that things didn't make sense, Hartley Coleridge reworked elements of Ejuxria; W. H. Auden did not allow "physical impossibilities and magic means" in his play-world of mines machinery; Stanislaw Lem constructed his "High Castle" and his pseudomachines with a "lust for realistic detail" and a "passion for precision."

In Meredith's case, I could trace the actual decision tree of playful yet consistent choices. Early on, she had decided that there was no metal in Kar Land. Subsequently, when she became interested in detailing the instruments of everyday life, it was necessary to imagine spoons, knives, bowls, and farming implements made out of nonmetallic materials. In their turn, cooking implements of wood, stone, and clay influenced Kar cuisine.

For all her research, however, there was reverie as well to my daughter's worldplay. After some experimentation in the kitchen, she decided that a staple diet of honey, nuts, and stone-ground cornmeal suited a simple people inhabiting round, one-room homes with an open fire and a minimum of cooking implements. But then again, so did smoked salmon mousse or goose Wellington paired with seaweed pudding and crushed pine needle tea! From my point of view, no surprise, this was Kar's charm. The drive for verisimilitude acted as a spur to the imagination in more ways than one.

Like so many other children, Meredith stitched together bits and pieces of the real world with naïve notions and untested prescriptions. As a matter of course, not everything she dreamed up was as realistic as she wished—though it certainly was original. Eventually these realizations became her own. When she was in her early to mid-teens she spent a great deal of time drawing up Kar flora and fauna (see figure 1.8).

Four or five years later, the college girl studying evolution realized that, as appealing as the animals she gathered on the island might be, they did not on the whole represent a viable ecology. They did, however, represent her fancy set free in a make-believe land that, finally, at age nineteen, she mapped *in toto* (see figure 1.9).

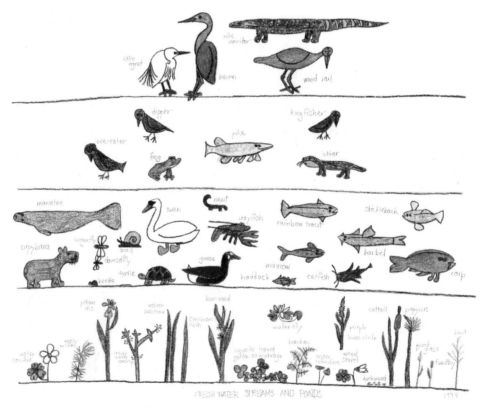

Fig. 1.8.   Kar ecology, "Fresh Water Streams and Ponds," dated 1997. Meredith, age 15 or 16.

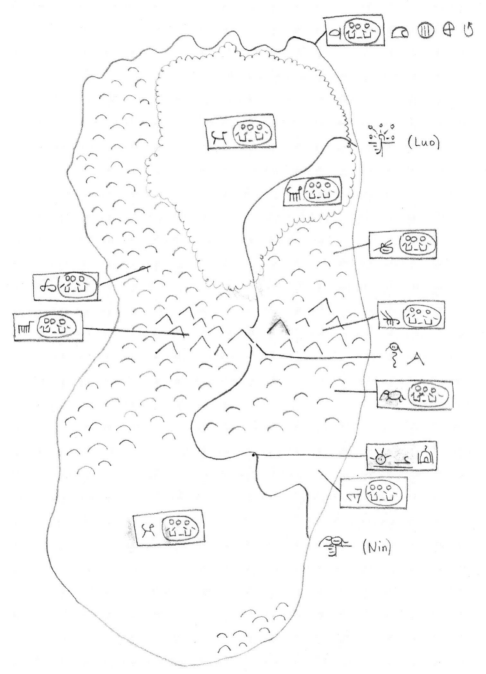

Fig. 1.9. A map of Kar, titled "The Drawing of Karrom," dated 2001. Meredith, age 19. The central mountains surround 'Mother Mountain', from which flow two rivers, the Luo (Peacock) and the Nin (Whale). The Nin cradles the capital city, Romfiz Village. Each geographic area is labeled by the people who live there: the fish people, the wolf people, hawk people, antelope people, and so on.

If Meredith were to write an account of her childhood worldplay, it would be different from mine. My description here of phonemes, fables, and foods does no more
than scratch the surface of materials she produced over ten years and more. The same
is true for the make-believe play of a Nietzsche, an Oldenburg, an Auden, and many
others, all of whom have safeguarded for themselves the deepest secrets of their play.
Yet I can clearly see that my daughter has been affected, like so many others before
her, by her experience of imaginary world invention.

Reverberations from Kar began surfacing in her early adult years. After studying
the evolution of communication and language in college, combining courses in linguistics, psychology, anthropology, and animal biology, she pursued a doctorate in
zoology and conservation. She also maintained a secondary interest in writing poetry
and in print making and other forms of visual art.

In "How the World Began" the adolescent had foreseen that the "person who made
all" would occasionally emerge from his house in the hollow to rearrange an invented
nature, illustrate it, and make a poem or two for the marketplace. The adult Meredith,
recognizing her own kinship with Moi Covcul, has remained, like that imaginary being, "glad" to have "made such a beautiful and wonderful world."

COMMONALITIES AND QUESTIONS

The psychologist Harold Grier McCurdy, a veteran investigator of creativity, believed
it possible to find in the documents of play "those things which children know and do
not as a rule articulate very fully." Inspired by intimate knowledge of my daughter's
invention of an imaginary world, directed by testimonies by or on behalf of many
other worldplaying children, I articulated in their stead a provisional profile for imaginary world invention.

Worldplay appeared to be a **solitary,** or perhaps **intimately shared,** pastime. Over
the years nearly everyone in my extended family heard or saw something of Kar,
yet immersion in that make-believe remained a solo pursuit for Meredith. Thomas
Malkin, Hartley Coleridge, Barbara Follett, and Stanislaw Lem also played alone.
Friedrich Nietzsche played in the imaginary world of King Squirrel with his sister;
C. S. Lewis played in Boxen with his brother.

Worldplay looked to be **constructive,** that is to say, creative in the broadest sense
of making things come into existence. Hartley related his dreams of Ejuxria out loud
to all who might listen; some of those stories he wrote down in long letters to family
and friends. Thomas composed histories and stories and music, as did Meredith, as did
Friedrich. Young Stanislaw sewed together play passports; young Claes Oldenburg
put together imaginary airplanes from sundry kits. Thomas, Barbara, Meredith, and a
young Maurice Baring constructed pretend languages and dictionaries.

Worldplay seemed to be **imitative**, involving the plausible transposition of knowledge gained in the real world. Thomas imitated the geographical patterns and fine
detail of real cartography in his map of Allestone. Meredith borrowed the plots and
structures of fairy tales. Friedrich transposed what he had seen of a traveling exhibition of artwork into a gallery for King Squirrel, taking care that the pictures were to

scale. Stanislaw invested his pseudomachines with the trappings of precise measurement and authenticity.

Worldplay appeared to be **complex** and **cumulative,** involving the ongoing collection of detail. Thomas elaborated the history of his Allestonians and their institutions, as did Hartley the language, laws, government, and political speeches of Ejuxria. Claes filled notebook after notebook with drawings and plans for the daily material culture of Neubern. Meredith catalogued numerous aspects of Kar culture, amassing a visual encyclopedia of substantial proportions.

Worldplay was apparently **integrative** and **synthetic.** Care was taken to fit ongoing elaborations into the fabric of the imaginary world in ways that made sense—hence the histories and compendiums, the dictionaries and lists. In the process of bringing so much of their learning to bear in one game of play, Thomas, Hartley, Warnie and Jacks, Stanislaw, Claes, and Meredith, too, all drew on their developing powers of wonder and imagination, of problem solving and creating.

Finally, worldplay seemed a **seminal experience**, remembered over the course of a lifetime. It touched not only the child at play, but the adult recalling that play. The memoirs of C. S. Lewis and Stanislaw Lem waxed poetic with regard to the lifelong meaning they had found in the imaginary worlds of their childhood. Observing and sometimes sharing the worldplay as a parent or sibling also had lasting influence. Benjamin Malkin, Derwent Coleridge, Elizabeth Forster-Nietzsche, all expressed their deep delight in the playful wonders of home-grown imaginary worlds. So, too, had I.

Such a profile of worldplay commonalities, provisionally drawn from the experiences of a dozen or so children, provided a start to my investigations. What it suggested was that worldplay, for all the uniqueness of each individual manifestation, is a phenomenon of recurring structure and function. Certain factors that characterize one case may also characterize the many.

How many? Is worldplay more common than we think, though commonly overlooked? Does it develop imagination in ordinary or extraordinary ways? Does it nurture creative potential that might in different circumstances lie fallow? Is that potential specific to the play or of a more general sort?

Exploring these questions led me to Robert Silvey, the first person to compare his childhood play with that of the famous Brontë siblings and the first to gather for study a significant number of anonymous men and women whose imaginary worlds would otherwise have gone unsung.

Chapter Two

Searching for Paracosms: How One Man Found the Imaginary Worlds of Childhood

> I discovered that miraculous worlds may reveal themselves to a patient observer where the casual passerby sees nothing at all.
>
> —Karl von Frisch, ethologist

IMAGINARY MATTERS

Imagine a man on a train absently fingering documents in the briefcase by his side, all the while gazing into a far distance. Sometime in the 1970s, lately retired as head of audience research at the BBC, Robert Silvey had embarked on a fanciful business that occupied both mind and heart. After a decorous exchange of letters with a person he had not yet met, he found himself speeding toward a summit meeting of two imaginary nations, precious state papers tucked under his arm.

Among those papers was the map of a large make-believe continent set in a remote expanse of the Atlantic Ocean (see figure 2.1).

Sixty years had gone by since Silvey had drawn that map. As a schoolboy enamored of atlases and almanacs, he had written up governmental budgets, financial tables, and lists of cabinet ministers, too, for a parallel world he called "The New Hentian States."

There had been a great deal of fun in this make-believe and a heady sense of creating order out of nothing. The histories, constitutions, and daily newspapers compiled for The New Hentian States, though figments of imagination, were real and genuine, Silvey believed, in the same way that a model train was as authentic as the actual train that carried him to his destination.

Picture, then, as our imagined train pulled into his station stop, how eagerly Silvey descended to the platform, how eagerly a gentleman sporting an old top hat stepped forward to shake his hand. Son of Heath Robinson, an illustrator well known for lampoons and jerrybuilt contraptions, Mr. "Top Hat" was to the playful manner born. Indeed, having invented his own imaginary world in childhood, he was well suited to the role of imaginary ambassador at this veritable meeting of Silvey's "United Nations" of imaginary countries.

Fig. 2.1.   Robert Silvey's map of The New Hentian States.

Playfulness aside, Silvey's purpose was serious. Whenever he heard that someone somewhere had invented a make-believe country or *paracosm*—a term for "parallel world" soon coined at his behest—he went to great lengths to look them up. For some time, in fact, he had harbored hopes of embarking upon a systematic survey of childhood world invention. His goals were modest: to get a feel for the lay of the paracosm's lands, the variety of its forms, and its impact on people's lives. He suspected that the invention of imaginary worlds was an uncommon form of pretend play. He believed that its greatest appeal lay with solitary children, especially boys. He felt, too, that worldplay had educational value—"not so much in the acquisition of knowledge," he wrote, "as in the stimulation of curiosity."

Silvey's pioneering inquiries would inevitably lead beyond these simple expectations. Willy-nilly, his search for paracosms ran into a tangled web of questions about the relationship of make-believe to creativity, creativity to genius, and genius to madness. Moreover, it fed into conventional assumptions that pretend play anticipated creativity of a certain sort, the kind that prepared a child for artistic endeavor.

Whether or not Silvey foresaw all these issues or related them to his own experience is uncertain; but sure enough, every Pandora opens her box. He opened his in 1977 with a curious appeal to the public that ran in several British newspapers. *"Was there ever a time, gentle reader, when you invented an imaginary world?"*

Within short order, over fifty people responded to this singular call for paracosms. We can channel Silvey's delight and also his circumspection. From his many years at the BBC, he understood that the individuals who contacted him did not necessarily represent the population at large. As a set of self-selected enthusiasts, they held the same value as a "post-bag" of letters to a radio show—they reflected some part of public experience, but what part or proportion was unknown. Nevertheless, here was an unprecedented opportunity to compile a collection of records that might be used to establish the general nature of imaginary world invention in childhood. Consequently, in 1979 he asked retired psychiatrist Stephen MacKeith to join him in devising a plan for further research.

For a start, the two collaborators set out to establish the criteria that distinguished paracosm play from other sorts of childhood make-believe such as the animation of toys, the enacting of storybook roles, or the Scheherazade-like spinning of bedtime tales.

They required that the child play with his or her invented world persistently and repeatedly over "an appreciable length of time," in order to distinguish it from make-believe that vanished at the end of the day.

They required that the child attach importance to consistency, "systematizing" his or her imaginary world so that it did not "change its spots" from one time to the next.

They required that the child value the play highly. Whether consciously or unconsciously, the paracosm had to satisfy certain emotional or intellectual needs; it had to "matter."

Many of these criteria derived from Silvey's play with his own New Hentian States. However, other elements characteristic of his experience were not included. There was no insistence that the worldplay be solitary, for instance; that it necessarily involve the making of maps or ministerial lists and histories; that it have recognized educational value; that it be realistic or at least, real-seeming. There was always the chance that certain particulars of Silvey's practice might turn out to be the anomaly, the unexplained deviation from more prevalent forms of worldplay. Indeed, he already knew enough of imaginary worlds other than his own to realize that the phenomenon had a variety of guises.

One exemplar stood out among the rest. Like many an educated Englishman, Silvey was well versed in the imaginary worlds of the Brontë sisters, whose unconventional tales of brooding heroes and passionate heroines had burst upon the literary scene in the mid-nineteenth century. Because of their enduring fame as writers, the play-worlds that Charlotte, Emily, and Anne shared with their brother Branwell had drawn repeated attention. In her *Life of Charlotte Brontë*, published two years after Charlotte's death in 1857, Mrs. Gaskell professed herself astonished at the "creative power" of the children's make-believe. Some ninety years later, Fannie Ratchford proposed that their imaginative play had been a hotbed for the sisters' genius.

Fairly or not, Silvey knew, all other childhood worldplay would be measured against the Brontë archetype.

GLASS TOWN, ANGRIA, AND GONDAL

The facts, most biographers agree, were these: in 1826, when Charlotte was ten years old, Branwell nine, Emily eight, and Anne six, Branwell received a set of twelve wooden soldiers from their father, perpetual curate of the village of Haworth on the English moors of West Yorkshire.

The toy soldiers immediately sparked a set of imaginary characters the children called the "Young Men" or the "Twelves." Three years later, Charlotte recalled the moment in one of her diaries:

> When papa came home it was night and we were in Bed so next morning Branwell came to our Door with a Box of soldiers Emily and I jumped out of Bed and I snat[c]hed up one and exclaimed this is the Duke of Wellington it shall be mine!!! When I said this Emily likewise took one and said it should be hers when Anne came down she took one also. Branwell chose Bonaparte.

The wooden Twelves were not the first toys to stimulate pretend play for the Brontë children. Nor were the adventures of the Young Men the only make-believe competing for their attention. At age thirteen Branwell counted up three sets of wooden soldiers, two of "Turkish musicians" and one band of "Indians" which he and his sisters had "maimed Lost burnt or destroyed" in play over a period of six years. For her part, Charlotte made note of "Our Fellows," a game based on Aesop's Fables, and the "Islander's," born in a bored moment when each of the children picked an English island and a "chief man." She and Emily also shared bed stories before sleep.

In time, the children abandoned the bed play and the Fellow's play and merged the Young Men and the Islanders into one all-encompassing game. Toy soldiers in hand, all four siblings spent long hours in and around their parsonage home staging battles for the wooden Twelves and sailing the seas in search of kingdoms. Eventually, the Twelves set foot in Africa, where the children conceived a fanciful "Great Glass Town" encompassing a confederacy of soldier-ruled lands. They made up a special language for their soldiers, based upon the local Yorkshire dialect. They created roles for themselves as "Genii," large guardian spirits who, when circumstances warranted, resurrected the dead and performed other godlike feats.

Even as the children moved into their early teens Glass Town play continued—albeit in modified form. Charlotte was thirteen and Branwell almost twelve when the two began to document the Young Men's adventures in miniature handmade books, some as small as two by one and one-half inches (see figure 2.2).

Absorbing material from books in their father's library and from newspapers and magazines purchased in the nearby town, they began to imitate what they knew of maps, histories, stories, poems, and editorial essays in their toy-sized *Young Men's Magazine*. And they spent a lot of time at it, Charlotte at one point taking five and a half hours over the course of two days to fill a tiny volume with a Glass Town narrative later estimated at three thousand words.

Toy soldiers gave way to drawings, too. By dint of self-study as well as formal art lessons, the Brontë siblings learned to sketch and paint exquisitely rendered portraits of their heroes and heroines, setting them in romantic scenery copied from book and magazine illustrations. Drawing was, in fact, such an important part of the Brontë worldplay that Branwell later harbored hopes of becoming an artist.

It is perhaps around this same time that the shared make-believe also began to assert itself in private daydreams. In adolescence, Branwell possessed, in his own words, a "springy mind" roused by ideas "clothed in sunlight." Emily experienced, in her

Fig. 2.2. A handmade book by Charlotte Brontë, age 14, opened to "Chapter the first" of "An interesting passage in the lives of some eminent personages of the present age, by Lord Charles Wellesley." Written by Charlotte in June of 1830.

words, the "Flood of strange sensations" that reflect "the heart's real feeling." Return-ing to school and eventually taking employment as a teacher, Charlotte "scarce dare[d] think" of the visions she had little time or privacy to indulge away from home. In the midst of tedious duties, favorite characters would suddenly appear to her with such vividness that she felt "quite gone" from her drab surroundings. "[W]hat a treasure is thought!" she wrote, "What a privilege is reverie! I am thankful I have the power of solacing myself with the dream of creations whose reality I shall never behold."

All told, collaborative play in Glass Town lasted some eight years. In the last four or five of those years the four Brontës largely generated their imaginary world by combining private daydream with shared artistic and literary endeavor.

Then, when Charlotte was eighteen and Branwell seventeen, the two turned their at-tention to an offshoot of Glass Town that they called "Angria." For another six years, according to one scholar, they "each attempted to outdo or outmanoeuvre the other" by wresting control of characters and storylines. What Charlotte produced in terms of emo-tional narrative—at least twelve volumes of romance and adventure—Branwell more than made up for in the extraordinary output of Angrian history, geography, and politics.

Emily and Anne, meanwhile, attended to another Glass Town outgrowth they called "Gondal"—a "unique society" with a strong-willed queen that proved even longer-lived than Angria.

Interestingly enough, though Emily and Anne appear to have read the Angrian stories of Charlotte and Branwell, they themselves were more secretive. Emily's poetry is said to bear the mark of Gondal inspiration—but it is only a trace. Most of the histories, stories, poems, and drawings that survive for modern scrutiny belong to Glass Town and to Angria.

THE GENII AND "MAD" GENIUS

In the late 1970s Silvey could hardly escape reference to the Brontës' "fantasy realms." In fact, he characterized his New Hentian States as another secret Gondal, and himself as a Gondalite. He did not claim juvenile genius on his own part nor pre-cocity. Rather, he based his identification with the Brontës on the play itself.

Unfortunately, this association carried other baggage that Silvey surely wished to avoid. At the time he began his worldplay inquiries, overindulged daydream worlds were generally considered to be pathological, especially if they persisted past early childhood. In a 1955 compilation of true stories, for instance, psychiatrist Robert Lindner recalled the crippling effects on one patient of an active fantasy life begun in "solitary childhood." The adult patient no longer distinguished between what was real and what was pretend; even the good doctor got sucked into the pretense. To toy with one's sense of reality, Lindner concluded, was to wield a "double-edged sword."

A few years later, Joanne Greenberg wrote of her schizophrenic surrender to the imaginary—and punitive—world of Yr. The flip side of imaginative genius, it seemed, was madness.

Echoing these sentiments, Brontë scholarship assiduously traced every indication of emotional instability among the four siblings. If the Brontës' creativity had blossomed in their worldplay so, too, most biographers reasoned, did their idiosyncratic refuge in hearth, home, and daydream.

The issue crystallized from one twentieth-century scholar to the next. In 1949 Fannie Ratchford had argued rather simply that the siblings' "exaggerated make-believe," though the "strangest apprenticeship" in the writer's trade, was highly adaptive to their creative needs as they matured. A few years later Margaret Lane stated more forcefully that if the Brontë fantasy life stoked the creative flame, it also extinguished the siblings' fitness for real life. Craving their dream world as if it were a drug, the Brontës engaged in "a profound turning away from, or refusal of, ordinary life."

Some ten years later, in an unconventional effort to rescue Branwell from scholarly disapproval—he was, after all, the only sibling to fall short of early promise—Daphne Du Maurier fanned the flames of Brontë madness. In spite of evidence that Branwell had fallen victim to laudanum and alcohol addiction, she speculated that the aberrant behavior keeping him from creative work was caused by schizophrenia or epilepsy, this last highly associated, in the nineteenth century at least, with insanity.

By the time, then, that Silvey referred to Branwell, Charlotte, Emily, and Anne as archetypal inventors of imaginary worlds, scholarly consensus took it as a given that the Brontës had preferred the inner imagination to reality and in some cases, at some times, had poorly distinguished between the two.

What madness may have to do with creativity and genius has continued to intrigue down to this day, with scholars arguing for and against the association, its benefits and its deficits. In 1995, in a large scale and statistically convincing study of 1,004 eminent individuals of the 20th century, psychiatrist Arnold Ludwig argued that no necessary or sufficient correlation, hence no causal connection, between mental illness and creative achievement was to be found. Individuals in artistic professions were somewhat more likely than, say, scientists to experience mild mental disturbance, but mental illness in its severe forms proved detrimental to their work.

At present scholars tentatively agree that creative eminence in general, across a range of professions, correlates with mental health—although a little eccentricity goes a long way, especially in the arts and literature, in promoting the novelty of experience and expression valuable to those fields. Indeed, Ludwig has suggested that a certain amount of mild psychological unease might actually accompany the onset of—and be relieved by—creative endeavors of all kinds. To the extent such tension heightens the pleasure of problem resolution, it may also result in "addiction" to creative thought processes and activities.

This craving for creative experience, rather than mad withdrawal from the world, seems to have been the case with the Brontë sisters, if not their brother. True enough, all four did prefer their worldplay to most other social activity. The girls pined away when sent to school and Branwell turned tail on the formal study of art. What's more, they all failed in their twenties to find congenial footing outside Haworth. Branwell lost job after job; Emily retreated home as family housekeeper; Charlotte and Anne took posts as schoolteachers and governesses—and suffered horribly under the regimen. "Stupidity the atmosphere, school-books the employment, asses the society," wrote Charlotte in her journal, "what in all this is there to remind me of the divine, silent, unseen land of thought." Home meant the freedom to enter at will the worlds of Angria and Gondal—and, for the girls at least, to write the literature those worlds inspired.

As Charlotte made clear in her journals and letters, the combination was intoxicating. Whenever she could, she devoted herself to conjuring up compelling daydreams and recording them in story. From an early age she thought herself possessed of "a mighty imagination" that freely flowed in play. When writing she knew herself inspired by "fervid flashes from one of the Muses' lamps that just then passed through my mind." Arguing from personal experience, as an older school girl she characterized genius as spontaneity of thought and vision. Years later, she called again on the spontaneous play of imagination to defend the passionate outpourings of *Jane Eyre:*

> When authors write best, or at least, when they write most fluently, an influence seems to waken in them which becomes their master, which will have its own way, putting out of view all behests but its own . . . rejecting carefully elaborated old ideas, and suddenly creating and adopting new ones. Is it not so? And should we try to counteract this influence? Can we indeed counteract it?"

Charlotte's question—ought the influence of imagination be counteracted?—was not simply rhetorical. For all the intense joys of daydreaming and writing, she also suffered intensely over what she believed to be the sinister attractions of her world-play—not the escape, per se, but the sacrilege of the experience.

Almost from the start, she and Branwell had referred to their imaginary land as their "infernal world." In contrast to the avowed Christian mores of their family circle, Angria was a place of violence, cruelty, and vice. While Branwell wrote dispatches of war and politics involving the ruthless Marquess of Douro, Charlotte explored Douro's licit and illicit affairs with love-obsessed women. By the time she was twenty and newly embarked on her career as a teacher, the moral conflict reached its climax. To a friend she wrote, "If you knew my thoughts; the dreams that absorb me; and the fiery imagination that at times eats me up and makes me feel Society as it is, wretchedly insipid you would pity and I dare say despise me."

Just what the tenor of Charlotte's pursuits ought to have been, according to contemporary society, is made abundantly clear in a letter she received the following year from the poet Robert Southey. Charlotte had sent Southey a sample of her work and begged an opinion of her talents. Southey's response was twofold. "Literature," he wrote, "cannot be the business of a woman's life: & it ought not to be." The duties of the sex, he opined, left no time to pursue true accomplishment in writing; in moments of leisure a woman might write poetry to elevate the mind but should do so with no thought for publication or fame.

Southey might have said the same to any female supplicant. But he also and particularly urged Charlotte to curtail her vivid daydreams, to step back from the abyss of a "visionary world":

> The daydreams in wh[ich] you habitually indulge are likely to induce a distempered state of mind, & in proportion as all the "ordinary uses of the world" seem to you "flat & unprofitable," you will be unfitted for them, without becoming fitted for anything else.

Southey felt reason for concern. For many years he had been uncle and surrogate father to Hartley Coleridge, whom we briefly met in chapter 1. As a brilliant child, Hartley had been much given to daydreaming; in adult life, he floundered at making a living and squandered his poetic gifts. Southey blamed unbridled imagination. Though Charlotte was no doubt unaware of this subtext, she took the advice to heart. Antagonisms mounting between her religion and her make-believe, between her allotted role in life and her creative desires, she made several half-hearted and at least one concerted effort to throw off her worldplay.

Not until her play partnership with her brother faltered, however, when she was twenty-four and Branwell twenty-two, did Angria truly dissolve. Mercifully for the literary canon, the writing did not. Still driven by her "addiction" to creative activity, Charlotte turned from the fervent narratives of her paracosm to English settings—and so did her sisters. Branwell, the imaginative equal of his sisters in childhood, never reached this artistic juncture. Indeed, the wreck of his talent, along with economic necessity, strengthened the sisters' resolve to sell their art. In short order, they published a joint book of poems, followed a year later, in 1847, by Anne's *Agnes Grey*, Emily's *Wuthering Heights*, and Charlotte's *Jane Eyre,* this last to instant success.

These first books proved as nothing else could that the Brontë sisters had not utterly lost themselves to secret daydreams. If madness is defined as an inability to function effectively in the real world, then—despite the misgivings of peers and progeny—these women were manifestly not mad. They had, in fact, the wherewithal to transform their vivid and private powers of imagination into public art of the highest order. They distinguished between what was imagined and what was real without sacrificing what was necessary to them of either one.

ORDINARY IMAGINARY WORLDS

When Silvey identified with the juvenile Brontës, he presumed madness no more than genius. Some children—like Lindner's patient, like Joanne Greenberg—may have invented imaginary worlds to cope with trauma, depression, or mental illness, but Silvey's instincts told him that many more did so as a means of exploring the fullness of ordinary experience. To focus on these children, he and his colleague MacKeith added one last criterion to paracosm play. Not only must it endure consistently and meaningfully over some period of time, it must be *understood as pretense.*

In this manner, the two researchers anticipated psychological studies showing that psychotic individuals rarely developed organized daydreams. Those who did lacked playful control of the fantasies and the ability to distinguish them from reality. By insisting on these distinctions, Silvey and MacKeith reclaimed from the "pathological" the play of a normally developing imagination.

At this juncture, Silvey's untimely death largely ended his contributions to the research. He had nonetheless accomplished much. Via questionnaire, fifty-seven inventors of imaginary worlds had provided a rich lode of information about their childhood paracosms, their juvenile sense of self, and the family and school environments within which they grew up. Despite the loss of his colleague, MacKeith persisted in writing up, first, a preliminary analysis and then, a joint report. Eventually he collaborated with the play expert David Cohen to bring the work Silvey had begun to posthumous culmination in book form.

Written in essence by two men and a ghost, *The Development of Imagination, the Private Worlds of Childhood* (1991), shed light on paracosm play in three ways: by establishing its developmental profile; by assessing its appeal to certain personality types; and by categorizing its forms and contents.

In the first instance, the trio of researchers argued that the invention of imaginary worlds typically begins around the age of nine, continues for some months or years, and then fades in the late teens. Because of early taproots in the invention of imaginary friends or ties to adolescent daydreams and structured storytelling, worldplay is akin to other imaginative activities that flourish throughout childhood. Unlike these common forms of make-believe play, however, the researchers considered the invention of imaginary worlds to be rare at every stage of development. They were well aware, of course, that this last point had not been proven, but the small number of known cases, when compared to the general population, seemed to argue in its favor.

The trio proposed, secondly, that the appeal of worldplay was restricted to certain personality types. Respondents had been asked to choose from a list of twenty-six adjectives, those that best described them in childhood. The two attributes chosen by three-fifths or more of the group were "imaginative" and "bright." Two-fifths or so selected "dreamy" and "curious." Roughly one-quarter to one-third described themselves as "bad at games," "timid," "unmechanically minded," and "solitary"; less than one-sixth chose "good at games," "outgoing," "mechanically minded," and "gregarious." From these data Silvey and MacKeith characterized children who invented imaginary worlds as "dreamy" personalities, though their type might equally have been described as "imaginative," "bright," and "curious."

Third, and finally, the researchers organized the sixty-four worlds invented by their fifty-seven paracosmists into five content groups or categories:

- *Toy-based lands,* including "Animal-land," a floating island "inhabited by Golliwogs, Humpty-dumpties, animals, [and] dolls." In the years before prep school, one "Philip" and his younger brother made Golliwogs from colored wool and, rather than act out the game, recited events for each other in bedtime stories.
- *Particular, local places,* including the pretend orphanage run by a terrifying warden and his wife. "Leonora" and two of her friends playacted "The Game" from age eight to adolescence.
- *Islands, countries, and peoples,* including the international railway system invented by "Denis" between the ages of eleven and fourteen. Two imaginary individuals, complete with back-stories and portraits, built a worldwide railway system that traversed continents and crossed oceans by means of an imaginary tunnel-building machine. Denis subsequently invented an imaginary school staffed by important personages, for whom he drew official portraits, wrote potted biographies, and researched uniforms, medals, heraldry, and peerage genealogies.
- *Systems, documents, and languages,* including Silvey's New Hentian States, a number of railway system worlds focused on timetables and maps, and the island

state of "Possumbul." Possumbul, played by two cousins "Dan" and "Peter" from the ages of five or so to thirteen, began as a toy-based world of stuffed animals and toy soldiers that incrementally acquired a democratic government, a language, and a religion, as well as maps, city plans, military medals, and uniforms.

- *Unstructured, idyllic realms,* including "Brenda's" amorphous utopian fantasies, one located in a thicket of bushes, another on a mapped imaginary island. "Creating places where things happened was the major preoccupation" when she was between nine and eleven years old; much of the play involved the "imaginary acting-out of social interactions."

Close consideration of content categories and the case histories included in each reveals a simple developmental progression in imaginary world invention. In general, the very youngest children make up paracosms revolving around toys, animals, or imagined people in family groups or other small communities. Children between the ages of seven and twelve invent countries and peoples, or build up languages, governments, and other systems.

As children grow up, their interest in human affairs tends to shift from the personal intimacy of toy families to the social interactions of larger establishments and to the increasingly abstract cultural, economic, and political systems characterizing society at large. Those who persist in worldplay over significant periods of time may invent new and different paracosms, or they may adapt an original paracosm to changing concerns.

Whatever the case, content categories begin to blur. Take the paracosmist Denis, for example, who invented at least two imaginary worlds. Silvey, MacKeith, and Cohen placed his imaginary school (as well as his railroad world) in their third category of islands, countries, and peoples, despite a focus on local place similar to Leonora's orphanage game.

Because of his interest in recreating medals and uniforms for that imaginary school, Denis also shared play activity with the inventors of Possumbul, categorized in the fourth group focused on systems, documents, and languages.

Due to its origins in play with stuffed animals, Possumbul likewise had characteristics similar to those of Philip's Animal-land, placed in the first group of toy-based places. Despite the neat categories, there is much variation and overlap in the age-related elaboration of worldplay content.

Well aware that the imaginary worlds they studied shared characteristics across categories, Silvey and MacKeith had early on set out an additional four "dimensions" of variation within and across types that had less to do with content than with the quality or style of play.

- First, they noticed, children either intend that their worldplay be *fantastic*, like fairy stories in which things and events are impossibly magical, or they intend that the play be *naturalistic*, in which things and events are meant to be consistent with the laws of nature and society.
- Second, children either create *idealistic,* utopian worlds, in which everyone is happy and everything goes according to plan, or they create *realistic* worlds reflecting moral and social dilemmas.

- Third, children focus on the social world of their characters, with its *high degree of personal interactions*, or they focus on settings and institutions, with a *low degree of personal interactions*.
- And fourth, children involve themselves as characters in their play or they stand outside it looking in (what the researchers termed *ego or non-ego involvement*).

For Silvey and MacKeith, these dimensions clarified important differences between, say, Animal-land (fantastic) and Possumbul (naturalistic) or between the railway world of Denis (high degree of personal interaction) and those focused on timetables and maps (low degree of personal interaction). We might even take these dimensions to clarify certain differences in worldplay between children who shared the same paracosm.

Recall that Charlotte and her brother Branwell collaborated on stories, drawings, and other documentations of Angria; their style of play, however, was not entirely the same. The siblings agreed that their imaginary land was a place highly naturalistic and realistic, scene to possible events and probable behaviors. Both made firm distinctions between themselves and their characters, remaining outside the play as creators, not characters. Yet Branwell focused content on the political and military histories of Angria (low degree of personal interaction), while Charlotte attended to the personal lives of Branwell's heroes and villains (high degree of personal interaction).

Interestingly enough, the Brontë pattern typified the worldplay of Silvey, MacKeith, and Cohen's fifty-seven respondents—(yet another indication, if need be, that the siblings' make-believe fell within normal parameters). The overwhelming majority of childhood paracosms were alive with moral and social dilemmas; over two-thirds were consistent with the laws of nature and society; two-thirds were outside the self.

Moreover, except for the fact that some girls had a greater preference for fantastic worlds than most boys, none of these first three categories varied much between the two sexes. With regard to personal interactions, however, the gender difference was remarkable. Most boys preferred to focus on groups and institutions. Two out of three girls focused on characters and their emotional concerns. All together, given the nearly equal numbers of boys and girls in the sample (31 boys, 33 girls), the imaginary world that was naturalistic, realistic, non-ego involved, and minimally concerned with personal life predominated.

THE PULSE OF WORLDPLAY

Silvey's search for paracosms opened a new window onto childhood imagination. Some of his initial suppositions had, unsurprisingly, failed to pan out. Worldplay was not just a solitary endeavor, for many of the paracosms he gathered had been shared worlds. Nor did it appeal more to boys than to girls. But on the whole, his presentiments had been sound. The basic impulse of paracosm play was to model a realistic and naturalistic universe. It belonged to children very much like himself. It was a phenomenon worth study.

What Silvey and his research partners achieved may, in fact, be considered a watershed in play studies. Before the search for paracosms there was little to corroborate their normality. After, there was much to confirm their invention as a pinnacle of the developing imagination. Individuals may now peruse *The Development of Imagination* for observations and insights that illuminate the worldplay of children in their care or the worldplay in their own past.

In my own reading of that book, I saw that my daughter had been a classic paracosmist: A bright, curious, somewhat dreamy child, more interested in solitary play than in social games, begins around the age of nine to invent an imaginary world. That world displayed the characteristics of paracosms based on islands, countries, and peoples and of paracosms based on systems, documents, and languages, the two types blending seamlessly into a working whole. Her worldplay had been naturalistic, realistic, projected outside herself with a high degree of personal interaction—and with a high degree of systematized, abstracted detail as well.

I also noticed that as Meredith matured, her paracosm play led her to develop interests in both art and science. And this outcome led me to question some of the book's other conclusions. Cohen and MacKeith made two particularly troublesome, contradictory claims: first, that paracosm play is linked to an affinity for the arts and second, that it is somehow at odds with the full development of imagination or creative potential. Certain suppositions and results over the course of the research apparently led to this paradox.

Before Silvey's death, he and MacKeith had compiled a list of imaginary worlds mentioned in memoirs, autobiographies, and biographies. (See the appendix.) This short list was comprised of fifteen well-known novelists and poets, with a few additional artists and writers. These included poet W. H. Auden, novelist Robert Louis Stevenson, artist-sculptor Claes Oldenburg, actor Peter Ustinov, and philosopher Alan Watts. Silvey and MacKeith understood that writers might dominate the list because they "easily write autobiographies"! Nevertheless, they took the preponderance of literary examples as fair evidence that the invention of imaginary worlds in childhood anticipated mature endeavor in the arts.

Silvey and MacKeith did not press the point, possibly due to Silvey's stated resistance to speculation based on self-selecting "post-bag" samples. But after his death MacKeith and Cohen took the tacit position that the invention of imaginary worlds *ought to prepare* the dreamy child for mature endeavor of an artistic sort, as it apparently had for writers and artists on the list and, of course, for the Brontës.

As things turned out, however, supporting evidence did not surface among their anonymous paracosmists. Although the researchers refrained from systematically describing adult careers, they did say that only a couple of their paracosmists achieved any kind of literary success and "few of [the] original sample of fifty-seven became artists." As their own data seemed to make clear, the invention of imaginary worlds in childhood did not *necessarily* lead toward adult careers in literature or the arts. As a result, the two researchers reversed course and argued that the invention of imaginary worlds in childhood was unrelated, perhaps even inversely related, to creative development.

In retrospect, Cohen and MacKeith made a number of questionable assumptions that undermine that conclusion. To be fair, these assumptions were quite common among psychologists at the time and still persist to a significant degree among the public. One of these assumptions is that some activities, such as the arts, are inherently creative, whereas others, such as science or engineering, are not. Another assumption is that creativity is a function of one's ability to fantasize, which is to say, to "think outside the box" and imagine impossible things. Psychologists often capture this novelty-producing capacity as "divergent thinking."

Put these assumptions together and you get what seems to have been Cohen and MacKeith's train of thought: first, a fanciful imagination is of value to artistic fields of endeavor; second, the preference for fantasy therefore epitomizes creative imagination; and third, the creative value of make-believe play in childhood must thus lie in its impossible whimsies. By these tokens, the ordinary invention of imaginary worlds, few of which were idealistic or impossibly magical and fantastic, simply didn't measure up.

What the researchers found instead was that most worldplay, highly naturalistic as well as realistic, more obviously involved what psychologists call the "convergent thinking" of a problem-solving endeavor. Moreover, only some manifestations of worldplay involved artistic fantasy, a significant portion focusing on the elaborate rules and plausible models of organization and analysis rather than the sole production of novelty. Hence the researchers' gist that, while worldplay appeared to be "the most complex form of imaginative activity children are capable of," inventing paracosms as a child somehow inhibited creative development.

We can challenge these conclusions and their underlying assumptions on two or three grounds. First, no one profession is inherently more creative than another. There are just as many hack writers and unimaginative artists as there are laboratory technicians and bean counters. Second, every invention and discovery requires much the same kind and degree of imagination as an outstanding novel or poem or new sculptural form. Moreover, the anonymous inventor exploits many of the same imaginative skills and creative behaviors as the most eminent of innovators. The idea that creativity only manifests in artistic genius cannot be accepted—and the arguments Cohen and MacKeith apparently based on the notion must be reexamined.

Indeed, Silvey's own career should have given his collaborators pause. Answering his own query, he described the boy he had been as imaginative, but not artistic. In fact, his mature achievements lay elsewhere. He pioneered opinion polling at the BBC by marrying the demands of statistical inquiry to sociological and psychological nuance, in part because he understood intimately that a valid sample—like an imaginary world—"had to be selected in such a way as to be a miniature, a scale-model, of the universe."

Recognized in 1960 as an Officer of the Order of the British Empire, an honor granted for valuable service in the arts, sciences and public sectors, he went on to jump-start the study of paracosms. By these measures, he proved himself more than capable, even creative, in teasing out patterns and possibilities in his particular walk of life. And that mature creativity had something to do with his childhood play.

When all was said and done, Silvey's experience suggested that worldplay may be valuable preparation not just for the arts, but for any profession, and not just to geniuses, but to people of more ordinary talents as well. Mindful of how I might build on his groundbreaking work, on the best of his collaborators' insights, and on a broader definition of creative undertaking, I set out to determine just how uncommon or common worldplay might be, whether or not it manifests among people who go into different professions and if so, what connection individuals may draw between this play and their adult creative endeavor, no matter the field.

In short, I dreamed up a worldplay project of my own.

Chapter Three

Memory Counts: MacArthur Fellows and College Students Recall Childhood Play

I think there are deep continuities between the functioning of the imagination in early childhood and its functioning later.

—Paul Harris, psychologist

SAMPLING AND ASSESSING WORLDPLAY

From: Bob <rrb@michstateu.edu>
Date: 15 Oct 9:00 (EST)
To: <mrb@michstateu.edu>
Subject: beans

How's the bean count going?

From: Michele <mrb@michstateu.edu>
Date: 25 Sep 11:02 (EST)
To: <rrb@michstateu.edu>
Subject: peas

More like pea counting. Remember how you told me umpteen years ago that Mendel had difficulty deciding if a yellow-green pea was yellow or green? I never thought it would be like splitting hairs to say, yes, this is an imagined place and, no, this is not. This is ephemeral or not; persistent or not; elaborated or not. This is worldplay, for crying out loud, and this is not!!! If mulling over this sample has taught me anything, it's that the invention of imaginary worlds is far from an either/or experience.

From:	Bob <rrb@michstateu.edu>
Date:	15 Oct 11:45 (EST)
To:	<mrb@michstateu.edu>
Subject:	fuzzy set

Sounds like a "fuzzy set." Which comes into play when you try to categorize things that vary continuously into discrete groups. Can't be done without ambiguity and bias. As a geneticist by the name of Pearl demonstrated when he had 15 scientists sort the same 532 corn kernels into yellow-starchy, yellow-sweet, white-starchy or white-sweet groupings. Each scientist came up with a different count. Instead of objectivity, Pearl discovered "personal equation," the slight nuance in perception each of us brings to observation. We may like to think of corn crosses—and kinds of play—as distinct from one another, but nature is more complicated than that.

From:	Michele <mrb@michstateu.edu>
Date:	15 Oct 2:30 (EST)
To:	<rrb@michstateu.edu>
Subject:	fuzzy memory

Human nature, too! If counting memories is subject to the bias of researcher perception, memories that count are also prone to the ambiguities of individual recall. Still and all, I think I can establish whether or not people *think* there's a connection between imaginative invention in childhood and adulthood.

From:	Bob <rrb@michstateu.edu>
Date:	15 Oct 5:00 (EST)
To:	<mrb@michstateu.edu>
Subject:	counting memories counts

Do tell!

From:	Michele <mrb@michstateu.edu>
Date:	15 Oct 2:30 (EST)
To:	<rrb@michstateu.edu>
Subject:	The Worldplay Project

Gladly.

As we now know, the search for paracosms in late twentieth century Britain raised but did not settle questions concerning the incidence of childhood worldplay, its effects on the developing imagination and its connections to adult creative activity and profession. Inspired to push forward what Silvey, Cohen, and MacKeith had started, in the early 2000s I undertook a complementary Worldplay Project investigating imaginary world invention among MacArthur Fellows. Recipients of the so-called "genius" grants, I expected, might reasonably provide data that clarified the relationship between imaginary world invention and creativity.

For over thirty years, by means of a private vetting process, the John D. and Catherine T. MacArthur Foundation has been regularly selecting individuals of exceptional originality and promise for no-strings-attached awards of money. (Full disclosure: my husband was named one of the very first Fellows in 1981.) Upon appointment, some Fellows have already reached the peak of their careers; others have only just begun the climb. In any case, they variously work in the arts, sciences, social sciences, humanities, and public interest professions. In terms of the Worldplay Project, I hoped that this variety of adult endeavors would provide a broad look at the role of imaginative play in the development of a creative life.

In sampling this group for childhood paracosms, the purpose of the Worldplay Project was to explore in a largely quantitative way certain hypotheses believed true on qualitative or anecdotal grounds. Earlier research had concluded that paracosm play was rare and indicated an affinity with the arts. I conjectured otherwise:

First, paracosm play would be relatively common, especially among demonstrably creative individuals.

Second, these individuals would work as adults in a diverse range of disciplines across the arts and sciences.

Third, many of them would perceive connections between childhood play and adult work, perhaps even articulate how the early invention of parallel worlds nurtured and trained creative capacities of general and lifelong use.

I launched the Worldplay Project in 2002 by contacting 505 MacArthur Fellows, about 90 percent of those given awards from 1981 through 2001. By mail or e-mail each of these individuals received a short query asking about vocations, hobbies, childhood play in general, the invention of imaginary worlds in particular, and perceived connections to adult creativity.

The information received from Fellows would be interesting only if it differed from information received from a population that was *not* demonstrably creative—or at least, *not selected* on those grounds. To that end, the Worldplay Project also involved a control group of students attending Michigan State University (MSU).

Although the entrance level for this large, land-grant institution is considered moderately difficult, the student body represents a group of individuals selected for ordinary academic achievement rather than creative productivity. Over the course of 2003, eight university classrooms in the sciences, humanities, arts, and general education departments were polled, using an anonymous questionnaire almost identical to that prepared for Fellows.

As a foil for the Fellows, the student population worked best if it could be assumed that creative aptitude was the *only* gross difference between the two groups. But the reality was not that simple. The two groups also differed markedly in age. Over half of responding Fellows were in their fifties and sixties. Nearly all students were in their early twenties; some were in their thirties or forties.

This age gap introduced a potential bias in study results. Students, closer in years to childhood, might have more accessible memories of early worldplay and Fellows, fewer. Yet Silvey had observed that childhood worldplay, as a seminal experience, held long-term significance for paracosmists. On these grounds, any effect the passage of time might have on the recall of worldplay in childhood would likely be mitigated by the importance of that play—and the age difference could be ignored.

In the event, out of 505 Fellow contacts, the Worldplay Project received 106 responses, a return rate of about one in five. Sixteen Fellows politely declined to participate in the survey altogether. Some cited personal discretion or protection of current creative inspiration. "This cuts too close to home," wrote one. "Sacred territory," wrote another, "these are subjects I prefer not to discuss for fear of disturbing the muse the wrong way!" The rest cited lack of time or interest. All together, 90 MacArthur Fellows answered query questions in whole or in part. Of these, 39 Fellows reported worldplay and 51 reported no worldplay. On the face of it, this meant that 43 percent of respondents from this group had invented imaginary worlds in childhood.

Out of some 1,000 students given the opportunity to fill out the query, 262 students responded, again about one-fifth of the sampled pool. One hundred and five student responses answered "yes" to worldplay in childhood; 157 answered "no." The positive self-report of imaginary world invention in this group was 40 percent.

These preliminary results were very surprising. On the one hand, Silvey and MacKeith had believed paracosm play to be rare. After all, they had received only 57 responses to their worldplay query from a very large, newspaper-reading population. On the other hand, I had expected the invention of imaginary worlds to be more commonplace only in creative groups. Yet Fellows and students both reported *similarly high rates* of childhood worldplay.

Upon closer evaluation, however, many of these responses proved to be "false positives." Self-reported play-worlds were not always paracosms—at least when compared to the Brontës' Glass Town, my daughter's Kar Land, or the various imaginary worlds described in *The Development of Imagination.* Because the query implied that worldplay was imaginative and often creative, many Fellows and students may have consciously or unconsciously characterized their play as such. Subjective self-reports had necessarily to be reevaluated according to more objective measures.

Most of the play described by Fellows and students fell into the three sorts typically recognized by psychologists: enacted make-believe (playacting or socio-dramatic play), make-believe reverie (daydreams), and constructed make-believe, this last including the modeling or crafting of props or other artifacts. In theory, these types of imaginative play were distinct from one another. In practice, however, the invention of a paracosm blurred the lines between one sort and another.

It didn't matter for worldplay whether the child enacted an elaborate pretense with or without other children, engaged in daydream, or modeled an imagined space with blocks and other materials. What mattered was make-believe that took on a life of its own. My task for the Worldplay Project was to recognize within a multitude of play experiences those that really did involve the wholesale invention of an imaginary place.

I established a checklist based upon the Silvey and MacKeith criteria: imaginary worlds must be persistent, consistent, and important to the individual. I also made provision for additional qualities of play. There must be evidence that the play-world in question actually involved imagined dimensions—places and/or people—beyond the here and now of props and playacting. There must be indication, too, that those imagined dimensions were conceived in some detail and involved specific rather than generic notions of place or persons. The difference I wanted to capture is the difference between playing dolls and playing in Lolly-Dollyland.

The project's worldplay criteria included as well the notion of solitary or intimately shared play with one or two intimates as a proxy for the personal ownership of the make-believe. Whether in the school yard or the neighborhood, I took it as given that group play with large and shifting numbers of children afforded much less individual control over the course of play and its imaginative dimensions.

Finally, I also looked for written stories, maps, drawings, and other constructions as corroborative evidence of worldplay. The presence of such artifacts of play made it possible to distinguish between persistent imaginary worlds and more ephemeral make-believe. It also allowed me to accept as paracosm play a couple of reported instances of imaginary friends, when these friends inhabited a fully conceived and documented place.

There were ambiguities inherent in these criteria. Childhood play *leaned* toward the ephemeral or the persistent. Make-believe places and people *tended* toward the generic or toward the unique. Play scenarios *tended* toward continual repetition or toward continuous development. Children *apparently* controlled play scenarios or apparently did not.

Moreover, recalled play rarely matched all criteria for the invention of imaginary worlds. The "palace room" one MacArthur Fellow recreated by herself with household knickknacks appeared to be persistent, consistent from day to day, and to involve a specific imaginary place, though she never documented that world or systematized it other than in imagination. Similarly, "a little 'subdivision' complete with street signs & everything," which one student described building in the woods behind her house with "brothers and neighbors," seemed to have the hallmarks of a parallel play world enjoyed for a number of years, though unelaborated in any way "other than what's left in the woods."

Ultimately, whether any particular instance of play might be recognizable worldplay was a more-or-less proposition. Certain traits were corroborative; others, however, were a must.

In the checklist's final form, bona fide worldplay 1) *required* the notion of a specific "other" place, either partly or wholly imaginary; 2) *might include* the notion of specific persons, either partly or wholly imaginary; and 3) *must include* the consistent return over some period of time to a specific scenario, as evidenced by the naming of place and characters or the elaboration of a continuous narrative or other systematization.

When these criteria did not resolve ambiguity, indications that the play had been private or intimately shared as opposed to communally practiced were considered. This and other evidence of the child's creative control helped tip the balance toward worldplay. When all was said and done, the Worldplay Project accepted the "palace room" as an invented world, but rejected the "subdivision" in the woods as such, for communal play with a loose group of children had not been offset by evidence of private or intimately shared elaboration.

RATES OF WORLDPLAY

As a first order of business the Worldplay Project established rates for researcher-assessed childhood worldplay. Thirty-nine MacArthur Fellows reported that they had invented imaginary worlds in childhood. After evaluating these responses in terms of the project checklist, however, sixteen responses were found to describe ephemeral playacting, imaginary companions, make-believe borrowed from books or movies, and other, minor forms of play. The remaining twenty-three reports qualified as recognizable instances of paracosm play.

These instances of worldplay included the model city that one Fellow built in the woods when he was around nine years old, because the city had institutions and a history. The invention of imaginary worlds was also to be found in another Fellow's play with a model theater that set the stage for imaginary operas. Finally, a more ambiguous, but acceptable example included the genealogical records kept by yet another Fellow for "a cast of imaginary characters" whose adventures in the "real world" had "evolving histories."

Given these 23 instances of recognizable worldplay, the invention of imaginary worlds among the 90 responding Fellows was 26 percent. Whether the 400 Fellows who did *not* respond to the query invented imaginary worlds in the same, greater, or lesser proportion remained, of course, unknown.

Assuming, on the one hand, that query responders did in fact fairly represent the sample as a whole, then 26 percent represented a maximum proportion of MacArthur Fellows inventing imaginary worlds in childhood. (In other words, out of the 505 Fellows contacted, some 131 might actually have invented worlds in childhood.) Assuming, on the other hand, that the 23 individuals assessed as inventing imaginary worlds represented *only* the sampled Fellows with this childhood experience, then only 5 percent or so (23 out of 505) invented worlds in childhood. Presumably, the reality lay somewhere within this 5 percent to 26 percent range.

In order to place these results in context, the incidence of worldplay among MSU students was also determined. Out of 105 self-reports of paracosm play, 73 actually described socio-dramatic play, make-believe borrowed from book and entertainment narratives, imaginary companions, ephemeral daydreams or bedtime stories in the absence of a consistently imagined place, language games in the absence of an imaginary world, and one or two irrelevant play forms. Thirty-two student responses qualified as researcher-assessed worldplay.

These thirty-two reports of bona fide worldplay included the invented land of "Mystica," inhabited by people and other creatures and replete with maps and histories. They also included a "rainbow house" where the child at play "lived with imaginary animals and cartoons I loved" and a paracosm of bed stories woven around people who "lived in the clouds and at night would come into your dreams."

By this count, the rate of recognizable worldplay among student responders was 12 percent. Once again, assuming that the proportion among responders was typical of all students given a chance to fill out the query, this 12 percent represented the maximum rate of worldplay in that group. Assuming the alternative, assuming that *all* students with childhood worldplay chose to respond positively to the query, then the rate for the entire group was a minimum of 3 percent. Again, the real incidence of worldplay among MSU students presumably fell between 3 percent and 12 percent.

For Fellows and students alike, the researcher-assessed incidence for worldplay came in considerably lower than self-report rates. Nonetheless, in its upper and lower limits that incidence traced the contours of a visible feature in the landscape of play.

By extrapolation, the student range at its high end suggested that as many as one-eighth or more of a general population might invent long-term imaginary worlds in childhood—about the same proportion, according to the U.S. Census for 2004–2005, that engage in photography as an adult hobby (11.4 percent). The Fellow range at its high end suggested that as many as one-quarter of demonstrably creative people might invent worlds, this corresponding roughly to the frequency of yearly attendance at art museums among American adults (27 percent).

Even at the lower limits of incidence, extrapolation suggested that childhood worldplay is at least as frequent in the general population as the adult hobby of flying kites (3.2 percent) or, in creative populations, as adult yearly participation in hobbies such as chess (4.6 percent) or drawing (6.7 percent). Contrary to the suppositions of Silvey and MacKeith, the invention of imaginary worlds in childhood could no longer be considered rare, but rather noticeably common (see figure 3.1).

The same project data also suggested that childhood worldplay might indeed be linked to mature creativity, for if early worldplay had no relevance at all to creative activity in adulthood, one might expect its incidence in both regular and creative

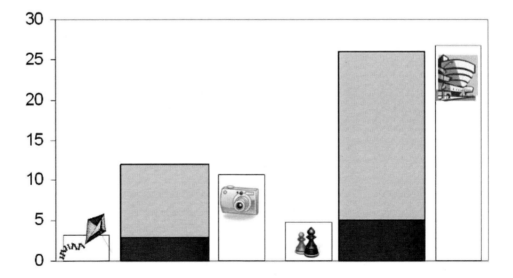

MSU Students   MacArthur Fellows

Fig. 3.1. Minimum (black) and Maximum (gray) Rates of Worldplay for MSU Students and MacArthur Fellows Compared to U.S. Hobby Rates (kite flying, photography, chess, and attendance at art museums, 2004-2005).

populations to be more or less the same. In fact, whether at lower or higher ends, Fellows had engaged in recognizable worldplay about twice as often as MSU students.

Demonstrable creativity was *not,* however, the only difference between the two groups. If the age gap between MacArthur Fellows and MSU students had not obviously favored student *recall* of bona fide worldplay, it might still have favored the worldplay *practice* of Fellows, so that they, more so than students, were pushed towards complex make-believe.

In effect, the two groups appeared to straddle both sides of a watershed in childhood play. In the last thirty to fifty years the introduction of certain twentieth century entertainment technologies, such as television and, more recently, personal computers and the Internet, have profoundly altered possibilities for make-believe. (What effect computer games, in particular, may have on the worldplay impulse will be taken up at length in chapter 11.) Fellows may have invented more imaginary worlds as children because they had less entertainment options and more free time for make-believe. MSU students may have invented fewer worlds because they had more entertainment options and less free time.

Taking these possible generational effects into account, there looked to be an affinity between childhood worldplay and free time for make-believe and between early worldplay, time for make-believe, and adult creative endeavor.

DISCIPLINARY INCLINATIONS

In addition to incidence, the Worldplay Project tracked adult careers associated with the childhood invention of paracosms. Silvey, MacKeith, and Cohen had tied the invention of imaginary worlds to the artistic professions—though they did not investigate in any systematic way the actual distribution of adult endeavors among their sample of paracosmists. The Worldplay Project purposefully collected such data.

In the interests of simplicity, the project utilized the disciplinary categorization of Fellows employed by the MacArthur Foundation (see figure 3.2). Over the years 1981–1996, the MacArthur Foundation appointed about one-fourth of Fellows in the arts, a few more than one-fourth in the sciences, one-fifth each in the humanities and in public-issues professions, and one-tenth in the social sciences. The professional breakdown of MacArthur Fellows responding to the project survey closely mirrored this disciplinary complexion, except for one-third fewer responses from individuals in the humanities than might have been expected and about a third more responses in the social sciences.

As anticipated, MSU students expected to engage in a similarly wide range of adult careers. Because so many students intended to make a living in law, business, and education, however, the public issues and social science professions together represented almost two-thirds of all students, whereas arts and sciences claimed little more than a third. Six percent of students had not yet made a career choice.

Consideration of the professional distribution of students and Fellows with worldplay in their background turned up additional differences. Students in the humanities, arts, and public issues fields were more likely to have invented imaginary worlds in

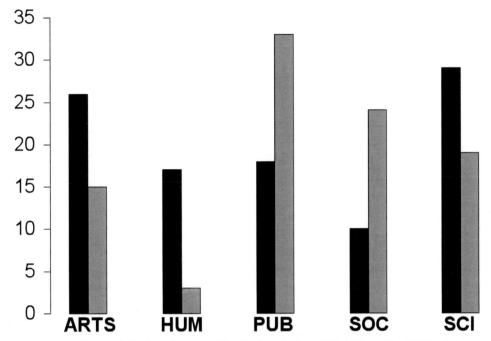

Fig. 3.2. Professional Fields and Intended Professions in the ARTS, HUManities, PUBlic Interest Professions, SOCial sciences and SCIences, by percent: MacArthur Fellows (black bars) and MSU Students (gray bars). (See chapter endnotes for variety of fields within categories.)

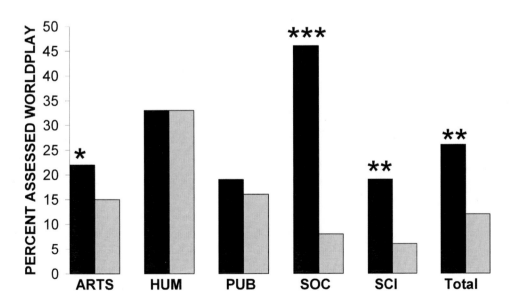

Fig. 3.3. Childhood Worldplay: MacArthur Fellows (black bars) and MSU Students (gray bars). * = p<.05 ** = p<.001 *** = p<.0001 (See figure note in chapter endnotes for explanation of p-values and their significance.)

childhood than students in the social sciences or sciences, by a factor of two or more (see figure 3.3). This finding seemed to mirror the presumption entertained by Silvey, MacKeith, and Cohen that paracosmists would find the arts (and, by extension, closely related careers in the humanities) especially congenial.

As figure 3.3 indicates, however, the same association did not hold true for MacArthur Fellows. In that group, artists were somewhat less likely than individuals working in the humanities and half as likely as individuals working in the social sciences to have invented imaginary worlds as children.

Moreover, these same artists were barely more likely to have invented worlds than Fellows working in education, journalism, and public policy fields or in the sciences. These results appeared to corroborate the expectation that creative individuals inventing imaginary worlds in childhood would find other professions as rewarding as the arts. Judging by the Fellows sampled in the Worldplay Project, the childhood invention of paracosms anticipated an affinity not just for the arts and related studies in the humanities, but for the sciences and social sciences as well.

Subsequent analysis confirmed this reading of the data. Comparing the professional distributions discipline by discipline proved some of the differences between the two groups highly significant. In particular, Fellows in the social sciences, the sciences, and the arts were more likely to have invented imaginary worlds in childhood than students planning to enter these same professions. In all three of these disciplinary fields it looked like childhood worldplay might be a *predictor* for mature creative achievement.

PERCEPTIONS OF CONNECTION

Both in general and in certain particular professions, the invention of imaginary worlds in childhood was strongly associated with creative achievement in adulthood. Still, that statistical correlation begged explanation, for in and of itself it could not prove that childhood worldplay *caused* adult creativity in any direct way. The actual influence or effect of paracosm play on mature endeavor was much more likely to be indirect and relational, such that a network of factors operating in tandem affected eventual creative outcomes. For its third and final order of business, then, the Worldplay Project explored what Fellows and students thought about the value of childhood play in imaginary worlds to ascertain a possible system of factors at work in individual experience.

When questioned as to whether childhood play *of any kind* had been important to vocation or avocations, some 40 percent of MacArthur Fellows replied yes. This included the Fellow appointed in the humanities who wrote: "My childhood was fairly rough and tumble, always racing around the neighborhood, building things, starting 'businesses,' coming up with new 'inventions' (that never worked), launching ourselves into outer space, saving bugs in jars, digging holes to China—in memory, at least, all fresh, unfettered, and teeming with possibility. My work today is pretty much the same thing." Other Fellows focused on prescient role-playing, on hobby interests such as astronomy or history, or the early-learned joys of taking things apart and putting them together again.

Some 53 percent of the student sample also indicated that childhood play of some kind had influenced current hobbies and intended professions. In fact, most extended comments in this group involved personally drawn connections between early play and ongoing leisure activities, which ranged from sports activities to music listening to game playing and movie watching.

In addition, many Fellows and students reported ongoing worldplay—understood as the invention of, or the participation in, imagined worlds. The query had referred to the "make-believe realms" of paintings, plays, films, and novels or to the "possible worlds" hypothetically constructed by scientists and others. Slightly over half of the Fellows who responded answered that they, in fact, did create or participate in such worlds; similarly, half of students already did or expected to do the same.

Interestingly enough, just about two-fifths of all responding Fellows, and more than a quarter of all responding students, specified that adult worldplay involved the *professional* invention of imagined or possible worlds. (Just what MacArthur Fellows meant by worldplay at work is investigated at length in chapter 8.) Fewer respondents in both groups reported ongoing worldplay in hobby or left the context of ongoing worldplay unspecified.

It was not necessary to have invented worlds in childhood to participate in, create, or anticipate creating invented worlds in adulthood, especially when this mature worldplay involved public—or at least socially sanctioned—activity. For some individuals, however, adult worldplay thrived in a more private space. Five Fellows revealed some tendency to "still return occasionally" as adults to imaginary realms first invented in childhood. Twelve MSU students also responded variously that they "still [play] in this world today," or "still slip into parts occasionally," "but only in my head."

In addition, a few Fellows disclosed paracosmic fantasies newly minted in maturity. These included the Fellow who thought of the tendency to practice "my skills by debating adversaries or giving speeches when I'm alone (in the car or walking to the metro)" as "imagined versions of real-life settings in which I find myself." They also included the Fellow who confessed, "My [spouse] and I play an elaborate imaginary world game all the time."

By and large, Fellows and students referred to worldplay in ongoing fantasy lives with a great deal of reticence. As one Fellow commented with regard to his childhood daydream world, "I feel awfully bashful about it. I am embarrassed by the childishness of it." The same embarrassment attended private worldplay in maturity. "As you get older," wrote one student, "they [parents/others] are less likely to think highly of it."

Social pressures of this sort go a long way in explaining the observed decline of juvenile worldplay in the late teens and early twenties. Though Silvey and MacKeith had noted the late-blooming "Mortmere" of Christopher Isherwood and his college pal, they found few additional young adults clinging to old paracosms or inventing new ones. Even in the Mortmere case, the worldplay did not outlast the young men's schooling.

In this light, the fact that some Fellows, well into middle and late adulthood, should continue to engage in childhood worlds seemed all the more remarkable. Or was it? Psychologists and others have long noted strong links between the tendency to daydream and originality of thought. Many argue, as well, that "creativity does not suddenly spring to life in adulthood." Perhaps MacArthur Fellows and others who extended their childhood worldplay into maturity continued to nurture an active imagination. By the same token, perhaps those who perceived their vocation or avocation *in terms of such play* also did so, whether or not they had invented paracosms when young.

What we do know is this: among those who engaged in worldplay as children perceptions of connection with adult forms of worldplay were high—61 percent for Fellows and 72 percent for students. A series of follow-up interviews clarified the nature of such connection among Fellows.

The poet Galway Kinnell provides a first example. As a child of seven or so, Kinnell built a little cardboard box village in the basement with two older siblings in a game called "Little Men." The children made houses out of cardboard boxes, cutting out doors and windows, putting up wallpaper inside, and making little pieces of furniture for each room. And they populated their town with an assortment of cast iron soldiers, sailors, pirates, cowboys, and Native Americans. In his Worldplay Project interview, Kinnell remembered the salient feature of his sibling play as profound absorption, fueled by the ability to empathize, "to go out of yourself and into other beings":

> Nothing was choreographed beforehand. We just went down there . . . we just began and . . . the thing is we soon fell into that world. I don't know how far [my siblings] fell, but I fell all the way into that world. That was the first time in my life that I really experienced transcendence of consciousness. . . . When my mother's voice came down the stairs telling us it was time to go to bed . . . it was a shock to me . . . that one or two or three hours had passed while we were doing this. . . . I was really in the trance of another world when I played that game. And then, later in my life, when I started writing, I noticed something that I connected with that trance. When I was really involved with a poem I entered the world of the poem.

Economist Alice Rivlin similarly remembered engaging in a "fairly sophisticated" bedstory for much of her middle childhood. In a world devastated by flood, she had imagined a self-sufficient community of families living on a string of barges. The problems were practical—how to get enough to eat—and the solutions were pragmatic—some families grew corn, some vegetables, others raised cows. As a child, Rivlin found "satisfaction in feeling that we could make it work."

In fact, the chief point of the make-believe involved "thinking about how to arrange things and what was happening in this world," that is to say, the patterning and modeling of a social system, as well as the discovery, synthesis, and organization of knowledge. Consequently, Rivlin saw its relevance to her mature work in public policy analysis, city and neighborhood planning, and "with other kinds of problem-solving in economics that I've done with my life." Whether at the local or national level, whether analyzing the effects of existing policy or "envisioning" new policy, "I think there's a connection," she observed in her project interview, "between figuring out how a system works . . . and this kind of [childhood] imagining."

Finally, scientist R. Stephen Berry allowed that worldplay may have served him as early, general practice in research, especially in experimental modeling—and in the imaginative task of plausible speculation. As a teen during World War II, Berry constructed an analogue world as war game with some of his friends:

> A few of us really loved maps and the sense that you could have these portrayals of what was going on in the world in the form of a map was somehow fascinating. . . . We would imagine say two or three or four countries in an imaginary continent that were typically at war or would sometimes be at war and without having definite characters we could have one country invade another and take over a big piece of it and you'd erase part of the map.

The link between this play and his science was indirect for Berry, yet compelling:

> I would be curious about the extent to which imagining a possible world, but still consistent with the real world, awakened an awareness in doing science later on [that] you could be inventive by doing just that kind of thing. I think that a lot of original ideas in science come from some kind of mind play that stays within the bounds of reality, but still asks about something that you have never seen or known to happen.

There's a pattern here: three Fellows, three paracosms, three professions, one overall perception of connection. Personal testimony such as that recounted here and that encountered in chapters to come demonstrates that worldplay can carry over into mature endeavor across the arts and sciences. Moreover, it does so through a network of imaginative skills and creative behaviors—the first including empathizing, patterning, and modeling; the second including mental absorption, persistence, problem finding and solving, plausible speculation and, finally, the construction, synthesis, and organization of knowledge. If we cannot say that worldplay causes or guarantees creative achievement in maturity, we can surmise that it cultivates a number of factors that may work *in some combination* to promote adult creativity.

The model presented in figure 3.4 hypothesizes that childhood worldplay may affect adult creativity by cultivating the following network of intermediary factors: 1) cognitive capacities that include imaginative skills as well as facility with creative process and attendant behaviors; 2) strategies for learning and discovering, such as knowledge construction and problem finding and solving; and 3) compositional facility in expressive culture, particularly constructive forms such as stories, histories, drawings, maps, handmade books, outdoor forts, or other models.

In any particular instance, childhood worldplay may nurture all or only some of these intermediary factors and to a greater or lesser degree. A paracosm may or may not involve the invention of culture in the form of written stories; it may or may not prolong play with knowledge construction over many years, heightening emotional investment in the activity.

This variation in kind and quality of impact on the child necessarily results in variable influence on mature creative capacity and productivity. The more factors that

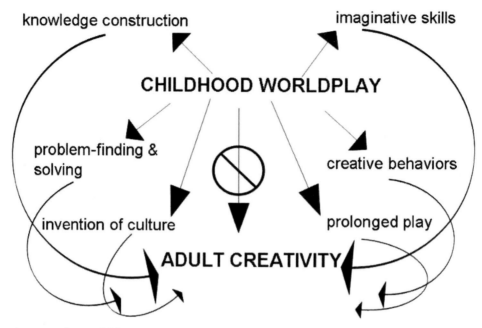

knowledge construction   imaginative skills

CHILDHOOD WORLDPLAY

problem-finding &
solving   creative behaviors

invention of culture   prolonged play

ADULT CREATIVITY

Fig. 3.4. The Worldplay–Creativity Network. The childhood invention of paracosms may indi-rectly influence adult outcomes.

childhood worldplay nurtures in combination and the more intensely, the model suggests, the greater the likelihood of mature creative outcome of some kind. Put another way, the weaker the exercise of fewer factors, the weaker the creative impact.

The model thus resolves the apparent paradox that worldplay may lead to a range of outcomes, from modest personal and/or professional creative achievement in maturity to eminent levels of creative production. Depending on cognitive, creative, and compositional emphases, paracosm invention may lead in diverse directions. Yet, at the very least, the connections drawn by individuals tell us that play can and does function in ordinary and extraordinary ways as a cognitive strategy for learning, discovering, and creating throughout a lifetime.

PRELIMINARY CONCLUSIONS AND CONJECTURES

There are difficulties with self-report in any study of human experience. People choose to respond—or not respond—to surveys according to their interests or, simply, their schedules. What they have to say about worldplay refracts consciously and unconsciously through the prism of their beliefs concerning imagination and creativity. When they were born and in what circumstances they grew up also skew life histories and their explanation. Yet despite the tug of bias, memory counts. The additive weight of shared behaviors can establish significant correlations; the accumulation of singular, anecdotal explanations can pose tentative causations. Altogether, the memory counts gathered here suggest a number of conclusions.

Worldplay *is* much more common than hitherto realized. It may be most prevalent among creative people. There seems to be a strong link between childhood worldplay and mature creativity in a wide range of disciplines, significantly so in the arts, social sciences, and sciences. More than half of paracosmists in the Worldplay Project saw some connection between early play in imaginary worlds and adult work. Moreover, whether or not the invention of imaginary worlds figured prominently in early years, over half of all study participants—Fellows and students alike—recognized elements of worldplay in their adult vocations and avocations. Creative imagination in maturity, it turned out, can look remarkably like child's play.

Indeed, repeated testimony suggests that childhood worldplay is of particular relevance to mature creativity when some combination of the six following outcomes is manifest:

- worldplay exercises imaginative skills;
- worldplay develops creative capacities and behaviors;
- worldplay serves to prolong imaginative and creative play in older children and teens;
- worldplay exercises the capacity for problem finding and problem solving within a make-believe or conjectured system;
- worldplay nurtures the ability and the audacity to imagine and construct new knowledge—and to address perennial human challenges; and
- worldplay stimulates the invention of culture by bridging the gap between imagined idea, playful enactment, and the durable documentations of art, music, experiment, theory, or invention.

In chapters to come, each of these outcomes is taken up in its turn, first in childhood, then in maturity. After counting memories here, in Part II we can count on a history of research into play, giftedness, and creativity to expand our understanding of imaginary world invention—and vice versa.

From:	Bob <rrb@michstateu.edu>
Date:	Nov 24 3:27 (EST)
To:	<mrb@michstateu.edu>
Subject:	whadsneggst?

So far, so good. To paraphrase the last student to see me in office hours, whadsneggst?

From:	Michele <mrb@michstateu.edu>
Date:	Nov 24 4:11 (EST)
To:	<rrb@michstateu.edu>
Subject:	Re: whadsneggst?

The foundations of make-believe play—what it is, how it develops. There's a (fuzzy) set of play behaviors that seem to coalesce around place-making and, given the right nudge, imaginary world invention. Both place-making play and worldplay spring from the same nest, so to speak.

From:	Bob <rrb@michstateu.edu>
Date:	Nov 24 3:27 (EST)
To:	<mrb@michstateu.edu>
Subject:	Re: Re: whadsneggst?

Ah, a continuum of play "crosses." Like the cardboard castle I built in my early teens, though I've kept it all these years boxed up in the laundry room, was NOT EXACTLY THE SAME THING as Meredith's invention of Kar. For one thing, making up stories for my knights was a Tolkienesque endeavor that never occurred to me. Yet I, too, was constructing something imaginary. If not a whole, parallel world, then a part of a world, brought to life in the mind.

From:	Michele <mrb@michstateu.edu>
Date:	Nov 24 4:11 (EST)
To:	<rrb@michstateu.edu>
Subject:	Re: Re: Re: whadsneggst?

Egg-xactly. ☺

Part II

EXPLORING THE
GARDENS OF MAKE-BELIEVE

Chapter Four

Pretense and Place: The Poetics
of Play in Middle Childhood

The mind is its own place.

—Patrick Brontë, curate

THE PLAYFUL MIND

Come with me to the Smithsonian Institution for a symposium called "The Playful Mind" that took place in the fall of 2000, for it is here we gain two insights. On one level, all play is pretense and on another, the development of childhood make-believe takes a natural turn toward the making of imagined spaces and places.

The day-long symposium cuts the ribbon for a new exhibit called "Invention at Play" with a gathering of artists, scientists, and other researchers. There's the artist whose mechanical sculptures tickle the funny bone, the anthropologist whose sound/light synthesizer toys with the fusion of our senses, and the scientist, Sue Savage-Rumbaugh, who begins her talk on the play habits of bonobos with what might be called a frolic.

Called to the stage, Savage-Rumbaugh's grown son bounds up the steps, chases his mother around the lectern and over the table. At a standstill to catch their breath, they pant hoarsely, mouths open, lips covering their teeth. Suddenly, the scientist turns on her son and he scoots away behind a chair.

I exchange a quick glance with the older gentleman seated to my left. Not a word is spoken, yet we—and the rest of the audience, too—respond with smiles and laughter. We see a bonobo "play face" in the teeth-covered open mouth We hear bonobo laughter in the hoarse pants. As if we really were watching young chimpanzees, we recognize in the pretense of pretense signals that are familiar to us. All of us in the lecture hall accept the "simulated actions in place of real actions." We know ourselves at play.

This is not privileged knowledge. Whether observing children, people from another culture, or other animal species, human beings know play when they see it, when they "get" the ironic stance that makes behavior a kind of commentary on itself. Of course, not all pretense is play; deception in many of its guises would not prompt us to smile and laugh. The pretense of play, however, is without guile. What we grasp immediately in the mock chase is that quality that the anthropologist with the synthesizer has called "galumphing."

Borrowed from Lewis Carroll's oh-so-playful verse, the word *galumphing* suggests exaggerated, reiterative, frivolous, daring and, above all, joyful behavior. In the case of the "chimpanzees" onstage, the physical aggression that serves serious purpose in the regulation of social life is taken out of that context, stripped of its threat and elaborated for no apparent reason. Unlike physical chase in the "real world," chase play has no obvious goal. Play, I remind myself as I watch Savage-Rumbaugh and her son, is just for fun.

Play may have no immediate purpose, but animal behaviorists have long argued that mock chase and similar activities are biologically adaptive in the long term. According to Niko Tinbergen, one of the founders of ethology, animal species that supplement innate or instinctive capacities with learned abilities depend on the self-education of physical play. The kitten pouncing on a ball of yarn, for example, hones behaviors necessary for the hunt well before its survival depends on the outcome.

More recently, researchers have emphasized additional adaptive consequences. Play develops the "welfare" of the individual, not only by building physical capacity, but by calibrating defensive responses to various levels of challenge and by cultivating intimate social bonds. The young bonobos in mock chase manage intragroup aggression and build relationships, too—both of which affect individual survival and reproductive success as well as group welfare. Animal play among primates and other mammalian species is a sign of flexible intelligence, one that cultivates a problem-posing, problem-solving responsiveness to the environment.

As Savage-Rumbaugh begins her talk, my mind skips from playful chimpanzees to playful children. I've seen kids engaged in mock chase, but there is almost always another narrative unfolding at the same time: two horses run with the wind; three winged cats pursue a magic feather.

Human beings spend a great deal of childhood in such imaginative dimensions, where things in the real world stand in for conjectured ideas and situations. We recognize the cues in the use of props, such as scarves that serve as cats' wings, and in vocalized conditions, such as "let's pretend that we're horses." By these and other means, we discern in the play a suspension of objective truth in favor of imagined entities, events, and narratives. We *believe* that in tandem with the actual world of actual things there also exists a simulated world of imagined beings and imagined places.

Some researchers have proposed that make-believe play, much like the bipedal gait or opposable thumb, sets humans off from the rest of the animal kingdom. But where does simple pretense end and make-believe begin? Savage-Rumbaugh is just now explaining that make-believe play also appears among apes—at least those studied in captivity at the Language Research Center of Georgia State University. Although the imaginative games of chimpanzees and bonobos are not as elaborate as those of human beings, they do involve sustained interaction with imaginary toys, imaginary food, and even imaginary monsters.

Because the apes in her care acquire language from an early age, they also "sometimes . . . use language to pretend" and to draw fellow bonobos or human beings into their pretense. For Savage-Rumbaugh, as for many psychologists who study play in animals and children, there is close connection between language acquisition and make-believe, between pretend play and the projection of other minds and realities.

Thanks to Savage-Rumbaugh, I am reminded what ties so much of childhood pretense to paracosm play. The invention of an imagined world is, in its most elemental form, the bedrock of *all* make-believe. With this understanding in hand, it should be possible to characterize a continuous spectrum of elements that link everyday play to worldplay. And I know just who can help me—the older gentleman at my side.

THE DEVELOPMENT OF MAKE-BELIEVE

Jerome Singer, an academic psychologist lately retired from Yale University, is a doyen among specialists in make-believe. Indeed, he has spent a lifetime, as he has put it, in study of "the most ephemeral phenomena of human thought." He began, in the 1960s, by looking at imagination and daydreaming among adults and establishing its widespread occurrence. With his wife, Dorothy, who is also a psychologist, he has focused since the early 1970s on make-believe play in childhood.

Singer and Singer are by no means the first to study children at play—concerted efforts to tackle the phenomenon may be found among nineteenth and twentieth century scholars of many persuasions. Among psychologists, Karl Groos argued at the end of the nineteenth century that play functioned instinctually—and in humans often consciously—to prepare and sustain mature skills. It was not mere diversion. Some fifty-five years later, Jean Piaget narrowed that focus in his work on the development of cognitive function. In close, years-long study of his own children, he searched for the emergence of rational thought from the subsoil of infantile play.

Initially, Piaget argued, pretend play enabled the child to construct internal pictures or schemas of reality. Once the ability to think logically took hold, however, make-believe became superfluous to further cognitive development (and thus held no long-term significance for adulthood). Other psychologists, such as Carl Jung and Erik Erikson, at work in the psychoanalytic tradition, focused on childhood play as personal, therapeutic mastery of social, emotional, and physical realities.

For the Singers, all these influences converged in what is known as the "cognitive-affective" model of play. The model makes several assumptions. First, human play involves some physical challenge, some experiential novelty, or some situational incongruity—or any combination of the three. Second, people are information-processing creatures who use the lessons of experience to constantly adjust their notions of reality. And third, the courting of novelty and the processing of reality are closely tied to—may depend upon—a positive emotional response. Indeed, emotional reward encourages the child to explore in ever-widening circles, from nursery to family to neighborhood, and to embrace thereby a growing sense of autonomy and identity.

Within this very broad terrain of human exploratory play, the Singers have focused on the growth of imagination itself. "[C]hildhood fantasies," they observe, ". . . are not purely idiosyncratic but are indeed a reflection of our common humanity." Indeed, there is a consistent pattern to imaginative development.

The ability to pretend first emerges in the two-year-old as simple, usually solitary behaviors. By age three, when make-believe really blooms, the very young begin to engage in social pretend play and continue to do so for at least another two years. This is the kind of interactive make-believe that parents readily observe in play groups and teachers in preschool and kindergarten. Its content and quality has been memorably rendered by the master teacher Vivian Gussin Paley. In *A Child's Work: The Importance of Fantasy Play* (2004), she watched children taking care of a baby, exploring outer space, and poignantly saving those who fell from the Twin Towers.

As different as the content of these scenarios may be, social pretend play invariably involves familiar activities performed *in the absence* of real-life materials and contexts. One object may substitute for or symbolize another: the child pretends to drive to the store by sitting in a big cardboard box rather than a real car. Activities usually performed by someone else are often appropriated: Mom or Dad normally drives, but the child takes on that role. Reenactment of appropriated activities may not unfold logically, either: another child suggests that the box/car can sprout wings and fly. Distinctions between the animate and inanimate begin to blur: the cardboard box becomes a giant bird, the two children riding on its back. Finally, flexible transition from the known to the unknown allows for flexible exploration of emotional reaction: when flight proves too scary, the children come to a safe landing in a box in the middle of their preschool classroom.

Social pretend play is an important part of behavior in the fourth, fifth and sixth years of life. Around the age of seven, however, children turn increasingly toward socially constructed, rule-bound games. As Piaget saw it, this change in play reflects the child's increasing ability to distinguish between what is real and what is not real—and to prefer reality.

In particular, the seven- to twelve- or thirteen-year-old demonstrates a quickening desire to organize physical things in the real world. Concrete operational thought grows apace with an expanding sense of self as an independent agent in family, school, and neighborhood. Altogether, the emergence of rational thought and self-awareness, coupled with a rule-bound focus for social games, marks the transition from early to middle childhood. Because that transition can be so dramatic, many researchers, Piaget among them, have assumed that make-believe largely disappears along with pretend play.

The Singers have demurred. Appearances to the contrary, pretend play may not disappear—though its social dimensions surely wither. As children move from kindergarten to grade school, unstructured play time decreases noticeably in the classroom, on the playground, and in the home, largely replaced by structured sports and organized entertainments as well as reading, watching television, or playing on the computer. Children who persist in pretend play are often pressured by peers and parents to "grow up." Yet despite such social and institutional pressures, make-believe may not disappear, but only go into hiding.

Singer himself should know. In *The Inner World of Daydreaming*, published in 1975, he offered up his personal experience as a preliminary reference point. Like the Brontë siblings, like Robert Silvey, he too had invented imaginary people and places as a child. In elementary school years, he dreamed up an ancient Greek senator in beard and toga inhabiting a made-up Greco-Roman society. Singer also dreamed up an imaginary musician-composer and wrote down his music in a made-up notation system. It was the baseball board game the young Singer played with several friends, however, that demonstrated how and why social pretend play might disappear in the first place.

Housed in a miniature stadium, with "little metal baseball characters who could pitch the ball and actually hit the ball and even hit it over the fence and make a home run," the game played out the sport in concrete and realistic terms. The boys chose different real-life baseball teams for the enacted contest. Bit by bit, however, imaginary baseball players and then entire make-believe teams crept into play. When Singer's friends "stopped doing that kind of thing together," turning instead to real sports play, he continued solo and in his head.

As Singer has put it, he incorporated what had been social play into daydream—and tucked it out of sight. Instead of manipulating toy players in a toy stadium, he visualized fly balls and home runs. He scribbled out deft cartoon illustrations of players in action; he wrote out box scores and kept statistics. What's more, the fantasy stuck with him over the years. Visualizing his favorite players on the baseball diamond, the adult Singer has confessed, is a great way to fall asleep.

Pondering this kind of transition from pretend play to daydreaming, both Singers have suggested a connection to the ongoing development of conscious thought. Initially, they point out, pretend play emerges with a facility for speech. Vocalization of the play—the chatter that sets the narrative—seems to represent the child's developing stream of consciousness. Make-believe undergoes significant change about the same time that that stream of consciousness becomes silently expressed or internalized. When the child learns not only to read, but to read without moving the lips, make-believe can become the stuff of internal discourse beyond the direct gaze of peers or parents. "As skill in internal speech and thought develop," the two psychologists have written, "make-believe play may become an ongoing fantasy activity."

Singer and Singer hypothesize that make-believe play persists through middle childhood into adolescence and even adulthood in internalized form. If it actually does, we continue to know little about it. Pick up almost any book on play and the focus will be squarely set on the preschool and kindergarten crowd. Very few studies target the years from seven to thirteen or beyond. This may reflect the residual influence of theorists such as Piaget, who found play of little interest in later stages of life. It may also reflect the difficulty researchers have observing a phenomenon that is no longer—objectively—observable.

Simply put, older children no longer make believe in the presence of adults without self-conscious distortion of the play. Nonetheless, middle childhood may harbor a stage of "let's pretend" as critical as any other, one in which the child's withdrawal into internalized pretense, her growing sense of self, and too, her growing mastery of the material world, all interact and influence one another to produce complex forms of prolonged make-believe play.

THE POETICS OF PLACE-MAKING

Some part of the evidence for that complex and prolonged play lies in all those self-reports gathered from MacArthur Fellows and Michigan State University students in the Worldplay Project. Whether or not reported pastimes were considered worldplay, they testified as a whole to the felt-experience of alternate reality in *all* childhood make-believe.

One Fellow made the very argument when he pointed out that, though he did not invent a long-lived paracosm in childhood, he certainly "visited, in play, various imaginary worlds borrowed from movies, books, radio and TV programs . . . cowboy games, war games, Robin Hood games, pirate games—the visitable worlds were many." Another Fellow made a similar claim: "[I]t wasn't just one imaginary world," she wrote. "We'd invent new worlds for new games. . . . Each world was brief . . . lasting a week or so or just the duration of an afternoon's play." A student similarly insisted on a sense of imagined place: "My friends and I would always create new worlds every time we got together. Our worlds never stayed the same."

These games may have been temporary and fleeting, nevertheless they took place in an imagined space that was remembered—and valued—as such. Indeed, what these reports speak to is a place-making play that includes, but is not limited to, the paracosm. As a much larger and much more common phenomenon, place-making play sets worldplay to one side as, simply, the internalized and often solitary pursuit of externalized, socially shared inventions revolving around secret and special spaces.

In *The Poetics of Space* (1964), the philosopher Gaston Bachelard noted how we intuitively draw together special places, secret seclusions, and generative imagination: "Every corner in a house, every angle in a room, every inch of secluded space in which we like to hide, or withdraw into ourselves, is a symbol of solitude for the imagination; that is to say, it is the germ of a room, or of a house." Sifting through the combined reports from MacArthur Fellows and MSU students and hunting for patterns within that pool of make-believe experience, we find the following elements in the "poetics" of place-making play:

- the prolongation of make-believe after social pretend play gutters out,
- adaptation to varied social contexts,
- withdrawal into private activity vis-à-vis the adult world,
- the organization of found and constructed environments,
- the internalization of place to one degree or another in a variety of imaginative or play styles, and
- the potential for wholly imagined place-making.

Let's take a look at each in turn.

Onset and Duration of Play

Place-making play manifests in early childhood, peaks in middle childhood, and subsides in late childhood (see figure 4.1).

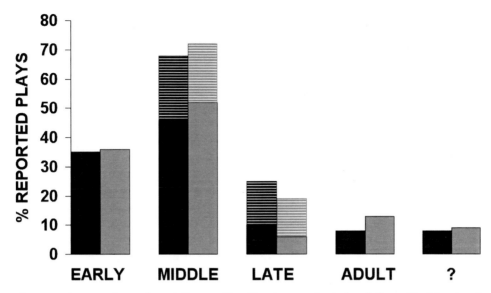

Fig. 4.1. Onset and Duration of Place-Making Play Among MacArthur Fellows (black bars) and MSU Students (gray bars). ONSET of plays or games = solid shades; DURATION of plays/games begun at an earlier stage of childhood still being played = horizontal lines. Number of reported plays/games: Fellows, 48; Students, 113. Age ranges as follows—EARLY (3-6 years), MIDDLE (7-12 years), LATE (13-19 years), ADULT (20+ years). ? = Onset and duration of play unknown.

Among students, a bit more than one-third of reported games had their onset between the ages of 3 and 6 (early childhood). Just over half began between ages 7 and 12 (middle childhood). The number of games beginning at age 13 or later (late childhood) was negligible. The pattern among MacArthur Fellows was similar.

In addition, for both groups over half of the games invented in early childhood persisted, increasing the considerable bulge of place-making play in middle childhood. Only about one-quarter of student games and about one-fifth of Fellows games endured from middle into teenage years.

Overall, the duration of place-making play, particularly high from early into middle childhood, lends support to the Singers' speculation that the highly visible make-believe of the very young does not entirely disappear, but rather shifts in manifestation. Some of the parameters of that shift can be traced in the social dimensions of place-making play, its facets of privacy, and the formation—whether physical or imagined—of place itself.

Social Dimensions

Almost all the play reported by students or Fellows occurred in or around the home, in a diverse set of social groupings: solitary, shared with one or two intimate friends, or in large and fluid groups of children.

For students, the play was more often shared than solitary, and more often solitary than group. Just over two-fifths reported playing with a brother or a sister or a "best friend"; just under two-fifths reported playing by themselves; a remaining one-fifth reported playing "with kids in the neighborhood" or "all my friends."

For Fellows, in contrast, place-making play was predominantly a solitary activity, rather than a shared or group one. Three-fifths of their reported games were solitary, one-fifth were shared; fewer than one-fifth occurred in groups (see figure 4.2).

An additional set of differences between Fellows and students played out over time. Among students, social play (in the form of shared or group games) dominated solitary play in early childhood by more than two to one, though by middle childhood solitary play made modest inroads into that social context. For Fellows just the reverse was true—solitary play took a dramatic lead in early years over social (shared and group) games and only slipped from over three-quarters to a bit less than half in middle years.

What these data reveal is that the students—though not necessarily Fellows—behaved very much as psychologists might expect. The Singers have suggested that as children abandon social pretend in middle years, those who remain attached to this kind of make-believe may "withdraw" into solitary play. The student data would seem to corroborate this, at least with reference to place-making play, by a rise in solitary activity in middle childhood.

What the Fellows data suggest, however, is that some children may *already* demonstrate preference for solitary rather than shared pretend play in early childhood, whether due to isolation from other children or personal preference. Indeed, for the student who confessed she was "a bit possessive regarding 'the world,'" control of

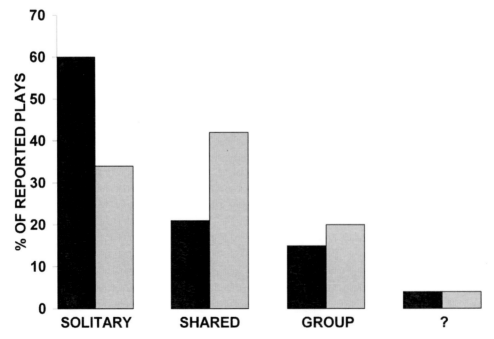

Fig. 4.2.   The Social Context of Place-Making Play for MacArthur Fellows (black bars) and MSU Students (gray bars). Number of plays/games: Fellows, 48 plays; Students, 113 plays.

imaginative invention seems to have been paramount in solitary play, as it was for the Fellow who deliberately withdrew to a backyard swing: "No one ever played with me in it," she remembered. "It would have ruined everything."

Secrecy and Privacy

The disclosure or nondisclosure of play to parents and guardians reveals much about secrecy and privacy in childhood make-believe. Broadly speaking, students and Fellows either never told their parents (i.e., their play was secret), did not tell their parents though their parents clearly knew about the play (their play was semi-secret), or did or probably did tell their parents (play was not secret).

Among students, the number of recalled games that were directly disclosed to parents (not secret) roughly equaled the number of games that were either indirectly disclosed (semi-secret) or never disclosed (secret). Due to the large number of non-responses to this question among Fellows, the relative proportion of secret and non-secret games is unknown. What data do exist for the Fellows suggest that keeping play secret from parents rises in middle childhood. This is certainly true for students, whose disclosure to parents in middle childhood declined from two-thirds to one-third of reported games, while secret and semi-secret games surged.

This surge may reflect the child's cognitive discovery of secrecy, usually after the age of five or six. Not only are children of this age able to conceal their thoughts and feelings, they may do so to avoid parental interference with play. Disclosure, after all, involves risk of quelling disapproval, indifference, or even enthusiasm. To illustrate the two ends of that spectrum, one Fellow recalled telling his parents about his play: "I received contempt for some of the details and didn't mention it to them again." Upon disclosure to her father, one student found him overeager "to visit the playworld" she shared with a sibling—"it didn't work out very well."

Disclosure of secret play, it would seem, is not meant to erase a fundamental privacy from unwanted interference. As one Fellow recalled, when her mother tried to play along and involve other family members in disclosed make-believe, "I was completely enraged and felt betrayed." Even in semi-secret or nonsecret play, a child may seek physical seclusion or play in plain sight in a psychologically withdrawn state of mind. For every student or Fellow who kept make-believe play hidden, another found full or partial secrecy unnecessary because the privacy of play was still honored.

It is likely that secrecy in play may, like solitary play, also reflect a predisposition on the child's part. In fact, solitary play and secret play often go together. Among students, over half of those games reported to be solitary were also secret; over half of secret games were also solitary. Conversely, shared play with one or two intimates and nonsecret play were also associated one with the other more than half the time. The onset of solitary, secret make-believe play increased with middle childhood; the onset of shared, nonsecret make-believe play decreased at the same time.

Recent work suggests that some degree of secrecy or privacy may, in fact, benefit the child of middle years. By inviting conception of an internal or psychological space, an amalgam of the two in play aids in the growth of identity distinct from and independent of parent and family members.

Found and Constructed Places

As a support for internal or psychological space, children of eight, nine, ten, and eleven seek out special places around the house and beneath the bushes or construct "forts" or "hide-outs" at some distance from the family home.

Reports to the Worldplay Project include the teepee a student built with help from her parents and the town another constructed in the playroom. They also include the found "homes" one Fellow contrived in the "dark eaves of the attic" and beneath backyard bushes. Other special places took shape farther afield, like the house a student conceived within "a metal rocket ship on my elementary school playground" or the "model city" a Fellow built "out of small stones in the woods near my home."

Physical construction dovetails with a third kind of place—the miniature or modeled place that was particularly common among Fellows. One recalled whole days spent building a Bronx Zoo on the dinner table out of "small animals, trees, Lincoln logs, jeweler's wire, etc. etc." Another remembered constructing a make-believe place for paper dolls by cutting out pictures of home furnishings featured in old Montgomery Ward catalogs. In her play with doll houses, one student wrote, "I loved rearranging the furniture and setting everything up." Indeed, she experienced herself as a maker of what some researchers call "small worlds."

That same personal agency informed the recollections of many others, too, whether in found or constructed or life-size or miniature locales. The student who built forts in the woods with her brothers retained vivid memories of the "life we created." Similarly, one Fellow recalled his valiant attempt to shape an entire neighborhood of children into a "Republic" patterned on the Roman model.

Even the Fellow who communed with the found environment around his rural home experienced that given world as a dynamic space of his own making, primarily due to the overlay of imagined interaction with trees, fields, and haystacks. Place-making play invariably involves the shaping and organizing of material things and—though this is more difficult for an outsider to see—things immaterial and interior as well.

Play Styles and Imaginative Trend

The internalization of place-making play appears to vary in degree according to the child's propensities for companionship, privacy, personal agency, and the physical props of place. Indeed, we may conjecture, as is indicated in figure 4.3, that the greater the opportunity for solitary, secret play, the greater the degree of interior place-making.

Consider the example of one MacArthur Fellow, who recalled at least two kinds of place-making. "I had a girlfriend who joined in this and we had Indian names . . . and rampaged around the woods pretending to be Indians," she wrote. The strong current of interior experience that permeated this play was further nurtured in private moments. "At night when I went to sleep," she added, "I would imagine that I was lying on a bed of leaves in my Indian dwelling." In effect, this Fellow continued the shared and physically enacted make-believe in solitary and interior fashion, engaging in imagined realms in the absence of physical props or social companionship.

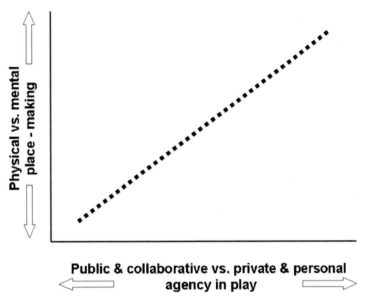

Fig. 4.3. Imaginative Trend in Place-Making Play.

What her experience suggests is that place-making play manifests at least two broadly distinct imaginative styles as it is more or less social, more or less private, and more or less dependent on the organization and manipulation of physical objects in physical settings.

The first style is characterized by shared, public playacting in which children take on the roles of varying characters in constructed and found settings. The Robinson Crusoe–like building of community referred to by many Fellows and students may serve as example.

The second style is characterized by more intimate, private place-making only partly attached to physical place or companionship, as exemplified by the Fellow playing Indians. Much play in miniature places also falls into this second style, especially when some part of the make-believe is mentally rather than physically experienced.

This second style appears to form a bridge between social playacting and wholly interior daydreaming. Indeed, Fellows and students engaged in solitary and private place-making play trend toward an increased internalization of make-believe—one in which the physicality of place gives way to figments of the imagination.

Wholly Imagined Place

Among Fellows and students, around a third of place-making play blossomed in wholly imagined locales. These existed not as overlays of found and constructed environments, but as internally evoked places for make-believe to happen.

Among Fellows these included visions of times and places in a historical past, where imaginary companions and characters played out their lives in borrowed circumstances; in a hypothetical, made-up past, such as that invented for a Chinese Native American Empire; or in a future world of space travel to realms only visible to the imagining mind. Among students they included the wholly imagined medieval fantasy realm of "elves, magic, mountain-top kingdoms, undersea lairs, etc" and the partly imagined city of Pettit.

The Janus-face of such wholly imagined make-believe is that, cut free from the physical instantiation of place, a great deal of it is nevertheless re-externalized in art and craft. Many Fellows and students who reported the invention of wholly imagined places also reported supporting their play with stories, drawings, maps, character lists, and historical chronologies—or in the case of the younger participants, audio and video tapes. The student who, at age five, played alone and without disclosure in a world of "little imaginary people & society," also drew lots of pictures of "mouse houses" to accompany her play. The Fellow who immersed himself as a teenager in J. R. R. Tolkein's *Lord of the Rings* spent many hours alone painting model medieval knights and building a cardboard castle set up in the family living room.

In the absence of physical enactment, this fabrication of pictures and cardboard castles seems to perform a dual role: to enhance the imagination of place and to anchor and sustain those interior elements. As Singer pointed out with reference to his own play, drawings, musical compositions, and box scores served as *structures* for his daydreams, providing acceptable articulation in the form of art or music or sports statistics of what might have been deemed unacceptable make-believe play. By drawing pictures or writing stories or building models, other children, too, enable themselves to indulge in internally imagined forms of make-believe long after social playacting has been proscribed.

Which brings us, finally, to the poetry at the heart of place-making play. We began this investigation of imagined places and spaces with the understanding that it is in the nature of all pretend play to stimulate some notion of alternate dimension. We end with the understanding that it is also the function of place, especially fabricated place, to stimulate make-believe play within the imagining mind.

Whether in the basement playhouse, the backyard tent, or the city in the woods, whether in stories, drawings, or maps, place-making is an act of absorption in some other plane of existence. It is a repeatable organization of mental experience. That experience may manifest itself in the temporary manufacture of props or in the more durable fabrication of artifacts and art forms. It may remain a social game enacted in physical place or move into solitary dimensions of ethereal space. It may fade from mind or become a touchstone memory. It may, finally, take the fabricated place into paracosm.

Viewed from the perspective of place-making play, worldplay reveals itself as a natural outcome in the spectrum of imaginative styles that characterize middle childhood make-believe.

PROLONGED PLAY AND BEYOND

Whether we consider the rough and tumble play of our fellow apes or the pretend play of our own young children, we see the first signs of ability to substitute what is imagined for what is real. Clever animals that we humans are, our early powers in play grow increasingly complicated as we mature. From the ages of six to twelve, we take our make-believe into found and constructed places in and around the home, learning as we go. Play tied to such places and spaces fosters a sense of independence, nurtures feelings of agency, and combines physical and imagined experience.

Such place-making play provides a frame for our understanding of pretense and place in the more ethereal worldplay. As children enter school many begin to forsake external enactments in favor of solitary and internalized make-believe. And the more that internalization gains ground, the more make-believe involves the invention of partially or wholly imagined worlds. Indeed, the juvenile games of MacArthur Fellows and MSU students, as well as the evolving ballgame fantasy of Jerome Singer, exemplify the range of imaginative engagement that ties concrete and enacted forms of place-making play to internalized and abstracted forms of worldplay.

These games speak as well to the way in which interior fantasizing may draw out the developmental course of imaginative play, thus contributing to the network of factors linking childhood worldplay to adult creativity (see figure 3.4). Place-making in six- to twelve-year-old children exercises the capacity for prolonged pretend play well after the intense exploration of make-believe in early childhood typically fades. Perhaps, too, the more internalized paracosm signals a further development of imagination, as interior play and its fabricated structures mutually reinforce one another. Perhaps again, as the most complex instance of childhood place-making, worldplay may serve as an early predictor of creative potential.

Like secret places in the woods, these propositions beckon, leading us, in the next chapter, to two more pioneering psychologists and their seminal studies of creative giftedness in children.

Chapter Five

Imaginary Countries and Gifted Play: First Investigations of "Creative IQ"

I dwell in Possibility—
A fairer House than Prose—
More numerous of Windows—
Superior—for Doors—

—Emily Dickinson, poet

TERMAN AND THE CHILD GENIUS

Our first brush with the gift in worldplay begins in the summer of 1917 in New York City, when a young researcher by the name of Lewis Terman walked into a class on the psychology of exceptional children at Teachers College, Columbia University. On summer leave from Stanford University, he had come to demonstrate a new battery of intelligence tests to his professional colleague, Leta Hollingworth, and her students.

Terman had derived the battery in question from a set of intelligence measures developed in the early 1900s by the French psychologist, Alfred Binet. Testing for memory, imagination, attention, and comprehension, Binet had succeeded in distinguishing levels of intelligence in samples of French schoolchildren. Terman revised Binet's measures and added some of his own for use in American school populations.

By means of an ascending series of tests for each chronological age, this Stanford-Binet revision enabled the computation of "mental age" or level of achievement. Terman then divided mental age by chronological age to produce an intelligence quotient. The eight-year-old with a mental age of four had an IQ of 50; the eight-year-old with a mental age of ten had an IQ of 125 and so forth. These scores were used to report the battery's outcome.

We may presume that Terman nodded in Hollingworth's direction and, turning to face the class, unconsciously tugged at his collar. Outside the thermometers had climbed to over 100 degrees and inside, as he later recalled, the room was "close, ill-ventilated and wretchedly hot." But his discomfort had also to do with the concern he felt for the seven-year-old boy who sat waiting for him by the table set center stage.

Child D, as Terman and Hollingworth referred to him in subsequent research reports, had already attracted considerable attention for his precocious intellect. To test him in such severe heat—and before a crowd of staring onlookers—seemed neither fair nor likely to yield as high an intelligence quotient as the boy might be capable of in quieter, more comfortable circumstances. Nevertheless, the questioning began.

Some forty-five minutes later, Terman confessed himself amazed. At each successive level, beginning with the year 9 tests all the way up to those for the average adult, the boy failed some, yet passed most. At 7 years, 4 and 2/3 months, he demonstrated a mental age of 13 years and 7 months, the ratio of these two figures producing an IQ of 184. Terman had yet to find a higher intelligence quotient. Indeed, no other child in his list of testees equaled D "in all-round intellectual ability."

Two years later Terman published a brief profile of D in *The Intelligence of School Children* (1919). This dossier, like others in the book, comprised a strange mix of data concerning D's family background, his early childhood development, and, of course, his intellectual precocity. Believing as he did in the biological inheritance of superior intellectual abilities, Terman took pains to demonstrate the economic and social success of the boy's parents, grandparents, and extended family. Child D had distinguished rabbis on both sides of the family. His father was an advertising man and a writer; his mother, also a writer, had completed some university course work; his paternal grandfather had had unusual mechanical ability.

As for the boy himself, D stood upright at five or six months, walked at nine months, talked at twelve. Like children everywhere, he played with "ball, bats and skates;" he also built toy models with dexterity. Though educated at home, he spent time every day on the playground of a local school—experience which did much to "normalize" the social skills of an only child. Equally important in Terman's eyes, D had no physical defects and few childhood illnesses. Teachers as well as parents testified that the boy was conscientious, obedient, and unselfish.

Today family heredity, health histories, and character evaluations may seem irrelevant to the assessment of intellectual capacity, yet D's case gave Terman an opportunity to make a point. Contemporary prejudice had long associated intellectual giftedness with a long list of distasteful qualities: physical puniness, ineptitude, sickliness, unhealthy preference for social isolation, a disinclination to play, moral aberration, and general nervous instability. Having been something of a sickly nerd himself, Terman took it as his mission to reverse these stigmas. Intellectually superior children, he argued, were more often than not superior in every way—physically healthy, socially well-adjusted, and morally mature.

D was certainly all of these things, a kind of poster boy for the best, the brightest, and the prodigious. According to Terman, D played with anagrams as a baby and learned to read at the same time he learned to talk. By the age of three he read and understood books suitable for children of nine. By age seven, he had plunged deep into the plays of Shakespeare, Gibbon's history of Rome, and Grote's history of Greece.

D also taught himself to print and to typewrite rapidly, "using only two fingers on each hand." He kept notes on subjects that intrigued him; he wrote stories; he taught himself to count by playing with a deck of cards. Commencing his home school study of arithmetic around the age of seven, by the age of eight he had progressed to algebra and geometry.

Terman also recorded D's extracurricular interests in solitaire and chess and in idiosyncratic projects of his own devising. These included accurately mapping the family apartment and recording voluminous data on automobiles, baseball teams, and the trolley system of New York City. D made up his own games focused on sports, literary characters, and cities and rivers. He also composed and typed up a weekly paper for his playground companions, complete with sections for news, advertising, and jokes.

By chance, Terman noted as well that D played with an imaginary country called "Borningtown." The boy spent many weeks on a geographical map of that land and began two books, complete with table of contents and chapter headings, detailing its characteristics: "Of the text so far," Terman noted, "there are five typewritten pages and one illustration." This play impressed, but only after the fact, as a kind of corroborating proof, if that were needed, of the boy's exceptional intelligence and maturity—for Terman had already decided, at first testing, that D was destined for creative eminence.

Thinking back to that hot summer day in 1917, Terman later remembered feeling himself in the presence of "real genius." Indeed, he compared D with Francis Galton, that half cousin of Charles Darwin who had initiated the study of eminent men in the late nineteenth century and made seminal contributions of his own. Terman had retroactively assigned Galton the extraordinary IQ of 200, based on the exceptionally young age at which the young Francis had begun to read, do his sums, memorize the multiplication table, and tell clock time. "[A] child of four years who is able to do the things characteristic of a child of seven or eight years," Terman wrote, "is a genius of the first order."

In D, Terman recognized the same accelerated acquisition of intellectual skills and knowledge, the same sustained pursuit of personal interests, the same early maturation of character. Whether D might follow in Galton's footsteps and achieve eminence in some adult field of endeavor remained to be seen. But Terman was more than hopeful. "[C]onsidering [D's] fine balance of personal, moral and intellectual traits, there is every reason to believe that he will become a distinguished man." Every reason to believe, that is, that high IQ and creative destiny went hand in hand.

LOCATING CREATIVE GIFTEDNESS

Terman felt sure that in IQ he had found the key to locating and identifying giftedness in childhood. Before rejoining him in his quest, however, it behooves us to consider some part of the difficulties that lay in his path. Intellectual aptitude and precocious talent are relatively easy to spot—people notice the child who can best adults at chess or mathematics or musical performance. Creative capacity, however, proves more elusive. This is the category of early signs and behaviors that involve originality and inventiveness and raise hopes of mature contribution in fields not yet mastered by the child. And if these capacities are hard to spot or predict, some part of the difficulty has to do with the concept of creativity itself.

Thus far, the term "creative" has been used in these pages without qualification, despite the fact that its common usage differs from the more restrained meanings employed by those who study the phenomenon. People commonly say someone is creative when they make things—when they knit their own sweaters or write poems, for example. The composer Igor Stravinsky largely shared this assumption. In his estimation, the moment the private and interior imagination bodied forth into a machine, a theory, or a symphony, it became both public and creative.

Psychologists and other students of human culture do not usually consider such products of the imagination as creative, however, unless something about symphony or theory, poem or sweater is both *novel* (i.e., never before conceived or constructed) and *effective* (i.e., useful or valuable to others). Some insist that this novelty and effectiveness hold for the very reaches of human knowledge and achievement. Others are content that it be true for the individual alone.

Consider the naïve poet, who imagines and then constructs with words what is for her some new connection between love and roses. If her poem proves a well-worn combination of ideas, her personally creative behavior will not be publicly recognized as such, except perhaps by her parents and friends. Imaginative acts and outcomes may thus be deemed more or less creative depending on their impact across ever-widening social contexts. "Big *C* creative" refers to those outcomes that alter whole fields of knowledge as practiced by the largest circles of people; "little *c* creative" refers to those that alter the understanding of one individual or smaller circles of family, school, neighborhood, etc.

When it comes to childhood play, "little *c*" holds sway. To the extent that a young girl communicates a pretend world to other children as a subject for socio-dramatic play, she begins to instantiate, albeit ephemerally, what she first imagined in the privacy of her mind. To the extent a young boy writes stories or draws pictures that express and capture some part of an imagined world, he crafts his vision into a concrete, somewhat permanent structure. Except in the case of prodigies, however, it is rarely the case that the products of a child's imagination will be evaluated outside the family circle or school environment.

Nor do we usually hold children (even prodigies!) to the same expectations of novelty or effectiveness that we do adults. Children have had less experience writing or painting or acting or making or doing; in short, less experience of the real world. They may reinvent imagined wheels new to themselves, but rarely do they invent the next new technology or the next new artistic form that proves effective for society at large. A child is almost never culturally ("Big *C*") creative.

This has made—continues to make—efforts to locate early signs of creative giftedness difficult, to say the least. By and large, scholars choose to search for indicators among large groups or single individuals, to look retrospectively to the childhood of eminent adults or to track forward, prospectively, from childhood into maturity. In the early decades of the twentieth century, where we left him, Lewis Terman is about to take on a prospective study of large groups of children and his colleague, Leta Hollingworth, the prospective study of a handful of individuals.

Together, they forge a synthetic path into the mysteries of creative destiny—not due to plan exactly, but to the overlap of their child subjects and professional interests. And if that were not reason enough to interest us in their research, we owe it to them for demonstrating (even if inadvertently) first, that intellectual and creative giftedness are not synonymous and second, that the invention of imaginary worlds and other forms of complex play may help distinguish which is which.

HOLLINGWORTH PICKS UP THE BATON OF "CREATIVE IQ"

Matters did not rest with Terman's glowing evaluation of the singular Child D. At the end of that hot summer in New York, he had returned to Stanford, relinquishing further professional interest in the boy to his colleague. Like Terman, Hollingworth had been drawn to the study of the gifted by a sense of her own giftedness in childhood and a firm belief that intellectual talent, though biologically inherited, required special assessment and nurture to bring to fruition. She interested herself especially in children with IQs above 180, for genius, as she understood it, depended upon precocious and extreme powers of the rational mind.

She also proved sensitive to the play interests of her very high IQ subjects. In her estimation, the stuff of play might not represent intellectual capacity *per se*, but it did represent an imaginative capability of equal importance to genius—the creative quotient, so to speak, embedded in IQ.

To bolster the point, Hollingworth took the work of A. H. Yoder as her bible. In the early 1890s Yoder had studied fifty great men and found in their boyhoods evidence of strong attachment to play. Yoder understood play to be any sustained interest on the part of the child, though he took particular note of the vigorous exercise of imagination, which capacity, he wrote, "may show itself in various ways." Among his group of great men, these often solitary ways included serial storytelling, playacting on a consistent theme, constructing toys and mechanical devices, experimenting for curiosity's sake, staging puppet shows, drawing, and versifying.

Yoder thus located imagination in the making of things under one's own aegis, whether these things were the ephemeral stuff of make-believe or more durable material constructions. And his argument boiled down to this: looking backward, it may be seen that great men possessed more imagination in youth than the average child, as evidenced by particular play pursuits; looking forward, it followed that similar play in childhood might pinpoint children destined for adult greatness.

Hollingworth endorsed Yoder's thinking wholeheartedly—and just as wholeheartedly investigated the play lives of her gifted subjects. As a result, worldplay began to swim into focus as an indicator of giftedness. D was not the first child she had come across with an imaginary country, nor was he to be the last. By the time *Gifted Children: Their Nature and Nurture* (1926) was published, she had compiled a case book of six very high IQ children; later she expanded that case book to an even dozen.

All twelve subjects had solitary, unusual, highly imaginative play interests of the kind suggested by Yoder. "Reading, calculation, designing, compiling statistics, constructing an imaginary land," wrote Hollingworth, "stand out prominently among the recreational interests of such children." Indeed, two of her study subjects had imaginary friends and three others provided ample evidence of worldplay. At the age of three Child A invented "Center Land," where children stayed up all night, played with fire, and used the elevator whenever they wished. Child E imagined a private country on the planet Venus inhabited by people and in possession of a navy. And Child D, of course, had Borningtown.

In Hollingworth's hands, the dossier on D expanded considerably. So too, did her documentation of the boy's imaginary country and his related interests. From the ages of four to seven, Hollingworth reported, D spent hours "laying out roads, drawing maps of its terrain, composing and recording its language (Bornish), and writing its history and literature." Evincing a zeal for calculation and classification, he counted the nouns, verbs, and adjectives in what he read to determine the frequency of different parts of speech. He invented words for concepts that, so far as he knew, had no name and placed them in his Bornish dictionary.

Even after his interest in Borningtown faded, D continued his "wordical work," inventing names for subtle variations in colors, assigning them numerical values, and classifying them according to their beauty. He also renamed and reclassified numbers and musical notes, as well as moths and birds. Practical experiments, too, reflected a certain amount of whimsy. At the age of eleven he determined the average geometrical path of a tack propelled by rubber band and wrote up the results.

The conclusions Hollingworth drew from such a data base do not surprise. Because her high IQ subjects surpassed their peers mentally, they tended to play by themselves. Because they played alone and had only themselves to please, their games were intellectually sophisticated and imaginatively complex. Highly complex pretend play, including imaginary friends and imaginary lands, thus belonged to children of extreme intellect and precocious learning—or so she thought. Interestingly enough, however, Terman already had data that suggested otherwise.

TERMAN'S TURN WITH ONE
THOUSAND SMART CHILDREN—AND WORLDPLAY

Upon his return to Stanford in 1917, Terman had embarked on the first large-scale, longitudinal study of intellectually gifted children. Relying upon teacher reports and grade acceleration, he tested the IQ of hundreds of thousands of the best students in local California school districts. In order to have a pool large enough for statistical analysis—his goal was one thousand participants—he accepted IQs of 140 and above or about one out of 200 tested children. Some provision was made for children below 140 IQ with special and precocious talents, such as those often found in the arts, but these were small in number (less than 2 percent of his initial group). As a result, his final study group represented compliant children who performed well in school or under special tutelage and on the IQ test.

In this large-scale project, Terman collected much the same kind of data that he had done with Child D. As part of an overall effort to describe the sociability of gifted children, he and his team gathered information from teachers, parents, and children on their play interests. Chiefly concerned with the physical versus intellectual and the social versus solitary aspects of typical childhood play, most questions dealt with very common playground games and home hobbies.

No doubt because of his involvement in D's case, however, and Hollingworth's ongoing demonstration that complex play characterized the upper reaches of gifted-ness, Terman also saw fit to scout out further terrain. In a questionnaire filled out by parents he asked, first, whether the child had "imaginary playmates" and second, "imaginary countries."

In the first volume of his *Genetic Studies of Genius,* published in 1925, Terman laid out the resulting data. Out of 643 parental queries, he received 136 (21 percent) positive responses to play with imaginary friends and 48 (7 percent) positive responses to play with imaginary countries.

These were remarkable results. Despite contemporary prejudice associating severe maladjustment with solitary make-believe, more than a few parents willingly revealed their children's idiosyncratic play with invisible companions and unreal lands. On a subjective basis Terman concluded that "a good many gifted children have had imaginary playmates or imaginary countries."

Unfortunately, he made no provision to obtain comparative data for these forms of play from his control subjects. Nor did he ask how or why the invention of imaginary lands should show up in the lower ranks of the gifted, despite Hollingworth's supposition that they would be found only among very high IQ children. The data, neverthe-

Table 5.1.   Reports of Imaginary Companions and Imaginary Worlds in Terman's 1925 Study of 643 Gifted Students. Based on data on pp. 41, 435–437 in Terman, Lewis M. 1925, Genetic Studies of Genius, vol. 1, "Mental and Physical Traits of a Thousand Gifted Children," Stanford U. Press, Stanford, CA.

		*If 100% report rate assumed**	*If 85% report rate assumed**
# boys in gifted group	352	—	(299)
# boys w/ imag companions	51	14%	17%
# boys w/ imag countries	23	6.5%	7.6%
# girls in gifted group	291		(247)
# girls w/ imag companions	85	29%	34%
# girls w/ imag countries	25	8.59%	10%
TOTALS:			
# children in gifted group	643		(546)
# children w/ imag companion	136	21%	25%
# children w/imag countries	48	7%	9%

* See figure note in the endnotes for this chapter.

less, begged that very question. Only fifteen of Terman's gifted children had tested at or above an IQ of 180 , yet at least forty-eight of them had invented imaginary worlds. Even as Hollingworth rallied her argument, here was tantalizing evidence that such play had a larger jurisdiction.

How much larger has since become evident. Over the last several decades psychologists have determined that play with imaginary companions, for instance, occurs among one- to two-thirds of *all* young children, not just the intellectually gifted. The invention of imaginary countries, as the Worldplay Project has found, also shows up in the general population—perhaps among 3 to 12 percent of all children.

We may look at Terman's play results today and see that the invention of imaginary worlds had a presence among children of "all-round intelligence," not just among those with very high IQs. We may go one step further and interpret his data as the first piece of evidence that logical power and vivid, even original, imagination occur independently of one another. Terman, however, did not make that determination. Though he was privy to the notion, current in some contemporary quarters, that creative qualities were likely distinct from the kinds of intelligence measured by IQ tests, he did not distinguish between intellectual and creative capacity.

Quite the contrary. By calling his longitudinal research the "genetic study of genius," Terman openly asserted his initial expectation that at least some of his intellectually gifted subjects might attain creative eminence. By eminence in general, he meant the kind of public success attained by the very high achievers Galton studied in the late nineteenth century—men (very, very few on Galton's list were women) who represented perhaps one out of four thousand adults.

Individuals who found some permanent footing on the public stage—world-renowned politicians, military leaders, intellectuals, artists—must invariably have smarts, Terman believed, and no matter the field or the achievement those smarts must be detectable by IQ testing. Of course, this did not mean that all high IQ children would earn some degree of eminence—or that all instances of eminence would involve creative achievement. But if such optimism was, in Terman's opinion, unwarranted, he still had cautious hopes for his select population.

Statistically speaking, Terman predicted that no more than 50 of his 1000 gifted children might actually attain the same degree of eminence as Galton's geniuses. It was much more likely, he felt, that some 200 (20 percent) might find their way into the lesser ranks of eminence to be found in *Who's Who in America*, a compilation of contemporary biographies based on notable (but not necessarily outstanding) achievement of general interest. In the event, follow-up studies through the 1950s did not bear out either expectation.

By 1959, some forty years after Terman began his study, only 31 men and 2 women from his gifted group (5 percent) had made an appearance in *Who's Who*. While it was clear that many of Terman's high IQ subjects were successful in the pursuit of intellectually demanding careers, others had suffered setbacks during the Great Depression of the 1930s and World War II. Even seventy-five years later it remained the case that few had made notable contributions and none had achieved outstanding eminence. Terman's study group, largely selected for "superior intellectuality . . . defined as ability to make a high score on . . . the Stanford-Binet" intelligence test, largely played out that talent. In the end, as in the beginning, creative capacities that flowered in genius had slipped the net.

HOLLINGWORTH DISTINGUISHES BETWEEN THE INTELLECTUAL AND THE CREATIVE

The same might be said for Hollingworth's much smaller sample of very high IQ children—though she, too, had had high hopes for the future eminence of her subjects. Unlike Terman, however, Hollingworth attempted to assess the creative potential of her twelve children independently of IQ scores or academic achievement. "Are their distinctive achievements only the phenomenal reproduction of things they have learned?" she asked. "Or do they also exhibit signs of originality and creativeness?"

At the outset, she rejected contemporary notions that did no more than equate creativeness with the pursuit of the conventional arts. Creativity in childhood, as Yoder had already suggested and Hollingworth now insisted, was to be found in a much wider range of demonstrated originality and inventiveness. What went missing from the "ordinary records and histories," focused only on IQ scores and academic precocity, often surfaced in made-up games and languages, idiosyncratic classifications of knowledge, spontaneous collections of things, mechanical constructions, and other forms of unusual extra-curricular activity that exercised imagination.

In a summation of her research published posthumously in 1942, Hollingworth rated one-third of her high IQ cases as notably creative and one-third as moderately creative; the final third, in her opinion, demonstrated no marked creativity at all.

No surprise, the invention of imaginary countries in childhood, related as it was in many cases to "constructive originality" (i.e., the drawing of maps, writing of stories, or the classifications of invented language) figured largely in her calculations of the "creativeness" of her subjects. So did play with imaginary companions. Two of the four children in the notably creative group—Child A and Child D—had invented imaginary worlds when young; A had also had an imaginary companion, as did one other child in the group. In the moderately creative group Hollingworth placed yet another child with an imaginary friend and Child E, who, like A and D, had had an imaginary country. All in all, five of the eight subjects who demonstrated originality in their play invented people or places for their amusement.

Interestingly enough, having endorsed worldplay and other forms of "constructive originality," Hollingworth proved somewhat uneasy about the blind indulgence of make-believe. The gifted child with imaginary friends, for instance, must be encouraged to find companionship with real people as well. But exaggerated academic study, she conceded, also left developmental gaps.

Child E served her as a case in point. An acknowledged prodigy by the age of eight, E sped through his schooling, completing 9th grade at age 9, high school at 11 years, 10 months, college at 15. At age 16 he received a masters degree and enrolled in a PhD program; at 18 he entered seminary; at 23 he earned his PhD; and at 25 his masters in theology.

There was much to marvel at in E's rapid academic certification, and Hollingworth did so. Yet something, she felt, was missing—and that something led her to assess E, despite his erudition, as only moderately creative. Harnessed to the organized pursuit of degrees, he had had little leisure for play. True, he invented an extraterrestrial country as a young boy, but this had been a time-starved affair. He had no other hobbies of any kind. By the time E finished his theological studies, Hollingworth had given up any expectations she may have had that the young man *Time* magazine called "New York City's most famed prodigy" would make a creative contribution to the world.

Hollingworth followed Child E for many years, from his first testing at age eight to his last at age eighteen, and knew his development well. Other of her cases also suggested that high intelligence might be cultivated academically, with little or no cultivation of creative potential. In the end, she observed, "the problem of the correlation of originality with intelligence scores perhaps deserves more careful study than it has received."

Creativity, it appeared, also required nurture—but of a distinctly different sort than the usual round of private tutors and school acceleration that served academic achievement. Among her own sample of high IQ subjects, those children appeared most creative who had had the time and support for self-initiated imaginative play and its attendant passions. These were the children she believed most likely to achieve creative eminence as adults.

As yet Hollingworth had no proof. The most promising of her subjects had been child D, the very same boy who had so impressed Terman in 1917. D had studied chemistry in college and pursued a career in industry. Sadly, he had died in 1938 at the age of 28, well before great achievements in that science might typically materialize. The other three children believed to be notably creative were also unproven in adult careers. By 1938 Child A, who would then have been 24, had completed college with high grades in math and science, but Hollingworth's published notes gave no indication of his career path. Child H, a young girl of 14 in 1938 and Child L, a boy of 11 in that year, were not yet near adulthood. The same was true for two subjects in the moderately gifted group; a third subject from that group became a medical doctor.

Whether these six individuals went on to achieve some sort of eminence Hollingworth was never to know, for she died in 1939, at the early age of fifty-three. Nor are we ever likely to know on her behalf, despite attempts to trace the lives of her study subjects—all of whom remained anonymous in her published papers. The only one of her high IQ children ever publicly identified was E, the church historian Edward Rochie Hardy Jr.

Like many of Terman's subjects, Hardy did well in an intellectually demanding career, climbing the academic ladder, writing and editing a number of books, earning himself a place in *Who's Who in America*. By Terman's criteria anyway, he made it into the lower ranks of eminence. No doubt, if she had been alive to assess the achievement, Hollingworth would have felt her expectations validated. The child whom she had found to be enormously intelligent and moderately creative made a commensurate contribution to the world as an adult.

When all was said that could be said in her own lifetime, Hollingworth distinguished between creative and intellectual capacities—and based her hopes for future eminence on a balance of both. Perhaps if her career had not been cut short, the role of worldplay as an indicator of creative potential might have moved front and center in the study of childhood giftedness and its relationship to adult genius. Hollingworth as well as Terman made it into *Who's Who* for pioneering work. Yet as things turned out, psychologists interested in assessing creative potential followed Terman's lead instead.

To plug the holes in Terman's intelligence tests, they developed other sets of timed tasks meant to identify original thinking. As faith in these structured laboratory tests soared, attention to complex, idiosyncratic play in real-life waned. Hollingworth's body of work in this regard went overlooked. Her growing appreciation for extraordinarily imaginative play—especially that complex make-believe involved in the invention of imaginary worlds—went out, like the baby, with the bathwater.

WHAT WE KNOW NOW: CREATIVITY PREDICTS CREATIVITY

Much has been learned in the years since Terman and Hollingworth opened up the field of giftedness research. Now, we generally recognize, that part of giftedness which is inherited with the color of our eyes does not segregate by social class; children of great potentiality are to be found everywhere, among the poor as well the rich, among the historically oppressed as well as the historically privileged. Other assumptions have changed as well. Almost to a man and woman, psychologists now recognize that creative giftedness is not the same thing as intellectual giftedness and cannot be found by the same measures. Yet efforts to identify and nurture children with the potential for future innovation and invention largely meet with disappointment.

Why this should be the case is something of a conundrum. Like the proverbial connoisseur, we think we know creative accomplishment when we see it. It may take years, even decades, to assimilate, but generally speaking, the world comes round to recognizing many (though certainly not all) of the innovations in thought, expression, or material culture produced by adults.

Nonetheless, when it comes to precedent behaviors or activities in childhood—insofar as they differ from adult achievement—we haven't a consistent or obvious clue. Batteries of tests developed in mid-twentieth century, chief among them the Torrance Tests of Creative Thinking (TTCT), have attempted to measure fluency, flexibility, and originality in thinking. Yet, as many critics have pointed out, the tasks set in these structured tests resist truly creative solution and bear little or no relation to real-world creative accomplishment. Overall, tests of any kind have proved inadequate in identifying creative talent, potential or otherwise.

This being the case, some researchers have proposed that creative ability in children be assessed by prodigious behavior itself. Typically identified in math, music, chess, or language, prodigies obviously demonstrate near-adult levels of talent at an early age. For some psychologists, such precocious accomplishment is a powerful indicator precisely because, as one of these researchers put it, "it is *openly masterful now* rather than *a remote* symptom of promise for the future."

The prodigy, however, is not necessarily creative. Unusual capacity for music or math performance, for example, is not the same as unusual capacity to produce new music or solve new problems. Moreover, when it comes to actual creative activity, the child is at a disadvantage in adult fields of endeavor, only capable, largely, of contributions at or near the "little *c*" end of the spectrum. It makes far more sense to identify creative potential in children by tracking behaviors that are *particular to childhood itself* and that *incidentally* develop skills and know-how useful in maturity.

Hollingworth seems to have had the same thought in mind when she suggested a link between the childhood play of imagination and the development of creative capacity. In essence, she argued, creativity appropriately understood in one context (e.g., childhood play) predicts or prepares for creativity in another (e.g., adult art or science).

This insight was not entirely lost to subsequent researchers in the field. Six years before he wrote about the literary, worldplaying prodigy Barbara Follett in 1966, the psychologist Harold Grier McCurdy looked for developmental patterns in a retrospective study of some twenty historical geniuses (all of whom had been retroactively assigned high IQs, all of whom were indisputably creative). He found "a rich efflorescence of fantasy" in childhood to be a likely element. "My point," he wrote, "is that fantasy is probably an important aspect of the development of genius, not only in those cases where the chief avenue to fame is through the production of works of imagination in the ordinary sense, but also in those where the adult accomplishment is of a different sort."

McCurdy supposed that eminent individuals such as the polymath Johann von Goethe, the writer Alfred de Musset, the philosopher Jeremy Bentham, the politician William Pitt the Younger, and the statesman and historian Barthold Georg Niebuhr, to name a few of his subjects, bridged many a hole in their accelerated acquisition of knowledge with make-believe, though the biographical information he consulted in his analysis lacked definitive evidence. Similarly, in her analysis of the Brontës' childhood pastimes, educator Ann McGreevy recognized a "learning laboratory" chiefly and productively characterized by high tolerance for self-paced, self-choice fantasy play.

In more recent years, researchers have likewise turned attention to the leisure activities of intellectually gifted or specially talented children. As with many an eminent exemplar, many gifted children freely devote extracurricular time to activities that satisfy their curiosity and develop their interests. They read voraciously; they practice skills related to particular talents; they spend time drawing or dancing or making music; and they play intricate board games and solve challenging puzzles. More to the point, as one researcher put it, they engage in elaborate make-believe, typically joining "complex clusters of diverse concepts and facts" and flights of fancy into "internally consistent conceptual structures."

Studies such as these confirm Hollingworth's initial findings that gifted children favor complex imaginative play, but there is more to know about the link between giftedness and make-believe activity. It is time to pick up where Hollingworth left off—at the brink of worldplay as an indicator of creative potential in and of itself, independent of other signs of giftedness. She herself was optimistic about what would be found:

"Since gifted children are . . . on the whole a stable and rational group, perhaps no effects, or good effects only, result from this play of the imagination." Yet if we are to heed her call to focus on complex play, a new approach is necessary—and not just among those children already recognized as gifted.

First, worldplay and other sophisticated make-believe can be studied as factors *independent of* intellectual giftedness. Despite the suppositions of Terman and Hollingworth, no systematic study has as yet linked any form of complex pretense to intelligence quotients or, for that matter, to prodigious talent. It may well turn out that the invention of imaginary lands does indeed require normal or even above normal intelligence, but it is time to look for the play among those who play well, rather than among those who test well.

Second, worldplay can be studied as an indicator of creative potential *in and of itself*. Terman and Hollingworth considered worldplay as an incidental sign of creative potential among precocious children only. But worldplay may in fact prove to be source as well as sign of creative giftedness among any and all children, *regardless* of mental ages and IQs.

Third, and finally, worldplay can be studied as a kind of self-apprenticeship in creative practice, rather than prodigious application in discipline or craft. The childhood inventor of imaginary lands often elaborates his or her world in multiple ways at once. He or she may write stories and compose music, draw maps and build models, design games, and possibly construct a secret language—all within the context of play. It is likely, therefore, that childhood worldplay confers benefits that differ substantially from the accelerated acquisition of mathematics or from the training of precocious skill in music or chess. Indeed, the most important difference may be this: Prodigies are usually specialists in learning and talent. Children who invent imaginary worlds may well develop the multiple skills and transferable practices of the generalist.

This is not to argue that all children who invent imagined places will grow up to revolutionize fields of endeavor or carve out new disciplines. But then again, as Terman and others have found, neither do most children with high IQs or remarkable talents. Additional factors, such as motivation and opportunity, also play an important role in the development of creative genius. We should not expect any one measure, including the complex elaboration of an invented world in childhood, to translate automatically or consistently into extraordinary achievement in adulthood. The assumption that gifted children become gifted adults is, after all, only an assumption.

What we *can* expect is that a close look at the actual practice of worldplay, such as that awaiting in the next chapter, will translate into a greater understanding of imaginative capacity and creative potential in childhood and perhaps, too, their connections to creative endeavor in maturity.

Chapter Six

A Learning Laboratory in Creative Practice: Plumbing the Plausible Imagination

And this matter is of absorbing interest; to trace the process by which an attic full of commonplace children's toys became a world as consistent and self-sufficient as that of the Iliad or the Barsetshire novels, would be no small contribution to general psychology.

—C. S. Lewis, writer

A CHILD'S MIND

A few years before Terman and Hollingworth took note of imaginary countries, an idea of their importance had already surfaced at the small New England campus of Clark University, where Terman himself had studied. G. Stanley Hall, an early pioneer in American psychology, had long been on the lookout for anything and everything to do with the child mind. He and his students (Terman had briefly been one of them) pinned labels on curiosity and on wonder, on play with dolls, on the collecting instinct, and more. Hall himself collected testimonies of extraordinary childhood play as others collected butterflies.

In the fall of 1914, well before Child D was to take his IQ test, Hall spotted yet another specimen—and pulled out his net. "My dear Mr. Folsom," he wrote to one of his new graduate students, "the childhood you describe is unique. If you are willing to write it out pretty fully to the extent of say not over some twenty pages of four hundred words each, I should like very much to print it in the *Pedagogical Seminary.*" Forthwith Joseph Folsom, eager to "do or create something of permanent value to society, and give a personal influence to the world," penned for the professor an obscure, yet compelling essay on his early paracosm play.

Publishing the piece in his journal, the first devoted to the psychology of children, Hall privately praised "The Scientific Play World of a Child" as "an addition of real value to the growing body of autobiographies of childhood" and its author as "gifted," as "a man of marked ability and promise." The level of detail in the student's play memoir was certainly unusual, as was his understanding of factors already considered relevant to precocity.

Even in youth Folsom had found himself ahead of his peers in the "mental grasp of impersonal things;" he had also found himself isolated from other children by his mother's refusal to allow him to play "in the streets." His was an intense imaginative life in a temperament suited, early on, to introspective review of its own play. To our benefit, he analyzed for the good professor how the boy he had been constructed his play-world; how he elaborated its many and idiosyncratic concepts; how, in effect, he devoted himself to the exercise of creative imagination.

Ever since he could remember, young Joe had had the habit of personifying inanimate things. Around the age of six his mother gave him some empty wooden spools, which he had immediately dubbed with names and personalities. He also infused broken chess pieces, blocks of wood, and stones of different sizes with imaginary being. Soon enough, the number of make-believe people grew so vast he organized individuals into families and families into "systems."

Eventually there were twelve systems all told, including, in addition to the "Spool System," a "Doll System" for his sister's dolls, a "Mystery System" for paper fairies and flying moons, and a "Volcanic System" for cratered mounds of earth that later became disembodied spirits. There was even a real person system for his family, the household servants, and the family dog.

Due to its grounding in physical objects, the grown-up Folsom referred to this system play as his "concrete play." As a boy, however, physical materials naturally merged with imagined constructs. Young Joe fashioned the concrete locales for his system world out of shelves and boxes, toy railroad tracks, and earthen works in the back yard. He connected these various places in his mind by imagining "a network of 'currents,'" which were hollow pipes or tunnels running underground, through the beams of the house, and through railroad tracks and sidewalks. These served as lines of communication between different parts of the play-world, as passageways for fire, water, electricity, and as routes of travel for the vaporous Volcanoes.

For much of middle childhood, Joe elaborated his system play according to his own enthusiasms. Yet he depended on the cooperative presence of his sister, younger by four years, to stimulate narrative pretense in this "universe of play people." Together the siblings improvised play scenarios for the system people revolving around family life and the rites of marriage, birth, and death.

Joe also depended on his sister as the primary audience for serial stories he set in yet another paracosm, an imagined place somewhat like the northeastern United States, "with New York, Chicago and Buffalo fairly well located, but all the intervening country distorted, reconstructed and given imaginary names." In this make-believe landscape he and his sister took express trains hither and yon, meeting with important personages, as well as "railroad wrecks, great fires, volcanic eruptions, and crime."

In both imaginary worlds, Folsom later recalled, "I truly lived and moved and had my being." After four or five years of shared play with his sister, however, a new home, a new school, and parental pressure convinced young Joe that "it was best I should give up these childish things." In the event, however, he did not give up his play so much as he internalized it.

Though most of the system people were boxed and put away, from the ages of eleven to fourteen young Joe set about writing "a full account of the whole play-world" he no longer enacted with his sister. By the time he had finished, this history comprised over ten thousand words, drawings, maps, and diagrams, all "carefully divided into chapters, and paragraphs with headings, . . . tabular classifications and footnote references." He turned, too, to the documentation of his imaginary rail travel. "Some years after I had outgrown the concrete play," Folsom wrote in 1915, "I was still mapping the cities and sketching the railroad trains of this realm. Even to-day in spare moments I sometimes imagine myself riding through that mysterious country."

PLAY PRACTICE ANALYZED

Folsom traced the development of content in his make-believe play. He also teased out imaginative and constructive practices inherent in its elaboration: "The general process," he wrote, "was in most cases first an idea taken from experience; second, an association of ideas and feelings into complexes; third, the expression and further elaboration of these complexes of ideas by play creations; fourth, the synthesis of all these separate creations into a consistent play-world." Following his lead, we too can unpack those practices one by one. We can begin to specify how worldplay may serve as a learning laboratory that exercises imagination and cultivates creative potential.

Ideas Taken from Experience

When Folsom considered his thinking as a child at play, he realized that the "material content or subject matter of my play-world was necessarily taken from my real environment." As a young boy, he formed ideas about the natural world, about the stones and ashes on the family property, for instance, that he experienced firsthand. He drew as well from the experiences of others—from what he was told of his father's work as a clergyman, and from books he read about volcanoes, the moon and stars, and electricity. He then used the ideas of firsthand and secondhand experience to imagine the powerful eruptive spirits which ruled his make-believe world.

How exactly was that accomplished? It is worth taking a moment to consider first just what it means to "take ideas from experience." For most of us, the word "stone" very likely stimulates a visual image of the object, a kinesthetic image of its weight and heft, and/or a tactile image of its rough surface. Although these images are indicated here with words on the page, the foundation for all thinking lies in the interior flow of these and other sense impressions. Even in the absence of words—especially in the absence of words— we can call to mind sights, sounds, smells, tastes, and body feelings of touch or pressure or balance that were once experienced, but not immediately present.

We may also imagine a conjured experience. We can form mental images of things *never before wholly perceived* in reality. We can suppose, like young Joe, the essence of volcanoes flowing like electricity through a network of underground pipes. Just like him, we can construct a fantasy out of "a universe of objective facts" by attending to "the striking, the unusual, the violent, the vigorously moving, and the mysterious elements" of experience—and mentally combining them.

Associations of Ideas and Feelings

Folsom took pains to describe the genesis of his volcano people. Ideas and feelings about dirt mounds in the backyard, invisible electric currents, powerful personality, and moral authority were mixed into what he called a "complex." By associating two or more ideas or feelings taken from real experience, the "complex" produced an unreal composite—quite in the same way that the mythical beasts of ancient Greece and Rome, known collectively as chimeras, married diverse real animals into fantastic creatures.

Contemporary scholars such as the cognitive scientist Mark Turner discuss the imaginative operation as a cognitive "blending" of one idea with another, and "a mainstay of early childhood thought." A child might superimpose the imagined features of a pet dog upon a very real balloon trailed about on a string, for instance—and call it an "imagination dog." Conceptually, young Joe's volcano people were no different, blending material objects with remembered experience of people and imagined personality.

Joe's imaginary worlds as a whole also represented compounded ideas, perceptions, and feelings. Anthropologist Stephen Nachmanovitch has referred to the serendipity of the admixture in play as a "bricolage," a tinkering with and repurposing of materials at hand. Instinctive tinkers, children "will incorporate anything into their play—whatever piece of stuff is lying on the ground, whatever piece of information they picked up at breakfast." Joe drew upon what he learned at home and at school, absorbing into play "certain rather striking or mysterious elements such as comets and mastodons, which somehow became associated with strong ideas, feelings, and curiosity."

For the ideal geography of his railroad world, for instance, he took an accurate mapping of distance between New York, Chicago, and other major landmarks and imagined in the interstices a sprawling network of make-believe train lines, each with its own set of travelers, hazards, and emblematic colors. As the imaginative play developed, simple blends linked up to form composites that compounded again into the repurposed "complexes" of make-believe pretense.

Blends and bricolage can tell us much about the young imagination and its potential for mature creativity. No one is surprised when a child substitutes a little toy truck for a big red fire engine or engages a set of dolls in a story setting derived from a television show—though perhaps we should be. No matter how unremarkable, all blends reflect the imagination at work. That said, our notice of make-believe chimeras generally increases, the more unlikely the juxtaposition of their elements. What we notice and notice again in child's play are the blends and complexes that are unusual to us—balloon dogs, spool people, and "greenly" dignified express trains whistling through a mysterious landscape for scheduled arrival in Chicago.

Divergence from conventional thinking is not the only measure of vigorous imagination, however. Those blends that surprise most also reveal hidden likenesses and relationships between hitherto unconnected things. Pet dogs and balloons, as unlike as they are, may suddenly be seen to share an inclination for companionship as well as a tendency to take off on their own. Similarly, volcanoes and authority figures share a great deal of physical and emotional force. In either case, the metaphoric connections invite us to contemplate a convergence of ideas about dissimilar things.

Indeed, when it comes to evaluating imaginative blends, the more unexpected and also the more insightful and apt, the more creative we may deem the child who puts them together.

Recall from chapter 5 that children exercise their creativity in personal, "little *c*" ways. Nevertheless, the more inventive their imaginative fancies, the more they demonstrate a *potential* for creativity *beyond* the personal context.

Young Joe surely demonstrated such potential. He blended material and immaterial elements of play into considerably unusual and perceptive juxtapositions. He instantiated these blends by constructing things—railroad setups, waterways in the dirt, systems people, marriage licenses, a written record of play—in accord with internal imagination. And by combining and recombining knowledge, experience, and emotion into a fanciful quilt of his own devising, he systematically elaborated "an original imaginary creation upon facts" in play.

Elaboration by Play Creation

Young Joe possessed an insatiable curiosity for bits and pieces of the world around him; he also possessed an all-consuming yen for organizing those bits and pieces. "Especially noticeable," he later wrote as an adult, " . . . was my interest in objects which admitted of comparison and classification. . . . I took great delight in the contemplation of orderly series of unlike but related objects and phenomena."

In early and middle childhood, certainly, Joe found much in the natural world to stimulate this appetite. He compared the shape and position of the moon from night to night, classified different types of locomotives, identified local trains by the sound of their whistles, pored over time tables and railroad lines, and memorized their stations. In adolescence he made lists of birds sighted and trees and flowers observed, thus comparing, classifying, and cataloguing his sensibilities.

The same appetite for managing the materials in his mental and physical environment characterized Joe's make-believe play. What he called his "classifying fever" reached its pitch with the Volcanoes, those mounds of earth that quickly morphed into ethereal, madly proliferating creatures. First he associated a whole host of Volcanoes with numbers up to a million "and so on to the unheard of number Madrackankantillion." He then joined other Volcanoes with letters; yet others with dinosaurs until, having run out of known prehistoric creatures as suitable totems, he made up "the Gondrondontherium, the most terrible of all nameable Volcanoes."

Joe's fever for organization did not stop there. He relentlessly compared all his system people according to certain traits and dispositions, including "fiercity," a temperament both noble and good. Constructing "a sort of paper machine for measuring the degree of fiercity of any individual," he took the temperature of them all: "The Pets . . . were between 5° and 20°. . . . The Dolls and lady Spool people were mostly between 35° and 70°; the male Spools, Towers, and Yucatownals were 40° and up to

100° or more." He also tabulated the "fiercity" of his innumerable Volcanoes, visualizing them (since they were wholly imaginary) in a circular hierarchy reflecting more or less of this trait.

Systematic arrangements and classifications played an important role in Joe's make-believe, but they did not form its sum total. He also lived and moved—literally—within the narratives that he and his sister spontaneously contrived in shared socio-dramatic play. The two made their play people talk "by our using several different tones of voice" and actively participated with them as characters in "play events." They stretched their imaginative wings by empathizing with one after another of their systems people and enacting ideas about individual, family, and community behavior.

In truth, the narrative organization of materials forged in shared play proved as critical to young Joe's imaginary world invention as the classificatory organization honed in solitary play. "I might lay plans and think over the affairs of the little world alone," he later wrote, "but never was there any pleasure in actually playing without her [my sister's] sympathy and cooperation."

At this juncture we may appreciate how narratives and classifications serve to *organize* play materials. They also function to *elaborate* those materials, to spin out simple pretexts into compound pretense, and in so doing, to *construct* knowledge and understanding.

Consider narrative first, which operates at the crossroads where knowledge and imagination intersect. Whether we recall the past, plan for the future, or postulate an alternate reality, it is through story that human beings vicariously explore and manage the chaos of experience. We explain our lives and other processes as a series of events in time involving particular actors motivated by particular impulses in particular places. That narrative impulse runs deep in childhood play. Children infuse toy props or themselves or some imagined entity with a declared existence, they inform these entities with imagined causal powers, and they link imagined events by consequence.

For some investigators—Turner chief among them—the narrative impulse is "a basic principle of mind," a "mental instrument" that shapes our ability to think. We can see what he means by considering Joe's simple blends as the smallest of story units, as building blocks for constructing larger narrative structures. The imaginative blend of volcano and human being implied at least two short narratives, one about geological eruptions, the other about people. The volcano erupts. The man gets angry. By mapping these two small stories together, the boy was off to a start in impromptu tales about awe-inspiring volcano beings.

In the process, we may assume, Joe enlarged his thinking in the same way that clichés articulate the thinking of communities and cultures. To say that a man squirrels away savings for hard times ahead is to imply a small story of blended elements: The squirrel/man buries/deposits nuts/money. Enabling us to imagine future need, narrative in this instance constructs knowledge about the benefits of delayed gratification and planning. From blends, to story fragments, to the improvised scenarios of play, narrative allows the child to make sense of experience, real and imagined.

Consider, as well, the knowledge construction that attends classification, which involves fundamentally the recognition and formation of patterns. Just as narrative imposes causal order, pattern recognition imposes analytic order on the flow of experience. Things and processes may be grouped by sensual quality, by functionality, by emotional association, etc., according to personal experience and perception. As a boy at play in the physical world, young Joe *discovered* patterns in the shape and size of stones and spools. He discovered patterns of personality, emotion, and behavior in the social world, too. By assigning these social patterns to his toys, he also *formed* patterns; he invented his own ways of organizing—and understanding—things and processes.

Tying systemic organization of his imaginary world to narrative elaboration, Joe in fact built for himself what philosopher Michael Polanyi has discussed as tacit, personal knowledge. Reliant on the individual's particular skills, biases, and passions, tacit knowledge is necessarily idiosyncratic and largely intuitive. To the extent that it is grounded in shared experience it may also connect with explicit group knowledge.

Young Joe's understanding of the interrelationships between imaginary beings, personality, letters, and emotion provides example. At times his play narrative called for imaginary persons to be scared to death. Only those system people low on the scale of "fiercity" could be thus frightened; only those high on the same scale (i.e., the Volcanoes) could do the frightening. And the Volcanoes did so by yelling certain letters at their victims, the letters also ordered by their effectiveness. The adult Folsom explained:

> In other words, the possibility of inflicting death by fright varied directly as the fiercity of the executioner, as the fear potency of the letters used, as the number of repetitions, loudness, etc., of the yelling, and inversely as the fiercity and general resisting power of the victim. I never as a child expressed it in this way, but I certainly had such a conception, and if I had known algebra at the time, would undoubtedly have formulated something like the above statement.

Joe's personal conception of inverse proportions might reasonably be described as a naïve discovery of principles he later recognized in algebraic mathematics. This is not to say that all the patterns the boy invented in play were meaningful explanations *outside that make-believe.* Volcanoes in the physical world did not erupt for emotional reasons; the sound of certain vowels and consonants did not extinguish life. Within the sphere of play, however, these chimeric blends did make sense. By the logics of narration and classification, they connected with one another into one over-arching pattern.

The Synthesis of a Consistent Play-World

While a boy, Folsom regarded his classifications and comparisons, his measurements, lists and stories, as so many "facts" pertaining to his imaginary world. Information, whether learned or imagined, required organization; more to the point, it required consistent, real-seeming organization. Looking back he observed, "My mind,—and I am led to believe this is true to a large extent of most children—although highly imaginative, was at the same time intensely realistic and logical."

In his case, he was willing to concede, the loyalty to consistency was absolute. Everything in the worldplay Joe shared with his sister had to be connected. Systematic arrangements had to line up with one another in logical as well as soul-satisfying ways. All his play journeys by rail, for instance, "were narrated so as to be consistent with the railroad schedules and the distance between the places in question." Because Volcanoes topped the charts in "fiercity" and expressed preference for the noble color green, they alone were suited for the role of philosophers. Other system people, endowed with different personality types, took the parts of lawyers, doctors, criminals, or silly creatures who "'talked with their tongues half out'."

Whatever new doll or imaginary being could not be convincingly placed within these classifications of personality and profession, Joe summarily rejected. The resulting imaginary world, as he later put it, was "like a system of geometry built upon unreal premises, but conforming accurately throughout to the arbitrary conditions." If, to the outsider, his play appeared marvelously fantastic, the boy himself found it marvelously believable, precisely because the imaginary world retained and refracted something of the real world—and did so consistently.

Even as a child, Folsom considered his imaginary countries built on "scientific" grounds; they were, in effect, plausible or real-seeming. And that plausibility holds an important key to what may be most valuable in the play practice—not just for young Joe, but for all children who invent imaginary worlds.

In making this claim, it is necessary to revisit, if only briefly, the paracosm research begun by Robert Silvey and the conclusions drawn from that data by Stephen MacKeith and David Cohen. Many individuals who supplied Silvey with materials commented upon their childhood drive to invent an imaginary world that was logically consistent—or what amounted to the same thing, *believable*.

For example, "Leonora," who shared an imaginary orphanage and its inhabitants with two girlfriends, remembered that "The Game," as they called it, "was frequently interrupted for an ongoing discussion of our actions, e.g., 'No, you can't possibly do that, it wouldn't be possible in the circumstances.'" "Ambrose," too, set about "establishing regularities" for the world he imagined on one of the moons of Saturn. "I had to invent all sorts of reasons for how the people got there;" he wrote, "why the language developed as it did, and why so many particulars resembled things on Earth." And "Jeremy," who also invented an imaginary language, "constructed rules for forming everything . . . from English."

All pretend play involves some degree of rule-governed behavior, of course, but in worldplay reasons and rules frame the imaginary venture as a problem-solving exercise in the persuasive and credible "what if." The island state of Possumbul, based on the "possible world" that five-year-old "Dan" and his cousin "Peter" had heard about from their socialist fathers, had necessarily to conform to political processes (as the boys understood them). "Once created," Dan wrote, "the elements could not just be demolished and a fresh start made: they had to be amended just as in the real world." With reference to two of her "mystical harmonious" worlds, "Brenda" wrote, "It was very important indeed to be plausible, in that everything had to connect into a coherent system, or whole pattern."

Interestingly enough, in analyzing these and other materials, Cohen and MacKeith suggested that "[t]his kind of systematic imagination is psychologically very curious. On the one hand, children are playing, fantasizing, imagining; on the other hand, the fantasy is very logical. Events in their world have to follow rules. It looks much more like work than play."

In so saying, they drew upon the viewpoint of psychologist Jean Piaget, whose son "T" had, from the age of seven, busied himself with the elaboration of an imaginary land called "Siwimbal." According to his father, T drew maps of Siwimbal and its towns, peopled the place with schoolchildren, and narrated numerous adventures on its soil. At age ten, he also began drawing tiny bears and monkeys in historical costumes and placing them in historically accurate settings. In both cases, Piaget considered the make-believe activity a constructive game "halfway between play and intelligent work." T's maps and drawings, he wrote, reflected a "merely imitative reproduction of the corresponding reality."

Arguing much the same for their group of paracosmists, Cohen and MacKeith characterized the plausible play as "imagination on a half-grand scale." Unfortunately, this assessment misunderstands the role of rule-making and plausible imitation in complex make-believe—and cannot be accepted as a generalization. Instead of curtailing the imagination, the imitation, or rather, the *transposition* of real world elements into an alternate, make-believe setting leads to their narrative and analytic *re-invention*.

Folsom referred to his play as "the real world modified to suit my tastes"—and modified it was. Subject matter may have originated in elements of objective experience, but boyish imagination diversely combined those bits and pieces into fantastic "facts" and phenomena. Transposition led him to generate a world in which every real thing looked strange and fantastic and every fantastic thing made some real sense. In effect, there may be stone creatures and volcano beings, but they think and feel like you and me about fires or electricity, and they obey certain natural and social laws. Rules, including the rule that everything be plausible and real-seeming, establish the integrity of the play-world by setting the constraints of the play improvisation.

Within constraints the imagination is set free to suppose and synthesize. Indeed, as numerous practitioners and some psychologists have argued, imagination *depends upon* constraints. Among these, Stravinsky is most famous for stating that if "everything is permissible to me . . . [then I would be lost] in this abyss of freedom." To the contrary, he wrote, "the more narrowly I limit my field of action and the more I surround myself with obstacles," the greater "my freedom [and]... precision of execution."

As with adult creators, so with young inventors of imaginary worlds. The writer Jacques Borel recalled how adopting the rules and grammar of Latin for Ladahi, an imaginary language constructed in childhood, let loose the floodgates of his linguistic imagination: "[A]t the end of a few weeks I possessed not only an adequate everyday vocabulary...but also sufficient syntax to enable me to talk and write...with some degree of ease." The poet W.H. Auden similarly observed that the constraints of his worldplay—particularly the "rules" that tied it to "reality and truth"—had taught him "certain principles which I was later to find applied to all artistic fabrication."

Children who constrain their make-believe do not thereby exercise a "half-grand" imagination. To the contrary, the constraints of plausibility can and do provide impetus for much inventive practice.

MODELING AND MNEMONIC INVENTION

When all is said and done, rule-making constraint and plausible re-invention channel the imagination in one particular and potentially creative direction. To invent an imaginary world is, in fact, to acquire practice in the art and science of modeling—a point Silvey made when he compared his New Hentian States to "highly complicated models in Meccano."

By and large, we model things or processes too vast, too small, too distant, or too close for direct observation and manipulation. Models simplify the complex; they simulate what can only be imagined. So do imaginary worlds. Indeed, modeling a secret country or a system of chimeric families presupposes two things: first, an intense curiosity for patterns and relationships difficult to examine directly and, second, the desire to conceptualize those patterns and relationships in imagination, to handle and organize them in an alternate realm of play.

If there is a particular name for this kind of make-believe model surely it is "analogon," a term Derwent Coleridge used in the mid-nineteenth century to refer to his brother Hartley's imaginary world, Ejuxria. Analogon means analogue, a thing or process that functions similarly to something else, though looks may be deceiving. A gill, for instance, is an analogue or analogon of a lung. According to Derwent, Hartley's Ejuxria was an analogon "to the world of fact, so far is it was known to [him], complete in all its parts," just as Joe's system world was an analogon to the real world as he knew it.

As models for conceptualizing and manipulating what is only partially known and understood, analogons serve to test understanding of *the way things work.* And they serve, too, to stretch that understanding beyond the here and now, as the logic of the make-believe setting suggests other and *different ways things might also work.* Herein lies a large part of the creative benefit to be had from worldplay. Successfully organizing and modeling the content of their paracosms, children learn to conceive and explore the possible.

Indeed, children at play in imaginary worlds learn to *articulate* the possible. In their hands, modeling begins with what may be material (a special place, a family of dolls, a pile of dirt), elaborates what may be imagined and immaterial (a chimeric landscape, a volcano people, underground tunnels) and often produces what may document the inner play (a drawing, a map, a story).

As suggested in chapter 4, artifacts such as these provide an acceptable format or structure for private, internalized make-believe. Moreover, according to psychologist Jerome Bruner, in drawing or writing down a figment of the imagination we do two things. We produce a record of our interior life and that record, which "embodies our thoughts and intentions," enables reflection. "The process of thought and its product," he has written, "become interwoven. . . ." By this token, the make-believe becomes the drawing becomes the paracosm play. Any and all artifacts evoking an imaginary world enable a persistent return to imagined place, a further elaboration of that alternate realm and, too, a check on its internal consistency.

Indeed, drawings, story fragments, and maps safeguard make-believe beyond its own generative processes in ways that remain accessible and relevant for long periods, sometimes throughout life. Reviewing his juvenilia in old age, the writer C. S. Lewis, for example, remarked that "the solitary memory is defective: and even where it seems to remember, it cannot claim authority." In his effort "to trace the process by which an attic full of commonplace children's toys became a world," the surviving maps and stories of Animal-Land and Boxen both revived and supplemented the "oral tradition" of memories and made-up words he shared with his brother, Warren, well into adulthood.

As mnemonic aids, stories, drawings and maps also contribute, Lewis understood, to "the conviction that one is dealing with a sort of reality." Indeed, they validate that imagined reality, a point the visual artist and sculptor Claes Oldenburg made when he recalled that his early drawings for the make-believe Neubern—"the first serious drawings that I did"—helped authenticate that something, "an imaginary universe which you have created with your pencil and watercolor," in fact "really looks like it exists."

For both men, the artifacts of childhood worldplay spoke to the origins of their mature creativity. This may have had something to do with early introduction to craft, in Lewis's case with writing, in Oldenburg's with visual art. But the creative benefits of the worldplay lay elsewhere as well. Tracing his originality to what he "made . . . up when I was a little kid," Oldenburg appears to have consciously borrowed the imaginative and creative processes of childhood play for his mature work: "I always begin from a real thing . . . and send it in the impure soup of myself and all associations and in a direct, naïve way, reconstruct the world."

Lewis certainly argued that generating the many artifacts of play involved something "essentially different from reverie;" it involved "invention." In turn, that invention involved multiple expressive forms—stories, drawings, maps—that conveyed information in different ways—visually, spatially and conceptually as well as verbally, intuitively and sequentially. Moreover, it involved the *integration* of story with drawing with history. For Lewis, "the mood of the systematizer" that drove him as child to make everything in his worldplay fit together proved far more important to his training as a novelist than any amount of juvenilia.

Modeling and documenting an imaginary world, then, children who play like a young Lewis, Oldenburg or Folsom learn to construct or invent culture in three senses of the term. First, they generate cultural artifacts (stories, drawings and maps); second, they generate an imaginary culture, an integrated system of beings negotiating place, experience and time, which the play artifacts represent, authenticate and sustain; and third, they generate a personal culture of creative process and practice. Constructing imaginary worlds, children construct, too, a sense of the self as creator.

THE CREATING SELF

In his 1915 essay, Folsom insisted upon the many "unusual features [of his play] which I have been unable to find developed to a like extent in the experiences of other persons." Professor Hall soon put the student straight: other childhood play worlds, though very different in their particulars, were surprisingly similar to his in their generalities. In a 1907 essay, Hall had already reflected upon the modeling play shared by two brothers in a sand pile behind their house. Now he directed Folsom to one Una Hunt and her evocation of the make-believe land she called "My Country." He also introduced Folsom to Lorey Day, another graduate student hard at work on recollections of an imaginary country called "Exlose."

In matters of chimeric imagination, narrative and systemic construction, modeling and mnemonic invention, Hunt and Day shared much with Folsom. In particular, they fashioned in worldplay a creative identity. For Hunt, play in the magical, "half-fairy" country of her imagination allowed her to explore feelings she associated with a private part of herself called Una Mary. It also allowed her to link "the known and the unknown . . . pressing in upon me from every side;" to blend fables, ballads, and fairy tales with strong emotional responses to forest glades and mountain sunsets; and to forge a psychological space "where all our wishes came true in a flash. . . ."

Day, too, projected an alter ego into Exlose, a world he developed "according to my own personal interests and desires" (see figure 6.1.). At the same time, he experienced all the headiness of an extrinsic and primal "child god." "Exlose was an imaginary world," he wrote, "and I was . . . the First Cause of everything."

In the case of Folsom, identity developed in make-believe had likewise much to do with a sense of creative power. Because he played with his sister, he had had to grapple with shared control of materials and narratives—both he and his sister "were of course the rulers of the universe." Moreover, like Day the "child god," like the Brontë genii, Folsom was acutely self-conscious as a boy of having *made* his imaginative game and in his own way.

His sister, he early understood, was far more biddable than he when it came to the spontaneous inventions of play. She "tended more to enjoy passively the myths created by others; . . . while I must rather create my own world of fancy to suit my personal tastes." More often than not, he found the narrative constructions of others unpalatable: "To me truth was much more wonderful than the fiction invented by others," he wrote, "but my own fiction was better still."

Because the sense of a creative self is so compelling for so many children who invent imaginary worlds, we might almost include it as a defining characteristic of worldplay. Take, for example, the many testimonies to be found in the case descriptions of Silvey's paracosmists. For "Andrea," who shared two imaginary worlds, the "ultimate pleasure" of such play "was in having created something." "Erica," who elaborated her imaginary land of "Crab" at great length, also recalled that its primary appeal lay in the "chance to be creative; to invent, imagine and channel what I had been reading and thinking into some definite form."

In addition, "Rosalind" remarked that in her worldplay "creation and further creation was more important than imaginary happenings and acting them out." And Ambrose understood that the invention of his imaginary country on an "earth-sized moon of Saturn" had been "an attempt to get some kind of control over the real world by reproducing its appearances; to find order in it, and to put myself in relation to that." In the process, he learned "how the imagination works."

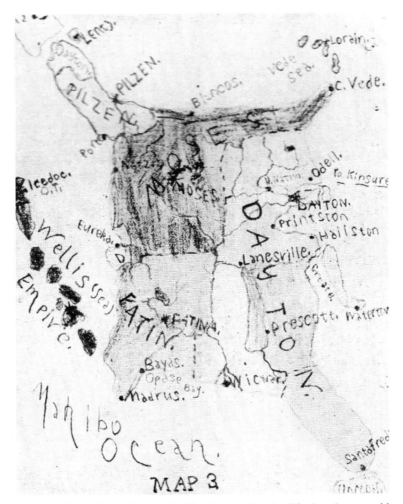

Fig. 6.1. One of several maps detailing the continents of the imaginary world of Exlose. Childhood drawing by Lorey Day.

Ultimately, the child as creator exercises a whole range of capacities that set the stage for original thinking. We find the imprint of creative practice in the blending of experiences and ideas, the classifications of real and imagined things, the organization of systemic patterns and narrative sequences, the modeling of worlds, the generation of artifacts, and the synthesizing of all that is known and felt into one grand design.

The creating self "owns" the processes and products of make-believe, the elaborations of narrative, and the systematic arrangements of people and place. More, it revels in aesthetic satisfaction for what has been wrought. In his design of medals, uniforms, and maps that brought to life the long-evolving world of Possumbul, Dan felt "ravished by my world, especially by its beauty and its order." And, interestingly enough, that aesthetic wonder may have something to do with yet another characteristic shared by Hunt, Day, and Folsom—the fused perceptions of synesthesia.

WORLDPLAY AND SYNESTHESIA—A CONNECTION?

In their autobiographies and memoirs of play Hunt, Day, and Folsom all reported childhood synesthesia, a perceptual condition in which sensory modes cross and combine with interesting effects on cognition. For example, music may be spontaneously experienced in visual images as well as sound. That fused perception may in turn promote metaphorical, this-is-like-that thinking. Richard Cytowic, author of *The Man Who Tasted Shapes* (1993), has additionally characterized synesthetic perception as emotionally charged and noetic, by which he means "experienced directly, an illumination that is accompanied by a feeling of certitude. It breaks through surface reality and gives a glimpse of the transcendent."

In instances considered true or clinical synesthesia, sensory and noetic fusion occurs involuntarily and is probably inherited. In non-clinical synesthesia, cross modal thinking depends on a fluid sensitivity to perceptual experience that can be learned—and unlearned. Whatever the case, the particulars of fused perception differ from individual to individual, as does the intensity.

As many as four in one hundred adults may see as well as hear sounds, feel textures along with tastes, or otherwise mix and fuse real sensations with associated ones. Somewhat larger proportions of children, between 5 and 15 percent, may combine colors with sounds, letters, or numbers or otherwise cross senses, though these numbers dwindle with maturation and schooling. Many children never remark on their synesthesia; for others sensory associations present so vividly and persistently as to play a central role in their young lives.

This was certainly the case for Hunt, Day, and Folsom. Hunt, for one, filled her account of childhood with synesthetic remembrances. "[N]early everything had color," she wrote, even people had distinctive hues "that I feel at once as soon as I see them." Additionally, letters and numbers had personality.

They did for Day as well. Capital letters especially, he wrote, had "facial and other motor expression." Some of these expressions suggested vague emotion, others much more specific feeling and personality. Capital D, for instance, was "proud and haughty. E was rather ugly, ill-natured and inclined to be ferocious at times. . . ." Later, in his work for Hall, Day devoted an entire article to his "Alphabet Friendships."

Folsom, too, associated letters and even colors with emotion and personality. In his railroad world the most important passengers clambered aboard the Greeniarten Express to speed from one town to another. An engine of any other name would hardly have traveled so fast or carried VIPs. "Green," he wrote in his adolescent account of the play, "was the most dignified, noble, and important color."

Whether Hunt, Day, and Folsom exhibited a clinical or a learned synesthesia is not entirely clear, nor does that necessarily matter. What counts is that all three children experienced their sensory fusions vividly and spontaneously. They incorporated synesthesia into their play and they made it a pretext for the elaboration of play.

In young Una's case, My Country had its start on a Persian rug possessed of a "tawny orange zigzag" flower stem that she associated with the Amazon River, "because its color was like the sound of the word." Other designs in the rug held similar synesthetic associations with woods, fields and summer homes.

Young Lorey peppered Exlose with place names chock-full of favorite letters. As Exlose grew to encompass more and more imaginary territory, he filled his maps with over one hundred locales, "each traceable to its source in alphabet friendship."

As for young Joe, sensory fusions of color, letters, and emotions characterized each of his imaginary families. "Each system, like a political nation, had a flag, on which its letters and certain other emblems were placed," he later remembered. "Each had also certain colors which were used in the flag."

Synesthetic and synthetic associations figured so largely in the childhood play of Folsom, Hunt, and Day that the question almost poses itself: Are other worldplaying children besides Folsom, Day, and Hunt synesthetic? Sometime in her early adolescence, my daughter Meredith revealed that numbers and letters each had their distinctive color. Though this synesthesia apparently played no organizing role in her worldplay, it did influence a consistent and long-lasting love for learning languages. Certain passages in the memoirs and notes of paracosmists Leo Lionni and Stanislaw Lem (both featured in chapter 9) suggest that they, too, may have been synesthetic in childhood.

Given the testimony reviewed here, certain speculations present themselves. Vivid cross-modal associations experienced in childhood may set the stage for—even help explain—the chimeric blends of make-believe play. Synesthesia may enhance pretense by spontaneously generating fusions which, though physically unreal, are yet perceptually, cognitively, and emotionally true. Turn that thought around and one purpose of childhood make-believe, especially in its more complex forms, may be to make sense of synesthetic perceptions and blended associations by exploring their plausibility. Further understanding awaits systematic study of synesthesia and imaginative play in combination.

TRANSITIONS TO ADULT ENDEAVOR

Inventing imaginary lands, children explore their potential for a creative life. In terms of the worldplay-creativity network (figure 3.5), they develop creative behaviors, they construct personal knowledge, and they invent or generate artifacts of culture in the form of drawings, stories, and maps that document and structure ways of being in imaginary worlds. In other words, they learn, in a laboratory of their own making, what it means to bring something novel and effective into existence. What's more, some part of this creative practice may outlast childhood. It did in young Joe's case.

After receiving his doctorate from Clark, Folsom held various positions in small New England colleges, teaching anthropology and economics as well as psychology. He contributed to the synthesis of all three disciplines into the new and hybrid discipline of social psychology, a field he believed would help "make human life more worth living." He also developed a research interest in marriage and the family, which cannot surprise anyone familiar with his childhood play. In 1934 he published *The Family, Its Sociology and Social Psychiatry* and four years later edited *Plan for Marriage*, a practical approach to sex, courtship, and parenthood well ahead of its time.

Censored in 1941 for reference to contraception, *Plan for Marriage* soon slid into obscurity—though many of its ideas did not. Valued by colleagues for his "creative, experimental and [...] liberal outlook," Folsom, too, slid out of sight after his death in 1960—though the field of study to which he devoted his life remains. What remains as well is his record of worldplay and how it mattered to him. "We do not wholly lose our childhood," he declared while still a student at Clark; "pressing interests" do not disappear as we grow older, but are "merely transformed."

This transformation was and is no mean achievement. If the privately imaginative child is to become a publicly creative adult, he or she must eventually channel interests and skills into endeavors valued by society at large. Creative practice gained in worldplay must be harnessed to the needs and concerns of adult disciplines. Somehow Folsom understood this as a young man on the brink of professional life. Somehow he—like Child E, like C.S. Lewis, like many others who invented worlds in childhood play—managed the maturation of creative imagination and practice. That "somehow" is the subject of the next chapter.

## Part III

GRAFTING WORLDPLAY
TO ADULT WORK

Chapter Seven

The Maturation of Creative Imagination: Robert Louis Stevenson as Mentor

I have always believed that the games of children are an absolutely essential preparation for life; thanks to them the infantile brain hastens its development, receiving, according to the hobbies preferred and the amusements carried on, a definite moral and intellectual stamp upon which the future will largely depend.

—Santiago Ramón y Cajal, neuroscientist and Nobel laureate

IN PRAISE OF THE PLAYBOX

In 1877, at the age of twenty-seven, Robert Louis Stevenson declared his adult allegiance to childhood play. In the essay "Crabbed Age and Youth," he supposed a boy "remarkably fond of toys (and in particular of lead soldiers)" who had grown to an age when the "playbox" ought to be left behind. Nothing, however, could induce the boy to give up "the very pick of life." Wrote Stevenson in his stead: "[S]o soon as I have made enough money, I shall retire and shut myself up among my playthings until the day I die." In this way, with a light touch, the writer protested the suppression of childhood play and asserted, too, its ongoing value in maturity.

The observation that play gets short shrift as children come of age in the Western world is surely as old and as perennial as that civilization itself. The Bible puts it thus: "When I was a child, I spake as a child, I felt as a child, I thought as a child: now that I am become a man, I have put away childish things." Turning their attention to the phenomenon, psychologists have asked what might be the causal factors.

In the early 1900s, for instance, G. Stanley Hall argued that as children become "alive to [the] fictitious nature" of their play, it loses its charm. Jean Piaget argued mid-century that developing powers of rational thought make pretend play irrelevant to learning and growing. More recently, scholars have considered other pressures that give pretend play the squeeze. Make-believe succumbs to what one psychologist has called a cultural "canalization" towards conventionality. That same canalization describes an apparent tapering of personal imagination and creative potential in older children and adults.

There are two typical pressure points managing the flow of imaginative play in childhood. Early on, the acquisition of language and of toys diverts make-believe in certain socially sanctioned directions. Whether a child plays with a rag doll or a commercialized action figure can have as much effect as access to fairy tales or video games. Again, in late childhood and adolescence, preparations for adulthood choke idiosyncratic make-believe in favor of peer-accepted games and pastimes. For those children and youth especially involved in complex play of their own making, this last funnel may provoke very conscious leave-taking of imagined worlds.

We have already witnessed Charlotte Brontë make determined efforts to shake off Angria, among them penning, at age twenty-four, her "Farewell to Angria." "God-frey," one of Silvey's paracosmists, wrote out a similar farewell at age seventeen describing his reasons for giving up "Dobid," an imaginary island state whose ancient language and contemporary transportation systems had engaged him for seven years. "Thinking out, writing and drawing a nation in full detail," though it was "party [*sic*] of my very self," the young Godfrey wrote, had become "absurd." Consequently, he wrote, "I have determined to sever any connection with these men and devote myself to my studies and to the things of the world around me."

There was more a shift of focus than finality in these two formal farewells. Neither Charlotte nor Godfrey abandoned worldplay so much as they grafted its elements onto acceptable adult endeavors, and in much the same way that Joseph Folsom turned from shared play with his sister to writing it up, to a career in marriage counseling and academic research.

Charlotte stopped placing her stories in Angria, settling instead on nominally English characters in a nominally English landscape—hence a plain Jane Eyre with all the passions of an Angrian heroine; hence the mysterious and foreboding Thornfield Hall and that supreme force of nature himself, Mr. Rochester. And Godfrey sketched out plans to become a visual artist, which profession he anticipated as "a means of uniting my every craze and hobby into one great nation of friends." Like young Joe, both Godfrey and Charlotte did not "lose their childhood" as the adult Folsom put it, but due to "the more pressing interests of later practical life," transformed it.

All of which brings us back to Stevenson and his paen to the playbox. Some people give up on "childish" things without necessarily giving up on play. Some fewer still manage to alter early creative experience in ways that matter to adult endeavor in spheres of public culture. Not surprisingly, Stevenson was one of these. Moreover, his story also becomes the story of his stepson Lloyd Osbourne, with whom he played and with whom he worked. The relationship between the two tells us much about how the transition from childhood play to adult creativity takes place.

Or, rather, how the transition may incompletely take place, for we know that not all children engaged in worldplay go on to significant achievement as adults. Osbourne, the record would have it, was one of these. Both stepfather and stepson engaged in worldplay; both took on the writing profession, but with different results. Indeed, in their twined yet divergent stories, certain factors come to the fore that tell us much about transpositions of worldplay beyond childhood and the maturation of creative imagination.

A LIFELONG PASSION FOR MAKE-BELIEVE

By all accounts, Robert Louis Stevenson possessed a charming, magnetic personality, equal parts serious artist and waggish schoolboy. The twin disposition suited him perfectly to the self-conscious appreciation of childhood make-believe—and its subsequent role in adult professional imagination. He was, he said of himself, "one of the few people in the world who do not forget their childhood," and he placed his memories in the service of his art.

Who has not heard of *A Child's Garden of Verses* (1885)—as well-known today as Grimm's fairy tales or Mother Goose rhymes? Who does not recognize the lines, "I have a little shadow that goes in and out with me" or "Let the sofa be mountains, the carpet be sea/There I'll establish a city for me"? In these simple verses published at the age of thirty-five, Stevenson personified shadows and toys, evoked invisible friends, and conjured up lands where imagination took flight. He staked his claim as a bon vivant of make-believe, as a connoisseur who had tasted of all kinds.

The Playful Child

Born in 1850 to a Scots family of lighthouse engineers, Stevenson engaged from an early age in "brilliant episodes of play" that remained with him for the rest of his life. In *Memoirs of Himself,* he recalled playing hunter in the gardens, toy gun on his arm, and feeling "myself so hotly into the spirit of my play, that I think I can still see the herd of antelope come sweeping down the lawn . . . it was almost a vision." Equally vivid in his memory were the bed stories or "songstries" he intoned just before falling asleep. When these were not dominated by the fire and brimstone of his pious nurse, they took the shape of serial stories, invented over multiple sessions, in which he and his toys went adventuring.

As an only and sickly child, much of Stevenson's childhood play was naturally solitary. But whenever he saw his cousins (of whom there were many), he eagerly included them in his play. His description of shared play with an older cousin Bob is particularly redolent of worldplay. Wrote Stevenson:

> We lived together in a purely visionary state. We had countries; his was Nosingtonia, mine Encyclopedia; where we ruled and made wars and inventions, and of which we were perpetually drawing maps. His was shaped a little like Ireland; mine lay diagonally across the paper like a large tip-cat.

The boys converted everything in their lives, even mealtime, into similar "game[s] of play":

> When my cousin and I took our porridge of a morning, we had a device to enliven the course of the meal. He ate his with sugar, and explained it to be a country continually buried under snow. I took mine with milk, and explained it to be a country suffering gradual inundation. You can imagine us exchanging bulletins; how here was an island still unsubmerged, here a valley not yet covered with snow; what inventions were made; how

his population lived in cabins on perches and travelled on stilts, and how mine was always in boats; how the interest grew furious, as the last corner of safe ground was cut off on all sides and grew smaller every moment; and how in fine, the food was of altogether secondary importance, and might even have been nauseous, so long as we seasoned it with these dreams.

Stevenson recalled other pretend play with Bob as well. The two cousins played dress-up. They drew pictures together. And, perhaps most important of all, they played with a commercially available pasteboard theater that proved, for the nascent writer, "one of the dearest pleasures of my childhood."

So loathe was Stevenson to give up this theater play that long after he had set it aside in mid-adolescence, he dedicated an entire essay to the cardboard backdrops and melodramatic skits of *Skelt's Juvenile Drama*. He had loved coloring in the various sets; even more, he had loved the stories meant to take place onstage. From Skelt's scripts of historical derring-do, he "acquired a gallery of scenes and characters" that in later years had a decisive influence on his imagination. So, too, did the act of playing itself, for even as an adult, he devoted himself to it.

The Playful Man

Like many an expert, Stevenson was in the habit of constant practice. Perhaps to compensate for long hours in his sickbed or at his desk, among friends he was "excessively and delightfully silly." After his marriage at the age of thirty to Fanny Osbourne, a divorced artist with two children, Stevenson's playfulness knit a lifelong bond with his stepson. For two long winters in the Swiss mountains, where he had retreated to regain his health, he restored flagging energies by playing with Lloyd.

Stevenson introduced the boy, at this time around twelve years old, to the painting of toy theater scenes and the arranging of toy dramas. The two also involved themselves in the production of small books and magazines on Lloyd's printing press. Much of the written material for these books came from Stevenson's pen, accompanied by woodcuts that he taught himself to carve for the occasion. According to one acquaintance of the family, these printing press productions made for "a kind of literary horse-play, yet with a certain squint-eyed, sprawling genius in it, and innocent Rabelaisian mirth."

In later years, Lloyd, too, recalled the "abiding spirit of the child" and the eager pretense with which Stevenson perfused their shared play. He remembered his stepfather helping him "slide the actors in and out on their tin stands, as well as imitating galloping horses, or screaming screams for the heroine in distress." Man as well as boy fell deep into make-believe. The two reserved their most passionate immersion, however, for the "kriegspiel" they played with hundreds of tin soldiers.

According to Lloyd, the war game began as a pretext for knocking down soldiers with well-aimed marbles. Very quickly it acquired elaborations of all sorts: "rules innumerable, prolonged arithmetical calculations, constant measuring with footrules, and the throwing of dice." At its height, stepfather and stepson mapped a landscape upon the attic floor in chalk of different colors, marking mountains, rivers, towns, bridges, and roads. The war in miniature took place, in effect, in a miniature and modeled world.

Indeed, the kriegspiel had all the hallmarks of worldplay. The play was persistent. Stepfather and stepson spent long hours at a time, over many days, to complete one game—and there were many games over a two-year period. The play was also consistent. Not only were the rules of engagement religiously observed, but a history of military heroes and their campaigns evolved from game to game. Stevenson actually documented some of these in war reports from the imaginary front for two imaginary newspapers.

The resulting "war correspondence" was a delightful send-up of serious matters. And matter the play did. According to Lloyd, the modeling of "real conditions and actual warfare" required "on Stevenson's part, the use of textbooks and long conversations with military invalids." The two tried to take into account, not just the effect on their troops of tactical maneuvers and ammunition supply, but the effect of terrain, weather, and even "miasma" and other sickness. The play was plausible.

The game exhibited other characteristics of worldplay as well. It was private, a pastime Stevenson shared with Lloyd and no one else, though five or six years later Stevenson briefly corralled his cousin Bob into the game, thus repeating in maturity some part of their shared play when children.

Initially the kriegspiel seems also to have been secret—not from other members of the family, but from adults on the outside. In the first winter of their game, when an unexpected visitor caught Stevenson "in the act of playing," he "crimsoned to the ears" and cut off the day's make-believe. But as the play grew in complexity, as it mattered more to him *as an adult*, he relinquished embarrassment. "I should like to make you understand," wrote one acquaintance, "how he spoke (now with a very conscious pride) about the strategical soldier-games which, in scientific ways, he and his stepson were in the habit of playing."

No doubt Stevenson reaped familial benefits by playing with his stepson in these early years of his marriage. But play was also important in and of itself, just the sort of occupation, he wrote, to change "into the most pleasant hours of the day those very vacant and idle seasons which would otherwise have hung most heavily upon my hand." More than that, play with Lloyd allowed Stevenson to remain in touch with what he valued above all—"the capacity," as the novelist Henry James put it, "for successful make-believe."

In "Crabbed Age and Youth," which was written and published in the first years of his association with Lloyd, the boy "supposed," the boy who would retain his "playthings until the day I die," was surely Stevenson himself. For in his stepson, he had found the playmate that made that pledge to lifelong play possible.

FROM CHILD'S PLAY TO LITERARY CRAFT

Given its role in his personal life, it comes as no surprise to find fascination with childhood play running like a leitmotif through the long row of Stevenson's collected works, which include essays, stories, novels, and correspondence, as well as verse. Overall, his portrait of childhood was idyllic; it was also ironic.

As he sketched out in his *Memoirs*, Stevenson had exulted in sensual, "animal" happiness when young; he had also suffered bedridden days, night terrors, and the harsh disciplines of schooling. Something about the compound experience made him want to mock nostalgia for the halcyon days of play. Something about his own mature dependence on continued play made him want to plumb its psychological and artistic depths. Thus, the wistful iconoclast set about his task, his "respects to Woodsworth," as he put it in one essay, notwithstanding.

Stevenson did not refer to the great poet lightly. Two generations removed, William Wordsworth had been a leading figure in the Romantic idealization of childhood. He had particularly valued the child's unitary imagination, the consciousness that lacked boundary between self and world and identified vicariously with all things animate and inanimate. In an exchange of ideas with the poet Samuel Taylor Coleridge, Wordsworth connected the holistic vision of children to natural creative genius. To retain some part of that unspoiled genius was the adult poet's ambition—in imaginative matters, he wrote, "The Child is father of the Man."

Interestingly enough, Wordsworth's understanding of the child's imaginative experience was based in part on his intimate acquaintance with Coleridge's son, Hartley. Already met with in these pages, Hartley had demonstrated his highly wrought imagination from an early age. In the poem "To H.C., Six Years Old," Wordsworth marveled at the boy's "fancies from afar," his "self-born carol" as ethereal as it was real, and the "blessed vision!" that made of him a "happy child!"

Unfortunately for the poet's philosophy of genius, Hartley failed to carry early promise forward. After flunking out of college, he squirreled himself away in the countryside, a dependent drunk and minor poet. Yet despite disappointing family and friends, he did remain something of a happy boy or boy-man—and was curiously celebrated as such by society.

His contemporary, the essayist Thomas De Quincey, was also famous for a robust childishness—and for much the same reasons. Both men were physically small. Both preserved additional elements of immaturity: De Quincey the clothes and manners of the child and Hartley a childlike insouciance and, it seems, the secret nurture of his worldplay. Coincidentally, De Quincey had also invented an imaginary world when young, a fantastical island called "Gombroon."

Within decades, the social lionization of these two men, as well as their childhood play, helped stimulate the writing of literature for children, especially those stories revolving around adventure on remote islands and imaginary places. One practitioner was none other than Stevenson himself.

In truth, Stevenson fit so squarely within the Romantic idealization of the child that his effort to distance himself from that tradition was less a divorce than a trial separation. In the essay "Child's Play" (1876), he insisted on the ambivalence. If he had not been entirely happy as a child, he had "never again been happy in the same way." The visionary delights that Wordsworth imputed to childhood in general, Stevenson very specifically located in play.

More to the point, Stevenson concerned himself with the distinctions to be made between the child's imaginative play and the adult's playful imagination. The first was sensory, spontaneous, cathartic, material, and externalized; the second perceptually aware, aesthetically sensitive, artfully reflective, intellectual, and internalized. "There is all the world between gaping wonderment at the jargon of birds," he explained, "and the emotion with which a man listens to articulate music." For all the empathic visions of immersive play-acting, the child's "power of imagination" remained "in some ways, but a pedestrian fancy." In words we might use today, it lacked creative value of the "Big *C*" variety.

For Stevenson what made childhood make-believe "pedestrian" was its improvisational nature, its very "playability." Props made things happen by suggesting characters, situations, or challenges for pretense. Mustaches conjured up pirates, chairs "substituted" for sailing ships, and rugs for open seas. Places, too, unerringly evoked distinctive stories. "Certain dank gardens cry aloud for a murder," Stevenson maintained; "certain old houses demand to be haunted; certain coasts are set apart for shipwreck." In the end, however, playable props and places failed to shake off their provenance. They stimulated highly engaging play precisely because they came laden with all the inspirations of embedded story.

That he himself shivered with delight over coves and ships was, Stevenson believed, a measure of how fully his toy theater and Skelt's dramas had "stamped [itself] upon my immaturity." Children borrowed their make-believe transparently, lifting story fragments wholesale for their own pastiche. Theirs was an inexhaustible "power of adoption," the flip side of which was an impotent "weakness to create."

If children had a natural genius, it was not an artistic one, though artists such as Wordsworth and Coleridge may have yearned for some part of it. Creative achievement Stevenson reserved for the adult. "It is the grown people who make the nursery stories," he concluded; "all the children do, is jealously to preserve the text."

LITERARY MAKE-BELIEVE

One of his biographers has labeled Stevenson a "master of the psychology of childhood." There is, in fact, much to admire in his analysis of play. But the artist's concerns were far from disinterested or objective. Rather, he sought to articulate what he saw as a very real gap between the creative impulses of the child and the creative achievements of the adult. As a writer, he knew that play narrative incompletely anticipated literary narrative. The immature imagination, as manifest in play, was *not yet the instrument* it might become in adult hands. For an individual to turn the imaginary worlds of childhood into the imagined worlds of literature, what was necessary, first and foremost, was training in craft.

In Stevenson's case, craft practice began early. Almost as soon as the boy embraced the enacting and telling of stories, he sought to document his imaginative adventures, to preserve them in words. "Long before he could write himself," his nurse recalled, "he used to get me to put things down to what he called his dictation." These "funny stories," as she remembered them, were all "burnt or lost." More serious affairs survived, like the "History of Moses" that little Louis dictated to his mother and aunt at around the age of six.

In this, as in other juvenilia, Louis demonstrated an early skill at handling the basic elements of narrative. He also demonstrated the derivative imagination that he later attributed to childhood play in general. There was no wild deviation from the biblical plot. Except for his blended drawing of ancient Israelites wearing chimney pot hats and smoking pipes like many a Victorian gentleman, Louis "jealously preserved the text" of the Bible story as he had imbibed it at his elders' knees.

Be that as it may, Louis's early experiences committing story to the page whet his appetite for more. By his early teens he regularly engaged with school friends in "literary activities" during leisure hours, including the production of a school magazine. Moreover, he had already fashioned for himself a course of self-education: "Whenever I read a book or a passage. . . in which there was either some conspicuous force or some happy distinction in the style," he later recalled, "I must sit down at once and set myself to ape that quality." In this manner he copied—or as he put, "played the sedulous ape to"—a whole host of British, American, French, and German authors.

Stevenson pursued this private study independently from the schooling his father prescribed for him in engineering and then in law. Eventually it proved the more compelling. In 1875, at the age of twenty-five, he gained admission to the Scottish bar and then took off hotfoot for the artist colonies of France. There his assiduous imitation of great writers continued apace. With a great deal of "industry and intellectual courage," he taught himself to expunge what was useless, accentuate what was important, and convey what he wished the reader to see and feel. Over ten years and more, as he liked to joke, he generated enough written exercises and practice drafts to fill a clothesbasket—and in the process he learned to write.

At no time did Stevenson privilege literary craft over creative vitality. Both were necessary to sustain artistic endeavor. But if technique could be learned, creative force was another matter. Stevenson wooed his muse in the continued animations of play. Both writing and reading, in his estimation, called upon the fantasies of the internalized imagination. Accordingly, he sought to tap into the "daydreams of common men" by tapping into his own. When we read unreservedly, we call upon our innermost daydreams, he argued; "we push the hero aside; . . . we lunge into the tale in our own person and bathe in fresh experience." When we write, we do the same. "Fiction is to the grown man," he concluded, "what play is to the child."

Treasure Island (1883), Stevenson's first big success, provides a case in point. Henry James called the book as "perfect as a well-played boys game." And as a game, it had begun. Neither Stevenson nor his wife nor his stepson ever tired of recounting how, in a moment of leisure with twelve-year-old Lloyd, the writer first doodled a map of an imaginary island. Places on that island conjured up plots and plots, characters. "The next thing I knew," Stevenson later revealed, "I had some paper before me and was writing out a list of chapters." Ink barely dry, he read the chapters to assembled family and friends, one of whom arranged for its serialization—and the rest, so they say, is history.

What "they" leave unsaid, however, is that play, especially play with Lloyd, continued to serve Stevenson as ballast for the rigors of sailing the seas of literary composition. *Treasure Island* itself ran aground after the fifteenth chapter. Ill again and drained of inspiration, Stevenson went for weeks unable to write. Instead, according to his wife, "he chose play with the ardour of a boy," spending long hours with Lloyd in toy theatricals, printing press ventures, and games with tin soldiers, until once again the ship that was *Treasure Island* regained its buoyancy and sailed on.

STEVENSON PLUS OSBOURNE: SOME FACTORS IN PLAY

Stevenson's history of play with his stepson goes a long way toward explaining several collaborations between the two when Lloyd reached his twenties and professed a desire to write. These included *The Wrong Box* (1889) and *The Wrecker* (1892), novels the two completed together; *The Ebb-Tide* (1894), begun in partnership, but finished by Stevenson alone; and a fourth project indefinitely suspended.

For the most part, scholars do not know what to make of this co-authorship. The adult Lloyd is commonly assessed as a ne'er-do-well, content to take advantage of Stevenson for monetary and professional support. Critics and commentators have considered the partnered books vastly inferior to Stevenson's work proper and dismissed them as evidence of "blind love" for an undeserving stepson. Seen through the lens of Stevenson's passion for play, however, he may have taken equal advantage of Lloyd.

Understood as an attempt to extend their make-believe play by other means, collaboration seems to have rekindled for Stevenson "the intoxicating pleasures of imagination." Lloyd certainly thought so. *The Wrecker* he remembered as "a pastime; not a task," conceived in "high spirits." His descriptions of evenings spent gaily discussing character and plot with his stepfather recalled the hours the two had spent a decade earlier sprawled on the attic floor.

Indeed, like the kriegspiel, the shared fiction involved a great deal of serious fun. Stevenson himself made mention that the two "spent five days weighing money and making calculations for the treasure found in 'The Wrecker.'" The partnership allowed him to take on the revision of Lloyd's first drafts with similar enthusiasm. "It's glorious to have the ground ploughed," he wrote, "and to sit back in luxury for the real fun of writing, which is rewriting."

The collaborative effort it took to produce *The Wrecker* was by no means carefree, however. Co-authorship was not just play, but also work, not just art, but also livelihood. While Stevenson voyaged around the South Seas, often apart from Lloyd, drafts and revisions of the book sailed back and forth at a sluggish pace, placing strain on the give and take of shared composition. All that weighing and calculating of treasure, enjoyable though it may have been, shored up only "a single chapter of a measly yarn." Well into the second year of writing, the "bother" Stevenson had with the book was "not to be imagined," or so he told one colleague privy to his dogged pursuit of manuscript completion, publication, and remuneration.

Nevertheless, the fact remains that Stevenson did not give up the teamwork, planning after *The Wrecker* another two shared projects. The question has been why. Sometime before his sudden death from cerebral hemorrhage in 1894, in a letter penned from his final berth on the island of Samoa, he himself suggested an answer. When drained of inspiration, he wrote, it was his habit to turn to his "old cure of a change of work," if not play. The collaborations with Lloyd, though crippled by as many aspects as Dr. Jekyll and Mr. Hyde, were meant to serve up the "old cure" in double dosage.

After Stevenson's death, Osbourne continued to write. Though his monetary inheritance from the Stevenson estate was considerable, and he involved himself in Samoan politics, he produced three short story collections and eight novels between 1900 and

1929, as well as several dramas in collaboration with his nephew, the playwright Austin Strong. By and large these were somewhat racy and page-turning in nature. *Baby Bullet* (1906), for instance, follows a young woman and her governess on lighthearted travel across Europe in an old car; *Infatuation* (1908) takes a look at "modern" romance; and *Wild Justice: Stories of the South Seas* (1906) deals with the intertwined lives of native islanders and the westerners who came to colonize them.

Stevenson biographers generally dismiss these works as potboilers devoid of psychological insight, thematic development, or literary taste. Contemporary reviewers had a more varied response. Some admired: the "simple pathos" of Osbourne's entertaining fiction testified to a "versatile imagination." Others found fault: "In spite of talent, the best of teachers, and the widest of opportunities," Osbourne had produced only lightweight literature. It is the negative assessment that has lasted down to this day, one Stevenson biographer recently joking that "[Osbourne's] post-collaboration career as a writer can be expressed mathematically: Stevenson-plus-Osbourne, minus Stevenson, is less than Osbourne."

With a bit more sympathy we might observe that despite intimate association with his mentor's particular genius, Osbourne developed a different set of imaginative and compositional skills. Moreover, this outcome offers us a unique opportunity to compare and contrast certain formative experiences for both men, much as Stevenson compared the creative imaginations of child and adult.

Consideration of Stevenson's transition from personal to public creativity, from childhood worldplay to the invention of imagined worlds in adult work, brings three experiences to the fore: first, thorough training in a disciplinary craft or field of endeavor (psychologists often refer to a "ten year rule" for full mastery); second, continued play in adulthood; and third, the harnessing of the play to the work. Figure 7.1 shows how these three factors may flow from childhood preparations by grafting them onto the worldplay-creativity network discussed in chapter 3. The degree to which these experiences are self-motivated during transition comprises a fourth factor.

Given the biographical assessments of the stepson, we might expect to find that Osbourne missed the boat on most or all of these factors or their mobilization. But closer examination reveals a more complicated portrait. Let's take as given that shared worldplay experienced in adolescence introduced him to the pleasures of personal creativity and that collaboration in young adulthood helped prepare him for public endeavor as an independent writer. In both instances, however, it was his stepfather who provided the lion's share of imaginative inspiration and artistic craft.

To be fair to Osbourne, this was not entirely his fault—not, at least, while he was a child. With his interests in mind, we might observe that Stevenson meddled constantly in Lloyd's play, dominating not just the kriegspiel, but other activities such as the boy's printing press productions. That his stepfather should undertake to provide a great deal of written material and illustrations, too, for small books and journals cannot have surprised, for Stevenson was already in the habit of painting the theater scenes purchased for Lloyd's toy theater and otherwise coloring his play. The pattern of dependence, once established, held throughout the pair's association.

Even Osbourne's training as a writer played second fiddle. Abbreviated, at best different, it looked much less like his stepfather's decades-long, self-guided cultiva-

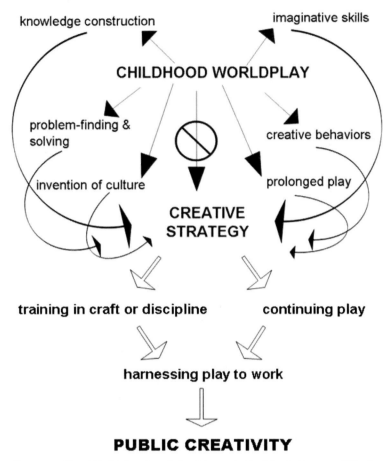

Fig. 7.1. The Worldplay-Creativity Network Revisited: Factors Affecting Public Creativity. Self-motivation affects every aspect of the transition from childhood worldplay to public creativity.

tion of formal craft than it did the informal play the two had once shared. Moreover, collaborations with Stevenson did not involve the conventional narrative aims of a *Kidnapped* or a *Treasure Island*. In *The Wrecker* and *Ebb-Tide* the two tied the classic adventure story to newly emerging genres—the mystery story and the detective story. Stevenson attempted to correct for what he called the "shallowness" of these new forms by developing character and atmosphere first, and plot second, but with mixed results.

There was also the matter of setting. Both *The Wrecker* and *Ebb-Tide* left the European scene behind to explore the multicultural drama of the South Seas. These and a number of Stevenson's solo works written in the same period expressed outright sympathy for islanders and implicitly critiqued Western prudery and imperialism. Stevenson's *The Beach of Falesá* (1891), for example, explored the sexual relationship between a British trader and a native girl—and suffered heavy expurgation at the publisher's hands as a result.

Propriety and politics, then, as well as disdain for new genres, motivated much critical dislike of Stevenson's South Sea tales, both those written alone and those written with his stepson. No surprise, these same new genres and themes unalloyed with the stepfather's literary sensibilities proved Osbourne's cup of tea. He became, as befit his apprenticeship, a competent writer of titillating, popular fiction.

Osbourne never did achieve (nor did he deserve) the literary fame of his mentor; nevertheless it appears that Stevenson scholars may have done him some disservice. Whether the stepson would have turned his hand to the writer's trade without the stepfather's support can only be surmised. What we do know is that Stevenson mentored Lloyd's "playable" imagination to an unconventional fare-thee-well, cultivating two of the factors favoring transition from childhood imagination to mature creativity: ongoing relish for play and a knack for harnessing that play to professional endeavor.

And the tutelage worked—not to produce the writer Stevenson's acolytes might have wished (that third factor, disciplinary training, proving quite different for the two men), but the writer who ploughed small sections of the fields first cleared by the master. Osbourne gained his own mention in the 1950 edition of *Who Was Who in America* for that achievement at least. We might also like to think he deserved recognition for bridging the gap between the invention of imaginary worlds in play and the invention of imagined worlds in some formal realm of adult work—a feat in itself.

A BRIEF LOOK AT "OUTSIDER PLAY"

Lloyd Osbourne was lucky, first, because he had a brilliant stepfather willing and able to mentor him into a writing career and, second, because there was, in fact, an adult field of endeavor that fed off the complex play activities they both shared. Not all individuals for whom play is also "the very pick of life" are able to transition, as Osbourne did, as Stevenson did, from private play to public endeavor.

Many an unknown hobbyist, many an eccentric dreamer and guarded genius of play has avoided craft training or otherwise missed out on disciplinary exploitation of their personal creativity. This may, of course, be a benefit. For the persistent paracosmist who resists the "canalization" of imagination, private activity can prove highly original. There may also be a cost, however, which is a life of creative isolation.

Indeed, society remains largely unaware of these individuals and their worldplay—with the exception of those "discovered" and subsequently appropriated into the canon of "outsider art." Outsider art refers to the material output of individuals untrained in and uninfluenced by conventional arts, yet whose originality in form or technique nonetheless compels attention and respect. By no means does all private worldplay qualify as outsider art, yet a noticeable amount of outsider art does depend upon private worldplay. This was—and is—the case for American outsider artists Henry Darger, Renaldo Gillet Kuhler, and "Mingering Mike."

Henry Darger, a janitor, spent a lifetime elaborating an imaginary world of off-planet children that was only discovered after his death in 1973. The "Vivian sisters" waged war with their human enemies and forged uneasy peace with winged beings called Blengins. Darger wrote two immense tomes documenting their story in "The

Realms of the Unreal" and elsewhere. He also drew several hundred illustrations in accompaniment. These illustrations, in watercolor on paper, have received widespread acclaim as some of the finest known examples of outsider art.

Similarly, in the early 2000s, the scientific illustrator Renaldo Gillet Kuhler gradually revealed his imaginary "Rocaterrania" to a persistent and sympathetic colleague. Over many decades Kuhler had constructed a language and designed an alphabet for his world as well as a substantial body of pen-and-ink drawings and watercolors documenting its cities and people. Since coming to light, this art has been praised for its density of vision.

Much the same may be said about the recent discovery in a flea market of handmade record albums, eventually traced to an odd-job man named Mike S. As a teen in the 1960s, Mike S. fed his passion for rhythm and blues by composing songs, singing them with friends, and recording them a cappella, on tape. Unable to pursue a music career, he imagined one as a recording artist named "Mingering Mike." Documenting the fantasy, he fabricated over eighty cardboard records inserted into hand-drawn album jackets, complete with fictitious liner notes, copyright information, and catalog numbers. Admiration for the sheer volume as well as the originality of this achievement has resulted in exhibits of the album covers.

The fact that decades of worldplay by Darger, Kuhler, and Mike S. might be unearthed and appreciated in retrospect speaks to the value of naïve and idiosyncratic expression in the visual arts. Similar discoveries have also occurred in the literary arts, chief among them the posthumous publication of the utopian novel *Islandia* (1942/1966), cut down from voluminous worldplay materials—language glossaries, population tables, gazetteers, climate notes, and maps—left by the lawyer Austin Tappan Wright.

For every Darger and Kuhler, for every Mike S. or Wright, however, we can surmise yet another worldplaying individual who does not get "discovered"—in part because no conventional discipline values *as such* the artifacts of his or her play. In this category we might place computer programmer and senior systems analyst Wyatt James, who left behind at his death in 2006 an array of drawings, maps, histories, stories, game boards, and websites that testified to much imaginary invention.

Beginning in childhood, and extending over his lifetime, James made a hobby of worldplay, some of it shared with by his brother, Chris. Over a six-month period in the late 1960s, when the two were in their twenties, they invented a board game they called "Gerousle." They crafted handmade boards and handmade cards for scores of play characters, as well as tokens, markers, and maps necessary to actual game play, which took about six days to complete. During their thirties, they shared maps, histories, and geographical descriptions relating to yet another imaginary place, the "Planet Blenkinsop," rotating in retrograde fashion around its own sun. Eventually, after ten years or so, Chris's accumulation of play documents filled two briefcases (see figures 7.2 and 7.3).

When shared interest in "Blenkinsop" petered out, Wyatt turned to the design of imaginary castles, complete with tour guide commentary and the maps and histories of numerous make-believe towns, counties, and countries. At first he drew plans by hand on graph paper, but by the 1990s he was using a personal computer to generate his

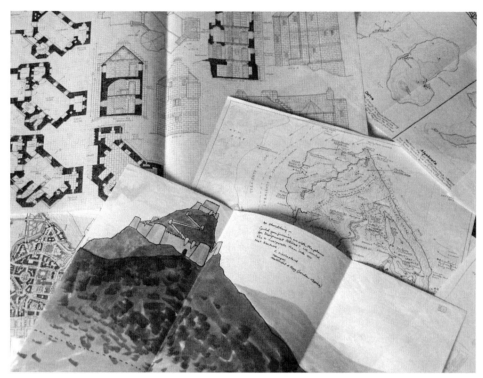

Fig. 7.2. Drawing, map and architectural plans for the planet Blenkinsop, by Wyatt and Chris James.

Fig. 7.3. Play that matters: The papers of Gerousle and Blenkinsop preserved by Chris James.

architectural drawings and post them, along with supporting documents, on a website he devoted to imaginary places.

In this semi-private, semi-public space, a pseudonymous Wyatt invited visitors to design their own imaginary castles and submit them for inclusion on his site: "You have to be a compulsive sort of person to do this sort of thing," he wrote, "but it is a lot of fun, rather like making balsa model airplanes from scratch, or making a quilt or tapestry. In a way, if you do it right, it combines the mental skills of architecture and historical fiction research."

Perhaps Wyatt hoped to build, not just imaginary worlds, but a community of individuals building imaginary worlds. We can only guess. Occasionally one finds unassociated websites similarly devoted to the stories and cultures or the arts and architectures of imaginary places. Diverse and homegrown languages crafted to go along with science-fiction worlds come to mind, as do the cityscapes drawn by the autist Gilles Tréhin.

By and large, paracosmists like these lack either the craft training or the disciplinary field that might allow them to harness their private play to public creativity. Despite the imaginative complexity of James's castle play and his mastery of its visual and verbal presentation, there exist no public fields of endeavor, no arts or sciences, exploring the intersections of architecture, social planning and historical fiction. His private pastime remained, perforce, "outsider play."

FROM PRIVATE PLAY TO PUBLIC CREATIVITY

By no means does public culture take full advantage of the human potential to imagine and create. There are challenges to bridging the gap between child's play and adult professional endeavor. Stevenson successfully harnessed his passion for imaginary world invention to the craft of writing and the artistic needs of the novelist. Much, but not all, of what he learned he passed on to his stepson. The worldplay impulse did not peter out or die, for either of these men, nor did it persist in unadulterated form, as in the case of private paracosmists like Kuhler, Mike S., Wright, or James.

To the contrary, for Stevenson and Osbourne worldplay provided a strategy for playful work in the real world. In as much as mature storytelling and its playable preparations recalled the storytelling artifacts and improvisations of complex make-believe in childhood, this strategy was an obvious one. But worldplay may also be yoked to less obvious mature outcomes in a wide range of disciplines, as demonstrated by many of the MacArthur Fellows who participated in the Worldplay Project discussed in chapters 3 and 4. To their understanding of worldplay at work we turn next.

Chapter Eight

Worldplay at Work: MacArthur Fellows Straddle a Creative Divide

The bulk of the world's knowledge is an imaginary construction.

—Helen Keller, author and activist

AN IMAGINARY BEAST IN REAL GARDENS

Many creative adults have sought to recapture the curiosity and wonder of childhood in mature play. Some among them have even conceived of that play in terms of inventing imaginary worlds. For John Gardner, to write a novel was to make up a "separate reality." For Leo Lionni, to design a children's picture book was to conceive of "orderly predictable alternatives" to reality. For Gustav Mahler, to compose a symphony was "to construct a world." As a means of generating hypotheses and courting insights, according to primatologist Sarah Hrdy, "[i]maginary worlds have a place in science." Certainly, for Nobel Prize–winner François Jacob, to advance scientific fact and theory was to invent "a possible world, or a piece of a possible world."

Many MacArthur Fellows among those participating in the Worldplay Project have also reported the imaginative invention of alternate worlds in adult work. One of these is Laura Otis, a professor of literature and the playful creator, when she was a child, of the Globbershnuckle.

The Globbershnuckle is "built much like a Shetland pony with donkey ears and a rabbit tail it is a bright green with pink spots." This statement is fact, as the drawing of the chimeric creature in figure 8.1 attests. It is also fiction, since the Globbershnuckle hails from "Zarf," "a magical planet inhabited by women only" where "no one ever gets any older and there is no record of time."

Home to things only dreamed of in our philosophies, Zarf is a wondrous place, and the Globbershnuckle, which gives "milk like a cow at 12:00 noon . . . and strawberry milkshakes at 4:30 in the afternoon," is a marvelous amalgam of the pragmatic and the visionary. In short, the blended beast is a perfect mascot for vocational worldplay, not just for Otis, but for all individuals who explore elements of make-believe in adult endeavor.

Fig. 8.1.   The Globbershnuckle. Crayon drawing by Laura Otis, age 10, in illustration of the story "Jenny of Zarf."

Otis put her imaginary pet aside around the age of twelve, but something of the play experience with Zarf and the girls who lived there has remained with her, reverberating in mature activity. As she explained it in a Project interview, "The ability to concentrate and focus on an imaginary situation so that I can describe it in detail and put myself in the place of any character in it I really developed when I was 6–10 . . . I have found this ability important as a historian of science and a literature teacher, trying to describe past or imaginary situations so that other people can see and feel them."

Otis has found that her research and writing also resembles childhood worldplay in its persistence, "because to write a book—it takes about five years for me to produce a book and you have to keep going back to the same world . . . and remember where all the pieces were." Most of all she finds herself negotiating a give-and-take between the discovered reality that comes "from outside of you" and the inner, imagined "system that you are organizing"—just as she did when "planning things [on Zarf], picturing what [the girls' houses] would look like, how they would get food, how they would make food."

For Otis, certain habits of mind such as heightened attention, task persistence, and empathic projection connect childhood worldplay to adult pursuits. And she is not alone in recognizing these links. As explored in chapter 3, other Fellows who invented worlds in childhood have felt these and other echoes of early play in maturity. Indeed, over half of Fellows in the Worldplay Project have claimed engagement with imaginary worlds in their adult lives *whether or not* they recalled childhood worldplay. Moreover, a great deal of that adult worldplay has had an explicitly professional context. Four out of ten Fellows, in fields across the arts and sciences, reported that their mature participation in worldplay occurred at work.

Does the writer mean substantially the same thing by imaginary world invention as the historian or the policy advocate? Are speculative blends of the real and the imaginary equally useful to the scientist as to the artist? With the Globbershnuckle as guide through professional gardens, we'll take a look at the cultivation of factual/fictional inquiry.

WORLDPLAY ACROSS THE PROFESSIONS

In published writing and in query response and private interview for the Worldplay Project, MacArthur Fellows across the arts and sciences revealed perceptions of mature worldplay at work functioning as an imaginative and creative strategy—with predictable and not-so-predictable variations from one disciplinary group to another.

The Arts: Fabricating Truths

Most people readily tie the invention of make-believe worlds to narrative fabrication. So did Fellows appointed in the arts. Choreographer Paul Taylor has explored "places," "countries," and "manufactured worlds" in his dances, the best of which bear the trace of "paths or patterns that started in childhood." In a somewhat different vein, choreographer Susan Marshall has explored "the narrative of the dance" that "involves creating a world with characters." In her case, she clarified in query response, worldplay fictions were "defined by specific movement vocabularies and the evolution of these vocabularies" according to a "unique, specific logic" shaped by the body.

Fellows in the literary arts had as much and more to say about narrating imaginary realities. One, a writer who remembered playing with toy soldiers, saw a connection between that childhood make-believe, ephemeral as it was, and his adult creation of character. Of his novels, he wrote, "I'm still manipulating tiny figures in my head." At times he has taken additional pains to create an entire imaginary country, much in the vein of the paracosmist Austin Tappan Wright. Although most novelists hardly go to these extremes, this Fellow felt, "it's arguable that all fiction writers are necessarily involved in imagined worlds."

The same might be said of poets, for whom each poem is in some way a consistent "fantasy." As Fellow Galway Kinnell has put it, writing a poem means conceiving of "an inner world." In his case, the game of Little Men shared with siblings involved a "disappearance from normal space and time" into a "consciousness" of alternate persuasion and place. Entering the world of the poem, he revealed in interview, requires the same "capacity to concentrate . . . That ability I sometimes have to totally disappear into whatever I'm writing about." Poetic vision depends on the capacity "to go out of yourself and into other beings and write about them almost as if from within."

This empathizing—what Kinnell and others refer to as "negative capability" or capacity to overcome self-consciousness—enables the artist to reach for a generalized sense of being and universal meaning. "The best poems," Kinnell has written, "are those in which you are not this or that person, but anyone, just a person. If you could go farther, you would no longer be a person but an animal. If you went farther still you would be the grass, eventually a stone. If a stone could speak, your poem would be its words." The stone becomes, in literary terms, a symbol, some aspect of human being—and vice versa. The poem that is the stone's poem comes closest to expressing in unique terms an abstract reality.

Despite, or because of, the artist's drive to articulate alternate worlds of general significance, the relationship between the real and the imaginary is sometimes problematic. As many poets and writers have pointed out, it is their stock-in-trade to fabricate particulars in order to tell some universal truth. In his own work, Kinnell has found the mental territory between the two "a little dangerous. I might be making up something that I'm letting the reader believe is true and I don't believe that that should happen in poetry. I should make it clear, make that difference clear" to the reader. Still, a poem that "makes me wake up to something and see something" true may be forgiven the false means. Indeed, when the poem has "the same effect on a lot of people, then it becomes a well-known poem."

Herein beats an apparent contradiction at the heart of art. We sense universal truth in the singular authentic voice that resonates with many people. That authentic voice builds its authority, at least in part, upon imaginative pretense. As articulated by many Fellows, reality and make-believe thus interpenetrate in intricate and subtle ways. Indeed, for yet another Fellow and poet, that interpenetration is so profound as to become one entity. "The world a child lives in," he has argued, "*is* an invention, whether she/he invents a specific alternative world or not."

The same invention holds true for the adult and artist, whether that artist is elaborating a fantasy world à la Tolkien or, as the poet Wallace Stevens would have it, conceiving a transcendent vision of this world that momentarily constructs and clarifies reality. Fictional and factual realities blur at some fundamental level. As one more Fellow who is both photographer and writer summed up the thought: "All art worth the name is simultaneously a vision of this world and another."

The Humanities: Documenting Imagination

For professionals in the humanities, that dual vision of the real and the imaginary also describes disciplinary worldplay. As one Fellow noted, "Any historian, especially one who works with human societies that thrived 3,000 years ago, is involved in re-imagining the past." In his case this often entails what he termed the "fictional reconstruction" of ancient ceremonies, "but based, as closely as possible, upon the documentary evidence."

Another Fellow historian also found it necessary to question and explore the relationship between the factual and the fictional in historical study: "How much of what we do can be directly observed? How much must be imagined? . . . I deal with Tibetan history and Sino-Tibetan relations in the 13th to the 17th centuries. Whether reading or sitting at the computer writing, I have to be able to imagine this world and time constantly."

In interview, two other Fellows in the humanities also elaborated at length on the relationship between imaginative interpretation and documentation of the evidence. The first of these was Peter Jeffery, a musicologist specializing in the early music of Europe and the Middle East, especially the origins of Gregorian chant. As a boy Jeffery projected himself into various historical settings with all the vividness of a movie. He did much the same thing as a historian of music. "If starting with a document or artifact and trying to recreate its context counts," he supposed, then his adult work, too, involved the make-believe invention of imaginary worlds. It certainly involved "the imaginative interpretation of actual artifacts."

Professionally, Jeffery has dealt with musical forms that are fragmentary. The earliest chant repertories, as preserved in medieval manuscripts, contain texts only. How, then, to reconstruct the music? He turned to Koranic and Buddhist traditions, still transmitted orally today, to recapture essential melodic features of the Christian tradition and to infer how the needs of eighth–century monastic schools might have shaped them.

Jeffery's purpose was to "hear" the historical sources on their own terms: "You can start to see," he remarked, "how [Gregorian chant] really originated with monks trying to memorize the psalms, and [other] parts of the Bible." Imaging visually as well as aurally, he has reconstructed mental pictures of the monastic milieu; recognizing and forming patterns, he has characterized that milieu in terms of other historical periods and traditions. The end result, he said, "is an imaginary world"—but not an arbitrary flight of fancy: "[Y]ou have to fill in the blanks in a documented way. . . . You don't want to be just imagining things . . ."

Laurel Ulrich, historian of eighteenth- and nineteenth-century America, has similarly concerned herself with, in her words, "the interface between imagination and what I would call documentation." That interface has informed her work; it has also informed her teaching—in such a manner that certain imaginative processes become clear. In a small museum course, for instance, she counseled her students to "Look again, look again, look again" at a corset or a pair of stays and consider them, first, "in relation to your body" and second, in relation to another artifact from the same milieu—a novel, perhaps.

"I guess there are two strategies, right there," Ulrich remarked in interview. "One is . . . look more closely, get your magnifying glass out, measure, do all of that; the other is trying to connect seemingly unrelated things. That's a literary strategy, that's poetry and metaphor and simile, but I also think it's a wonderful analytical tool for historical analysis and I use it constantly."

When the strategy succeeds, metaphoric thinking results in creative leaps that set off a "kind of detective work of trying to find evidence" to explain and support the intuition. As Ulrich put it, "[T]he seemingly arbitrary rules about documentation create the challenge and the fun because you have to work within those rules." The historian has to tack down the facts that keep her imaginative recreation of the past moored to public record. "It's taking the data, the source material that's not quite there . . . and then trying to make inferences and judgments about that to create something that didn't exist before." That something that didn't exist before is, in Ulrich's words, "an imagined world," as close as we can come—really—to understanding the past.

As children, Ulrich and her sister used to cut out pictures of "furniture and gadgets and whatever you needed for the house" from old catalogues and spread them across the floor with an assortment of paper dolls to make "houses, like a community, a town." The play world was realistic, "an extension" of the world they lived in. "Is that why I became a historian instead of a fiction writer or physicist?" she mused.

Quite possibly. The eight years and more of research she spent on the diary of an eighteenth-century midwife had much in common with her childhood play. In order to grasp the substance of one ordinary life, an entire New England community had, quite literally, to be mapped in space and time. The effort was an exercise in realistic historical reconstruction. It also involved the full absorptions of play. As Ulrich put it, "[T]he notion of being able to map a town and know who's in what house and what they're doing, that is just so intriguing to me and I'll spend endless labor to do that. So . . . there is that level of just deep play about my work."

By "deep play," Ulrich alluded to the endless fascinations of historical reconstruction—and something more. Originally the term referred to high-stakes gambling, but in the hands of anthropologists and others, it has come to mean any cultural activity in which personal, professional, even ideological values are placed at risk. In worldplay at work in the humanities, professional risk involves the precarious balance struck between reality and make-believe, documentation and imagination, fact and fiction.

"I know that my own imagination as an adult is so engaged by this whole enterprise of wanting [the historical reconstruction] to be real," Ulrich said. At the same time she was "in the business of telling stories" and engaging others in a kind of make-believe. Too little imagination, and the historical effort falls flat. Too much, and the reconstructed world seems improbable rather than plausibly probable and true. In 1991 Ulrich took the risk with *A Midwife's Tale: The Life of Martha Ballard Based on Her Diary, 1785–1812* and won a Pulitzer Prize.

The Public Issues Professions: Engaging the Plausible Pragmatic

Fellows in the public issues professions expressed an understanding of worldplay at work that differed from the artist's emphasis on imaginative vision or the humanist's careful recreation of other times and places. For individuals engaged in community affairs or education, human rights and public policy, imaginary worlds served vocational purpose by honing advocacy skills and by illuminating possibilities for change in the real world.

"I do a lot of public speaking, often debating public figures on television or other high profile settings, or giving speeches to large audiences," one Fellow, an immigration rights lobbyist, wrote in her query response. "I am constantly, almost involuntarily, honing my skills by debating adversaries or giving speeches when I'm alone (in the car or walking to the metro). They're not exactly imaginary worlds, but rather imagined versions of real-life settings in which I find myself."

Equally important to advocacy work, this Fellow carried around an internal "image of the kind of world I am trying to achieve." So, too, did the Fellow whose job has involved managing "a collaborative, mutually supportive, challenging teaching-and-learning environment." A sense of the possible flowed from deep spiritual understanding for her: "I feel I am constantly 'traveling' back and forth between the deeper, inner world which is very close to the Divine, and the outer world which is sometimes congruent with this and often not. I am always trying to pull the two worlds closer together—first of all for me personally, and then for those with whom I live and work."

Other Fellows concurred that the ability to imagine a better world was necessary to their own motivations and to the social persuasion of others. One of these was the health policy specialist Carol Levine. Since the age of eight, Levine had "wanted to be a person who could create the kinds of worlds" she read about in books. "Perhaps not utopian worlds, but better, nicer." She has become so by infusing her policy concerns with human immediacy. Although at work in a field driven by medical and statistical evidence, she has connected rigorous policy prescriptions to emotional narrative.

"Seeing the world as a series of stories," Levine said in interview, ". . . has served me well in my current world in that I have brought into what is often a very arid and philosophical and abstract kind of discussion the stories of real people and the feelings of real people and how policies and programs really relate to life." At least one of these stories was hers; Levine was a primary caregiver for her disabled husband for seventeen years. This personal experience helped galvanize her efforts to address the vulnerabilities of people thrust by accident or illness into the essential care of a parent, a child or a spouse.

Levine's particular talent has been to link personal narrative to objective analysis, to connect stories of mishap and need to viable visions of social repair. The challenge in health care planning is first, to identify a problem; second, to understand the parameters limiting possible solutions; and third, to anticipate the consequences of a chosen course of action. In her words, "It's a fairly complex set of decisions for which you don't really have clear-cut answers, but for which you have to create a plausible scenario." Because a scenario, "thought through and to that extent . . . imagined," harbors the potential to set "in motion something that could create an alternative world that you don't want," the policy maker is obligated to explore fictionally, well before implementation, what the consequences may be in human terms.

For another Fellow involved in global problem solving, narrative techniques in the service of plausible scenario building have also played a primary role. A combination of visualization, research, analysis, and intuition is a necessary basis for world-changing inquiry—both personally and for his profession as a whole. "I work in imaginary worlds that entail visualizing alternative states of being for communities, politicians, organizations," he wrote in his query response. "I employ scenarios dialogue and narrative construction methods to do this work in group contexts."

Indeed, part of this Fellow's work has involved the development of world-building workshops for policy professionals and others. By considering long-term trends in environmental insecurity or nuclear warfare, for instance, and by taking imaginative leaps from the known to the unknown, workshop participants challenge assumptions, bridge divergent perspectives, create an array of possible worlds, and explore the means to develop preferred futures.

In this Fellow's hands, the make-believe aspect of scenario building is constrained, not by historical facts, but by desired ends and the means available to achieve those ends. "The basic principle," he has written, "is to embrace uncertainty, describe driving forces and construct alternative visions of the world; backcast narratives that are plausible; and identify strategies for engaging the real world that exploit decision-points or crossroads in the imaginary narratives." In public issues professions such as his, the point is not that the plausible world be predictive, but that it build a virtual familiarity with possible events and consequences—and in the process nurture a resilient response to the real world.

The Social Sciences: Constructing Probable Possibles

For much the same reasons as the policy maker, the educator, and the advocate, Fellows in the social sciences and related fields most often conceived of professional worldplay as the projection of alternative ideas and hypothetical situations. A number even framed their pragmatic efforts as "possible worlds."

One anthropologist modeling the medical needs of underserved populations saw worldplay in her attempts "to set up a possible health care world." So, too, did the economist who envisioned "a world that is more humane, more just and more egalitarian." Social scientists promoting equal pay for equal work, universal child care, or family leave also planted their advocacy work in the rich soil of utopian vision. Archaeologists and others practicing in political science, geography, or sociology sifted through enormous amounts of empirical data for the tell-tale patterns that characterize the world as it is—and as it might be.

A compelling example of this kind of vocational worldplay can be found in the work of Fellow Robert Kates, a geographer who has spent forty years and more exploring human use of the earth. Kates has recalled a childhood "penchant for engaging in fantasy, a willingness to create imaginary worlds and to live within them." He has felt its influence in his adult "willingness to explore alternative hypotheses, views and futures" in a wide range of problem areas, from natural hazards and disaster mitigation, to the prevalence and persistence of world hunger, to global environmental change and its impact on society.

Fundamental to Kates's inquiry is the empirical field study, both observational and survey based. The data thus acquired are subject to comparison across space and time; from these comparisons, general principles are abstracted and reviewed. "In searching for conceptual insight," he wrote in a 2001 article, "I have drawn flow diagrams and built models . . . and grasped a few important insights or theories of the middle range." Middle-range theory refers to explanatory hypotheses closely tied to measurable pieces of reality, as defined by bodies of data. To the extent that these empirical hypotheses model complex reality in simplified analog form, they strike Kates—and others, too—as possible alternative worlds.

Kates has especially identified worldplay at work in the scenario construction that characterizes his research in the field of sustainability science. As a member of the Global Scenarios Group (GSG), a team of environmental scholars convened in 1995, he helped write *Great Transition: The Promise and Lure of the Times Ahead* (2002), a lay essay that investigates several dramatically different pathways for the global development of civilization in the next century. The word "dramatically" is used advisedly here, for as the authors of *Great Transition* pointed out, "a scenario is a summary of a play" and the essay itself is a "stor[y] with a logical plot and narrative about how the future might play out."

This story (a "history of the future" as the GSG team called it) draws upon science, with its focus on natural and human patterns unfolding through time and its generation of middle-range theories, to explain those patterns. It also draws upon imagination to go beyond data patterns and principles and give "voice to . . . non-quantifiable . . . values, behaviors and institutions." Through the make-believe projection of an imagined world, the authors write, "we can tell plausible and interesting stories about what could be . . . and provid[e] insight into the scope of the possible."

Ultimately, both analysis and imagination are necessary to professional worldplay of this kind. "Where modeling offers structure, discipline and rigor," Kates and his co-authors conclude, "narrative offers texture, richness and insight. The art is in the balance."

There is, indeed, an "art" to worldplay in the social sciences that fuses narrative with analytical technique. There is also a kinship with the arts in the relationship between imagined world and reality, a point brought home by political scientist and Fellow Robert Axelrod. In the early 1960s the teenage Axelrod won the Westinghouse Science Talent Search for a very simple computer simulation of hypothetical life-forms behaving in an artificial environment. Ever since, he has worked on the application of computer simulation to biological, economic, political, and social systems, investigating such diverse phenomena as the arms race, the development of ethics in children, and the evolution of decision making.

For Axelrod, the imagined worlds generated by simulation are, in at least some respects, equivalent to the pictures he used to watch his father paint in watercolors:

One way to think about this is, he is putting on the canvas his representation of what he sees. Now is that real or not? Well, it's not a photograph...but it certainly looks more or less like what he was looking at—a tree, for instance. So it bears relation to reality; it's his interpretation of which aspects of reality he wants to emphasize and how he wants to emphasize them. And to a substantial extent I see my model building, which I've done throughout my career starting with that high school project, as analogous to that. I'm making my picture of the world as I look at it, and inviting other people to look at it.

Axelrod's picture of the world is scientifically rigorous. "Computer simulation has very clear rules," he said in interview. "It's very explicit. And you have to tell the computer everything, so in fact everything is done as rigorously as a mathematical proof." But the simulation is also personal in the way that art is personal. You can change the rules or constraints as you wish. And much like the child at play in imaginary lands, the researcher derives satisfaction from this creative control. "If you make a mistake," he observed, "you can undo it" by recoding the assumptions that govern the behaviors of hypothetical animals or other agents in play.

In that sense, at least, computer simulation proves little different than a self-constructed game. As Axelrod recalled it, the Westinghouse project often felt like game playing. In his adult career the line between work and play has, similarly, been "very blurred . . . I might say all my work is play—but certainly my research is largely play, especially when successful."

Part of that play has involved the mind's eye. Recalling his first computer program, Axelrod remembered that "I was actually visualizing [the program] like a box on a table and the hypothetical animals were like mice that I put into this sandbox and they'd run around and I'd watch them and take that mouse out and put another one in." And because almost all of his computer simulations since then have also been "agent-based"—characterized by the presence of many individuals engaged in simple and reciprocal behaviors—he has continued to imagine his agents "in different parts of the memory of the computer interacting with each other." In effect, he has written, "Simulation is a way of doing thought experiments"—literally, as well as figuratively.

In fact, Axelrod argues, simulation is "a third way of doing science." Historically, the first two means of research and discovery open to scientists have been the deductive and inductive methods. As a research and discovery tool, simulation can be understood as a cross between both methods. Like deductive science, simulation "starts with a set of explicit assumptions" that, once set in train, "generat[e] data that can be analyzed inductively."

Simulation thus affords the social scientist a link to the real world that differs from most middle-range theorizing. Offering more than probable or predictive outcomes, simulated data sets function as "artificial worlds" for Axelrod. In the experimental vacuum of a computer program, the behaviors of multiple agents can be isolated and the systemic properties that "emerge" from their interaction studied. Sim-worlds may have no actual existence, yet they provide a "very useful way of studying reality."

The Sciences: Imagining the Provisionally Real

Like many of their peers in the social sciences or even the humanities, Fellows in the sciences value worldplay at work for nurturing imaginative qualities of mind and for modeling complex systems. One Fellow who elaborated on the make-believe-like processes required for knowledge construction was the physicist John Hopfield, who has studied the brain as a biological computing system. In this work, he has relied on his ability to visualize or "image" the brain's neural network, to develop analogies with known computer mechanisms, and to devise manageable simulation models to explore the resulting picture:

> My "imaginary world" is solely one of trying directly to imagine how things will work out, particularly the kinds of behaviors that a large system made of simple parts will dis-

play, imagining it in "pictorial" terms or thinking of its metaphorical connections with a system I already understand.

Other Fellows expressed similar reliance on visualizing structures or conceptualizing patterns to aid in the imaginative exploration of poorly understood phenomena. A Fellow at work on physiological control systems went one step further, empathizing with nonhuman objects of his study. "I imagine how I would behave as various molecules interacting and what the consequences would be," he has said. "I spend a great deal of time modeling [my scientific ideas] either in imagination or in reality, through games or actual physical objects." This level of imaginative immersion constituted a kind of worldplay, in his estimation, ultimately expressed in systemic representations of whole structures and processes.

For many Fellow scientists, then, the imaginary world at work refers to an internally imagined mental model, constrained but not entirely determined by known facts. At least in this "limited sense," one Fellow bet that all scientists create imagined worlds. Another tied scientific worldplay to the necessary simplification or abstraction of reality—in his own case, the "reductive version of imagining how the particular world of what I study scientifically *might* work." And a Fellow in biology insisted that the scientific abstraction had to remain "relevant to physical nature" (i.e., tied to the real).

For yet another Fellow, the scientist, like historian or social scientist, never has all the facts, so scientific abstraction has to also and necessarily retain something of the imaginary:

> In a real sense to do theory is to explore imaginary worlds because all models are simplified versions of reality, the world. Part of the art of it all is what gets put in and what gets left out. But it's "bounded imagination" in that one's experience, tool kit, etc. says…pay attention to these features. Since lots gets left out of any model, part of the art has been described as the suspension of disbelief. . . . I will, for a while, believe in this simple world, even though I know lots of ways it fails to capture nature.

The idea that theoretical models in science involve a temporary suspension of disbelief is an intriguing one. After all, the willingness to entertain or enter into an alternate or artificial reality *as if real* is most often identified with the storytelling arts. Nevertheless, a number of Fellows in the sciences characterized the worldplay in their work as the construction of *provisional* narratives. One microbiologist, for instance, "completely agreed" that scientists invent possible worlds, for "a lot of science is making up a good story that fits the facts."

Nonscientists unaware of such expedient fabrication may find this kind of statement a confession of fraud. It is anything but. Scientific fictions may be provisional in nature, yet they are no more arbitrary than those used by historians or social scientists, either in implementation or explanation.

Consider implementation first. As neurobiologist and Fellow Paul Adams has explained it, narrative is a strategy for understanding reality. "As a scientist I imagine possible worlds that are closely based on my understanding of aspects of the real world. In other words, I try to imagine a 'story', with a very strong plot and characters, that completely meshes with the real world yet reveals that world in a new way." He means story-telling quite literally, with all its fictional elements:

> How does one construct a narrative in which the actors are neurons and synapses? . . .
> To start with, neurons and synapses are as vivid to me as knights and pawns to the chess
> player: as vivid as food on the table, or flowers in the garden, to the average person (or,
> I might add, as notes and chords were to deaf Beethoven!) At that level of familiarity the
> imagination can start to play games . . . while still respecting the true character of the
> notes, or the pieces, or the synapses.

Ultimately, the game of science is to tell a new story that explains all the strange facts and odd anomalies overlooked in standard explications of some real system, such as the brain. As Adams put it, "I attempt to see how certain raw 'facts,' preferably facts that keep cropping up over and over again, can be explained in ways that are both economical and unexpected." This is easier said than done. It doesn't happen very often that one comes up with an unexpected and economical (read, novel, and effective) narrative; it is even more rare that this fresh explanatory narrative will survive testing.

Adams avowed that over the course of his scientific career he has come more and more to value the inventive—theorizing—side of science. But the testing side—the reality check—remains absolutely essential to the scientific enterprise. In the course of developing a good story, the scientist has "reinvented some of the rules" that structure the newly posited possible world. But these rules are not simply different for the sake of difference. Rather, "the new imagined rules have ultimately to correspond to reality—indeed," Adams concluded, ". . . they must provide a better fit to reality than the old rules!" The narrative elaboration of a possible world in science must meet the most stringent criteria—and satisfy the most stringent constraints.

For this reason R. Stephen Berry, Fellow appointed in physical chemistry, understands worldplay in science to be largely restricted to the early stages of theory conception. After that, "the work comes when you try to carry it beyond that to see whether it really is consistent, whether it really does have useful implications and isn't just simply a hollow tautology."

Other Fellows have agreed. The imagined world has necessarily to "lead to concrete hypotheses testable by experiments," wrote one biologist. After the pictorial visualization of some part of a possible world, physicist Hopfield explained, comes the work of "exploring the contact between that picture and mathematics and computer simulations of the mathematics." As for the physiologist who imagined behaving like molecules, "An experiment (or research in general) is an attempt to determine whether some thing that only exists in your imagination might also exist in reality."

It is that (re)search, rather than the imagined world per se, to which the scientist pledges allegiance. Indeed, for some, the truth-value of the scientific model is not only provisional, it must always be suspect as well, even as it drives the acquisition of knowledge.

"We create simple possible worlds that are not true, but give us insight into the real ones," wrote an epidemiologist Fellow, though "sometimes people stray by taking the possible worlds too literally." The imagined world, however so well constrained by experience and reason, is *never* the exact equivalent of reality, and each advance in science demonstrates how the explanatory stories we tell are always incomplete and sometimes wrong—that is to say, they are revealed as the fictions they always were.

Refractions of Worldplay

Through the lens of adult work, worldplay displays a spectrum of disciplinary forms, much like a beam of light through a prism breaks up into a rainbow of colors. At one end of the vocational worldplay spectrum, imaginary worlds in the arts most closely resemble childhood make-believe—or at least, its typical instantiation. Whether highly impossible or unabashedly realistic, imaginary worlds in the arts are explored and elaborated as "possible worlds of the mind," with varying emphasis on the fictional, logical, and organic elements of story.

At the other end of the worldplay spectrum, imaginary worlds in the sciences shift in conception toward a pragmatic, problem-solving strategy that powers the construction of effective knowledge about the probable universe "out there." Involving imaginative faculties every bit as fresh and vivid as those of a child—or an artist—at play, the scientists' simplified versions of reality also require a certain suspension of disbelief, in order to allow the "bounded imagination" room to explore.

In between the two poles described by arts and sciences, practitioners in the humanities, the social sciences, and the public issues professions invent imaginary worlds to suit an inter-related set of imaginative and pragmatic purposes. Worldplay at work is a game with rules that enables the reconstruction of times past and places lost. It is a modeling tool for extrapolating futures dimly perceived. It is also an inspiration that galvanizes the self and others to analyze and solve the human-made problems of local and global society.

Across many fields of inquiry, those who recognize worldplay at work, like the many Fellows cited here, also recognize that our understanding of the world we live in is mediated by the world we imagine.

CREATIVE DIVIDE IN INTELLECTUAL CULTURE

MacArthur Fellows across many fields share a penchant for worldplay. If we are not surprised, perhaps we should be, for this strategy and all it implies about the role of play in creative thinking is largely at variance with conventional understanding of disciplinary specialization. As revealed by Michigan State University students, that second group of participants in the Worldplay Project, conventional understanding—or in this instance, *expectation* of imaginary world invention—more often than not mistakes actual professional *practice*.

Students largely located vocational worldplay in the same skills and activities as did Fellows, but not in the same fields of endeavor. As figure 8.2 indicates, for Fellows the humanities topped the charts in the practical invention of imagined worlds, followed by the social sciences, the sciences, the public issues professions, and the arts. For students, in contrast, the arts stimulated the greatest expectation of imaginary world invention, followed by the public issues professions, the social sciences, the humanities, and finally, the sciences. Simply put, Fellows and students faced off across a gap between practice and expectation—and a presumed divide between the arts and sciences.

Consider that student anticipation of worldplay in the arts, higher than for any other professional category, reflects an assumption of playful, make-believe pretense among artists at large. Fully 50 percent of students majoring in various arts or applied

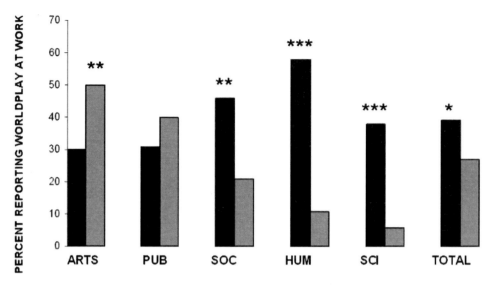

Fig. 8.2. **Worldplay in Adult Work: MacArthur Fellows (black bars) and MSU Students (gray bars), Arranged by Student Expectation. *= p<.01; **=p<.001; ***=p<.0001. (For discussion of p-value, see endnote for figure 3.3.)**

arts expected to invent imaginary worlds in their work. In contrast, only 30 percent of Fellows practicing in a variety of arts—dance, film, music, photography, theater, poetry, and fiction—recognized worldplay as part of their professional endeavor.

The relatively restrained practice of vocational worldplay among Fellows in the arts is perhaps atypical. Unrelated canvassing of scientists, engineers, and artists in an "ArtsSmarts" study has revealed upwards of 80 to 85 percent of artists reporting exploratory play and possible world speculation in their work (See figure 8.3). However, actual practice in the arts may also rein in play as easily as prolong it. Many artists—including those in the Worldplay Project—may preferentially focus attention on craft matters, especially in fields where the maintenance of technical skill is ongoing or disciplinary innovations are particularly abstract, nonrepresentational, or nonnarrative.

Outside the arts, students were most apt to recognize the vocational invention of worlds in the public interest professions. Forty percent of students anticipated engaging in some form of work-related worldplay as teachers, lawyers, and journalists; only 31 percent of Fellows in community affairs, education, human rights, public health, and other public policy professions did so.

Again, student expectation outpaced veteran practice, particularly among those preparing for careers as teachers. Fully 50 percent of education majors expected to create or participate directly in imaginary worlds with the children in their classrooms. In the absence of close contact or obvious resemblance between early and mature endeavor (i.e., in law and journalism) students were less prone to expect the invention of imagined worlds to play much of a role in their work.

Lack of intrinsic resemblance may also explain the rather dramatic drop in student expectation of vocational worldplay in the humanities and social sciences. Only 11

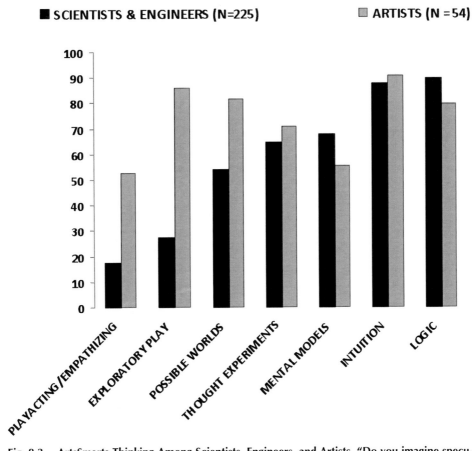

Fig. 8.3. ArtsSmarts Thinking Among Scientists, Engineers, and Artists. "Do you imagine speculative systems or 'possible worlds'?"

percent of students in the humanities recognized worldplay in the analysis of literary texts or historical reconstruction. Only 21 percent of students in the social sciences recognized elements of worldplay in the data-crunching projection of economic or political forecast. In contrast, Fellows working in these fields practiced imaginary-world invention in much higher proportions (58 percent among those in the humanities; 46 percent among those in the social sciences). Training in these fields, which tends to privilege reasoned adherence to evidence, apparently shortchanges student exposure to the imaginative pretense that animates documentation.

A similar educational omission occurs in the sciences, where veteran practice surpassed student expectation of worldplay at work by a whopping 38 to 6 percent. Despite the fact that Fellows in the sciences were *more* likely than Fellows in the arts to acknowledge worldplay at work, students in the sciences were much *less* likely than students in the arts—or any other professional category for that matter—to anticipate worldplay at work.

Student bias in this instance reflects the pervasive view that science is much less imaginative and playful than art. Though much research, including the study informing figure 8.3, indicates that many working scientists employ imaginative, subjective, and intuitive thinking styles, science training shows little overt acceptance of these cognitive processes. Indeed, one informal study of science textbooks from kindergarten to college found that many of the imaginative skills commonly used by adult practitioners are dropped from instruction as schooling progresses. Among those dropped skills is play.

On the receiving end of that schooling, students confirmed in their expectations some of the early arguments (covered in chapter 2) that childhood worldplay would be of primary value to writers and artists only. But expectations, as must by now be clear, can be deceiving. In practice, Fellows in the humanities, the social sciences, and the sciences *do* have pragmatic use for worldplay. Knowledge building in those fields *does* involve imaginative pretense just as surely as in the arts.

Indeed, worldplay is arguably a critical leavening agent in the acquisition and synthesis of *all* knowledge. The "make-believe worlds" of the arts, the "probable worlds" of the humanities and social sciences, and the "possible worlds" of science all articulate, at a fundamental level, one over-arching purpose. Within the limits described by data, documents, intuitions, or dreams, the worldplaying scientist, economist, historian, and poet push forward those new and effective visions of reality that create and recreate the human experience.

THE POLYMATHIC GARDENER

As well as mascot, the Globbershnuckle might also stand as muse for the many MacArthur Fellows whose method of work obscures accepted boundaries between different fields of study, between work and play, logic and imagination, science and art. No matter the professional field, creative individuals do not always choose *between* but often *blend both* sides of the fence into meaningful speculation.

Laura Otis is such a one. A professor in the humanities, she in fact began her education in science, training in biochemistry and neuroscience. After eight years of laboratory bench work and a master's degree, she switched to the study of literature. Yet far from abandoning her scientific background, her focus within the humanities has been to study the ways in which scientific and literary thinking share common ideas and shape each other's influence in the world. And when she isn't working at this endeavor, she's playing at it, like an artist. Otis has also explored her interests in as yet unpublished novels, the writing of which she pursues as an avocation or hobby, albeit a serious one.

In a word, Otis is a polymath, a person who pursues and combines diverse pursuits within a personally compelling network of enterprise. Like the Globbershnuckle, she blends talents and interests we normally associate with distinct areas of knowledge. So do other Fellows and other individuals profiled in these pages. As their particular muse, the Globbershnuckle reminds us that worldplay has a relationship with polymathy that is bound to be as idiosyncratic as it is useful. How does one weave diverse vocational and avocational interests into an imagined world? Is the knowledge gained personal, professional, profound? In the next chapter these and other questions lead to case studies of the worldplay (a)vocation.

Chapter Nine

The Worldplay Avocation-Vocation: Case Studies in Creative Polymathy

The master in the art of living draws no distinction between his work and his play, his labor and his leisure, his mind and his body, his education and his recreation, his love and his religion. He hardly knows which is which. He simply pursues his vision of excellence through whatever he is doing and leaves it to others to decide whether he is working or playing. To himself he is always doing both.

—James Michener, writer

ENCODED MONOLITHS AND IMAGINARY MUSEUMS

The *Encoded Monolith* is a sleek, stainless steel sculpture featuring three seven-foot-high, interconnecting columns with multiple drawers in each. The left column of drawers represents art, the right column science, and the third inner column where left and right drawers alternately overlap represents their virtual integration. The brainchild of visual artist and inventor Todd Siler, the *Monolith* contains over eight hundred visual notations, drawings, paintings, sculptural plans, and artist's books. The piece is a "metaphorm," a physical embodiment of Siler's multifarious explorations of brain and universe. It is also, he revealed in an interview exchange, a "physical embodiment of worldplay" (See figure 9.1.).

Let's take him at his word. Let's posit, too, a museum of imaginary worlds and a discovery cabinet of the same three-column design. After admiring any number of maps, secret dictionaries, and paper napkin speculations, we are drawn to our cabinet, the left column labeled "avocation," for private hobby pursuits, and the right column "vocation," for public and professional endeavors. The drawers, paired left and right, hold the papers, memoirs, and interviews of paracosmists and other world-playing individuals.

At random, we open an avocation drawer on the left holding the interview reminiscences of the cell biologist Barry Shur. Given to wacky fantasies with trombone-playing and song-singing ants, Shur has shared his weird world with an intimate circle of family and friends. We notice, however, that this avocation drawer reaches only half way into the cabinet. His private worldplay has no obvious connection with his

Fig. 9.1.   Todd Siler, *The Encoded Monolith*, 1980-1990, *left*. Todd Siler, *The Encoded Monolith Metaphorm #1*, 1980-1990, *right*. The two open drawers of the Monolith reveal the contents of Siler's creative process. The schematic *Metaphorm* allows us to see the inner, virtual column where the closed drawers overlap.

work, though it may serve as a marker of sorts for the creative verve he believes he brings to science.

Similar short drawers on the vocation side—those for Laurel Thatcher Ulrich, say, or Galway Kinnell—suggest that for these and other individuals met with in chapter 8, professional worldplay has no obvious or originating link with private, ongoing hobbies. There are two long drawers marked J. R. R. Tolkien, however, one for avocation and one for vocation—and both reach all the way to the back of the discovery cabinet, overlapping in the third, hidden column. So do the dual drawers for Gregory Benford and Desmond Morris and Todd Siler himself. For these individuals, worldplay permeates both vocation and avocation.

A few seconds' rumination and we realize that by rummaging through the long drawers and their twins, we can explore the manner in which worldplay vocations and avocations combine to promote polymathy, that is to say, the productive pursuit of multiple endeavors. We can also investigate how that polymathic breadth may help account for the creative outcomes of worldplay.

By and large, polymaths are the understudied cousins of gifted prodigies and other remarkable achievers. We all know how a Wolfgang Amadeus Mozart or a Pablo Picasso or a Leonard Euler, trained from childhood on in music, visual art, and mathematics respectively, reached the full flowering of their genius with single-minded devotion to one field of endeavor. Yet close examination of a wider range of individuals reveals other, if less well understood, patterns of creative development that are broader and more versatile.

For example, in a 1966 study of well-known achievers in the arts and humanities across 1,000 years of European history, 19 percent of those sampled had professional accomplishments in more than one field of endeavor. In yet another study of 2,102 historically eminent individuals, 24 percent achieved fame in at least two unrelated fields of endeavor.

More recent investigation corroborates this robust polymathy among scientists, social scientists, and others, particularly when avocations as well as vocations are thrown into the mix. The *(a)vocational* polymath makes two or more different kinds of things (poems and watercolors, say, or experimental hypotheses as well as music), and does so within varying degrees of private and public practice. And that broad and diverse practice, as uneven as it may be, can confer creative advantage.

Indeed, some scholars have argued that avocational pursuits directly stimulate vocational creativity. First, some of the earliest Nobel laureates proposed that the scientific imagination depended upon active pursuit of artistic hobbies. Then early twentieth century psychologists (including Lewis Terman) proclaimed that "geniuses" were more likely to be broadly talented than the average individual. Decades later, researchers found that the presence of at least one persistent and intellectually engaging hobby predicted career success far more accurately than IQ, standardized test scores, or grades. Other work has confirmed that in the sciences and in literature, successful individuals are more likely to be engaged in fine arts or crafts avocations than their less successful colleagues.

With this (a)vocational advantage in mind, we can begin to explore how worldplay may help promote polymathy, enabling the individual to integrate multiple "drawers" of interest and enterprise and reap creative benefit. Many people develop diverse interests as children and teens. Due to the pressures of disciplinary training and work, some inevitably abandon these extra-professional pursuits, while others manage to nurture them along as hobbies. In this last instance, private worldplay can provide the nexus that mixes the vocational with the avocational, and builds both into a unified vision of engagement. (A)vocational worldplay can also serve as a catapult, launching significant creative achievement in either hobby or profession or both.

How does that happen? Imaginary cabinet ready and waiting, let's take a look.

J. R. R. TOLKIEN: FAERY TONGUE AND ASTERISK-WORLD

Mention imaginary world invention and avocation in the same breath and almost at once J. R. R. Tolkien comes to mind. As he should. The "Middle-earth" he constructed in private while a busy Oxford philologist is still very much part of our public culture, whether we like to read *The Lord of the Rings*, watch the movie remakes, or indulge in the explosion of fantasy entertainment that has followed in the *Rings'* wake.

Indeed, Middle-earth seems so obviously akin to imaginary worlds fabricated in childhood, yet so novel in its dress and scope, that some have considered it an epitome of the unconstrained imagination. Unfortunately, they misunderstand their man. Tolkien undertook his private worldplay with the playful verve of the artist—and the painstaking thoroughness of the academic as well. And therein lay his road to creative polymathy.

The seeds for Tolkien's mature achievement were sown in childhood. His mother introduced him to French and Latin at the age of seven. A taste for the sounds and structures of these and other tongues followed him into his schooling, where he soon took on German, Greek, and Middle English.

He had a taste, as well, for secret languages shared with cousins and by his early teens was well on the way to developing a lifelong passion for "private lang." construction. After winning a scholarship to Oxford in 1911, Tolkien studied antecedent forms of English and other northern European languages, such as Gothic and Finnish. His interests were never merely academic; each new language he studied inspired the private construction of an analogue "faery" tongue.

To be sure, such construction was part and parcel of linguistic science. Philologists often filled gaps in the historical record with hypothetical "asterisk-words," suggested but not confirmed by existing evidence. By the same token they retrodicted an "asterisk-language," Indo-European, as the ancient root of subsequently disparate tongues.

For Tolkien, technical expertise in such reconstruction led to something more, as well. He had always loved reading the heroic myths of ancient peoples and civilizations, particularly those at the far reaches of historical record. By historical chance the English corpus of ancient tales had little of the depth and breadth he found so enthralling in German or Finnish traditions. Where linguistic patrimony ran dry, he hungered to construct an imagined language and an imagined world. He desired to restore what had somehow been lost—not just for himself, but for the English people.

This very private, yet remarkable, ambition came into focus just as Tolkien entered young manhood. In the interstices of disciplinary training, military service in World War I, and first steps into academia, he devised a "nonsense faery language" for a long-lived, beauty-loving Elven race. From an Anglo-Saxon poem, he took an unknown figure called Earendel, "brightest of angels, above the middle-earth" and constructed an "asterisk-myth," similar to those real myths with which ancient peoples explained celestial phenomena.

Tolkien's worldplay now began in earnest. He wrote up his myth as a poem and gave it a title in Old English, as if his verse were a translation from the original. More poems followed, as did the first of his imaginary landscapes in pencil and watercolor. These he placed, with the Elven language, among the documents and papers he called his "legendarium." In time, these included intertwined histories, genealogies, grammars, vocabularies, illustrative paintings, maps, and heraldic devices—all of them records of an engaging hobby.

Most hours of most days, Tolkien worked as a scholar in the humanities; he taught language classes, graded papers and literature exams, and engaged in linguistic research. Only at night or on vacation did he have time to turn to the languages and literature of his Middle-earth. The same interests that drove his vocation also drove his avocation, but by and large he kept the two endeavors separate. Indeed, for many decades his private passion—and, consequently, his polymathy—remained hidden from professional colleagues. Not until 1931, after a decade in philology, did he hint publicly at the enormity of his nonprofessional activity.

In a lecture initially called "A Hobby for the Home," and later titled "A Secret Vice," Tolkien admitted to an audience of his peers that "home-made or invented languages" and the "making instinct" took increasing amounts of his time and devotion. Yet that guilty pleasure, he argued, also afforded professional insight. Privately constructed languages imitated naturally occurring phonetics; privately constructed literatures borrowed piecemeal from culturally determined storytelling forms.

It followed that these private inventions might shed light on historically evolved phenomena. Imaginary languages and imaginary literatures functioned like so many experiments in the evolution of grammar, vocabulary, and narrative tradition. Construct a language for fun, he concluded, and "you will have had, *only more consciously and deliberately, and so more keenly,* the same creative experience as that of those many unnamed geniuses who have invented the skillful bits of machinery in our traditional languages."

Tolkien justified private language construction as a window onto creative process, and in his case, personal and professional inspiration intertwined. Believing as he did that "the making of language and mythology are related functions," his creative practice was nearly indistinguishable from the modus operandi of linguistic science. Typically, he began with a borrowed name or a made-up word such as "hobbit." Presuming hobbit to be a "worn-down form," he reconstituted with a bit of philological research the plausible asterisk-word *hol-bytla.* "If that name had occurred in our ancient language," he wrote, it would have meant, in Old English, "hole-dweller" or "hole-builder."

Tolkien found structure in this scholarly play, a kind of logarithm for elaboration and invention. Indeed, not until he had satisfied himself philologically did mythologies emerge within his imagination. "The stories," he told one correspondent in 1955, "were comparatively late in coming." But come they did. The "lost" tales later compiled in *The Silmarillion* were his "attempt to give a background or a world in which my expressions of linguistic taste could have a function."

The dense, academic play of the legendarium might have remained no more than a private obsession, if not for the fact that Tolkien also wrote for his children. Unlike the asterisk-myths, his Father Christmas letters and other homemade, self-illustrated picture books emphasized characters in the grip of adventure. They also used simpler, modern modes of narration. This release into new pastures worked wonders for the academic's literary craft and imagination. He wrote and illustrated *The Hobbit* (1937), his first novel, with children in mind.

Initially, *The Hobbit* had nothing to do with the legendarium, yet Tolkien soon realized that he had forged a kind of Rosetta Stone that would allow him to translate some part of his private mythology into a publicly palatable art. In due course, he absorbed the hobbit Bilbo and his accidental acquisition of a powerful Elven Ring within the corpus of tales belonging to Middle-earth. Seventeen years later he followed up with *The Lord of the Rings*, a darker, adult novel in three parts that traced the dangerous quest of Bilbo's nephew. In a company of men, dwarves, and elves, Frodo sought to destroy the corruptive power of the Elven Ring and restore the world to peace.

The Lord of the Rings trilogy garnered Tolkien much public acclaim. Nevertheless, private worldplay remained his primary bent as a writer. As he put it to the novelist Naomi Mitchison, he felt "a clash between 'literary' technique, and the fascination of elaborating in detail an imaginary mythical Age." Upon Mitchison's sensitive review of *The Lord of the Rings* in 1954, Tolkien wrote her that "[y]ours is the only comment that I have seen that, besides treating the book as 'literature' . . . and even taking it seriously . . . also sees it as an elaborate form of the *game* of inventing a country."

That game happily involved the "endless" adumbration of the stuff of hobbit life—of "clothes, agricultural implements, metal-working pottery, architecture and the like." It involved, too, endless documentation. The final volume of *The Lord of the Rings* included six appendices comprising royal annals, genealogies, chronologies, calendars, and linguistic guides. This was perhaps "too much" explanation, Tolkien admitted to Mitchison, but it served a primary purpose dear to the paracosmist's heart.

The pretense that the stories were not figments of imagination, but fragments of historical record, also contributed to the game. Back matter for *The Lord of the Rings* identified *The Hobbit* as, in actuality, "The Red Book of Westmarch," penned by the adventurous Bilbo. An accompanying "Note on the Shire Records" traced the preservation of this Red Book down through the asterisk-ages.

The literary establishment at the time found much of this authentication cumbersome. In first editions of *The Hobbit*, Tolkien had included ink-drawn maps as well as illustrations of Middle-earth (See figure 9.2.). Reviewers gave him a drubbing for what they considered the dilettante quality of the art. His publishers dropped all but the maps from subsequent editions and, except for maps and book covers, did not supply *The Lord of the Rings* with visual documents.

Recent reassessment of Tolkien's art suggests that this omission was a mistake—he was a better artist than contemporaries understood or he himself believed. Lamenting his inability to transpose line and color from mind to canvas with anything approaching fidelity, he nevertheless produced clear pictorial visions of Middle-earth that in many cases proved critical to narrative composition. Indeed, as more than one enthusiast has discovered, his visual and verbal descriptions of Middle-earth were of a piece. Vistas created in the reader's mind through prose reappear almost exactly as imagined in the rediscovered art work.

This coalescence of imaginative vision reminds us that all Tolkien's vocational and avocational interests became grist for the same synthesizing mill. He blurred the boundaries between visual and verbal expression of his inner imagination; he also blurred the edges between scholarship and fiction, and, ultimately, between scholarly fiction and spiritual understanding.

From the start, in fact, Tolkien had understood his constructed world as something outside of himself, amenable to rational research and principled elaboration. Fantasy had little to do with tree creatures or magic, he argued in a 1939 lecture, and much more to do with the "enchantment" of an alternate and possible reality. He wrote as much to Naomi Mitchison in 1954 and repeated the sentiment in a letter to another admirer:

> The name [Middle-earth] is the modern form . . . [of] an ancient name for . . . the abiding place of Men, the objectively real world. . . . The theatre of my tale is this earth, the one in which we now live. . . . Mine is not an "imaginary" world, but an imaginary historical moment.

Mitchison, for one, understood Tolkien's point. His was "a bigger bit of creation altogether [than fantasy]: perhaps a mythology," she argued at the time, and most appropriately done in the "whole-hearted and scholarly manner" he had adopted. With

The hill : hobbiton-across-the Water

Fig. 9.2. J.R.R. Tolkien, *The Hill: Hobbiton-across-the-Water*, 1937. Produced for publication in Tolkien's debut novel, this painting subsequently influenced description of Hobbiton in *The Lord of the Rings*.

these words, she put her finger on what was most remarkable in his achievement—the synthesis of literary and scholarly purpose. Following his own bent, Tolkien took two very different pursuits, rubbed them together and ignited a new and marvelous unity— fantasy adventure invigorated by philological technique and concern.

Both worldplay and polymathy were critical to the combustion. The whole art of his fantasy depended, as he put it, on "the power of giving to ideal creations the inner consistency of reality." In turn that inner consistency gave shape to a profound yearning that the faery world, with its clear-cut vision of good and evil, be true—a "sudden glimpse of the underlying reality" in the never-ending pattern of things.

Because Tolkien was an (a)vocational polymath, he built Middle-earth out of a mix of diverse materials whose blend proved highly unique and innovative. Because he was an old hand at world invention, he built a Middle-earth that seemed authentic and believable. Indeed, his use of techniques, skills, and purposes from one field of endeavor to reconceptualize another suggests a compelling pattern for creative practice. Professional vocation may influence a private passion for worldplay or vice versa. A quick look in other drawers in our imaginary cabinet tells us that this is particularly clear in the realms of science fiction and fictional science, kissing cousins to Tolkien's scholarly fantasy.

GREGORY BENFORD, URSULA LE GUIN, LEO LIONNI, STANISLAW LEM, AND SOME OTHERS: SCIENCE FICTION AND FICTIONAL SCIENCE

Let's begin with science fiction writer and physicist Gregory Benford. His particular brand of sci-fi concerns itself with "what if" speculations just beyond the edge of consensual science. Accordingly, he has used the building of fictional worlds to explore way-out ideas in physics. And he has used the extrapolations of physics to push forward his fiction.

Case in point, he based his first successful book, *Timescape* (1980), on a short story in which he quoted from one of his own scientific papers on tachyons—hypothetical particles that travel backward in time. The book fleshes out the implications, should these tachyons really exist, for sending dire humanitarian warnings into the past. His subsequent interest as a physicist in strange lightning-like structures at the rotational center of the Milky Way galaxy also found dual expression in his science and his fiction. "I got interested in doing the science because I was brought to the subject by the science fiction," he said in interview, "and then I turned it all around and put it back in the [Galactic Center Series of] novels."

Benford has won recognition for both his fiction and his physics, winning the Nebula Award for Science Fiction twice and receiving a Lord Foundation Award for his work in plasma turbulence and astrophysics. Interestingly enough, he owes much of that dual career to childhood worldplay. In a long-remembered game called "Moon and Mars" he and his twin brother explored "space travel and anything to do with the future."

The problem of living in a rotating space colony particularly engaged the boys, for they realized that a set of gravitational forces different from those on earth would necessitate alternate designs for the delivery of fresh water, the removal of waste, and other supports of civilization. These worldplay challenges led directly to intellectual interest in astro-physics for both boys and, in Gregory's case, to an abiding yen for inventing future scenarios "seen through the changing lens of science"—a yen he transformed into the writing of science fiction.

The ability to draw personally compelling connections between disciplines turns out to be an intellectual strategy of key importance to the polymath. Benford, like Tolkien in his time, has emphasized not the differences but the similarities between his twin pursuits. The kind of fiction he writes has, in his words, "severe constraints on it just like the science. That is, it has to occur in a real world with maybe different rules, different location, different time, but then you have to follow the rules." Whether the world in question is "real" or "imaginary," it follows that the exploratory part—working out all the implications of a thing or process within the given parameters—is much the same.

Science and literature also share a communicative structure for Benford. Despite its analytical organization, the science paper is as much a narrative as a science fiction story. Moreover, the more specialized and the more profuse scientific information becomes, the more need there is for the "connective tissue that story-telling provides."

As our discovery cabinet reveals, other scientists writing and reading speculative fiction have agreed that imaginative storytelling enriches the science. Physicist and sci-fi writer Robert Forward reserved his most daring scientific ideas for exploration in his short stories and novels. So did engineer and sci-fi icon Arthur C. Clarke. The physicist Freeman Dyson has also argued that such fiction "provides more insight into past and future worlds than any statistical analysis, because insight requires imagination." Open still more drawers and you find that physics is not the only science that lends itself to narrative worldplay.

Consider the work of Ursula Le Guin, who has woven award-winning science fictions and fantasies out of socio-political issues and archeological concerns. The daughter of famous anthropologists, she began around the age of nine to muse upon "Inner Lands" and explore their mythic properties by writing their stories. As an adult, too, she has remarked that the imaginary realms of "Outer Space, and the Inner Lands, are still, and always will be, my country."

Indeed. In the young-adult novel *Very Far Away from Anywhere Else* (1976), Le Guin brings to life a teenage boy named Owen who indulges in worldplay systematically. "I had this country called Thorn," Owen says. "I drew maps of it and stuff, but mostly I didn't write stories about it. Instead I described the flora and fauna, and the landscape and the cities, and figured out the economy and the way they lived, their government and history."

Owen calls that worldplay "kid stuff," but a mature Le Guin subsequently did the same thing in *Always Coming Home*, a science fiction novel published in 1985. This "archaeology of the future," as she described it, reads like a compilation of oral histories, stories, poems, and codices all having to do with the socio-spiritual organization of the Kesh, a people "who might be going to have lived a long, long time from now in Northern California."

A section called "The Back of the Book" looks a lot like Owen's description of his worldplay, with maps of the Valley as well as notes on Kesh food, clothing, arts, and crafts. In addition—and with reference to Tolkien's "secret vice"—there are samples of the Kesh language, including an alphabet and a glossary of words. Mimicking the documentary methods of the real world archeologist, Le Guin presents as science fiction an imaginary or asterisk anthropology.

Rifle through additional drawers in our discovery cabinet and you find one imaginary science or social science after another. Leo Lionni, the children's book author, also poured himself into drawing, sculpting, and casting in bronze a garden of strange imaginary flora. Along with an exhibition of that work, he published *Parallel Botany* (1977), a mock-erudite treatise on the discovery and classification of a hitherto unknown vegetal kingdom of plants, including the invisible *Tirillus mimeticus*.

Fictional the treatise may be, but it is littered with nuggets of fact and the serious inquiry of nonfiction. It is, as Lionni cites the poet Marianne Moore, an imaginary garden with real toads in it—much like the terrariums he arranged as miniature worlds for snakes and toads when he was a child. Indeed, lengthy introductory material in *Parallel Botany* takes serious issue with work by well-known scientists on biological growth and the aesthetics of organic form, raising questions about the relationship of art to science and the imaginary to the real.

With similar intent, the Scottish geologist and author Dougal Dixon imagined a hypothetical host of animals in his book *After Man, A Zoology of the Future* (1981). Likewise, the artist Beauvais Lyons proposed an artistically conceived excavation of artifacts from an imaginary past as an "archeological fiction." And, in the same vein, artist Norman Daly designed a multimedia exhibition of arts, literature, and material objects for a pseudo-civilization, posing for the purpose as "compiler" and "director of Llhuroscian Studies."

Both Daly and Lyons found verbal as well as visual inspiration in the short stories of Jorge Louis Borges, known for a narrative art that turns upon the archival relics of imaginary worlds. They might also have cited the Polish futurologist and writer Stanislaw Lem, who crafted a body of science fiction presented as bibliographic artifact. Short-listed numerous times for the Nobel Prize in literature, Lem was also widely recognized for his philosophical expertise in the science of interstellar messages. His output ran the gamut of fiction and nonfiction in at least thirteen distinct genres of writing. Moreover, a great deal of the art and the science of his trans-disciplinary approach was prefigured in childhood worldplay.

Recall from chapter 1 that, in youth, Lem crafted the bureaucratic papers of an imaginary castle and designed whimsical inventions; he also built working models of real electrical machines. In maturity, he proved the polymath he had always looked to be. He prepared for a career in medicine, worked as a research assistant for a science study group in Soviet Poland, taught at the university level, and reviewed scientific publications from beyond the Iron Curtain.

When, around 1950, Lem turned decisively toward a career in writing, his interests remained scientific. In his nonfiction work he focused on futurology, eventually gaining the respect of scientists and philosophers alike for his factual conjectures touching on advances in physics, astronomy, biology, and the emerging field of cybernetics, an interdisciplinary study of information processing and feedback.

In *Summa Technologiae* (1964), for instance, he explored the philosophical implications of certain technologies that were, at the time, still speculative. What he called ariadnology (the study of connective threads) anticipated data base search engines such as Google™; what he called phantomatics (imagination machines) anticipated computer-generated virtual realities such as those now realized in simulation training, robotic surgery, and online sites like Second Life™.

The concerns and interests Lem raised in nonfiction he poured into his fiction. This transfer or cross-fertilization of ideas is evident in what is perhaps his best-known novel, *Solaris* (1961), twice rendered into film. The 2002 Hollywood movie emphasizes the weird psychological effects that an unfathomable ocean-mind-planet has on a small group of scientist-pioneers. But the original story pays far more attention to the history of scientific investigations concerning that planetary entity, with their fits and starts and dead-end theories. Lem modeled the course of knowledge building in science and concluded that no matter how relentlessly we probe the unknown, our understanding will always and necessarily remain incomplete.

In other work, Lem pushed intellectual boundaries even farther by blurring the literary line between fiction and nonfiction—and he did so using the methods and strategies of the worldplay he had known in childhood. As he wrote in 1984, "I started to produce an increasing number of notes, fictitious encyclopedias, and small additional ideas, and this has finally led to the things I am doing now. I try to get to know the 'world' to be created by me by writing the literature specific to it."

In this paracosmic manner he developed his imagined worlds *before* composing their narratives. Eventually, he dispensed with the conventional storytelling altogether and shaped the worldplay itself into works such as *A Perfect Vacuum* (1971), *Imaginary Magnitude* (1973), and *One Human Minute* (1986), all of them compilations of prefaces and reviews for imaginary books.

To the extent that these and other of his short stories and novels modeled hypotheses that were, in his words, "too bold to claim scientific accuracy," Lem pushed on two fronts simultaneously: literary experimentation and futurological speculation. His creative polymathy was energized by scientific curiosity for the future, artistic imagination, and the interpenetration of the two in worldplay.

DESMOND MORRIS: EXPERIMENTAL INQUIRY AND THE SECRET KINGDOM OF BIOMORPHS

Versatility in interest and activity usually involves obviously aligned fields. Poetry and playwriting—or factual and fictional science—share craft concern for verbal communication and composition. But versatility can also involve less obvious disciplinary alignments. Painting and sculpture—as well as painting and narrative—may relate to one another in *meta*-craft concern with visual perception and form, though differently rendered.

In the hands of many practitioners, worldplay embraces these boundary crossings of craft and meta-craft concern with exuberance. Lionni explored an imaginary botany in drawing, sculpture, *and* writing. Tolkien gave expression to Middle-earth in poetry, prose, *and* painting and even drew music into his world building by collaborating with others to bring Elvish poetry to life. In some instances, however, blended disciplines can appear so different in cognitive process and purpose as to confound understanding, at least at first, of what binds them together to productive effect. The drawer marked Desmond Morris provides a case in point.

Morris has been known to the public as an Oxford University–trained zoologist, zoo curator, a producer and host of innumerable television programs on "everything from sex to understanding one's cat," and a best-selling author of popular classics such as *The Naked Ape* (1967), *Manwatching* (1977), and *Animalwatching* (1990). He is also, though this is less widely known, a successful artist.

Morris's multiple interests go way back. An only child and, in his words, "extremely shy," he absorbed himself in the study of insects, amphibians, and fish living in and around the pond near his home. Upon discovery of his great-grandfather's brass microscope in the attic, he spent hours peering at drops of pond water, drawn to what he instinctively felt to be another and "secret kingdom" of tiny creatures. His curiosity drawn in scientific directions, he thought he might grow up to be a naturalist.

In his mid-teens, however, Morris also discovered art, not the kind that reproduced nature or reality, but the surreal kind. First emerging in the 1920s, the surrealist movement in literature and art spurned rationality in favor of subconscious impulses. Its anti-establishment philosophy appealed to the young Morris. Particularly in the work of Spanish surrealist Joan Miró and others, he found what proved to be another microscope—automatism, dreams, and additional surrealist processes allowed him to explore the hidden and fascinating landscape of his own subliminal mind. He thought he might become an artist.

And he did do so, in a doppelganger sort of way. In 1950 he held his first art show, sharing exhibition space with his hero, Miró. He also earned an undergraduate degree in zoology and moved on to graduate study at Oxford with Nobel-prize-winning ethologist Niko Tinbergen. During student years and in the decade thereafter, Morris wrote numerous papers on the sexual behaviors of stickleback, other fish, and a variety of birds. He looked ahead to a career in academic science—but with his own particular twist. In 1952 he staged, at Oxford's Ashmolean Museum, a one-man show of drawings triggered by shapes seen under the microscope. Though Tinbergen thought this artistic effort a waste of time for a scientist, Morris refused to give it up—and set off down the polymathy path.

At the core of this journey lay the invention of possible places. Even when young, Morris had thought of his scientific and artistic endeavors in paracosmic terms. His childhood love for animals had plunged him into what felt like a "private world" of his own. Writing in a student magazine as a teen, he embraced as well the artist's passion for "develop[ing] a personal world."

Inevitably, poetic imagination aided by surrealistic ardor, guided by scientific enthusiasms, led Morris at age nineteen to paint *Entry to a Landscape,* a work of fictional/factual dimensions. "I slipped through this crack in the rocks," he later said, "and there I was, suddenly surrounded by a whole array of bizarre inhabitants." Colorful, globular beings eventually called "biomorphs" cavorted in a "secret, inner personal world" (See figure 9.3.).

Morris has described his biomorph world as "a fantasy version of the family lake" he explored as a child. Though his paintings reflect dreams and intuitions, they are also heavily influenced by zoological interests. Biomorphic shapes echo cellular and amoebic forms, like those found in pond water. Biomorphic colors and markings carry ethological as well as artistic associations. Biomorphic behaviors parallel the action patterns of real animals.

The biomorphs's world is one of animal activity, Morris has written, of "relationships and interactions, where one figure will be in love with another or aggressive towards another or playful with another or colluding with another or escaping from another or trapping another." Nothing about the imaginary creatures is arbitrary or implausible. They "mutate from canvas to canvas, growing, developing, changing" according to general biological principles. "The goal is to invent a new fauna and to nurse it through a slow evolution of its own, from picture to picture."

Significantly enough, the science in Morris's art reflects only one direction in his two-way street of meta-craft concern for evolutionary theory and for creative process and purpose. If his paintings have revealed his biological interests, his zoology has yielded, in turn, to artistic insights and processes. In the belief that exploration and discovery proceed from deep emotional engagement, he has employed in his science as in his art an empathetic, intuitive, and, ultimately, surrealist approach.

No surprise, this integration of artistic and scientific strategies first came to him in a dream. As a teen he had hoped to court the surrealist muse by painting biomorphic shapes on the black walls of his bedroom. He later recalled the outcome in the autobiographical *Animal Days* (1979):

> It was a strange little scenario. Not only was I surrounded by animals, but I changed into one myself. In essence, this was what was going to happen to me in my future research, when I became a full-time student of animal behavior. With each animal I studied, I *became* that animal. I tried to think like it, to feel like it. Instead of viewing the animal from a human standpoint—and making serious anthropomorphic errors in the process—I attempted, as a research ethologist, to put myself in the animal's place, so that *its* problems became *my* problems, and I read nothing into its life-style that was alien to its particular species. And the dream said it all.

So did a number of his paintings, in particular *The Zoologist, The Entymologist*, and *The Scientist*, all painted in the early 1950s. In these portraits, the human being is revealed *as* animal, not just because the observer empathizes with the observed, but because he *is* animal. This was exactly the point of Morris's first breakthrough book, an ethological examination of the species *homo sapiens*.

Suffused with the iconoclastic energy that he had hitherto confined to his art, *The Naked Ape* (1967) equally shocked and enlightened readers by focusing on the biological bases of human behavior. In true surrealist style, Morris juxtaposed verbal chitchat to fur grooming, sunglasses to aggressive threat-stares, and men's ties to their sexual organs. He magnified the visual, unspoken, often unconscious signaling and

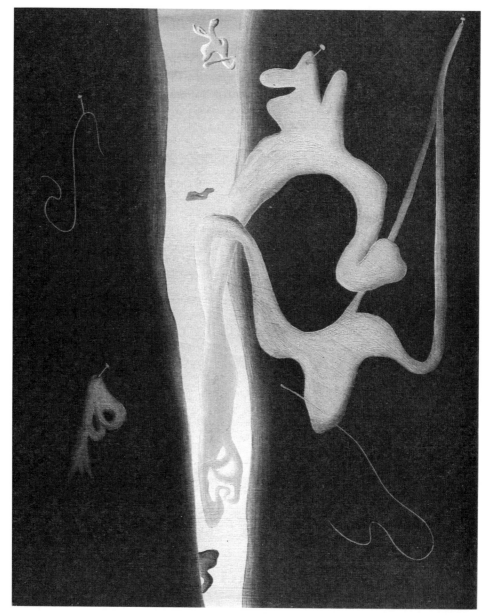

Fig. 9.3. Desmond Morris, *Entry to a Landscape*, 1947. At age 19, Morris painted his first vision of a biomorphic world.

display in our daily lives and drew out the evolutionary implications of these basic actions.

The Naked Ape made a very big splash in the late 1960s. An instant best seller, the book sold millions of copies and was eventually translated into some twenty-three languages worldwide. Morris had already written half a dozen books on animals (many with his wife, Ramona), notably including *The Biology of Art*, a pioneering work on chimpanzee art and the origins of human aesthetics. Still, *The Naked Ape* effectively ushered in a third career for Morris alongside those of scientist and artist, that of science writer. In that role he has published almost more books than can be counted on popular zoology and human ethology—fields he has dominated for decades, at least in the public mind. Nearly fifty years after first publication, the *Naked Ape* remains in print.

Morris's integration of animal behavior studies and surrealistic art paved the way for his unique vision as a painter and his unique contributions as an ethologist and writer. Although he understands scientific enterprise and artistic endeavor as "basically different," they are yet profoundly related for him by cognitive skill and exploratory style. Science largely draws on his reasoning, analytical mind. Art largely draws on his intuitional, imaginative mind. Nevertheless, he has written, "irrational, intuitive leaps are used during the brief creative moments of scientific research, and also there is a certain need for mundane planning and organization in the execution of a painting." A common trust in childlike curiosity suggests that "at a basic level, perhaps artists and scientists are not so different after all."

More to the point for Morris, both his art and his science share foundation in the creative impulses of play. For either endeavor to "thrive," in his view, "the playfulness of childhood must survive and mature as an adult mode of self-expression. . . . There must always be time set aside for playful innovations, for subjective explorations; in short, for the poetic and the mysterious alongside the objective and rational."

Not only must we encourage ourselves and others to foster the play in our work, we must dare to cross boundaries between the arts and the sciences, for "in reality," Morris has written, "people today are not scientists or artists . . . they are explorers or non-explorers, and the context of their explorations is of secondary importance." In his own case, he once wrote, "I never thought of myself as a zoologist who painted or as a painter who was interested in zoology," but as both simultaneously, a visual observer of outer and inner worlds.

In this joint venture, polymathic worldplay has had a key role. For sixty years and more Morris has generated hundreds of paintings, elaborating what one colleague has referred to as "a parallel world . . . and his documentation of its inhabitants and their customs is myth-making on a grand scale." His achievement in popular science may be similarly described as an accumulating narrative that shapes our understanding of the biological, animal nature of mankind. Whether in the service of the real or the surreal, the invention of rigorously imagined worlds in multiple pursuits exactly captures his polymathic achievement.

TODD SILER AND THE ARTSCIENCE ENTERPRISE

When creative polymathy is at its best, multiple avocations and vocations, no matter how diverse, stimulate one another in ways that make sense to the individual. Such fruitful relationships between disparate interests have been called "integrated activity sets" and "networks of enterprise." The term "correlative talents" has also been used to track the kind of support an avocation might lend a vocation, or vice versa. How or when do these networks get their start? Imaginary world invention can serve as the junction where diverse interests emerge and converge. And for many, the artist Todd Siler included, that polymathic blending begins in childhood.

From an early age, Siler lived an intense imaginative life revolving around multiple places and spaces wholly conjured in the mind. Worldplay provided escape from the stress of growing up in foster homes and boarding schools. Eventually, as a means of exploring both animated fantasies and real-world phenomena, it proved "an amazing source of power" by fueling a lot of drawing, storytelling, self-choice learning, and "what if" thinking.

The young Siler liked comparing the energies of the sun to the energies of the human mind; he loved speculating about "sunspots of the brain." All came together when the fifteen-year-old experienced a profound moment of insight. As he recalled it, "my abilities to write or draw or think all crystallized and came into some kind of coherence for me that I knew I had to use in a purposeful, creative way."

The adults in his life considered Siler a drawing prodigy. Privately, in keeping with his epiphany, he saw himself as both an artist *and* a scientist, exploring connections between vast realms of knowledge. Documenting that vision, he imagined a "virtual dialogue" between a young "artscientist" and other characters in an ongoing story, finally crafted at age twenty-three into a "bag novel" (See figure 9.4.).

Fig. 9.4. Todd Siler, *Bag Novel*, 1976. Like many worldplay artifacts, this series of ten text-inscribed paper bags, stored one within the other, is of deep personal significance to Siler and despite offers of purchase, remains in his possession.

In this artifact as artwork, a number of paper bags inserted one inside the other contain "thought streams" or "chapters" in the life of a child "growing into someone who contributes to science." Symbolically, the bag novel portrayed Siler's own attempt, throughout high school and college, to connect his science training with his artistic development. This dual effort often proved problematic. The intuitive approaches of the young artist baffled science teachers; the calculative rigor of the young scientist confounded art professors. Nevertheless, he persisted, and in the mid 1980s became the first visual artist to earn a PhD in the interdisciplinary study of psychology and art at MIT.

As part of his doctoral project, Siler produced *Thought Assemblies*, a huge mosaic of visual and handwritten graphics that track cognitive trails through the brain with scientific accuracy. He complemented this art with written work on "cerebreactors," imaginary machines linking cognitive processes to the fusion and fission of stars. A few years later, he published *Breaking the Mind Barrier* (1990), a book exploring more fully the concept of an interfused "artscience" and the connection-making tools at its center.

Siler subsequently formalized these "metaphorming" (or metaphor-making) skills and practices, which he has successfully parlayed to educational and business environments. He has also pushed his artscience into the realms of technological and scientific innovation. As an inventor, he has procured patents for a canvas-stretching device, for a printing process producing large-scale, nonrepeating design patterns, and for a free form spatial-tactile graphic input device for computer-aided design. As a scientist, he has proposed a new and alternative nuclear fusion device meant to harness nuclear fusion to the generation of safe and renewable energy.

At almost every turn, private worldplay has powered Siler's public endeavors, nowhere more so than in the intuitive approach he took to conceiving and designing his "fractal fusion reactor." Channeling the "lucid dreaming" of childhood stories and dialogues, he developed a line of supposition that experimental fusion reactors, which have to date failed to achieve sustained power output, owed that failure to their basis in classical Euclidean geometry. Modern developments in mathematics suggested that most natural objects and processes, including the energy-generating sun, were far better described by a different, a fractal geometry—with implications, supposed Siler, for a fully functional fusion reactor.

In fractal geometry, objects exist not in the standard one, two, or three dimensions, but in the fractional dimensions in between. Mountains, trees, the sun itself are highly irregular and nonlinear forms structurally similar to themselves at every level of magnification. Like the radiating pattern of a tree repeated from trunk to branch to twig, at both macro and micro levels the sun is roughly (statistically) self-similar. What then, Siler asked himself, if we were to design reactors to "metaphorm" or mimic the fractal nature of the sun?

Siler's exploration of the necessary science involved the artistic modeling of concepts and connections. It also involved immersion in an imagined environment familiar to him from childhood, a world where he had first explored his passion for astronomy, time, and space and for wondering what it would be like to experience the core of the sun. In the year spent developing his concept paper on fractal reactors, he

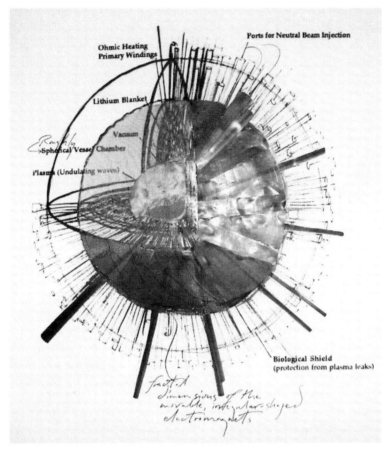

Fig. 9.5. Todd Siler, *Fractal Reactor: Visual Supposition and Premise for Re-Creating the Sun*, 2006. One of many drawings and models visualizing Siler's concept of a nuclear fusion energy device based on nature's fractal geometry and the dynamics of stars.

used this worldplay in "a strategic way" to envision and crystallize his initial insight. Subsequently, he presented his fractal reactor project to international gatherings of physicists and published three papers in the *Proceedings* of the Symposium on Current Trends in International Fusion Research (See figure 9.5.).

As exemplar, Siler epitomizes all that is salient in the link between childhood worldplay and mature worldplay polymathy. The connections he has drawn between early imagination and mature creativity may be traced in enduring content and interest, as with Benford; in craft apprenticeship or disciplinary technique, as with Tolkien; in speculative strategies and experimental inquiry, as with Lem or Morris. In addition, continued worldplay has helped Siler retain the childlike mind of the beginner or, as he has put it, the "'expert novice' (someone who learns to suspend what they know in order to discover what they don't know)."

Worldplay has also helped him develop the multiple and correlative fields of interest and practice typical of the creative polymath. Siler is a visual artist, one exhibited in museums around the world; he is also an author, an educator, an inventor, and a scientist. Moreover, he has been all these things at once, as recognized by his receipt in 2011 of the Leonardo da Vinci World Award of Arts. His consulting business has not been separate from his pursuit of the fractal reactor, nor are these interests tangential to his writing or his work in the fine arts.

These are not "disconnected, disassociated hobb[ies]," he has said, but "[o]ne integrated thing. I never say to myself, today I'm going to think as a visual artist, but tomorrow I'm going to act as a research scientist . . . I don't work like that. I see myself as just one tiny wavicle that's part of a beam of white light before it hits the prism of life."

The distinctions many of us draw between the expert work of vocation and the novice pursuit of avocation dissolve for Siler—and in much the same way that the two separate, yet interlocking, columns in his *Encoded Monolith* form a third virtual reality. Siler chose to safeguard in that sculpture many of the exploratory materials that went into the conceptualizing of his *Thought Assemblies*, his imaginary "cerebreactors," and *Breaking the Mind Barrier*. Significantly enough, he also enclosed his early *bag novel*. Making the *Monolith,* he observed in an interview, "was really a way to take the abundance of imagination and experiment and have a repository, a place where it all comes back to."

The imaginary worlds of childhood, the possible worlds of maturity, and the (a)-vocational polymathy sustaining and sustained by both—all take on equivalent roles within the same network of enterprise. The *Encoded Monolith* is Siler's enterprise made tangible, his artscience in embodied form. It is also a metaphor for the mind and its creative capabilities. Unless we fully open drawers and search deep within, the sculpture tells us, we cannot fully know ourselves, the universe, or, indeed, the benefits we derive from the avocation-vocation of polymathic worldplay.

SYNERGIES: WORLDPLAY AND POLYMATHY

Our perusal of an imaginary discovery cabinet in an imaginary museum of imaginary worlds began with a question, or rather, two: How is creative polymathy possible? What are the synergies between that polymathy and worldplay? Tolkien and Morris, two explorers of the human condition separated as much by philosophical purpose as by disciplinary endeavor, walk hand-in-hand with Benford, Lem, Siler, and others as inventors of plausibly imagined asterisk-worlds. Their secret vice—or simply, their secret—is that avocational creativity stokes vocational creativity and vice versa.

In the most effective networks of personal enterprise, avocation and vocation fertilize one another by combining ideas, techniques, and purposes across disciplinary boundaries. When these (a)vocational combinations produce unexpected explosions of transdisciplinary likeness and analogy, the result may reverberate, as the poet and mathematician Jacob Bronowski once suggested, in public ways. Avocations suddenly gain professional traction; vocations suddenly regain the open horizons of childlike wonder and exploration.

Playfully, we might ask what comes first in this creative combustion, the worldplay or the polymathy. Every individual profiled in these pages takes a slightly different path from childhood play to youthful passions to mature polymathy and the strategies that make that polymathy work. Yet, on the whole, it is the worldplay that provides the nexus supporting polymathic breadth of interest and promoting synthesis of avocation and vocation. The imaginative invention of a parallel place, followed by exploration of its many aspects, is what drives and sustains the polymathy.

This does not mean that all polymaths have worldplay humming in the background, or that all inventors of imaginary worlds become (a)vocational polymaths. Nor does it mean that all polymaths or all world-building individuals make publicly creative contributions to society. But certain conjectures are possible:

First, when worldplay and polymathy *do* converge, the *potential* for significant creative achievement heightens. The more polymathic the invention of an alternate world—that is to say, the more diverse the fields of knowledge, of craft and meta-craft concern that stimulate the imagination—the greater the chance of truly chimeric combination and novel contribution. And the more rigorous the creative strategy—think here of the drive to construct logically consistent and plausible scenarios that often attends worldplay—the more likely the novel contribution will also be effective in the real world.

Second, this pattern holds no matter what unexpected combination of knowledge and craft an individual may link into his or her integrated network of enterprise, no matter how possible or improbable, fictional or nonfictional the world they envision. Tolkien's Middle-earth is as trim as Benford's Galactic Center or the scientific ideas that support it, Morris's biomorph paintings as valid as Lem's futurological speculations.

By the same token, Siler's idea for a new kind of nuclear fusion reactor has as much catalytic potential as the art that explores and expresses his vision of mind in brain. Should the fractal reactor never make the leap from theoretical possibility to experimental reality, the concept yet serves physicists and others as a probe and a prod. And the artwork relevant to that scientific foray finds exhibit space at places like the National Science Foundation, educating even as it stimulates the senses.

A third and final conjecture is this: as a viable creative strategy, (a)vocational polymathy is more commonly, though privately, employed and more commonly productive than we yet know. Estimations that somewhere around 19 percent of artistic creators demonstrate polymathic achievement, largely in related fields, does not take into account scientists or social scientists or their (a)vocational accomplishments.

Nor does it take into account secret hobbies and unnoticed networks of enterprise. Despite professional compartmentalization, however, ideas, techniques, analyses, and intuitions can and do permeate within the mind—as in the third, interlocked column of Siler's *Monolith*. At times a secondary vocation proves more effectively novel in its impact than the primary vocation (certainly true for Tolkien), at times the reverse (considering the continuing influence of *The Naked Ape*, arguably the case for Morris). Worldplay can play a vital role in that disciplinary interpenetration and fusion.

Ultimately, worldplay as (a)vocational polymathy can prime the pump of innovative exploration and achievement. In Siler's words, "worldplay is not only central to

. . . creative syntheses; it often catalyzes them . . . [preparing] the mind for discovery through personally playful and purposeful acts of creative inquiry." Somewhat in the same vein, Tolkien once called for society to recognize the private invention of imaginary worlds as a "New Art, or a New Game" that might command gallery space in some future museum.

Until that day comes, we can envision our own imaginary museum of worldplay and then go one real step further. Turning to the fourth and final part of this book, we can ask whether the "New Game" of worldplay has a place in education as well as in the home. Can this integrated approach to work and play, to learning and discovering, energize formal and informal schooling of the creative imagination? In search of answers, we'll leave our imaginary museum behind and enter discovery rooms of another sort—classrooms.

Part IV

SOWING THE SEEDS OF WORLDPLAY

Chapter Ten

Imaginary World Invention Goes to School: An Argument for Playful Learning

Let my playing be my learning, and my learning be my playing.

—Johan Huizinga, historian

PROJECT NOTES: EDUCATING FOR CREATIVITY

Proposition: Part of the task of schooling is to nurture creativity. This may seem problematic in an educational climate focused on standardized testing, accountability, and the linking of the two. Nevertheless, the need to educate for creativity is more pressing now than ever. Mitchel Resnick, director of the Lifelong Kindergarten research group at the MIT Media Lab, is one of many who argue that healthy, competitive economies depend on innovation, and innovation depends on creativity.

As Resnick puts it, "[I]n today's rapidly changing world, people must continually come up with creative solutions to unexpected problems. Success is based not only on what you know or how much you know, but on your ability to think and act creatively." In short, we no longer live in an "Information Age" or a "Knowledge Economy," but in a "Creative Society." And the marketplace generally concurs. In one 2007 survey 99 percent of public school superintendents and 97 percent of American business executives identified creativity as an increasingly important workplace "skill" and schooling as crucial to its development.

To deliver the goods, education must balance two imperatives: the transfer of already constructed knowledge (such as reading, writing, and arithmetic) and the cultivation of capacity to construct new knowledge and solve outstanding problems (among them, poverty, disease, environmental degradation, and ways of being in virtual realities). Certain pedagogical trends already locate creative training in playful learning, arts-integrated instruction, and game-based modeling. The questions posed here are these: Should we add imaginary world invention to the toolbox? Can we harness the worldplay strategy to group education in creative imagination?

Deborah Meier and other individuals at work in the elementary and middle grade classroom, now and in the near past, suggest that the case can and must be made.

157

DEBORAH MEIER AND THE
CASE FOR CLASSROOM MAKE-BELIEVE

Deborah Meier, teacher, principal, learning theorist, and advocate for educational reform, has proven herself master of a special craft—she makes schools from scratch. Beginning as a kindergarten and Head Start teacher in Chicago, and moving on to Philadelphia and New York City, she wondered what were the essential ingredients for excellence in public education. In the 1970s, as founder and teacher-director of the Central Park East (CPE) elementary schools in Harlem, she grasped the opportunity to try out some new and innovative ideas in one of the poorest neighborhoods of New York.

Within a decade, evidence suggested that these ideas worked. By 1985 CPE's elementary graduates went on to finish high school at an elevated rate of 85 percent, as opposed to the citywide rate of 50 percent. Moreover, two-thirds of CPE students—an unprecedented number—were going on to college. Energized, Meier founded Central Park East Secondary School. Within six years, that high school was graduating 95 percent of its students; 90 percent were college bound.

Considered "one of the more original thinkers in American education," Meier had clearly brewed up something special. Success propelled her from the CPE schools to the organization of a network of likeminded schools, to the successful reform of two failing high schools, to advisory and research roles in academic and policy institutions, and back again to the hands-on launch of Mission Hill, a K–8 pilot school in one of the poorest neighborhoods of Boston.

There as elsewhere, she gave voice to a philosophy of teaching and learning that places the child in the center of the educational experience. Her schools demonstrated that it was possible, despite the constraints of public education, to buck typical, low expectations for students at the bottom of the ladder. "Each of the four [CPE] schools," she has written, "offers a rich and interesting curriculum full of powerful ideas and experiences aimed at inspiring its students with the desire to know more, a curriculum that sustains students' natural drive to make sense of the world and trusts in their capacity to have an impact upon it."

How did this philosophy actually play out? Classroom practice, as described by Meier and others, indicates that something very like the invention of imaginary worlds had an important role in her schools—and perhaps because she herself was no stranger to worldplay.

As a MacArthur Fellow participant in the Worldplay Project, Meier described her childhood play with an imaginary companion. Her invention had been so convincing, her family at first thought the "friend" was someone they had not yet met. Eventually she kept lists of names and family trees for a secret host of imaginary characters visited in daydreams and self-told stories. Their "ongoing saga," which followed her into adulthood, filled a lot of Meier's free time when she was young. So did play with her brother.

Like many other children, Meier and her brother constructed block cities, tree houses, roadways, and other physical sites. They also plotted train routes on the lawn and rode their bikes from one station to the next. "Sometimes," she revealed in interview, "one of us was the local and one of us was the express . . . we'd play it day after day." In hindsight, she realized a difference in the quality of their attention to the make-believe. "I was much more into peopling that world," she recalled, "and [my brother] was much more involved in very detailed environmentaling [of] it; thinking about how everything would fit together and so forth."

As Meier put it, her brother contributed more of the play *structure* and she, more of the play *story*. Both elements were necessary to the make-believe; both delivered a different meaning to the experience. It came as no surprise, really, that she and her brother continued to build places and spaces in their adult lives: her brother became an architect, focused on physical design, and she a teacher, focused on shaping interpersonal experiences within a very particular physical plant—the public school.

In Meier's case, the adult vocation was very much of a piece with the childhood play. She liked schools because "they are, sort of, private worlds." And the successful design of learning environments—like the successful design of imagined worlds—requires both structure and story. "I love all the things you can invest yourself in," Meier observed. "You can worry about the aesthetics of the school, you can worry about the lunchroom, about the food; . . . you can worry about how the light comes in the windows; you can worry about the curriculum, you can worry about the social life of the children. Within the school is every aspect of human life."

In other words, you can concern yourself with the physical environment and the daily narratives in each classroom, and you can imagine other, better ways of organizing both. The story of healthy growth and development for all children has given Meier deep satisfaction. "I'll [see] two kids skipping down the hall, giggling to each other and think, ah, we've made this little world here where these things are possible."

Among many things possible, Meier has been strongly committed to pretend play in elementary classrooms. "We need to give children enough space to have private and shared imaginary activities and to invent worlds," she said in the project interview, especially when so much of their day is spent within institutional walls. The hitch was, and remains, this: in recent years, educational policy across the United States has been squeezing imaginative engagement out of the school day. Time for play in preschool and kindergarten settings, not to mention elementary grades, has been severely curtailed over the last ten years and more as national efforts to mandate school readiness have pushed academic drill and testing to the fore.

Ignore play readiness, however, and you may well shortchange creative readiness, too. Meier has wondered what might be the effect on imagination when we "[cut] back on the places in which we naturally would have engaged in it, . . . when we change something that we've . . . taken for granted for hundreds of thousands of years." The "pleasure of imaginative play," she wrote in *The Power of Their Ideas* (1995), is not a "luxur[y] . . . suited only to the gifted few . . . [to be] offered after school on a voluntary basis." It is, rather, a necessity for all. Practically, this means protecting recess and time for free play. It also means weaving imaginative pretense into the fabric of classroom work, as teachers set the stage for guided play with curricular topics.

This proves to be a delicate undertaking. Pretend play can be fostered, but not really assigned. On the lookout, Meier has learned "what has to exist to maximize the chances that children will feel they can enter into [make-believe]," whether in the building block area, in arts and crafts activity, or between the pages of a book. Her rules of thumb are three, perhaps four.

First, give more time. The typical twenty minute period may not be enough for full immersion in art or reading or free play. Second, create spaces where kids can feel they are by themselves. Lofts, cubbies, designated areas, and other visual or aural screens offer "an illusion of privacy" that allows safe withdrawal into imagination. Third, support persistence by protecting repeated access to play constructions. The block area may belong to the same few children a week at a time; art projects may be completed after several returns to the same imaginative place. The overall goal, she told me, is to minimize interruptions.

Finally, allow for a range of focus and absorption, something Meier learned with her brother. Given the opportunity to play, children may prefer to make believe alone or in shared collaboration. They may choose to invent narratives or focus on the construction of other times and places. They may enter an imagined world a little or a lot, part way or full bore. Whether any one child prefers storytelling or system modeling— and whether and how that experience matters—depends upon individual temperament and proclivity. Classroom play is like a sandbox. Keep it ready and the children will come, each to their own patch, each pursuing different interests and goals. Put another way, classroom make-believe can be a pedagogical instrument of multiple entry points and multiple outcomes.

A BRIEF HISTORY OF CLASSROOM WORLDPLAY

From the late 1960s through the 1990s, Fred Rogers, writer, producer, and host of *Mister Rogers' Neighborhood*, invited his audience—many of whom were sitting in preschools and daycares across the country—to come with him to "The Neighborhood of Make-Believe." In the early 1990s the educator David Sobel championed the collaborative building of forts and special places in school settings. In 2000 and 2004, the U.S. government encouraged children, teenagers, and young adults to imagine viable space stations and planetary outposts on Mars as part of the Mars Millennium Project. Separated by time, place, even purpose, these initiatives nevertheless share in what might be termed "directed" or "guided" worldplay.

By placing diverse programs such as these under the same pedagogical umbrella, their common value can be more precisely understood. As a means of teaching the learnable processes of pretense, imagination, and knowledge construction, classroom initiatives in guided worldplay can purposefully take their place as part of a larger educational strategy to foster creative capacity.

Imaginary Cities/Imagined Civilizations

We begin with that tantalizing glimpse of worldplay which brought me to Deborah Meier's work in the first place. At CPE in Harlem in the late 1980s, third and fourth graders studied their urban environment by walking through their neighborhoods, talking with shopkeepers, mapping streets, modeling buildings, and painting murals.

Back in the classroom, they invented an imaginary city. They drew blueprints and modeled the construction of pretend houses. They made cooking utensils out of clay; they wove fabric.

True, monsters and gods populated the imaginary city, strumming musical instruments more fanciful than factual—but that hardly mattered to the learning. As well as the mythical narratives of make-believe, the children immersed themselves in the very real social and cultural narratives that required spoons for the table, houses to live in, grocery stores, and city maps.

Over the years, this playful blend of fact and fiction has continued to characterize many of the educational activities undertaken at the CPE schools and at Mission Hill in Boston. Frequent student-initiated projects have included building "a perfect island" and designing in group collaboration "a large playground of our desires." Class- or school-wide themes have similarly stimulated individual and group imagination about future, present, and past. Among these, count forays into marine biology, bridges, birds, neighborhoods, Greek mythology, and Shakespearean England.

At Mission Hill, students have also regularly recreated the possible world of King Tut, centered around "a blue, plastic, footwide Nile River" winding through the school hallways. For three months at a time, the whole school (each grade according to its ability) has involved itself in partially constructing, partially imagining a plausible past.

To be sure, not all children experience this imaginary historical world in the same way. When I spoke to her, Meier recalled one little boy making up a story of King Tut by "going back and forth between ancient times and today. . . . The characters in [his story] are real to him, . . . King Tut doesn't believe that he really exists, just as he's not sure whether King Tut really existed." This boy had wholly entered into an imagined world; through the microcosm of story an imaginary history had come to life in his heart and mind.

Meier contrasted his immersion to that of other children whose imaginative activities centered on the production of an ancient Egyptian newspaper. Fully cognizant of the anachronism in their pretense, "they were being playful," she said, "but not really being in Egypt." They engaged in the imaginative exercise as a "craft project," rather than a simulated reality.

Nevertheless, in both cases the play had served a didactic purpose. To posit an imagined world, no matter how thoroughly, is to stimulate critical thinking. As understood and articulated by Meier, this means students learn to question, test, and requestion evidence (how do you know that?); to establish viewpoint (who said it and why?); to puzzle out cause and effect (what led to what?); to engage in hypothesizing (what if or supposing that?); and to contend with relevance (who cares?).

Consider the young boy relating his make-believe encounter with King Tut. Within the space of that small story, he grappled with issues of evidence and viewpoint. How do I really know King Tut once lived? If I take his point of view, is my existence in doubt? Issues involving cause and effect and hypothesizing also pushed the narrative. What if Tut and I could talk to one another? What would happen? Would he believe in me? Finally, the boy confronted the relevance of the imaginative exercise. How does the directionality of time make me feel? What is my place in history? The make-believe bears evidence that important thinking skills were at work.

Improbable Geographies and Other Utopias

In the early 1970s, around the same time that Meier began weaving imaginative engagement into the curricula of her experimental schools in Harlem, the writer Richard Murphy took on a similar task working with sixth and eighth graders in a Manhattan public school, where he had pioneered a writing project organized around the idea of utopias.

He described his experiment in *Imaginary Worlds, Notes on a New Curriculum* (1974). In geography and social studies class, students were assigned the task of drawing maps for imaginary continents. Murphy also asked them to write essays and stories about the landscape, architecture, technology, government, and laws of their imaginary countries, in the hope that each might serve as a small "chapter" or building block for constructing a whole world.

Some projects involved individual story writing; others small group work, such as playwriting; and still others, larger classroom collaborations. In one, children contributed individually written chapters to an imaginary geography of the "Land of Withershins." Quite by accident, they also stumbled on the invention of constructed language, a typical feature of spontaneous worldplay, and in this instance a galvanizing one. The students made up words and wrote up dictionary definitions for blended ideas and things. Eventually, as Murphy had hoped, the relative freedom enjoyed by the children to invent outside and beyond the lesson plan had allowed the learning of geography to be more than an exercise—to become, in his words, a vision.

The arts-infused engagement with imaginary worlds that Murphy envisioned has echoed since in contemporary classrooms. Take, for instance, the children's book *Roxaboxen* (1991), which tells of a close-knit band of children who build a pretend town on a rocky hill strewn with sand, cactus, and discarded crates. Alice McLerran based her story on the childhood play of her mother, Marian Doan, who recorded a five-chapter "History of Roxaboxen" in the summer of 1916 when she was nearly twelve years old. Type the words "Roxaboxen" and "lesson ideas" into an Internet search engine today and you will find links to hundreds of learning activities that use the picture book.

Most of these lessons plans train student attention on specific curricular objectives. The study guide prepared by Magik Theatre of San Antonio, Texas, for instance, firmly ties the book and dramatic production of it to state standards in English language arts and reading, in social studies and science. However, the guide also suggests that teachers push beyond these knowledge basics by involving students in the collaborative construction of their own classroom Roxaboxen.

 The educational challenge posed by such classroom worldplay and the questions it raises may be assessed in terms of Bloom's taxonomy, a well-known pyramid of educational objectives. With regard to curricular content, the Magik Theatre study asks, "Who were the characters in the story?" and "What kinds of adaptations would an animal need to live in a desert?" The point of these questions is to exercise the recall of knowledge and its comprehension.

With regard to the classroom construction of an imaginary town, the guide asks, "How would you carry out your role as policeman or mayor?" "What made building your community easy or difficult?" "What kinds of rules do you think communities need and why?" Interestingly enough, these questions move up on Bloom's taxonomic scale into more complex levels of knowledge application, analysis, and evaluation. The world-building exercise also engages children in the taxonomy's highest level of intellectual behavior—synthesizing or creating a new whole from the disparate parts of acquired knowledge.

Vision Quests

Children reach for that creative synthesis when they enter the imaginative moment and discover something new and nonprescriptive about themselves and society. For this reason, drama specialist and master teacher Stacey Coates has worked hard to provide her students a special entrée into make-believe terrain. During the twenty years she taught at a private school in Washington, D.C., for instance, she integrated dramatic recreation into the literature, history, and science curriculum in a series of mission quests, the successful completion of which required subject knowledge, problem solving and cooperative behavior.

In the fourth grade, for instance, children journeyed into the land of Pompeii, where history, science, and make-believe converged. The children learned about volcanoes and Roman civilization. They also took on a heroic challenge, as Coates put it to me, "to go to the small town that was close to Pompeii—not a real town, but one that was invented by us—in an attempt to warn those people to move before the volcano erupted." To convince these imaginary people to believe them, it was necessary to speak in poetry. "So each group of children made up a poem to explain our purpose."

Too, the children girded their loins with certain tokens granting certain powers: a computer chip accessed any needed data; a geode conferred invisibility; a small toy animal made it possible to speak the language of any living thing. When, finally, both factual and fictional frames were in place, the children pantomimed entry into the imagined past, tiptoed through a valley of wolves, squeezed through chinks in the town wall, begged a wise owl for direction, found the sacred temple, read the Temple Goddess their poems, and convinced the ancient townspeople to flee from danger.

As Coates well understood, to bring fictional or historical events to life in this way is to build a temporary imaginary world within which all concerned—children and adults alike—suspend disbelief. She has always prepared carefully for the believe in make-believe. Hence the powers, the tasks, the mission—all of which ask the students to invest themselves literally and figuratively in the journey.

For this arts-integrated worldplay to work, the teacher must be invested, too. In early adolescence Coates shared a secret language and secret rituals with a best friend. In classroom worldplay she has worked to recapture the "tenderness and sensitivity" of that childhood pretense and commitment to it. "What I recommend to teachers," she told me, "is a great deal of seriousness. . . . A great deal of conviction, a great deal of belief in this imaginary world, so that it can be taken seriously by [the children] as well." Establish an atmosphere of support and respect, Coates argued, and "anything becomes possible in the way of make-believe. And within make-believe, then, anything becomes possible in the way of learning and problem-solving."

Games of Village and Globe

When problem-driven learning is tied to fictional pretense, students integrate "knowing about" with "understanding how." The "Game of Village" demonstrates this in spades. Initially undertaken in the 1970s and 1980s at a summer camp in New Hampshire, Village is presently incorporated into classroom practice at the Prairie Creek Community School, a public charter school in Castle Rock, Minnesota.

Led by Michelle Martin, the teachers of Prairie Creek set aside a month at the end of each year for fourth and fifth graders to construct a miniature world on a 1/24 scale. As the game begins, the children make little dolls, called "peeps." The peeps attend town planning meetings and stake out property in a field adjacent to the school. They—or, rather, their humans—build homes, develop the land, evaluate its worth in peep dollars, work up peep businesses, write proposals for community action, and grow a town government (See figure 10.1.).

Prairie Creek has played Village for many years and no two games have ever been alike. Students have designed democracies as well as socialist monarchies, and contended with flooding rains as well as marauding snails. The teachers play the game as members of a national government, but theirs is a light-handed, guiding role. Like Coates, they make sure the make-believe is respected; they also make sure that the game remains plausible and that emerging problems are solved realistically and materially.

Magic is not allowed in Village, but there *is* plenty of math (all that measuring to scale!), plenty of social studies and economics, and plenty of language arts. Students write peep biographies and peep community proposals. They publish miniature books or manufacture patentable inventions—baby carriers, egg carton furniture, or inflatable beds—and sell them in the marketplace. Some even send their peeps to the local peep university. A Village Fair rings in the game's finale, though for many—students and teachers, alike—the peeps live on, influencing academic interests and aspirations.

Fig. 10.1.   The Game of Village at Prairie Creek School, June 2011. A peep, *left*; a peep house, *right*.

A somewhat similar initiative premiered in Scotland in 2010 for an older set of students. Seven Scottish secondary schools (middle through high school in the United States) engaged in a week-long interactive web drama called *State of Emergency.* Five-minute "bulletins" pulled students deep into escalating conflict in an unidentified, fictional country. True to the name of the sponsoring program, Co-Create, students responded to the imagined events as journalists, aid workers, refugees, and harried civilians.

Experiences varied from school to school. Students engaged in direct conversation with fictional soldiers, politicians, and scientists. They learned how to broadcast news, generate electricity, deliver first aid, raise funds, and cope with a shortage of supplies. As the technologically enhanced make-believe played out, they plunged deep into problem-oriented learning in language and media arts, science, social studies, and economics.

Gaming Imaginary Worlds

Thus far, our exemplars of guided worldplay largely mimic the enacting and documenting activities of spontaneous worldplay and largely fall, too, under the banner of arts-integrated instruction. Additional examples suggest that other elements of worldplay, as harnessed by new technologies, may also be applied to pedagogical purpose.

Counted among these are the classroom computer games in development at the Institute for Learning Technologies (ILT) at Columbia University. Literacy studies suggest that readers who internally visualize "storyworlds" are more proficient at retaining narrative information. Drawing on that work, ILT Director John Black has investigated the role of what he calls "imaginary worlds" in elementary and middle grade science learning—and in the context of computer-aided instruction.

For Black, "imaginary worlds" refers to mental models and speculations about how the real world works. As personal "what-if" conjectures, construed in the privacy of the mind, these imaginary worlds might or might not conform to consensual, public understanding. Working with middle-school students designing possible colonies for the Mars Millennium Project, he demonstrated that student ability to construct an accurate, consensual mental model of physical, biological and social systems could be facilitated with computer-enhanced instruction.

Computer simulations that allowed students to manipulate system factors proved particularly appropriate. Especially in the lower grades, students were most apt to construct durable and accurate understanding when teaching materials included "graphic simulation using direct manipulation animation." In other words, young students learned physics best by controlling computer-animated roller coaster cars and receiving instant feedback on their kinetic energy. Imaginary world construction "seems like a very productive model of education when it can be made to work," Black concluded, especially in computer simulation and gaming formats.

In the laboratory, Black and his ILT team have worked on the computer game-based construction of mental models in a variety of curricular subjects. In REAL Planet, for instance, "students teach an alien how to design an ecological system on a make-believe planet that has environmental conditions similar to that of Earth." Like worldplay itself, the modeling is as fictional as it is factual. Indeed, the game allows users to design imaginary animals, even as they tag those chimeras as herbivores, carnivores, decomposers, and so forth.

Once they set their imaginary world in virtual motion, students learn in real time whether their make-believe ecology adequately accounts for predator-prey relations, food supply, population growth, and other factors relevant to real-world ecology. They reflect on, critique, and revise their understanding based on multiple simulation trials and feedback. The game converges on textbook knowledge and solutions—and imaginary worlds eventually conform to consensual reality.

Game-Based Classrooms

Black's work logically points in two directions, toward computer-aided mental modeling and toward expanded game-based learning. Experimentation in the latter is already under way. In New York City, a pilot program focused on nurturing the social, cognitive, and technological skills developed in game play opened its first demonstration school in 2010.

Using cardboard and tokens as well as computers, students at Quest to Learn (Q2L) Elementary School play already available games designed to facilitate learning in math, science, or language arts. And they participate in the ongoing proto-typing and testing of new educational games developed by their teachers in collaboration with in-house game designers. In the process, Q2L deliberately capitalizes on middle childhood's love of controlled, competitive challenge—and on its fascination with world invention. For Katie Salen, game designer and intellectual architect of this innovative program, building a game in the classroom "is equivalent to building a mini world."

Quite in the manner of Coates's dramatic journeys or the game of Village, Q2L students role-play their way into the ancient past or side-step into other, fictional realities. As denizens of an imaginary city called "Creepytown," for instance, students in Q2L's first year engaged in computer game-like quests to analyze economic crises, build revenue-raising businesses, and advance through multiple levels of grade-appropriate expertise in math and English.

In the school's second year, the same mix of fiction and fact permeated the game playing in teacher Ross Flatt's English and social studies classroom. In "Galactic Mappers" students worked collaboratively to map imaginary continents, pulling "feature cards" to guide them in the elaboration of geographic detail. In a follow-up game, "Inhabitation," students strategized the procurement of various resources necessary to early human settlement. Designed to target specific grade-level skills, these games also made space for "a lot of pretend" that, according to Flatt, created "a need to know" curricular knowledge in order to solve authentic problems for imagined characters and communities.

Building Mental Models in Cyberspace

Other pedagogical tools, such as *Think Like a Genius®* (TLG) software 2.0, take on computer-aided mental modeling in nongame fashion. Developed by artist-psychologist-inventor Todd Siler, met with in chapter 9, the TLG platform provides a 3D visual field and an array of objects, connectors, backdrops, and landscapes with which to build imaginary models or "worldz"™. It is particularly suited to symbolic modeling or what Siler calls "metaphorming," exploring connections between unrelated things for new and effective knowledge. In Denver classrooms, where TLG has been prototyped, middle-school students have related newly acquired biological information to something else they understand more fully.

By way of example, one such student model layers the basic constituents of a human cell onto a schematic map of the United States. A fence along the United States-Mexico border symbolizes the cell membrane; a waste treatment plant stands in for the lysosome. Suddenly, the cell becomes a socioeconomic community with familiar features. And the body politic becomes a living organism that must take in nutrients, support growth, and excrete waste. Understanding of both parts of the modeled metaphor just as suddenly expands. By teasing out the implications embodied in this and other cyber "worldz," Siler has argued, mental modeling can "tap the collective creativity and ingenuity of kids" in the modern classroom.

WORLDPLAY AND EMBODIED EDUCATION

By now it must seem we've come a long way from spontaneous worldplay. And we have. If Quest to Learn classrooms take game play to a level of consistent application not seen in isolated arts-integrated explorations of imaginary worlds, both approaches differ from private, self-choice play in countries of the mind—as well they might. When Siler refers to "worldz" and Black to "imaginary worlds" they focus our attention, not on play worlds *per se,* but on the mental or symbolic constructs that contribute functionally to mental model building and the educational transfer of knowledge.

In the process, both men make a pedagogical argument that applies to all forms of imaginary world invention, in the classroom and out. Siler has attributed the educational benefits of symbolic model building to its concrete, nonlinguistic representations—physical images, diagrams, and other constructed forms. Black has argued that student-input simulations such as REAL Planet involve a "grounded/embodied cognition approach to mental models" that demonstrably involves students in "a deeper level of understanding" of complex and dynamic systems.

Educational research makes sense of these claims. In one assessment of best classroom practices, nonlinguistic representation of information placed among the top five strategies affecting student achievement. Classroom transfer of knowledge typically tends toward the spoken and written word. However, when teachers help students generate nonlinguistic imagery that complements and supports knowledge, learning is enhanced.

Nonlinguistic representations may include graphic organizers, such as time lines, idea clusters, and diagrams of structure or process; they also encompass picture drawing, mental imaging, and whole body activities such as role-playing or re-enacting complex physical processes. Some of these representations may be found in game-based worldplay such as REAL Planet or Inhabitation; others form part and parcel of the enacted worldplay to be found in Creepytown, *State of Emergency*, or Withershins.

Cognitive theory offers us an explanation for the pedagogical effectiveness of non-linguistic imagery—and by extension, of enacted play. Neuroscientists postulate that the brain stores knowledge in two ways: in semantic, linguistic form and in simulated imagery and action—that is to say, in the perceptual, motor, and emotional states of what they call embodied cognition. Using brain imaging studies, they have begun to confirm that we "know" about things in terms of recalled sights, sounds, smells, tastes, motor patterns, and other bodily sensations and feelings.

Thinking about roosters and hens, for instance, we activate visual processing areas; thinking about knives and forks, we activate motor areas; thinking about scrambled eggs, we activate gustatory areas. What's more, the very words we use to express our embodied thinking provide further evidence of a brain-based link between the concrete perceptions of the body and the abstract conceptions of mind. We materialize the immaterial idea of communication, for example, when we say, "Wrap your head around this."

The same embodied, metaphoric processes apply to worldplay, where the plausible reenactments and imaginary models of pretense link personal experience to received knowledge. When students playact a vision quest to ancient Pompeii, hold a town meeting in the Village, or model a bank bust in Creepytown, they explore and store tacit understanding of ethical values, governmental procedures, and economic principles in that physical activity. And that same embodied storage makes understanding amendable to further reflection, elaboration, and extension. Indeed, not only does the imaginary world capture increasingly complex ideas about the real world, we might also say it serves to represent the way we think, especially when we think imaginatively and creatively.

Consider that the nonverbal, sensory cognition probed by neuroscientists and others depends on the purposeful articulation of imaginative skills or tools. Study of creative individuals and their thinking processes suggests that at least thirteen tools form a common core across the arts and sciences: observing, imaging, abstracting, recognizing and forming patterns, empathizing, body thinking, dimensional thinking, playing, modeling, transforming, and synthesizing. Generally implementing them all, worldplay particularly exercises a handful.

Inventing paracosms, children learn to image purposefully by internalizing the sensory simulation of imaginary place; they learn to empathize by personalizing stones or experiencing the lives of imaginary people; they learn to model by designing and implementing their own stories, newspapers, train systems, towns, and countries. They learn to recognize and form consistent, plausible patterns of play knowledge and narrative. They learn to synthesize all that they know and feel into one grand design. Moreover, teacher awareness of how these tools function in the classroom can lead to assessment of imaginative skill as well as knowledge acquisition.

Because worldplay in the classroom can involve multiple documentations of imaginary scenarios, children also explore their multiple "intelligences." Classrooms have traditionally privileged linguistic and logical-mathematical competencies, but there are additional and equally important musical, visual-spatial, bodily-kinesthetic, and personal competencies. These "intelligences" may be understood in terms of innate sensitivities as well as disciplinary skills. Classroom exposure to multiple representations of knowledge enables each child to discover cognitive talents (say, for musical or visual thinking) and to use those talents to reinforce cognitive weaknesses (bodily-kinesthetic or mathematical thinking, perhaps).

This exposure and this mutual reinforcement is exactly what worldplay provides. Classroom enactments like *State of Emergency* and time travel to Pompeii exercise verbal, kinesthetic, and personal skills; the game of Village prompts students to explore the full measure of mathematical, verbal, visual-spatial, bodily kinesthetic, and personal "intelligences"—and in combinations that suit and challenge the individual child.

Inventing an imaginary utopian world, a historically plausible world, or mental models of a logically possible ecology, students learn by integrating thinking tools and disciplinary competencies into open-ended inquiry. And they do so according to the problematic nature and needs of the imaginative endeavor. Some problems may deal with the make-believe dimensions of play itself: What kinds of creatures inhabit my alien planet? How do I get to my imaginary island? How will my peep make a living? Other problems may deal with the plausibility of applied knowledge: How does my alien ecology operate? What laws work best for my Roxaboxen town? How do I persuade my peers when to use the cloak of invisibility?

In addition, students confront problems of craft and expressive skill: How do I design my symbolic model visually? In two or three dimensions? How do I describe my imaginary island? Does a story best capture that parallel reality, or would I rather draw maps or pictures, craft its pottery, or design and construct its imaginary machines? Posing these and other problems, students naturally turn to relevant imaginative skills, relevant craft skills, and relevant subject knowledge to find solutions. They take a minds-on, hands-on approach to learning.

The imaginative challenge that works in elementary and middle school can also work in college classrooms and other adult-learning environments. Teachers, artists, and other participants in Worldplay Project workshops find themselves thinking and constructing in new or unusual ways—and having fun, too (See figure 10.2.). One of these, the art educator Ren Hullender, went on to develop a week-long unit on worldplay for childhood education majors at Central Michigan University.

At the beginning of the semester, Hullender guided his students into the open-ended invention of imaginary worlds, which they documented by drawing, writing, and constructing handmade books (See figure 10.3.). To Hullender's surprise many of the students, on their own initiative, integrated subsequent assignments within the worldplay. Over the semester-long course, classroom affect went up and involvement soared. If many of his teachers in training had been initially hesitant to engage in make-believe (and they were), by term's end they had recaptured something of Coates's "tenderness and sensitivity," not only for make-believe in classroom learning, but also for their own imaginations at play.

Fig. 10.2.   Martian Ent Doll. Adult worldplay workshop artifact, May 2011.

Fig. 10.3. Time Line for the Imaginary World of Coexistence. College classroom handmade book, fall 2010. "July 2nd, 1937. Amelia Earhart crashes her plane during her around the world flight and . . . inhabitant creatures utilize her brain and face to create the first mixed fish/person creatures of the abyss."

CREATIVE SCHOOLING: CAVEATS AND CALLINGS

The educational punch of worldplay may be summarized thus: the richer the sensory experiences involved, the more varied the manner of their expression, and the more personal and playful the connections linking new information to prior knowledge, the more long-term, effective learning takes place. As promising as worldplay may be for the classroom pedagogy in general, however, when it comes to reaping creative benefits, certain caveats must be kept in mind.

Guided worldplay that adheres too closely to curricular agendas and correct answers or that allows students too little imaginative influence on the parameters of the play may help impart knowledge, but it is less clear that it will help impart creative training. Pedagogical tools like REAL Planet may be less serviceable, in this respect, than Siler's symbolic modeling, and symbolic modeling alone less effective than multiply documented, lightly guided approaches such as Village or other world-building activities in arts-integrated classrooms.

That said, the classroom invention of imaginary worlds looks to be a powerful means of teaching for creative thinking and doing—*looks to be*, because for most children in most classrooms across the United States, worldplay is nothing more than a pipe dream. Elementary and middle schools that abandon recess, the arts, and other forms of playful learning—as many of them have done—retain no age-appropriate "locale" for the exercise of imaginative skills or creative vision. Worldplay, for all its promise as an educational tool especially suited to middle childhood years, remains noticeably absent from most contemporary classrooms.

One can impute this state of affairs to the cross tides of educational policy, which falsely pit learning against playing. One can blame the difficulties researchers have translating experience-based endorsements such as those provided by Deborah Meier, Richard Murphy, Stacey Coates, Michelle Martin, John Black, Todd Siler, and others into evidence-based studies of efficacious instruction. Certainly, as an organizing principle in educating for creativity, worldplay has yet to be implemented or tested in any systematic way. Nevertheless, the qualitative, experienced-based data harvested from creative exemplars and successful learning environments profiled in these pages tell us to give worldplay a try. It is time to envision a new paracosm and to advocate a new paradigm for creative schooling.

First, let's call loud and clear for playful learning in formal education. We can insist on a reasonable measure of make-believe in the classroom, not simply in kindergarten and the earliest elementary grades, but throughout middle childhood—and beyond. This means time for free play and recess; it also means judicious amounts of playful schoolwork and, yes, guided worldplay.

Second, let's resuscitate and protect pretend play informally, outside of school and at home. Like Deborah Meier, we can make little worlds for our children and youth where make-believe is possible for as long as possible. We can support the free play that each individual makes to their own order.

Finally, let's encourage the young to invent their own kind of private worldplay according to their needs and desires. Now and in the future, that worldplay may look much the same as it did for a Charlotte Brontë or a Claes Oldenburg. It may look different. Given the recent explosion in computer technologies, chances are good it *will* look different. How do we evaluate the creative benefit for children in up-and-coming entertainments? How do we support old-fashioned play in a new-fangled age? A look at the child's lived experience with computer games and other virtual realities in the next chapter—and review of nurturing tactics at the parent's disposal in the chapter after that—provide some answers.

Chapter Eleven

Worldplay the Computer Way: Children and Youth Reveal Their Lived Experience

Brooding, she changed the pool into the sea, and made the minnows into sharks and whales, and cast vast clouds over this tiny world by holding her hand against the sun, and so brought darkness and desolation, like God himself, to millions of ignorant and innocent creatures, and then took her hand away suddenly and let the sun stream down.

—Virginia Woolf, writer

IMAGINARY WORLDS AT THE CROSSROADS

With a rapid clicking of the mouse, fifteen-year-old Nate demonstrated how he played with simulated characters in an imagined world made real right there on his computer screen. It was a fun game, he assured me, and whenever he got bored with it, he'd make up a new Sim™ family with new personalities and new life wishes and set their daily lives in motion. Nothing was quite the same with a new family; nothing was all that different. He knew by now how to finesse the game.

"Do you ever feel like making an imaginary world of your own," I asked him. "Maybe write stories about your imagined people?" Nate pulled himself away from the screen. "Not really," he said. "But that's just because I have no real ability to create stuff like that. I know enough to get around, but no real drive to try to create a game. . . . And I don't really feel the need to write stories, especially since I could just probably have my Sim characters do it [act out the narrative] anyway."

For days after our discussion Nate's words rattled around in my head. Here he was, a mid-teen, playing with virtual dolls in a virtual space and place. Score one point for all the research indicating that early pretend play doesn't disappear, it just internalizes. Score another point for the new computer technologies that bring that play back out into the light. Yet I couldn't help wondering what impact computer game play might be having on Nate's imaginative and creative development. Were computer games and sims sounding the death knell of spontaneous, self-fashioned worldplay in

173

childhood? Or were they, rather, a new form of imaginary world invention? One that was even now pulling children and youth into complex make-believe?

Something's happening here. With the introduction of fantasy board and card games in the 1970s, with the advent of personal computers and simulation games in the early 1980s, with the proliferation of online sims in the early 2000s, play in imaginary worlds has gone increasingly commercial and readymade. Children no longer have to make up worlds from their own pastiche of influences, interests, and experiences. They—or their parents—have only to choose from the store shelf among hundreds if not thousands of card, board, and above all, computer games that structure play within fictional realms. They have only to go online to navigate make-believe places and participate in virtual realities.

Simply put, children have the option as never before to *consume* play designed for them by adults, rather than *create* their own. And they do so, in large numbers.

Indeed, in the same time it took for my children to wend their way from kindergarten to college and in roughly the same years—from 1980 to 2000—the enticements of computers and computer play have gone from nonexistent to ever present. In the last two decades children's overall access to computers at home has more than doubled, from 32 percent in 1993 to 75 percent in 2003. School access has likewise increased, from 61 percent to 83 percent in the same time span. Current estimates place computer technology in the hands of 90 percent of American children at home or at school.

This explosion in computer access has been more than matched by an explosion in computer play. Nearly half of all Americans play computer games and sims—most of them under the age of 35 or 40, a great many of them children. As of 2008 99 percent of boys age 12 to 17 played computer games, as did 97 percent of girls.

Not only do most teens play computer simulation games, they do so, as a 2008 Pew report puts it, "with relative frequency and duration." Nearly one-third of teen gamers play every day, an hour or two at a time. Even very young children get into the act. A 2011 report found 12 percent of children ages two to four and 24 percent of children ages five to eight also used computers for some form of play *every day*. No wonder, then, that one preeminent scholar calls computer media and games "the major cultural activity" of young people today, "the way movies and literature were for earlier generations."

Such a sea change in social behavior inevitably causes controversy. Sure enough, we find ourselves in the throes of debate about the influences electronic media may have on the well-being of children. There is, in fact, a vast literature on the psychological and physical impact of computer play. What concerns us here is that part addressing imaginative and creative development.

For those who fear that the effects are largely negative, electronic media may be "altering the very structure of how children think and imagine" and affecting "their potential for creative thought" by promoting a derivative and imitative imagination in individuals. For those who view the effects in a more positive light, computer simulation play involves trial-by-error learning and a tinkering mentality that fuels bottom-up, collaborative innovation by the many.

No doubt about it, we are in the midst of a great experiment. Will new technologies of virtual play threaten to degrade the individual imagination—or "produce a new kind of creativity?" Come down hard on one side or the other and chances are you buy Marshall McLuhan's notion that the media is the message. Yet for scholars of play it is the attitude and the derived value—not the material medium—that determines what play is and what one gets out of it, creative or not. The means for engaging in imaginary worlds is less salient than the child's *experience* of the activity.

With that proviso in mind, we'll turn to the worldplay possibilities in computer games—*and from the child's point of view*.

EXPLORING COMPUTER SIMULATED WORLDS

To focus on the lived experience of play is to privilege how children behave and what they say during the activity itself, or shortly thereafter. This means probing *in situ* for basic phenomena of the make-believe—for sensory impressions, bodily feelings, moods, and so forth. It means striving to understand the child's perceptions of space, body, time, and human relationship during play and borrowing their subjective responses to describe their experience. What is it *really like* to play in an imaginary place?

Based on the many recollections of self-fashioned worldplay already explored in this book, we might say that the child inventor of a make-believe world experiences his or her imaginative construct physically, as a felt projection of the found and constructed places typical of middle-childhood play. There is a kind of gravity in that space that holds the child securely and engenders feelings of safety and wholeness.

Because the play is private, and often secret, self-consciousness dissolves; the body is absorbed into the imaginative moment and is not separate from it. Time beats to the rhythms of inner attention. The demands of the physical environment and of other people, so long as they remain non-urgent, drop from conscious awareness. To the outside observer, the child seems lost in another world. The child, however, *finds* him or herself in another world. Within the narrative of the play, he or she experiences agency, power, and control as an independent and, often, creative being.

Do children who explore imaginary worlds in computer games and simulations share in the same lived experience? What *does* it feel like to dwell in a computer game? Like a book, like a movie, like an invented world of one's own? I asked these and other questions of eight young people chosen for interviews because they told me their favorite computer games made them feel like they were exploring—or creating—an imaginary world (see table 11.1).

My informants (names changed to protect their privacy) fell into two age groups: four children between six and twelve years old and four teens between fifteen and seventeen. All the children were boys; half the teens were girls. The games these youths elected to tell me about covered a wide range of types. Additionally, all the games were played in the home. All were played alone or online, though they were hardly private, but frequently discussed with family and friends. Finally, in the act of playing, all the young people, from the youngest to the oldest, were drawn deep into pretense.

Table 11.1. Simulated Worldplay: Genres, games, gamers. + Genres are listed in order of popularity among children and teens, as reported by the Pew Internet and American Life Project in 2008. Only game types discussed in these pages are included here.

GENRES+	GAMES	GAMERS
Adventure	Spore*	Aaron, 9
Strategy	Age of Mythology	Ian, 12
Simulation	Sims 3: World Adventures	Nate, 15
	Jurassic Park: Operation Genesis	Lee, 9
First Person Shooter	Halo	Thom, 17
	Call of Duty	Ian, 12
Role-Playing Game	Virtual Hogwarts	Molly, 17
	RunEscape	Andrew, 6
	Dragon Age	Thom, 17
Virtual Worlds	Second Life	Ellie, 17

* Marketed as a multi-genre game, *Spore* is also considered a strategy game and an RPG.

The Lived Experience of Simulated Worlds

During his interview, nine-year-old Lee began by sitting next to me on the sofa, across the room from a large television that screened his Xbox game, Jurassic Park™. A would-be paleontologist, he patiently explained that the game supposes the rebreeding of dinosaurs from genetic material found in their petrified bones. When and where or how this takes place, he was not quite sure.

"The real part [of the game] is dinosaurs," he told me, "and they make the not-real part, too." As he became more involved in the game than the interview, he stood up with the controls and inched closer to the television. Within short order he had moved right up to the screen, withdrawing from my questions and closing the distance between himself and his dinosaur zoo.

As a hallmark of play, this ready absorption signals the child's experience of what some have called the "vivid present" and others, immersion or "presence." A heightened awareness is focused on the engaging moment, dispelling all other conscious streams of thought. During their interviews, nine-year-old Aaron and six-year-old Andrew also lost track of me and the immediate environment, just like Lee.

Real time gave way, for these children, to a malleable inner time that compressed or expanded according to the needs of the pretense. Fifteen-year-old Nate, at play with his Sim family, learned to manipulate his game in order to speed through the tedium of daily affairs or to draw out moments of life-altering choice. Aaron, at play with made-up creatures in the game of Spore™, compressed eons of pretend evolution into a few hours of actual play.

Needless to say, the absorbed child also experiences a game space. When six-year-old Andrew played the online role-playing fantasy game RuneScape™ in my presence, he appeared to be navigating a constantly shifting landscape of villages and fields, of manmade and natural features. At some point, however, he clicked on a little map that showed his position from a zoom-out perspective. What was visible onscreen fit like a moving puzzle piece into a larger and stable territory.

How big was this world? I asked. "Pretty big," Andrew told me. "It doesn't look that big, but it's huge." The RuneScape world existed well beyond what Andrew saw onscreen at any one time. Yet, insofar as he remembered where he had been before, insofar as he knew where he planned to go in the future, the virtual world had imagined dimension in his mind beyond its moment-to-moment simulation.

Older children and teens articulated this ability to imagine the game environment beyond the screen as "being there." The primary cues, for twelve-year-old Ian, were visual and auditory. "With the computer," he told me, "you take everything in with your eyes and ears." The trick was to interpret these cues within an imagined context—in his case the first person shooter game Call of Duty™. For seventeen-year-old Thom, engaged in the first-person shooter game Halo™, this meant translating the two-dimensional onscreen visuals into a three-dimensional space in his mind. "When I'm in there I feel like the aliens are all around me, it's like I'm mentally in there."

Like a basketball player who knows what's happening on the entire court, Thom experienced a heightened awareness that enabled him "to know every part of the map," whether in the visual field or not. Seventeen-year-old Molly was similarly aware of the classroom she attended on Virtual Hogwarts™, though in her case, the triggers were verbal rather than visual cues. On a good day, she said, "I kind of feel I'm there. . . . I'll see what's going on around me."

Being there meant feeling involved. All my informants played their games because it was "fun" to do so—and for the most part their emotions were positive. Among the three youngest, I witnessed happy faces, cries of delight, ebullient chatter directed at play characters, and bodily expressions of excitement. Game playing, Andrew told me, made him "feel extremely good." In addition to "fun," the older children and teens also talked about "challenge"—and their emotional responses, as reported to me, were more obviously mixed.

This was especially so for the two boys playing first-person shooter games. "You get so emotional about certain things," Thom told me. Miss a shot and you feel "just angry;" but to play well you have "to cool yourself down. . . . So it's very trying." For Ian, fighting zombies felt so real it "actually triggers something in your mind that makes you want to run instead of keep going, but then you realize it's a video game . . . and knowing you can't die is actually the factor that keeps you going." Conquering fear in the simulated world by fighting "something you're normally scared of" gave him "a sense of security," and feelings of "pride and power."

Emotional engagement naturally involved identifying with the projected self or with other beings that populate the imagined and imaginary landscape. Ian's strong emotions had much to do with his subjective, "close" identification during play with his avatar. "Well, you are one [a soldier]. You're there. You also have a name. My name is SPD."

Molly also identified strongly with her character on Virtual Hogwarts, not as a projection of herself, however, but as a person for whom she spoke. "You create a character, give them a biography and a background and then you role-play certain situations, how they would react to certain things." This more objective, "far" identification seemed to be the norm among my informants. Andrew placed ten or more "persons" in the simulated RuneScape world, not as "an avatar that much" but as dolls manipulated and identified with during bouts of play.

Close or far projection of self also included attention to other beings—to social interaction and relationship. Molly not only imagined her character, but she also visualized how other characters looked or moved. "When I'm writing I'm picturing how she would react to facial expressions or bodily reactions of what's going on in the classroom."

At times, Molly also heard these characters speak the dialogue that she and other users typed onscreen. "It's not like that's what's dominating my hearing," she told me, "but I can kind of hear in the back of my mind a little voice saying what the other person has said." Other senses also get involved in the mental experience of people and things. Once Molly even tasted the magic potion she described online as "purple mud."

The imagined experience of objects and others in an imaginary environment had a second dimension as well for Molly. Beyond or outside of the verbal simulation of a Hogwarts classroom, she projected other users at computer consoles, describing actions and speaking for their characters. Such interaction appealed to Molly, not only as a means of crafting shared make-believe and testing writing skill, but as a venue for getting "to know people better." Thom certainly experienced real relationships with other users, relationships that heavily influenced the game simulation. "You're relating to three other people; you need to understand them, talk to them," he told me, in order to work together as a team in the simulated environment.

Awareness of other participants in the game world did not always translate into experienced relationship, however. Molly and seventeen-year-old Ellie, tooling around the online virtual world of Second Life™, both expressed disappointment that they had not, in fact, made any friends in their simulation forays online. In contrast, the much younger Andrew gave no thought to other participants in the RuneScape world, though he understood well enough that other users moved characters around just like he did. In his case, the make-believe simulation placed a veil over real interaction with others in cyberspace.

The same veil obscured relationship with game designers and producers. When I asked who made or created the game experience, most children and teens vaguely described some kind of collaborative effort on the part of themselves, co-playing peers, other users (if online), and those individuals who had invented the setting, the quest, the graphics, and so forth. Few, however, grasped the situation as clearly as Aaron. "The creators of the whole Spore game are Maxus and EA," the nine-year-old told me. (Maxus, an American company, develops video games, and is a subsidiary of Electronic Arts [EA], a major marketer of video games.) "The only thing I create is my stuff," though "technically," he realized, he was simply putting together parts that Maxus makes.

When at play in single-user games, the older Thom similarly understood himself to be in direct competition with the game designers (rather than other players) because it was the designers who "set up the whole game," the opponents and the obstacles that had to be overcome to reach the end goal. "Obviously, I don't consciously think about beating the game designers," he told me, "but I think about getting to the next level, what's the challenge here, what should I do."

Thom understood game structure well. He took pride in dealing with obstacles almost reflexively. Game play at its best for him—as for Ian, Aaron, and Andrew—involved an exhilarating match between challenge and skill. If game demands far outstripped player performance, the experience turned sour, turned frustrating, they told me. If player performance outstripped demands, the experience turned boring. Novelty and familiarity in balance, however, clearly pulled the player into flow—that positive state of effortlessly focused consciousness that often accompanies activities such as sports, hobbies, or vocational tasks enjoyed for their own sake.

For children and teens at play with computer games a clear understanding of the goals, immediate feedback, and feelings of competency set the stage for focused attention and intense concentration. In flow, their awareness of outer time, outer place, and outer self disappeared into inner occupation with imagined experience in a simulated world.

Digging Deeper: Agency in Game Play

No doubt about it, game play in cyberspace is engaging play. Children of all ages explore fascinations, challenge competencies, and hone knowhow in a hybrid of externally simulated and internally imaged experience encountered as if real—and socially shared on those terms. What concerns us here is whether the lived experience of computer-simulated worlds is enough like the lived experience of self-fashioned worldplay to substitute for it.

The free-play invention of imaginary worlds involves the child or teen in making and, often enough, creating. Are similar opportunities to flex imaginative and creative muscle available in play with video games and sims? The children and youth with whom I talked explored this issue in terms of agency, that is to say, user choices within the game and user control of outcomes.

First and foremost, children located agency in the choice and design of avatars and other characters. Asked what he liked best about Jurassic Park, Lee said, "You can make your own dinosaurs." He did not mean that he invented them; rather, he chose which species to "hatch." On occasion he distinguished between beasts by assigning them pet names—his personal addition to the game.

Other children and teens, given the chance to assemble characters from a variety of elements, were more confident that they had designed one-of-a-kind beings. Aaron looked forward, at the start of each new game of Spore, to putting together some new "cuckoo creature," some species of animal "unique" and "different." To play with the same creature in every game, he told me, "would be really boring."

Nate also enjoyed selecting facial features, clothing, personality traits, and life wishes for his Sim characters. Drop-down menus provided such a range of choices he was sure that any particular permutation he might make would almost never be repeated. He believed his characters to be unique because "it's something that's on your whim you create." Ellie likewise relished the freedom to choose what her onscreen self-representation would look like. On Second Life, she told me, she could design a "unique individual."

Players also experienced degrees of agency in guiding avatar or character response to action choices in the simulated environment. For Thom, engrossed in working out optimal strategies in his first-person shooter game, combat simulation was analogous to chess. "And every single bit of it, of everything, is me controlling it . . . when you're playing chess . . . where you put your bishop affects the game board. . . . In [Halo] where I choose to go is what affects the game."

For others, the simulated environment was more of a Pandora's box, and their sense of control less complete. Although Molly played in a multi-user online space like Thom did, she recognized that she had little or no control over what happened in Hogwarts classroom forums. What her character said and how her character behaved were wholly within her purview, but she was not the only puppeteer in the Hogwarts improv.

Nor did she want to be. "I don't think I would like to have it where I know exactly what's going to happen with everything," she told me. She wanted surprises. So did Nate, who routinely set his Sim characters at a midway point between full freewill and none. In this way, he could respond to the "random" game-generated behaviors of characters on freewill settings, even as he purposefully moved them toward achieving their life goals. Unexpected events added spice to a game in which moment-to-moment decisions set characters on a narrative path whose end could not entirely be foreseen: "You actually have control over what's going to happen . . . [though] not all the choices necessarily end well for you."

For Nate, control over "people's lives . . . gives me a god complex." Ian, too, reveled in his role as the outside manipulator of an imaginary world in Age of Mythology™. "In a way, you kind of act and think you're a god, because you're creating a village and protecting your village" from harm. At play in Jurassic Park, Lee similarly cast himself as the unseen zoo keeper in a master relationship with pet dinosaurs. "The best part about this game," he told me, "is to take care of your dinosaurs." His play duties—making dinosaurs, entertaining guests at the zoo—added up to the same kind of external agency relished by Nate and Ian: "You control the whole island," Lee told me.

Observing and acknowledging the satisfaction that these children and youth took in managing game worlds calls to mind similar satisfactions among those at play in self-fashioned realms of the imagination. But if computer play provides opportunity for agency, it does so with certain cautionary notes attached that some of my older game players, at least, well understood. For Thom, moment-to-moment choices were critical to his enjoyment of online Halo. They were also a deal breaker when it came to other computer play.

"There are some games that don't let you choose very much and those I don't really like," he told me. He enjoyed Dragon Age™, however, because it allowed him to make all sorts of "little decisions," from outfitting an avatar to exploring one area of the simulated world instead of another. These little decisions reminded Thom of books he liked to read when he was younger, the kind that "say at the very bottom, flip to the next page to do this, flip to the next page to do that," thus permitting variation in the narrative adventure.

At the same time, Thom realized that little choices described predetermined pathways or decision trees through the game narrative. "In Dragon Age, there's a main quest [within which] you get to do very many different things and there are many different choices to get through it, but it's the same quest each time you play it." No matter how many different paths he took, his final destination remained the same. He was not really "affecting what the game designers made." His freedom of choice, his control of the game outcome, his instrumentality were all, in other words, a misperception—but one he was willing to accept in order to experience and explore the game world. "It's kind of weird. I know I'm getting fooled. . . . But that doesn't bother me as long as it *appears* that I have an option."

Ellie also recognized—and accepted—certain imaginative and creative trade-offs in computer play. She preferred those simulation experiences that allowed her to indulge in what she called "an *illusion* of being productive . . . like I'm making friends or I'm learning things." She wanted something to show for her play, some experiential memory or virtual artifact that made her feel she had been creative—even if she had not. For both teens, personal agency in computer play—whether articulated as the misperception of instrumentality or the illusion of productivity—was no more than an acknowledged charade.

For Ellie, that charade contributed to her waning interest in computer games and simulations from its highpoint in middle childhood. Reasonably versed in computer technologies and a fan of emerging online forums such as Tumblr, she agreed to talk about her play in virtual worlds not as an enthusiast, but as something of a philistine. She enjoyed Second Life—but only up to a point. "The imaginative part stopped for me when I stopped designing my avatar," she told me.

Further opportunities for playful participation in that online world often involved design tools and computer applications with which she was unfamiliar. Upwards of 99 percent of the content in Second Life is generated by users, but Ellie was not among them. To learn how to use the necessary programs just for the simulated experience seemed too much like work, she confided. She much preferred entertainment forums for which she already possessed the requisite skills: "Maybe I'm a throwback or something, but I think that when I read or when I watch a movie, those are the things that are inspiring visually or creatively or thinking of new thoughts."

As a medium for play, Second Life lacked immediate affordance for Ellie—and, consequently, it lacked imaginative scope. Whether we speak of language or visual images, pen and paper or computer, mastery of any medium of exchange involves a learning curve. Up to a point on that curve, the medium remains opaque, a locked door; after that point, the door opens and the medium itself seems to dissolve, to become, in a word, transparent.

Just as a certain degree of reading literacy must be mastered before stories can leap off the page into the imagining mind, a certain degree of computer—and game—literacy is necessary before simulated worlds can come to life. One is no longer aware of reading words; one is no longer aware of negotiating menus and clicking the mouse.

There is only the lived story; there is only the lived game. Without such literacy, however, imaginative play in computer worlds is hampered.

As Ellie knew well, online illiteracy can be remedied. But to what purpose? "If you're just gonna go for a walk," she told me, "why would you go for a walk on your computer in Second Life? . . . I'd rather go for a walk in the real world, personally." Her critique of computer games did *not* just reflect her technological unreadiness. It also had its roots in her desire for a full, unfettered experience. And the relative lack of unfettered experience in computer simulations brings us right up against the shortcomings of computer worldplay.

Imaginative Literacies Compared

Comparing computer play with reading fiction reveals much about these shortcomings.

Reading stimulates the mental recreation of setting, characters, and actions in visual, auditory, tactile, kinesthetic, and other sensory images. One "sees" the pirate with the scar slashing across his cheek. One "hears" the sail flapping in the wind. One "feels" the swell of the waves on ship deck. Perhaps one also "smells" the salt air. And so on. The reader pulls all these sensory images together into a private, internal simulation of the reading experience.

In contrast, computer play is largely a visual experience stimulating visual-spatial imagery. To be sure, the games include auditory cues such as melodic tracks and sound "buttons," but these are usually unrelated in any real way to the visual simulation. All other senses remain largely untapped (Molly's one memorable experience of virtual taste being the exception that proves the rule).

This difference between reading and gaming helps clarify the difference between exploring simulated worlds and inventing imaginary ones. Ian, for one, found the sensory restrictions of game simulations somewhat frustrating. If he could improve the game experience for the better, he confided, he would add realistic sound and bodily awareness. Instead of relying on a "little white icon" to tell him a zombie was at his back, he would rather sense that presence. He would rather, in other words, that the simulated experience be as real as possible or, at the very least, that it be more like reading.

What makes books good, Ian told me, is that they "describe everything." They call on his ability to re-create *in his own way* what the author can suggest but not simulate. Chances are, the pirate a boy like Ian imagines is not the spitting image of some actor or avatar, but some mental composite pulled together from personal experience: the loud voice of a somewhat scary teacher perhaps, the remembered feel of a limp when he sprained his ankle, the black patch Mom jerry-rigged for Halloween. This imaginative effort amounts to a co-creation of the narrative, which, indeed, does not exist until the reader reanimates it internally.

In computer play much of this co-creative process goes lacking; the gamer's imaginative input is far more passive. "It's easier to visualize things when you're [actually] seeing them," Ian told me. Nate made a similar observation. His game play was not like reading a book "because here [in The Sims] you actually get to see what's going on so you don't really need to try and picture it in your head. You're already kind of watching a movie." Characters and actions are readymade; the game's imagery dominates—and obviates—any personal imaginative input.

This dominating image stream concerns a number of critics of computer play—and with justification. Exploring simulated worlds may involve imaginative elaborations beyond the given sights and sounds of the computer screen—a sense of three-dimensional space, for instance, or an emotional feel for relationship with virtual beings. But the game also restrains that imaginative embroidery. Except for the "illusions" of choice and agency within the sim world, there is little room for nonprogrammed possibility, for something other than expected variations and outcomes. Without personal imaginative effort, every pirate looks and acts the same—and every child who plays the game plays pretty much the same.

In and of itself, *based in the child's lived experience*, the exploration of simulated worlds in computer play is *not* fully commensurate with the invention of self-fashioned imaginary worlds. Yes, the game experience, as play, does share characteristics with intense make-believe: absorption, immersion, agency, and engagement. And simulation play does allow the player a measure of instrumental elaboration within the game world. But game play also restricts imaginative reach and casts an illusory pall on that agency and instrumentality.

At best, computer play in simulated worlds may be understood as a cooperative venture, dependent on the creative inputs of the game designer and the responsive recombinations of the child player. At worst, the child who explores imaginary worlds in computer games and simulations passively *consumes* a readymade experience. In either case, worldplay the computer way does little to facilitate active creative practice *during that play experience itself.*

Does it have to be this way? Can computer play still lead children toward constructive practice? The answer is a qualified yes.

THE DOING OF "UNTAUGHT" THINGS

Game design has been referred to as an art, and it is for the designers, calling upon all their powers of imaginative and creative production. For the child user, however, game play is not an art, but more of a sport. What we're talking about here is the difference between the free-form activity of pretend play and soccer on the playground or in organized leagues. In the first, child-determined goals and constraints respond fluidly to the whim of individual or group. In the second, externally enforced rules and purposes remain largely unresponsive. What we're talking about, in terms of worldplay, is that, unlike personal invention, the exploration of imaginary worlds via computer game is a highly managed—and adult-mediated—affair.

Does this adult mediation matter? Assuredly. Many parents and caretakers would argue that adult supervision of all kinds is a necessary trade-off for the guarantee of children's safety. Yet, psychologists—philosophers and educators, too—find cause for concern when children no longer have their share in the making of things and experiences. The philosopher-educator John Dewey, for one, observed that the self is "something in continuous formation through choice of action." Often enough, growth of self depends on exploring oppositional or slyly subversive action, on questioning the status quo and testing the limits of authority—all of which children tend to do in self-fashioned play.

As educational philosopher Maxine Greene has observed, however, when others limit the child's choice of action, imaginative or otherwise, the kind of self formed may very well be a conforming self. Children, she has argued, "must discover a sense of their own agency" if their experiences are to have deep personal meaning, if their experiences are to shape their capacity to imagine and, ultimately, to create the newly possible. "[T]hey must make their own use of what has been taught," she has insisted; "in fact, children must go beyond what has been learned—to do what might be called untaught things."

And in certain circumstances computer play can make that happen—off-line.

Stimulating Off-line Play

Of all the computer games and simulations played by my group of sim world enthusiasts only one—Virtual Hogwarts—demonstrated any overt nurture of personal imagination and creativity. Molly came to that online site because of her love for the books of J. K. Rowling. By means of verbal simulation she continued her play in the fictional world of Harry Potter—and fictionalized her play.

There were constraints, to be sure. Invented characters could not be lifted wholesale from the Rowling books; nor could they be substantially different from the book characters, either. They must be an "average human with magic powers," Molly told me, and aged ten or eleven and attending the Hogwarts School. Though these and other "rules" did not leave her "with a ton of creative space," they actually helped her develop a character with consistent personality and behavior. Because so much of the narrative structure "already exists and was created by somebody else," Molly found it easy to improvise dialogue and description—and to lose herself in the moment of play.

Molly's experience on Virtual Hogwarts gave her good writing practice. It carried over into her other storytelling, too, but with a difference. Well away from the Hogwarts world, she told me, "I get an idea for one particular part of a story, but *I* have to build a beginning and an ending around it." She had to create her own characters from scratch, invent choices, and fabricate plot lines and purposes. More than that, she had to build a backstory, a world that structured and supported the narrative. There were rules to that enterprise, too, just as there were in Virtual Hogwarts, but these were discovered rather than imposed. "If I can create the structure for my original fiction, then I'll be set," she said. Luckily, building the fictional world was as rewarding for her as crafting the narrative itself.

For Molly, computer play in a simulated world connected strongly with off-line play. It reinforced her desire to create fictional worlds of her own. And it helped sharpen her understanding of that creative endeavor. In evaluating the imaginative and creative worth of childhood activities, of course, this is the gold standard: that reading or watching television, that trips to the theater, to art and science museums, and yes, that play with computer games should stimulate personal enthusiasms and scaffold private, self-choice play. I looked for that gold standard among the children and teens I spoke with and found that nearly all, especially the younger ones, took at least some elements of their computer play beyond screen time.

Aaron told me that Spore was on his mind "a lot." He "plans ahead" what he wants his creatures to do, what abilities he wants them to have. When bored in school, Nate did the same for his play with The Sims. Away from his Jurassic Park game, Lee "wished that dinosaurs will still be alive. . . . I'd keep one as a pet—well, not a carnivore." He "made up this dinosaur called Dollyosaurus" and played with her in the backyard.

Ian and his younger brother Andrew also took their computer play outside, in their case mixing their several games together. "We never really just stay with one game," Ian told me. "We incorporate all of them that we've ever learned together. . . . So, for example, I could just take up the mission of Call of Duty and then replace it with spears and you have to get resources. That's kind of how we play."

Scaffolding on the visual images and narrative scenarios of sim games, Ian and his brother engaged in very intense make-believe, the kind where objects in the real world substitute transparently for objects in the what-if universe. "Once you've seen something a certain number of times [in a game], you can visualize it in your mind," Ian informed me, "and so everything around you becomes something, becomes the world although you can still see the real world. So it's kind of strange." It is also precious, for children engaged in the possibilities of pretense find themselves only a step away from the material construction of imagined artifacts, only a step away from their own inventive practice in the real world.

In addition to repurposing found objects into "spears and resources" with his brother Ian, Andrew liked to sketch pictures that drew him back into favorite imaginary worlds. Lee, too, sometimes drew pictures of his imaginary dinosaurs. And Aaron built Spore creatures with parts from Lego Bionicals™. Somewhat chagrined that the computer game only allowed for symmetrical creatures, he made sure that his Sporonicals, as he called them, were mostly "asymmetrical." This was rule breaking and rule making in one breath—a sure indication that off-line play involved untaught things.

A few children I spoke to also invented their own imaginary worlds—or expressed the desire to do so. Not surprisingly, most of this world building, actual or potential, was framed in terms of the game play that inspired it—and the rule breaking/rule making that constructing a parallel or analogue game implied. Aaron thought it *might* be fun to supersize all the things he liked about computer play. His game would be "basically Spore," but with greater powers both to inflict "damage" on hostile creatures and to befriend others.

Two children actually sketched out their plans. Andrew showed me the written rules and some of the hand-drawn cards for a fantasy game he made up with his brother Ian. Like their outdoor make-believe together, this self-fashioned game drew on bits and pieces of commercial games. The boys had worked out game procedurals, sketched a game board, and adapted to their purposes a dragon, a goblin, and a time bomb. Eventually, Andrew told me, his older brother intended to put the game on computer.

Toward Creative Computer Literacy

In fact, Ian did want to learn how to program computer games—"it's what I'm trying to do at the moment," he told me. He'd learned already that "everything consists of codes" and he had some basic commands under his belt. These did not directly translate into inventive prowess, however. As a medium of active craft and expression, game programming is, in fact, a complex and difficult art, dependent on the acquisition of specialized skills typically acquired in high school or, more likely, in college. With the exception of Ian, all the other teens I spoke with had already decided that constructing computer games was too rigorous. The difficulty of the form, as they understood it, shut down any desire to make sim worlds of their own.

Certain initiatives aim to change all that, to place programming knowhow and game design within the purview of children and youth. The Scratch™ Project headed by Mitchell Resnick and his "Lifelong Kindergarten" group at MIT comes to mind; so do Gamestar Mechanic™, a platform and community for seven- to fourteen-year-olds that supports game design and game sharing; Microsoft's Kudo™ Game Lab and Imagine Cup Kodu Challenge for children ages nine to eighteen; and the National STEM Video Game Challenge for middle and high school students, which encourages the use of Scratch, Gamestar Mechanic, Kudo, and other programming apps to design games of many kinds and on any topic. In video gaming camps and media arts centers everywhere there are undoubtedly many more such projects on the rise.

Given time, these kinds of opportunities will surely effect a facility for sim-world construction in middle and late childhood. We are not there yet. Like Miss Piggy, the Muppet character who famously enough could "hear" French, but not "speak" it, the children and teens I spoke to could "hear," even "read" computer games, but not "speak" or construct them—not, at least, in the originating tongue.

Did my game players feel that world invention in *other* expressive idioms remained open to them? For Nate, computer play with The Sims had dissipated any impulse to make up his own imaginary worlds in verbal or other forms, but this was not the case for the younger Ian. When "you have the sense you want to make a computer game really bad," he told me, "usually when it's fresh out of your head, then . . . you draw for a couple of hours and then you go back to playing or do something else." Lacking computer skills, he transposed the urge to make his own game world into a medium he *did* have at his command.

Such transposition demonstrates on the child's part that creative practice based on simulated worldplay remains an open possibility. And it strongly suggests that, should computer programming and related electronic media be placed within their ken, children and youth will utilize sim technologies to construct their own imaginary worlds.

That has certainly been the case, though belatedly so, for Kyla Gorman (her real name), finishing up a master's program in game design when we met. As a child of twelve and thirteen, Gorman began to make up an "alien world of water among the trees" that was inhabited by plausibly evolving animals and plants. By the end of high school, she had filled an official "scientific" notebook with the best of her doodles and speculations concerning the imaginary world of "Trisent," named for its three sentient forms of life—aquatic, tree dwelling, and amphibious (See figure 11.2.).

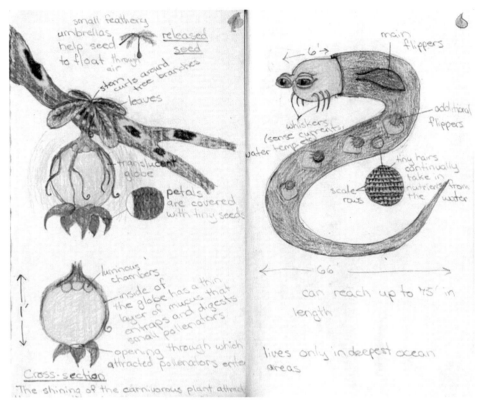

Fig. 11.2. Two Trisent creatures evolved by doodling from simple abstract shapes, with 'scientific' commentary. Drawings by Kyla Gorman in her teens.

That same notebook provided the environmental parameters with which she planned, as a graduate student, to build "a virtual world in which you can explore the landscape I'd always been thinking about, and be the creatures that I had designed." Beyond play, the point of her game will be to develop a scientifically valuable empathy and to exercise a "generally applicable skill set [useful for] real world problem solving." The same skills, of course, enabled her to make up all that "imaginary stuff" when a child, she told me. And "it feels oddly like returning full circle . . . to use all the brainstorming I did [as a kid] in a productive way" as an adult.

MAKING ROOM FOR THE MAKE IN MAKE-BELIEVE

Self-fashioned worldplay . . . or new-fangled "simplay"? In the best of all possible worlds, the future does not lie in the direction of "either/or" but "both/and." Balanced resources for play time are needed. So are balanced skills for making and creating in traditional media as well as in new technologies. We owe it to our youngest children to take care that electronic play joins but does not crowd out the pretend play of early childhood or the place-play and internalized make-believe of middle childhood. We owe it to our older children and youth to help them reflect upon and manage electronic play as a tool rather than a crutch for self-expression and personal growth.

That said, we can look forward to the day when advances in computer technology allow children to program simulated worlds for computer display with as much ease as playacting an imaginary person, drawing an imaginary landscape, or penning an imaginary story. We can look forward to the day when *all* these elements go into the construction of an imagined world. With a clear plan in mind, parents, educators, and caretakers can help shape a best possible future in which worldplay in all its forms becomes the stimulus for imaginative and creative development and a rich internal life. The next chapter takes a look at how.

Chapter Twelve

The Creative Capital of Make-Believe: How to Support Children Playing at Their Best

Play is the first poetry of the human being.

—Jean Paul Friedrich Richter, tutor and man of letters

ON THE LOOKOUT FOR WORLDPLAY

In the 1989 movie *Field of Dreams* an Iowa farmer gambles that if he builds a baseball diamond in a stand of corn, the athletes that fill his dreams will come to play. If this book has met its mark, I have built a field of understanding that will enable parents, guardians, teachers, psychologists, social workers, policy makers, and others to recognize worldplay when they see it and to value it for all it is worth. It has certainly been my experience since embarking on this study that the players have come. Mention the invention of imaginary worlds in casual conversation or in formal circumstances, as I have done, and you will find more than a few acquaintances, colleagues, and friends who say, with some surprise, "But I did that as a child!"

For me, there was the scientist who revealed herself over a dish of noodles outside Tokyo; the writer who told me of her troubled son in a chance remark; the professor of modern German history whose husband told my husband of the "parallel worlds" his wife created while growing up in the Midwest: "Alas, [she] burnt all the documents after much teasing from her siblings."

There were also the teaching artists, colleagues at a retreat, who let me know that they—or children they knew—had invented worlds. There was the friend who told me of a "subterranean" rabbit warren land that she "entered" in the "time between going to bed and falling asleep." There was the librarian who sent me an e-mail out of the blue, overjoyed to find he was not alone in inventing a private world; the web designer who posted numerous electronic pages devoted to an ancient warrior named Tollo; the conference attendee who tearfully recalled finding at his death the worldplay notebooks of a stepson in his twenties.

And there were the senior citizens, as well—the seventy-two-year-old woman who shared "Basementville" with her brother; the ninety-two-year-old man who remembered that as a young boy he "drew imaginary maps by the hour;" the sixty-seven-year-old woman who recalled inventing with a friend a world of the future "à la Flash Gordon." And, most recently, there was the Polish émigré who spoke of finally finding home in an imaginary republic situated in the parklands visible from her apartment porch.

Look sharp and you, too, may see the glimmer of imaginary world invention behind the sofa, in the backyard, on the playground, in a friend's hobby or a colleague's work style, in an art museum, a writer's archives, a scientist's memoirs—or in your own childhood play. The trick is to appreciate that glimmer for what it is—or may be.

That was certainly my challenge the day my niece took me into her confidence about Fairy Land and other make-believe play that filled her life. Megan, who was ten years old at the time, took me up to her room. I turned on my tape recorder and for the next two hours we looked through her toys, her dolls, her books, her artwork, and more.

At first I only understood that Megan engaged with great enthusiasm in the usual assortment of make-believe games. She played dolls with one or two friends at a time; she played "let's pretend" during recess at school with a few more. The girls made up fairies together; they also enacted scenarios from favorite books by modifying characters and combining plots for playacting. Occasionally, they would agree to write down the stuff of their play, but none of these stories ever materialized. Megan's make-believe, it seemed clear to me, emphasized social participation in diverse and unrelated episodes that disappeared at the end of the day.

But I was only half right. As Megan warmed up to my interest in her make-believe, as she told me of one doll and one play scenario after another, I began to perceive a persistent elaboration and coherence. With and without her friends, she had made up dozens of characters, some of whom were dolls, some of whom were "imaginary friends," play people conjured up in the mind. Sometimes she drew pictures of these imaginary people; sometimes she drew their family trees, in one case at least, tracing relationships back two generations on both maternal and paternal sides (See figure 12.1.).

There was "usually something real" about these doll people and imaginary friends, Megan told me. I could see why. Each and every one had a particular story—the story that she and her real friends had enacted together, in some cases as long ago as third grade, two years before.

Almost by accident, I learned that all this shared play had, for Megan, a private dimension as well. She counted up for me all the friends—five real and five imaginary—who played one particular game with her. Did all the real friends have to be together to play that game, I asked? "I guess not," Megan replied. So who knows the whole story? "I do." The conversation moved on, but eventually circled back. Since Megan knew all these stories by heart, did she ever play them alone? The answer, when I got it, opened up the door to her private synthesis of one, all-encompassing imaginary world.

From; Japan
Lives: Hawia
Sport; Vollyball
Name; Yoshy
Age; 15
Birthday: October
4 1992
Job; Asistent
coach for 5 year-
Old vollyball team

Volly Waves ball
05

Fig. 12.1.   An imaginary friend named Yoshy and her vital statistics. Drawing by Megan, around age 10.

All along Megan had been telling me in bits and pieces about Fairy Land, which had something to do with the big tree right outside her bedroom window that "looks like a kingdom rising with all the leaves, like the fairies lived in there," and just as much to do with notions gleaned from movies, books, and peers. At night, as she settled down to sleep, the fairies would "come in through my window and . . . they all start partying. And my American Girl® dolls come down and start playing too."

Of course, the fairies also lived elsewhere, in imagined places constructed with Megan's friends. But it wasn't until she and I had been talking for over an hour that she suddenly confided a larger, secret country:

My biggest imaginary world is, okay, my room is the kingdom and there's an entrance to the rest of the kingdom [See figure 12.2.] and I'm the queen and all my American girl dolls are, like the governors of the different places. So like Fairy Land is in my world somewhere, just like a different part of it.

Almost at once, Megan veered off again, detailing another set of doll characters and another set of adventures. But a little later she shed more light on the various parts of

Fig. 12.2.   One of several entrances to Fairy Land. Drawing and paper construction by Megan, around age 10.

"My Kingdom." "I make up stuff," she said, "like there's a place where all the water is . . . a place of wild woods and places for different books. Like I have a place for the *Lightning Thief* books and a place for *Aragon* and the dragons and everything." Though she had shared individual parts of her kingdom with one friend or another, no one in her peer group knew the whole. "It's kind of mostly private. . . . My Kingdom is—I don't tell a lot of people about it."

Finally I understood. All the different fairy lands Megan had been telling me about—all the different games she played with one real friend or another—belonged to one big imaginary space. What appeared on the outside to be ephemeral proved persistent on the inside, what appeared various and diverse proved interconnected and cohesive. Most important of all, what appeared to be—and often was—the result of social collaboration also served the needs and purposes of independent play. Though she invited friends in to co-construct one part or another, Megan protected the imaginary world in its entirety as a solitary endeavor. In extraordinary fashion, it seemed to me, she expropriated large amounts of social pretend play into private worldplay.

A Question of Nature and Nurture

In genesis, substance, and sustenance, my niece's Fairy Land differed greatly from my daughter's Kar Land, even as both shared in the general characteristics of worldplay. Born fifteen years apart and raised in cities distant from one another, the girls never directly communicated about their internalized make-believe. Nor might one have expected them to, given the private nature of imaginary world invention. Yet since the two girls were cousins, the question naturally poses itself: Does worldplay run in families? If so, is the tendency an innate one, or must it be learned—or at any rate, nurtured?

As with so many other nature/nurture propositions, the kinds of data at our command simply do not allow for definitive either/or answers. Considering the same question with regard to child prodigies, psychologist David Henry Feldman has argued that since "families share a communality of genetic, situational, cultural, and personal experiences, it should not be surprising that certain types and patterns of behavior would recur, particularly when there is some family tradition . . . preserving the value of these characteristics."

The same undoubtedly holds true for worldplay. Children may turn to paracosm play for a variety of reasons embedded in a variety of life events and conditions including (but certainly not limited to) emotional triggers, family dislocation, illness, social isolation, boredom, shyness, intense wonder, imitative drive. Only consider novelist Alan Garner or the anonymous paracosmist "Jane," both forced by illness to spend long hours alone, both finding imaginary lands in the cracks and surfaces of their ceilings. Or actor Peter Ustinov, who traced his worldplay to the messy wringing of a chicken's neck: "There was . . . only one way in which I could keep a grip on myself in this vile world of grown-ups," he later wrote, "and that was the establishment of an imaginary country. . . . The first article in the constitution of this land was that no chickens would have their necks wrung."

What we can surmise from any particular instance is that the invention of an imaginary world reflects something of the child's imaginative capacity and something also of the child's imaginative response to the immediate and family environment. And in many cases, that environment displays "values" or "traditions" rich in modeling and support for complex make-believe.

Indeed, shared worldplay with siblings, cousins, or other family members is a constant in the annals of imaginary world invention. Recall the worldplay of the young Brontës or of Robert Louis Stevenson, first with his cousin Bob and later with his stepson Lloyd, or of Gregory Benford and his brother. To these we might add, for the nineteenth century, the Winkworth sisters' play in interrelated fairy lands and "kingdoms of Natural History"; Friedrich Nietzsche and his sister's play with King Squirrel I; and Leo Tolstoy's play in the ant world "Moravian" with his siblings.

We can also add, for the twentieth century, Gertrude Stein's construction of an imaginary language and an imaginary world with her brother; Vera Brittain's invention of "The Dicks" with her brother; C. S. and Warnie Lewis at play in the shared land of Boxen; an anonymous Dutch family of children at play in the land of "Relevia"; and Fairfield Porter at play with a brother and two friends around 1918—the children christened their imaginary island (see figure 1.1) with the first two letters of all their names: EDward, FAirfield, LOuise, BArbara.

Given such a showing, it should come as no surprise that 36 percent of all the paracosmists assembled by Robert Silvey invented their imaginary worlds with a sibling or cousin. What's more, four of these individuals, or 10 percent, also reported some kind of generational history with worldplay. "David" had a father who invented an imaginary world in his childhood; "Alice" had two nephews engaged in worldplay in theirs.

Several well known examples of elaborate worldplay also display a generational proclivity. In 1942, Sylvia Wright ushered into publication the novel, *Islandia*, based on voluminous materials left by her father, Austin Tappan Wright. A lawyer by profession, Wright had throughout adult life devoted himself to the maps, climate notes, population tables, gazetters, and so forth, of an imaginary place. That worldplay, which he began as a child, found reflection in a brother's play—and in a parent's play as well. According to his daughter, "Occasionally [my father] shut my uncle, who was younger, out of *Islandia*, and my uncle created his own world, *Cravay*. After my grandfather's death, they discovered that he, too, had mapped an imaginary world." Her father's mother, she noted, also wrote several novels "which took place in a college town of her own concocting."

In the Wright family's case, the generational transfer of worldplay seems to have occurred without overt suggestion from parent to child. That may also have been the case for Robert Louis Stevenson, whose father apparently told himself bedstories as a child. In other instances, however, generational proclivity obviously involved a great deal of parental modeling and support. For paracosmist "Ambrose" the invention of imaginary worlds was a family tradition. Not only did his own worldplay begin at his father's suggestion, but his father had also had an imaginary world when he, too, was a boy.

Take, in addition, the familial experience of artist Claes Oldenburg. The young Claes invented an imaginary country just around the time the family moved from Sweden to the United States. According to one biographer, Oldenburg's parents appreciated the boy's play in Neubern as a means of coping with a series of transitions: the birth of a younger sibling as well as the move into a new language in a new home. Indeed, in this regard, Claes's father appears to have modeled worldplay actively. Not only had he himself, in collaboration with his brother (Claes's uncle) once built a miniature village, he purposely invented a country called "Nobbeberg" to amuse his sons and pass on to them a love of worldplay.

Adult Modeling of Make-Believe

What these examples suggest is that worldplay, or its ethos, can be learned in a family context. Indeed, some theorists suggest that *all* play is learned. Much evidence suggests that proper stimulation enhances imaginative abilities in young children. According to psychologists Dorothy and Jerome Singer, imaginative play benefits from a certain amount of initial guided learning, as the parent or adult role models and scaffolds play from very simple to more complex activities. They and other psychologists, too, have pursued this line of research by developing play intervention for at-risk parents and toddlers. Preliminary results indicate that parents can learn to model and young children can learn to play in support of cognitive and imaginative skills.

By the same token, parents and other adults can model and encourage more complex forms of pretend play such as worldplay in support of aesthetic and creative skills. Aesthetic understanding, based on a habitual and heightened awareness of one's perceptions and feelings, does not necessarily come naturally. Many children experience moments of wonder when the sounds of a summer morning or the patterns in a tiled floor suddenly surge into awareness and ineffable significance. But these moments come unbidden and sporadically. More often than not, regular aesthetic response requires a learned attention to outer and inner experience.

Unlike the "passive gaze" that registers an experience with minimal participation, aesthetic response to what has been seen, heard, or felt involves active reflection about what it means to (re)imagine and (re)create what has caught the attention. Worldplay that elaborates upon books, movies, or video games is in this sense an aesthetic response. And that response can be—ought to be—nurtured and cultivated. As educational philosopher Maxine Greene has argued, "It is still necessary to empower children to invent their own extraterrestrial creatures, to play with words and shapes in their own authentic ways, to learn what it is to summon up illusioned worlds."

Luckily, adult modeling for worldplay does not require extensive personal experience. Among Silvey's paracosmists, nine out of thirty-nine individuals reported some other kind of parental support. "Allan" received encouragement from his father in the form of a "map of an island drawn for me by my father and containing such imaginative concepts as a Land of Lost Toys and a Land of Upside Down People." Allan altered the world to suit himself and the play took off.

Similarly, Patrick Brontë, who harbored literary dreams of his own, gave his children free rein to write and read whatever they liked. And even though he seems never to have read any of their minuscule manuscripts (indeed, scholars speculate that the tiny writing may have been a purposeful deterrent on the children's part), one biographer of the family has called him "probably the greatest single influence on his children's early writing." We might speculate that that influence also encompassed the play that gave birth to the writing—after all, it was Patrick who provided his children with the toy soldiers that journeyed from real-world Haworth to imaginary Glass Town.

ENCOURAGING WORLDPLAY

Suppose you want to encourage the sustained invention of imaginary worlds in a six- or eleven-year-old, regardless of your own play background. Ought you to try? How might you go about it? The short answer is yes and with a great deal of tact.

In *The Brightening Glance: Imagination and Childhood* (2006), the art theorist Ellen Handler Spitz argues that "[t]he topic of adult participation in children's play is delicate, complex, and controversial," largely due to the overwhelming influence a parent or a teacher or even adult-generated entertainment media can have. Adults must work hard not to impose their own interests, methods, or judgments upon play activity.

The act of modeling and encouraging can, indeed, be fraught with missteps. As Spitz observes, it is "difficult" to wear the two hats of modeler/encourager and parent/adult at the same time. If adult expectations are too high, the child's frustration may turn off playful experimentation. If the adult adopts a judgmental attitude to elements of play that seem emotionally distasteful or intellectually frivolous, the play activity can get derailed—or go into hiding.

Wield a light hand, however, and when the child withdraws pretense from outside influence and critique—as children tend to do in the very years when worldplay is most likely to take root—the play will be private but not wholly secret, the kind adults know about but don't participate in. Welcome this privacy as sign of a job well done. The best approach to cultivating worldplay is to do so with little or no expectation in mind and then to step back. Or, as Silvey's collaborators put it, "Adults—keep out."

As must by now be clear, the whole point of worldplay is for the child to invent for him- or herself, according to personal needs and interests. This personal or intrinsic motivation will be far more effective in promoting originality in play than extrinsic rewards and assessments (even when subtle, rewards may make an activity seem like work). Indeed, research suggests that both excessive structure and adult interference suppress curiosity and creativity in children. "Adults," Cohen and MacKeith insisted, "ought to leave children to get on with their imaginary worlds by themselves."

When it comes to cultivating private worldplay, then, the optimal adult role is not that of playmate, but something far more important—behind-the-scenes play facilitator. By shaping a handful of conditions, parents and other caretakers can stimulate and support imaginative play and attendant creative behaviors. Psychologists suggest five easy rules of thumb for supporting pretend play in early childhood. Thinking back on all we've explored in these pages, I'll suggest an additional handful of tactics in support of worldplay through middle and late childhood.

Five Rules of Thumb for Pretend Play in Early Childhood

1. *Provide place.* Give children a place for pretend play. Physically, this place might be the living room rug, the kitchen table before and after meals, or a corner of the classroom. Wherever it is, that place must also be a psychological space where play does not have to compete with other activities in order to happen. Then and only then will you have what the Singers call a "sacred place" for make-believe.
2. *Provide time.* Set aside uninterrupted, "sacred time" for children to play in the play place. Schedule it daily. Let it last—twenty minutes, an hour, or more when possible. Note that this probably means curtailing electronic media use. Turn off the television. Establish a computer-game-free zone. And prepare to rethink the words, "I'm bored," when you hear them. One of the downsides of constantly available electronic distraction is that children no longer take advantage of tedium or dissatisfaction to craft their own imaginative engagement with the world. Yet boredom

can be a powerful stimulant for creativity. Help children welcome not knowing what to do as an invitation to do their own thing.

3. *Provide materials.* Give children access to a variety of materials for play and pretending, constructing and expressing. These may include crayons, paper, magazines to cut up, and miscellaneous craft supplies. They ought also to include toys and props that can be used in many ways and for different purposes, like dress-up clothes, building blocks, or puppets. The point is not to provide separate items for every play need, but to provide opportunities for repurposing toys, tinkering with materials, and constructing artifacts to suit the play at hand.

4. *Provide privacy.* Grant children a certain amount of autonomy and privacy to utilize provided space, time, and materials *as they wish*. Adults may find the need to model activities to get young children going, but the less involved they are in actual play, the more benefit that play has for the child.

5. *Provide permission.* Let children know you value and support their make-believe and constructive play. Listen. Laugh. Reinforce. Put pictures up on the refrigerator or the bulletin board, watch puppet shows, let the block castle in the living room or the classroom corner stay standing for as long as possible. Most importantly, respect the unusual thoughts that surface in play.

These five conditions are essential to imaginative and creative play in early childhood. They are also relatively easy and inexpensive to provide. As Robert Louis Stevenson and many psychologists and educators since have observed, pretend play thrives best when and where the imagination makes its own substitutions for reality. The web-based site for *Mr. Rogers' Neighborhood*, run by Family Communications, Inc., suggests that a place to play may be as simple as a sheet thrown over a table to make a cave. Materials for play may be as readily at hand and as inexpensive as old clothes, hats, and shoes or cardboard tubes and other scrap materials. Valuing play may be as easy as telling a child he or she has wonderful ideas.

All this may come as good news to those facing the plethora of toys now available for purchase. Which to buy? If the stimulation of a child's creative imagination is the goal, less can most definitely be more: fewer specialty items and more all-purpose toys means less commercially programmed activity and more personally imaginative play. Indeed, Spitz recommends that parents privilege "objects for children that are unique 'one-ofs' . . . rather than monotonous manufactured replicas." These may include hand-me-downs or borrowings, like the household chinoiserie which one MacArthur Fellow used to create a private "palace room," or things of nature, like the hollyhocks that yet another Fellow used to make flower dolls.

Five More Rules of Thumb for Cultivating Worldplay in Middle and Late Childhood

1. *Introduce children to the idea of worldplay.* Casually mention the imaginary world you invented in childhood. Or, like Allan's father or Robert Louis Stevenson, start a map of an upside down world or a treasure island and let the children in your care take it over. Observe the play that does engage them and occasionally ask

leading questions. I remember asking my daughter if there were people who spoke that language she made up, if they had stories they liked to tell, where they lived, what they wore. Soon enough she asked her own questions and the elaboration of Kar Land took off.

For those who feel a bit more guidance might do the trick, look for stories that model make-believe play in imaginary lands. Start with Alice McLerran's *Roxaboxen* (1991) or Norton Juster's classic book, *The Phantom Tollbooth,* originally published in 1961 and still in print. In that story, a young boy named Milo receives a mystery package, assembles a cardboard tollbooth, opens up a map of imaginary destination, and drives off into make-believe.

Copy that. Hunt up *Secret Spaces Imaginary Places: Creating Your Own Worlds for Play* (1986) by Elin McCoy for child-friendly instructions on how to build things like kid-sized tollbooths from stuff found at home. Or track down *Make-Believe Empire: A How-To Book* (1982) by MacArthur Fellow Paul Berman. Over twenty years ago now since the writing, Berman shares his enthusiasm for world building directly with children and offers playful tips for constructing miniature cardboard castles, legal documents, boats and maps—and for growing crops in small containers.

2. *Favor play stimulants that call out for imaginative reconstruction.* Imagination does not thrive in a vacuum. It needs experiential material with which to work—books, movies, computer games, trips to museums, cultural events, and other urban, suburban, and wilderness outings.

Keep in mind that the very best stimulants exude an air of mystery, adventure, or expectation and leave some part of the telling (and retelling) to the child. As the philosopher Gaston Bachelard would have it, "images that are too clear . . . block the imagination. We've seen, we've understood, we've spoken. Everything is settled." For just this reason, books may provide more inspiration than movies or computer games simply because they require rather than provide the mental reconstruction of sense images and physical enactments.

3. *Encourage material elaborations of imaginative play.* Children whose lives are rich with activities and experiences that stimulate the imagination will more likely than not recreate that engagement in play. Alone or in concert with others, they may playact a favorite scenario from the Harry Potter books, or better yet, a blended mash-up of Harry Potter with the movie *Toy Story* with the computer game The Sims.

In those moments when children share the delights of that play, parents and other adults can encourage them to document the make-believe with little books and written stories, with drawings, maps, photographs, game boards or other artifacts. As children and youth gain facility with computer programming tools, with the construction of videos and other emerging media forms, these can (and should) also serve as recording tools. Each newly minted drawing, story, video, or computer game creates and commemorates yet another piece of an imagined world.

4. *Make room for solitary play.* In support of the imaginative reconstructions and material documentations of play, one of the best gifts a parent or adult can give a child is solitude. Solitude is not the same thing as loneliness. It is, rather, alone-

time, the kind that fosters a rich inner life of daydreams, private thoughts, and personal knowledge.

Alone, a child is wholly free to imagine, dream, craft, and create *for him or herself.* As Bachelard put it, "Alone we are at the origin of all real action that we are not 'obliged' to perform." No surprise, many creative individuals from many periods in history have recalled spending long hours in youth thinking and dreaming by themselves. Toying with ideas, experimenting with material instantiations, children in solitary play take their first steps toward a truly personal and, therefore, original imagination.

Despite this great good, support for solitary play will mean bucking the trend. Society places enormous emphasis these days on the benefits of shared or group play—social skills and "emotional intelligence" chief among them. In addition, corporations and large-scale enterprises are particularly interested in a workforce trained in collaborative productivity. What is overlooked, however, is that shared play and group creativity both depend on the original input of individuals and, thus, on judicious amounts of solitary thinking and musing.

Consider, too, as does psychologist Luciano L'Abate, that solitary play in and of itself "implies a certain degree of interdependence" and is, like all other play, "an exquisitely relational activity." Actual role-playing and role-sharing need not occur for a child to rehearse pretend interactions with others or to posit and explore the narrative interactions of imaginary beings.

When documented in story, drawing, or other artifact, complex imaginative play also involves the exercise of arts, crafts, and communication skills and of inventive process behaviors that transfer to public spheres of learning and doing. And it is just this sort of segue between a personal creative imagination and its social relevance in school or workplace that the twenty-first century truly requires.

5. *Support children in complex make-believe for as long as that play remains important to them.* Although worldplay typically peaks in middle childhood and fades away thereafter, in some cases children may want to persist through adolescence and even the teen years. To do so, they may need an adult's tacit support in navigating pressure from peers and other authority figures to "give up childish things" for "age appropriate" games and activities.

Kyla Gorman, the young game designer we met in chapter 11, remembered discussing with her mother how adolescent friends no longer wanted to play make-believe games. Her mother confessed that she, too, had wanted to play pretend games longer than her peers. She helped Kyla realize that "the longer you do it, the longer the creativity muscles stay flexed and the more creative a person it makes you in the end."

But What If It Isn't Worldplay?

You do what you can to set the stage for worldplay. But like many a gamble, it doesn't pay off—at least not obviously. When the father of paracosmist Ambrose modeled worldplay for his children, the idea took hold for Ambrose, but not for his sister. Nor, in the next generation, did any of Ambrose's children create imaginary worlds at his suggestion. Robert Silvey, he who kicked off modern interest in imaginary worlds, also made the pitch for worldplay to his children, though to no avail. "When my own children reached the appropriate age," he acknowledged, "I told them about my private worlds: but though they seemed quite interested, the idea did not catch on with any of them: their imaginative lives took a different form."

To Silvey's credit, he did not insist. Nor should we feel we have failed if children in our care prefer other forms of make-believe. Play is fundamentally "a psychological attitude" and should not, as educational philosopher John Dewey reminded, be narrowly identified with outward behaviors. Give a child ample opportunity to imagine and create his or her own play and trust in the result—that part you can see and that part you can't.

My son Brian never did catch the worldplay bug from his sister, but like her he reaped the benefits of dedicated place, time, materials, privacy, and support for self-directed play. He, too, read a variety of books, saw lots of movies, took many trips (okay, too many trips, according to him) to art museums, even as he played many games (okay, too many games, according to me) on the computer. And because he was also cajoled into spending time in solitary off-line play, he adapted favorite games for single-player use and came up with new board games of his own (one of which we all thought was very, very cool). Years later, I saw just how right all this play was for him—both the computer play and the created play—when he studied game theory in college and pursued a keen interest in entrepreneurial business and marketplace strategy.

Playing Complexly, Playing at Their Best

Ultimately, how a child habitually makes believe depends, as Dewey put it, on "the free play, the interplay, of all the child's powers, thoughts and physical movements, in embodying, in a satisfying form, his own images and interests." This "satisfying form" may not take shape as worldplay. Nor should it necessarily do so. From the start of these investigations, worldplay has served as convenient shorthand for the study of complex imaginative play in general. Whether or not a child constructs a bona fide paracosm is of less import than the full development of personal capacity for imagination, make-believe, and creativity.

How might parents and other adults determine that children are indeed playing at their best? Dewey, himself, suggested asking three questions:

1. "Will the proposed mode of play appeal to the child as his or her own?"
2. "Is it something of which he has the instinctive roots in himself, and which will mature the capacities that are struggling for manifestation in him?"
3. "Will the proposed activity give that sort of expression to these impulses that will carry the child on to *a higher plane of consciousness and action*, instead of merely exciting her and then leaving her just where she was before?"

If the answers to Dewey's questions are positive, then adults may rest assured that the children in their care are truly playing. In the fullest sense of the word they are exploring, imagining, and making meaning. In complex imaginative play of all sorts, the young gain familiarity with the stages and strategies of original thinking; they develop their curiosities; they gain confidence in their powers of understanding. In activities of no (direct) consequence, they learn to risk, fail, and risk again. They imbibe a set of intuitions and attitudes that facilitate self-directed learning and problem solving and include the following implicit understandings:

- I know how to make my own make-believe play.
- Play begins with the question "what if?" It builds upon problems raised in the leap from something I know to something else I can only imagine.
- To make something else, ideas and things of all kinds must be connected, combined, blended, and rearranged—first in my mind, then through my body. What I imagine I can pretend. What I imagine I can enact or make.
- I know how to create something new and original to me.
- What has been imagined and made can be something new and original when a particular set of ideas, things and materials has never, to my knowledge, been blended before.
- The more I play in this way, the better I get at expressing—through playacting, writing, drawing, game making, and so forth—what is in and on my mind.
- I know that playing is a way of learning.
- The more I elaborate and document my play and the more I learn to work with complex and evolving ideas and systems, the better I am at handling open-ended tasks and the better I understand that problems can have multiple solutions.
- The more I try to organize and synthesize my play knowledge plausibly, the more I understand about the real world it reflects.
- I know that play can be a way of creating new possibilities for posing and solving real world problems.

These understandings, framed here in terms of the child's complex make-believe, might just as easily be framed in terms of the student's playful learning or the adult's professional productivity. Nurture a child's imaginative play, and you contribute to the social reservoir of ordinary everyday creativity. From this pool springs the rare genius or the publicly acknowledged artist, scientist, or inventor. From this pool also springs the many lesser known and anonymous thinkers and doers who add problem-solving value to the work of the world.

In the United States and other western countries heading full steam into the global economy of the twenty-first century, workers with this kind of creative capacity are fast becoming a necessity. Politicians, educators, and other policy makers now ask how creativity may be taught—in the workplace, in college, in secondary and elementary school. What is the optimal level of intervention and remediation? No one knows—yet. But surely it will not escape notice that so many of the attitudes, behaviors, and skills that characterize creative ability *first appear and subsequently develop in the make-believe play of early and middle childhood*. Long after active play in private worlds of make-believe comes to an end, even as it modulates into serious pursuits in the arts or sciences, in public affairs and practical endeavors, this knowhow continues to resonate.

HIGHER PLANES OF ACTION: A CHECK-IN

Three years after our first conversation about make-believe play, I talked with my niece Megan again. She had reached adolescence and I was curious as to whether she still played in My Kingdom. She did. She and most of her old friends, she told me, continued their make-believe together—but with some differences.

One or two of the girls were no longer interested in the game. For those who were, the focus had firmly shifted from fairies to Harry Potter and to Greek myths. And where a couple of years ago they would have acted out the play narrative with dolls, now they just talked about what would happen "if" a character did this or that. Sometimes they simply reminded themselves of what they used to play and how they played it.

Remembering that in earlier years Megan had been the ringleader when it came to worldplay with her friends, I suspected that she drove a great deal of their prolonged interest in shared make-believe. Even access to computer games such as Age of Mythology had not diverted her attention from dolls or daydreams. Though she enjoyed the simulated game world, she told me, "I felt like I could control *my* imaginary world better . . . I could control the plot." The video game never did inspire off-line play in the same way books did—and continued to do. Megan remained "fascinated with reading." And even though she had less time for free play, what with sports and other after-school activities, she was still keen on elaborating the narratives she loved the most.

The intensity of her earlier worldplay had begun to fade, but Megan still liked to mix, match, and connect things up. Whether fairies or gods and goddesses, each of these "different dimensions" still fit within a larger play universe. By herself she imagined different endings to favorite books or transposed the characters from one book into the plot of another just to see where things went. She did this at night, before falling asleep. And she liked to think about My Kingdom. She had a "good memory" for the "people" she had imagined and for the things that had happened in that imaginary play place. "I think it stayed around so long because it was so complex," she said. She had only just, but finally, taken down the picture of the castle door to Fairy Land that had hung on her wall for years.

Our chat over, I felt an overwhelming sense of privilege that Megan had, not once but twice, let me into her private play life. In the years to come, I thought, I will get to ask again how the play persists (or doesn't), how it colors (or doesn't) some of her choices and some of her pursuits.

According to her mother, Anne, in the three years between our two conversations Megan's interest in Greek myths had "really exploded." She had read a lot of Norse, Irish, and Roman myths as well and all of it stemmed from her early love of fairies. At the same time, she had fallen in love with science. She had some very strong science teachers, Anne said, "which is a big part of it. [But] intuitively, I think that the science interest is [also] the result of her imaginary explorations. I have no direct evidence, it is just a sense."

This observation surprised and pleased me. Anne and I had not spoken of these things before, but her gut reaction as a parent was to see in worldplay all the value that I had spent many years investigating. Parents and other caretakers *can* shape a family ethos supportive of worldplay and other forms of complex make-believe. Children *can* be empowered to integrate the lessons of creative play with maturing aspiration and endeavor.

Already, Megan had begun to see herself as a bioengineer who likes to write stories on the side. Maybe some of those stories (placed on the page or not) will hark back to her middle childhood make-believe. Maybe some of her inventive process in engineering (if that's what she actually ends up doing) will reflect the exploratory as well as the synthesizing impulses of her worldplay. The connections, indirect though they may be, will be there for Megan herself to feel, understand, and articulate when need be. As must also be the case for the children and youth in homes and schools everywhere whose best make-believe even now helps prepare them for mature creative endeavor, alone or with others, at home or at work, to their private satisfaction or to professional, even public, acclaim in some future time and place.

Even now, those of us who help nurture their play contribute to the creative capital of the world.

Conclusion

Wither the Worldplay Impulse?

It is never pointless to think about alternatives that may at the moment seem improbable, impossible, or simply fantastic.

—Vaclav Havel, writer, dissident and politician

Inside a large and unusual marble floats a cat's eye of metallic oxides melted into fantastic shapes and gorgeous colors. When you or I roll such a glass globe in our hands and peer into its depths, we see familiar things and familiar patterns. The flowing forms in vibrant blue become seas, emerald green crystals become mountains, tawny yellow contours become plains. We intuit an alternative space, a place of possibility. We imagine a scenario, a hypothetical model or a story. We invent a world.

Such a marble and such response to it are metaphors for worldplay, both as process and as outcome. They also stand for the development in our understanding of related conceptions and constructions over the past one hundred years and more. The invention of imaginary realms offers us a microcosm for exploring the complex nature of creativity and its maturation throughout the life cycle.

Building on the research and insights of others, I have argued that worldplay has a recognizable shape and impact. And because I believe in its value, I have tried to impart an "enlightened cherishing" of the worldplay impulse. There is an intriguing, often charming, history to the childhood invention of imaginary worlds, which coalesce around place-making, storytelling, mapping, and secret language games. As a phenomenon readily observed in biographical records—and in our own homes—worldplay comes to our attention as a naturally recurring behavior of seminal importance, with strong connections to adult endeavor in those arts that mimic imaginary world invention and in those sciences that posit possible worlds.

The first full study of worldplay, begun by Robert Silvey and finished by his collaborators, raised questions about its spontaneous incidence among children, its effects on their imaginative development, and its connections to adult profession and mature creativity. Subsequent research into the childhood play of MacArthur Fellows, college students, and individuals who have left rich records in their wake suggests that worldplay may in fact engage as many as one out of thirty to one out of ten children.

Moreover, it appears to function as a cognitive strategy for learning, discovering, and creating. There are strong connections—statistical correlations and experiential causations both—between childhood play and mature work in many fields of endeavor.

Why this should be so has much to do with the nature of play itself. In a landscape ranging from rough-and-tumble exercise to playacting to social games, the invention of imaginary worlds grows out of the tendency in middle childhood to make believe within found and constructed places. When such place-making play internalizes as worldplay, it signals a further development of imaginative and creative potential. Early twentieth century psychologists Terman and Hollingworth understood this intuitively, though they relied first and foremost on intelligence quotient tests to locate creative ability. A century later, we know that intellectual and creative capacity do not necessarily march hand in hand. Worldplay, as an activity organically germane to childhood, may indicate early creative potential with far greater accuracy than high IQ or even prodigious talent.

There can be little doubt that at sustained levels, childhood worldplay provides early immersion in a range of imaginative and creative behaviors. Among many firsthand accounts of imaginary world invention, we owe some of the most revealing to students of G. Stanley Hall, the turn-of-the-twentieth-century psychologist who actively sought and solicited memoirs of childhood play. Study of these memoirs, along with more recent autobiographies and interviews, reveals that the worldplaying child experiences deep absorption in self-directed activity; practices persistent and consistent modeling of a make-believe reality; organizes accumulating (play) knowledge by means of narration and other systematic pattern forming; develops skill in crafting documents such as stories, drawings and maps; and reaps the aesthetic satisfactions of a self-conscious maker and creator.

These are precisely the skills that accompany creative capacity in so many adult endeavors. Indeed, early immersion in worldplay may achieve a number of outcomes *of relevance to mature creativity.*

First, worldplay nurtures the capacity for continued pretend play, especially through middle and late childhood, well after the intense exploration of make-believe in early childhood typically fades.

Second, worldplay exercises a range of cognitive capacities involved in projecting alternate realities, including imaginative thinking skills such as imaging, empathizing, recognizing and forming patterns, dimensional thinking, and modeling. As well, it may develop and sustain attitudes associated with creative process and activity: persistence, independence, openness to possibility.

Third, the projection of an imagined reality involves self-initiated problem raising and problem solving—and at two levels of constraint. First, the transposition of real world elements into make-believe raises questions: Where is my imaginary country? What do imaginary beings do there? Second, the answers suppose chimeric, yet plausible solutions. These, in turn, require a balanced blend of imaginative and analytic skills. Put another way, worldplay exercises the capacity for consistent elaboration and synthesis within a modeled system. Regardless of that system's fantastical or realistic context, it provides a replicable strategy for learning and discovery.

Fourth, the active modeling of an imaginary world involves the construction of personal knowledge. As an intuitively charged form of comprehension, personal knowledge deals with make-believe "facts." It also deals with consensual understandings which we all share. The foundations of play-generated knowledge lie in the narrative elaborations of story and story frame. Ongoing and cumulative histories of chimeric beings, places, and systems reinforce the givenness of the make-believe realm. They also reflect its heuristic insights into humankind and nature.

Fifth, that givenness, that "self-sufficient reality" as C. S. Lewis put it, often involves instantiation in the form of stories, drawings, maps, and other artifacts. These external structures support further reflection and refinement of the imagined world as a thing in itself. Such documentation, and the synthetic efforts that may attend it, provide early experience in the invention of culture.

Sixth, the invention of culture, albeit in play, involves a developing sense of self as an independent creator. The creating self, with attendant strategies for make-believe projection, may transfer to a variety of mature endeavors—and at modest as well as eminent levels of achievement. Indeed, because worldplay at any age ties the effervescence of play to the exigencies of problem solving, it may nurture both the ability and the audacity to imagine effective solutions to challenges in all walks of life.

Worldplay in childhood does not, of course, guarantee later creative achievement. At the very least, however, it is a heads-up. Just as composers can only come from the ranks of musicians, mature creators can only come from the ranks of those with prior experience creating. The playful, imaginative, and problem-solving aspects of world invention make it just such an experience, a "learning laboratory" calling on behaviors and practices that may serve as predictors for mature productivity.

Whether creative potential fulfills itself as such depends on additional circumstance, on opportunity and desire. Indeed, the transition from worldplay in childhood to worldplay in maturity would seem to depend on several factors: among them, ongoing relish for the play, a knack for harnessing it to professional activity, and long-term commitment to disciplinary training. Recall that Robert Louis Stevenson successfully harnessed his passion for imaginary world invention to the art and craft of writing. Lloyd Osbourne, on the receiving end of his stepfather's "brilliant bouts of play," proved far less committed to professional discipline and, ultimately, far less a writer.

The connections between childhood play and adult work, so clearly seen in a Stevenson, hold true for many other individuals as well, and in less obvious ways. Among MacArthur Fellows who reported a worldplay impulse in their professional endeavor, the links have to do with the generation of speculative scenarios, what-if reconstructions of incomplete data, and the imaginative modeling of the unknown.

Moreover, worldplay at work is often associated with, even integrated with, worldplay in hobby or avocation. Many individuals who use the invention of imaginary worlds as creative strategy are also polymaths, adept in more than one field of disciplinary activity. For J. R. R. Tolkien, Desmond Morris, Gregory Benford, Todd Siler, and others, the synthesis of private worldplay and public work has proved instrumental in priming the pump of discovery and achievement. In principle, when worldplay and polymathy do converge, the potential for creative achievement heightens.

Given its origins in childhood play, as well as its role in developing and advancing disciplinary knowledge in maturity, worldplay can serve as an appropriate strategy for child-centered learning. Educator Deborah Meier offers guidance on the judicious use of make-believe worlds in elementary classrooms, echoed elsewhere in the use of playacting, storytelling, material craft, and computer simulation. Where implemented, classroom worldplay appears to bolster mental modeling and effective learning.

Equally important, schooling in worldplay may help reverse apparent decline across the United States in make-believe play as a whole. One of the unintended consequences of electronic entertainment has been to strengthen trends away from self-directed free play in childhood toward adult-directed and managed play. Computer games and simulations mimic the worldplay impulse (which is part of their appeal), but by and large, they do little to exercise creative muscle. At present, unless and until children combine computer play with enacted make-believe, narrative craft, or accessible forms of computer game or simulation programming, their creative development in a wired world remains limited.

Outside school and in the home adults can, of course, take steps to encourage a thoughtful balance of consumer play with creative play. Whether children take to full-blown worldplay or not, parents can gift them with ongoing opportunities to "play at *their* best" and to develop certain understandings: how to imagine their own make-believe; how to make the stories, drawings, games and other artifacts of play that reflect their imagining minds; how to think for themselves; how to construct knowledge. Whether or not children carry elements of worldplay into their mature work, these understandings of what it means to imagine and create will serve them well in a constantly innovating knowledge economy.

For all that worldplay can and does contribute to the creative resources of society, questions yet remain. We might, for instance, canvass children currently inventing imaginary worlds, prod their play for salient features now, and follow them into maturity, quite like Lewis Terman did for his studies of IQ. We might ask questions about paracosms and the development of social or moral understanding, as some researchers have recently begun to do. We might also ask how dependent is worldplay on the socioeconomic environment? How widespread is worldplay really?

This study has largely fixed on European and American exemplars. If we were to find a relative lack of childhood worldplay in nonwestern countries, that might call into question its universality as a play behavior, despite its value as learning laboratory and creative strategy in our own culture. How indebted is worldplay, anyway, to the kinds of thinking to which we expose children in their youngest years? The cultural expression of worldplay may be affected not only by parental attitudes, but also by indigenous forms of make-believe, narrative, and logical reasoning.

Developing and varying over time, individual, familial, socioeconomic, and cultural constraints probably set certain historical conditions that may or may not privilege the invention of imagined worlds. The MacArthur Fellows and college students sampled in this study recalled recognizable worldplay at statistically significant different rates. The higher incidence of childhood worldplay among Fellows appears to reflect that group's concentration of individuals of proven creative potential and achievement. Yet it is also true that Fellows and college students largely represented two generations divided by tremendous change in childhood pastimes and entertainments. The advent of movies and television—and the attendant opportunity for passive leisure—might also account for the drop in recognized worldplay among children growing up after the 1950s or 1960s.

Further study of incidence, whether for complex make-believe play in general or worldplay in particular, may yet confirm the historical trend. Will the late twentieth century introduction of personal computers, computer games, and Internet simulations prove yet another watershed between generations? Will self-invented worldplay give way to commercially available games and group simulations—not just for children, but for adults, too? Most players in virtual worlds, it turns out, are not children, but male adults "with a wide variety of occupations and demographic characteristics." Worldplay in virtual worlds, at least, is "not simply a childish fad." Nor is it simply a leisure pastime; it is also a professional one.

Consider that applications of simulated worlds and simulated games to science and social science research are on the increase. Businesses build virtual worlds for commercial purposes. Scientists utilize video games to crowd-source solutions to protein folding, to investigate complexity theory and artificial life, to visualize the physics of black holes, and to research economic, social, and psychological behaviors. Call of Duty, Second Life, World of Warcraft—and the software that makes them possible—are, it is claimed, "destined to be the future chalkboard of science." As this trend continues, will we see a shift to collaborative forms of innovative knowhow at the expense of personal inventive drive? Or will we see instead the development of new, perhaps hybrid, forms of creativity?

What we can be sure of is this: As society changes, so does childhood play; and as the toys and tools of childhood play evolve, so will the worldplay impulse. However, just as society influences childhood play, so too does childhood play influence society. Indeed, this insight has run through this study of imaginary world invention like the two *f*s that, as the poet Ron Padgett wrote, "run through giraffe / like 2 giraffes."

Over a hundred years ago, Alexander Francis Chamberlain argued in a remarkable work entitled *The Child: A Study in the Evolution of Man* (1900) that the evolution of culture has made it possible for humans to tap into child's play as the source of ever-progressive creativity. The book reads like a *Who's Who* of philosophers, scientists, and educators observing that the purpose of prolonged immaturity is to allow the child ample and sufficient scope to play, that is, to experiment, to learn, and to discover. Chamberlain taught anthropology at Clark University at precisely that moment in time when G. Stanley Hall and his students—Folsom and Terman among them—pushed forward psychological investigations of childhood and adolescent play.

Jump a half century or so forward to ongoing scientific interest in play as an adaptive mechanism. Animals of flexible intelligence, it was proposed in the mid-twentieth century, use play to cultivate malleable responses to a changing environment. Niko Tinbergen, Nobel Prize winning ethologist, argued from the animal evidence that play was critical to the education of children precisely because the cultural environment alters from generation to generation and at an accelerating rate. For worldplaying artist and scientist Desmond Morris, who studied zoology with Tinbergen, negotiating that cultural change requires that "the playfulness of childhood must survive and mature as an adult mode of self-expression." "[A]dult play," he has said, "is what gives us all our greatest achievements—art, literature, poetry, theatre, music and scientific research."

Clearly, Chamberlain was not the last to advance the idea that play lies at the heart of creative culture; nor was he the first. Yet we may credit him with articulating the idea that child's play holds the key to the future course of civilization. The evolutionary imperative, as he saw it, was to preserve and further develop in maturity "resemblances" to childlike playfulness. "Rather the parent strives to be like the babe than the babe to be like the parent," he wrote. "The things often but dimly foreshadowed in the child seem to be those which will one day be the most valued possession of the race." The childhood invention of imaginary worlds is surely one such possession. And if current trends in computer gaming and in research simulations continue, some part of that worldplay may become more and more an instrument of adult play and adult work.

Whether the private invention of imaginary worlds will persist alongside the public play of virtual realities, only time will tell. Consulting my marble globe, I am optimistic about the chances. If children continue to seek autonomy in solitary play, if adults continue to insist on the power of personal knowledge, there will be an opening for the do-it-yourself invention of imaginary worlds both in childhood and maturity.

Some would say these are big "ifs." That may well be. In the last quarter of the nineteenth century the brilliantly playful Stevenson lamented that "there is something radically wrong in a generation that does not know how to play." In the decline of play as he knew it, he saw the decline of England itself. Over a century later, we might make the same observation and voice the same fear—though perhaps the perennial nature of that foreboding should give us pause. Material alterations to play we may accept, even as we insist that society cannot afford to let the technological tools at our disposal master us or rob our children of creative practice. Rather, we must use our computer-extended imaginations to advantage, without losing sight of the concrete experiences and make-believe challenges that develop inventive capacity in young and old alike.

If we can manage this, if we can train the young to responsible use of powerful simulation technologies, then their personal invention of speculative realities will surely privilege chimeric imagination, plausible modeling, and creative powers of mind, though in ways we cannot yet foresee. One thing is certain. A society that wishes to promote and sustain creative capital for the future will look to the present nurture of self-fashioned make-believe in all its many forms and to the ongoing and playful invention of imaginary worlds.

Appendix

A Childhood Worldplay List

Appendix Note: This list builds upon the one published by Silvey and MacKeith in 1988. I have included additional "paracosmists" as found in biographies, autobiographies, and other print sources, as well as some of the individuals who granted me interviews over the years, specifically those willing to go public with their childhood play.

As Silvey and MacKeith found, childhood worldplay described in published biographies and autobiographies tends to belong predominantly to writers. Many factors may be involved, without necessarily assuming a special connection between childhood worldplay and adult endeavor in the literary arts.

First, all fields of endeavor are not equal when it comes to who writes autobiographies, or who has biographies written about them. In an update to his parents' book, *Cradles of Eminence*, a mid-twentieth century sampling of biographical materials, Ted Goertzel noted "that writers are over-represented because they write interesting autobiographies and because biographers may enjoy writing about other writers, not because they are more important than the other groups." Ludwig also argued that professions vary in acknowledging the relevance or impact of private experience on occupational activity. The under-representation of visual artists, scientists, social activists, and business leaders in biography and memoir may also reflect public disinterest rather than the overall value or contributions of these groups to society.

Second, not all autobiographies (or biographies) are equally revealing about childhood experiences, especially the kind and quality of childhood play. Individuals who recall pretend play as particularly important in their lives may do so because it obviously resembles or prepares for their adult endeavors. The writer who recalls early worldplay offers an acceptable explanation of his imaginative development. In contrast, the scientist may not consider that background critical to her development of rational or experimental skills. The social scientist or political activist may not find early make-believe relevant to mature concern for the real world. These groups may be under-represented in the annals of worldplay due to personal, cultural biases.

Third, this list is in no way comprehensive. Silvey and MacKeith found that "privately reported" paracosms continued to "trickle in" after their analysis had been completed. Like them, I fully expect additional examples to come to light. The publicly known cases in this list are just that—publicly known. As such, they hint at without necessarily representing the full contours of a much wider phenomenon.

Appendix: A Childhood Worldplay List

NAME	IMAGINARY WORLD	ADULT ENDEAVOR	REFERENCE
Adams, Paul b. 1947	sci fi universe	neurobiologist	personal communication (see ch. 8)
*Auden, W. H. 1907–1973	"private, sacred world"	poet, writer	Auden, 1965 & 1970; Silvey & MacKeith, 1988
Axelrod, Robert b. 1943	computer sim life forms	political scientist	personal communication (see ch. 8)
Baring, Maurice 1874–1945	"Spankaboo"	poet, dramatist, writer	Baring, 1922; Singer & Singer, 1990
Benford, Gregory b. 1941	"Moon and Mars"	physicist/writer	Personal communication (see ch. 9)
Berry, R.Stephen b. 1931	bedstory; war game	chemist	personal communication (see chs. 3 & 8)
*Borel, Jacques 1925–2002	imaginary country, aka "Ladahi"	writer	Borel, 1968; Silvey & MacKeith, 1988
Brittain, Vera 1893–1970	"The Dicks"	writer	Goertzel & Goertzel, 1962
+Brontë, Anne 1820–1849	"Glass Town" & "Gondal"	poet, writer	Ratchford, 1949; Barker, 1997
+Brontë, Branwell 1817–1848	"Glass Town" & "Angria"	artist, poet	Ratchford, 1949; Barker, 1997
+Brontë, Charlotte 1816–1855	"Glass Town" & "Angria"	poet, writer	Ratchford, 1949; Barker, 1997
+Brontë, Emily 1818–1848	"Glass Town" & "Gondal"	poet, writer	Ratchford, 1949; Barker, 1997
Coleridge, Hartley 1796–1849	"Ejuxria"	poet, writer	Coleridge, H., 1851
Day, Lorey C. b. 1890s?	"Exlose"	psychologist	Day, 1914 & 1917
*de Quincey, Thomas 1785–1859	"Gombroon"	writer	de Quincey, 1853; Silvey & MacKeith, 1988
de la Roche, Mazo 1879–1961	"The Game" / "The Play"	writer	de la Roche, 1957; Hambleton, 1966

Name	Paracosm	Occupation	Reference
Doan, Marian 1905–1980	"Roxaboxan"	housewife	McLerran, 1998
Follett, Barbara 1914–disappeared 1939	"Farksolia"	writer	McCurdy, 1966
Folsom, Joseph K. 1893–1960	multiple "Systems"	psychologist	Folsom, 1915
Garner, Alan b. 1934	imaginary landscape in the ceiling	writer	Cooper, 1999
Gorman, Kyla b. 1986	"Trisent"	game designer	personal communication (see ch. 11)
*Grahame, Kenneth 1859–1932	imaginary "City"	writer	Grahame, 1895; Green, 1982; Silvey & MacKeith, 1988
Hardy, Edward Rochie (Child E) 1908–1981	imaginary country on Venus	Anglican priest, historian	Hollingworth, 1942
Hunt, Una 1876 – ?	"My Country"	visual artist, writer	Hunt, 1914
*Isherwood, Christopher 1904–1986	private world/town, aka "Mortmere"	writer	Isherwood, 1947; Silvey & MacKeith, 1988
Jung, C. J. 1875–1961	imaginary medieval castle, secret keep	psychiatrist	Jung, 1961
Kaye-Smith, Sheila (Fry) 1857–1956	"The Lodge"	writer	Kaye-Smith, 1956; Goertzel & Goertzel, 1962
Kerouac, Jack 1922–1969	fantasy baseball, football, horse races	writer	Kerouac, 1960
Kinnell, Galway b. 1927	"Little Men"	poet	personal communication (see chs. 3 & 8)
Kitchen, Alexa b.1998	"Kirsy-Lirsy Land"	(gifted child)	Mechling, 2006; alexakitchen.com
Lee, David b.1931	imaginary railroad	physicist	Lee, 2000–2001
Lem, Stanislaw 1921–2006	"High Castle"	writer, futurologist	Lem, 1995
*Lewis, C. S. 1898–1963	"Animal-Land" & "Boxen" w/sib.	writer	Lewis, 1955; Silvey & MacKeith, 1988

NAME	IMAGINARY WORLD	ADULT ENDEAVOR	REFERENCE
Lewis, W. H. 1895–1973	"India" & "Boxen" w/sib.	popular historian	Lewis, 1955
Lionni, Leo 1910–1999	"miniature worlds" in terrariums	designer, artist, sculptor, writer	Lionni, 1997
MacDonald, Betty 1908–1958	"Nancy and Plum"	writer	Goertzel & Goertzel, 1962
*Malkin, Thomas W. 1795–1802	"Allestone"	(gifted child)	Malkin, 1806/1997; Silvey & MacKeith, 1988
McBride, James b. 1957	"mirror" world	memoirist	McBride, 1996
Meier, Deborah b. 1931	"ongoing saga" of imaginary characters	educator	personal communication (see ch. 10)
Morris, Desmond b. 1928	secret lake world	zoologist, artist, writer	Morris, 1980. Levy, 1997
Mozart, Wolfgang A. 1756–1791	"Kingdom of Back"	musician, composer	Cox, 1926; Solomon, 1995
* Nietzsche, Friedrich 1844–1900	kingdom of "King Squirrel"	philosopher, composer, poet	Forster-Nietzsche, 1912; Silvey & MacKeith, 1988
*Oldenburg, Claes b. 1929	"Neubern"	visual artist	Rose, 1970; Silvey & MacKeith, 1988
Otis, Laura b. 1961	"woodsgirls" world, planet "Zarf"	neuroscience, lit professor, writer	personal communication (see ch. 8)
Paolini, Christopher b. 1983	"Alagaësia"	writer	Smith, 2003
Porter, Fairfield 1907–1975	"Edfaloba"	visual artist	Cummings, 1968
Rivlin, Alice b. 1931	"barge" world	economist	personal communication (see ch. 3)
Sacks, Oliver b. 1933	"kingdom of numbers"	physician, neurologist, writer	Sacks, 2001
Shur, Barry b. 1950	"Kadyu"	biologist	personal communication (see ch. 9)
Shaler, Nathaniel S. 1841–1906	imaginary war, heroic companions	paleontologist, geologist, poet	Shaler, 1909

Name	Paracosm	Occupation	Source
Siler, Todd b. 1953	multiple "dream worlds"	artist, inventor, scientist	personal communication (see ch. 9)
Silvey, Robert 1903?–1981	"New Hentian States"	statistician, sociologist	Silvey, 1977; Cohen & MacKeith, 1991
Singer, Jerome b. 1924	multiple; imaginary sports league	psychologist	Singer, 1975; personal communication (see ch. 4)
*Sorley, Charles H. 1895–1915	imaginary kingdom	writer	Silvey & MacKeith, 1988
Swainston, Steph b. 1974	"Fourlands"	writer/teacher	VanderMeer, 2007
Stein, Gertrude 1874–1946	imaginary world/language	writer	Goertzel & Goertzel, 1962
*Stevenson, Robert L. 1850–1894	"Encyclopaedia"	writer	Stevenson, 1923–1924, v. 29; Silvey & MacKeith, 1988
Osbourne, Lloyd 1868–1947	kriegspiele w/stepfather	writer	Stevenson, 1923–1924, v. 30
Taylor, Paul b. 1930	"fantasy world" of crib; puppet theater	dancer/choreographer	Taylor, 1987
Tolstoy, Leo 1828–1910	"Moravian" or ant world	writer	Goertzel & Goertzel, 1962
*Trollope, Anthony 1815–1882	"Castle in the air"	writer	Pope-Hennessy, 1971; Silvey & MacKeith, 1988
*Ustinov, Peter 1921–2004	"Concordia"	actor	Ustinov, 1976/1998; Silvey & MacKeith, 1988
Watts, Alan 1915–1973	"Bath Bian Street," an island kingdom	philosopher, writer	Watts, 1973; Silvey & MacKeith, 1988
Winkworth, Catherine 1827–1878	"kingdom of Natural History"	translator	Winkworth, 1908.
Winkworth, Susanna 1820–1884	"All-mood"; Natural History kingdom	translator	Winkworth, 1908
*Wright, Austin Tappan, 1883–1931	"Islandia"	lawyer	Silvey & MacKeith, 1988

* Included, by Silvey & MacKeith, 1988, pp. 190–194, in their list of "published paracosms," (i.e., those mentioned in published biographies or autobiographies).

+ Mentioned in Silvey & MacKeith, 1988, but not included in their list.

Endnotes

Introduction: The Story of Worldplay

Supposition of a "separate reality:" Gardner, 1991/1983; of "a possible world. . . :" Jacob, 1988, 8-9. On decline in play time, see: MacPherson, October 1, 2002. For "nature deficit disorder:" Louv, 2006. On imagination deficit: Levin in MacPherson, August 15, 2004. For a succinct review of current pressures on play, see Whitebread & Basilio, 2013. On less play/less practice developing skills, see for e.g.: Gopnik, July/August 2012, 13; Stout, 2011; Meier & Oschshorn, 2006; Singer & Singer, 2005; MacPherson, 2004; Cowie, 1984, 27. Imagination and creativity "like muscles:" David Elkind, cited in Wenner, Feb/March 2009, 29. Deborah Meier on how the marginalization of play "cheats" our children: Meier, 1995, 63; on our national "inventiveness . . . at stake": Meier, 2006. Imagination as defined in Webster's.

PART I: DISCOVERING WORLDPLAY WHERE IT GROWS

Chapter 1. Hidden Worlds of Play: A Journey Through the Land of Kar

For most of the child inventors of imaginary worlds cited in these pages, basic resources may be found in the appendix to this book, *A Childhood Worldplay List*. Additional citations for quoted material will be found in these notes. Ustinov on secrecy of imaginary worlds: Ustinov, 1998, 278. List of imaginary worlds, unless otherwise noted: *A Childhood Worldplay List*; for 'Abixia' and 'Rontuia', see Levernier, et al, 2013.

"I Made It Up When I Was A Little Kid": On Thomas Malkin's "visionary country," see Malkin, 1806/1997, 93; on "enlisting every circumstance," Malkin, 130; on "early promise" of his play, Malkin, 140. On "visionary boyhood" of Hartley Coleridge, see his brother Derwent's memoir in H. Coleridge, 1851b, xi; on Hartley's many nations, Derwent in H. Coleridge, xliii. For Hartley on his early story-telling, see H. Coleridge, 1851a, 346. On Friedrich Nietzsche's play with "tiny china figures," see Forster-Nietzsche, 1912, 46; on his toy building "in classic style," see Forster-Nietzsche, 46-47. For C.S. Lewis on "mapping" Animal-Land, see Lewis, 1955, 15. For Claes Oldenburg on "everything I do is completely original," see Rose, 1970, 19; on "a parallel reality," see Rose, 189; as creator with vision, Rose, 52. For Stanislaw Lem on his "passion for inventing," see Lem, 1995, 47; on "a shape began to emerge," Lem, 106; on imaginative invention as "play and also a creative act," Lem, 127; on his anticipation of the anti-novel, Lem, 109; on his concern with man-machine interface, see Ziegfeld, 1985, 144.

How the World Began: For Fairfield Porter pretending "everything . . . runs by sunlight," see Spring, 2000, 14. For W.H. Auden on "private sacred world," see Auden, 1970, 424. For Anthony Trollope on "nothing impossible," see Pope-Hennessy, 1971, 28. On stages of creative process, see Csikszentmihalyi, 1996, 79-80, as a representative text; on creative spiral, see Milne, 2008, 26. For Bronowski on "explorations . . . of hidden likeness," see Bronowski, 1956, 30-31.

Commonalities and Questions: Harold Grier McCurdy on "those things which children know," in McCurdy, 1966, v.

Chapter 2: Searching for Paracosms:
How One Man Found the Imaginary Worlds of Childhood

Imaginary Matters. For Robert Silvey on the educational value of imaginary world invention, see Silvey, 1977, 18; on the value of a "post-bag," Silvey, 1974, 29; for Silvey and collaborators on criteria for paracosms, MacKeith, 1982-83; Cohen & MacKeith, 1991; Cohen, 1990. For Gaskell on the "creative power" of Brontë worldplay, see Evans & Evans, 1982, 89; for Ratchford on that play as "hotbed for genius," Ratchford, 1949, xv, 189. Charlotte's diary entry, "when papa came home" (*The History of the Year*, 12 March 1829), is reprinted in Barker, 1997, 12. For Branwell on toys "maimed" (*Introduction to the History of the Young Men*, 15 December 1830), see reprint in Barker, 1997, 14; on other games, see Barker, 1997, 12. On the Brontës' one encompassing game, see Alexander, 1987, xiii; on their special play language, Barker, 1994, 156; on their roles as Genii, see citation in Barker, 1997, 10. On length of Charlotte's Glass Town narrative, see Lane, 1980/1952, 22. For Branwell on his "springy mind" etc., see Barker, 1994, 515; Emily on her "Flood" of feeling, see Barker, 1994, 276; Charlotte on visions she "scarce dare[d] think," see Ratchford, 1949, 105 and on the "privilege of reverie," see Barker, 1994, 237 and, generally, Barker, 1997. On Charlotte and Branwell attempting to "outdo" one another, see Barker, 1994, 193; on Charlotte as emotional and Branwell as political, see Ratchford, 1949, 67 and Du Maurier, 1961, 79. On Emily and Anne as secretive in their play, see Barker, 1994, 272; on the trace of Gondal inspiration, see Ratchford, 1949, 183.

Genii and "Mad" Genius. On the paracosm as a "double-edged sword," see Lindner, 1955, 279, passim. For the world of Yr, see Greenberg, 1964. On Brontë worldplay as "strangest apprenticeship," see Ratchford, 1949, 149, 189; as "refusal of ordinary life," Lane, 1980/1952, 19. For Branwell's supposed insanity, see Du Maurier, 1961, 293 and passim; for current consensus on Brontës, see Barker, 1994, 156. On the creativity/madness association, see Cropley, et al, 2010; on mental illness detrimental to creativity: Ludwig, 1995, 161; on eccentricity promoting creativity: Simonton, 2010, 225-229; on addiction to creative thought: Ludwig, 1995, 192-194. Charlotte cited on "stupidity the atmosphere," in Barker, 1997, 40; on "mighty imagination," in Barker, 1994, 161; on "fervid flashes," in Barker, 1994, 164; on genius as spontaneity, in Barker, 1994, 414; on "when authors write best" in Barker, 1994, 547; on her misgivings, "if you knew my thoughts," in Barker, 1997, 37. Southey on woman's business and on daydreams habitually indulged is cited in Barker, 1997, 47. On Hartley Coleridge squandering his gifts, see Plotz, 2011; on Southey blaming imagination, see Hartmann, 1931, 43. On dissolution of Angria, see Barker, 1994, 350.

Ordinary Imaginary Worlds. On psychotic individuals and fantasies, see Singer and Singer, 1990, 115. Silvey and collaborators on imaginary worlds as rare: Cohen & MacKeith, 1991, appendix 1 and 2; on small number of cases in favor: Silvey & MacKeith, 1988, 175. For adjectival descriptions of personality types, see Silvey & MacKeith, 1988, table 3; for paracosmists as 'dreamy', see Silvey & MacKeith, 1988, 195. For the paracosm "inhabited by Golliwogs," see Cohen and MacKeith, 1991, 30; for Brenda's utopian paracosm, see Cohen and MacKeith, 1991, 98; for more on other paracosms and content categories referenced in this section, see Cohen & MacKeith, 1991, generally. For the four "dimensions" of variation in paracosms, see Silvey & MacKeith, 1988.

The Pulse of Worldplay. For childhood worldplay list, see Appendix to this book. On writers dominating the childhood worldplay list, see Silvey & MacKeith, 1988, 191; on "few" of their paracosmists "became artists," Cohen & MacKeith, 1991, 22, 89; on worldplay unrelated to creative development, see Cohen & MacKeith, 1991, 104. For creativity as ability to fantasize, see MacKeith, 1982-83, 263. For "divergent thinking" in general see, e.g., Runco, 2007, 3-4, 10-11. For convergent thinking in paracosm play, see Silvey & MacKeth, 1988, 195; in general, Runco, 2007, 3-4, 10-11. The paracosm as "most complex form of imaginative activity" in childhood, see Cohen, 1990, 30; for paracosms inhibiting or suppressing creativity, Cohen & MacKeith, 1991, 104, 53 and passim. On commonality of imaginary skills and creative behaviors across disciplines, see R. Root-Bernstein & M. Root-Bernstein, 1999. For Silvey on similarity of data sample and paracosm, see Silvey, 1974, 46.

Chapter 3: Memory Counts:
MacArthur Fellows and College Students Recall Childhood Play

Sampling and Assessing Worldplay: For Mendel's pea-counting and Pearl's "personal equation," see R. Root-Bernstein, 1983, particularly pages 281-282. Readers interested in the query text, as well as other survey instruments and/or the tables of data that inform this discussion of the Worldplay Project are referred to M. Root-Bernstein

& R. Root-Bernstein, 2006, 423-425. On the three sorts or categories of make-believe play, see Cohen & MacKeith, 1991, 110-111 and Piaget, 1962/1946, 110-113.

Rates of Worldplay: Rates for adult hobbies such as photography, flying kites or chess are taken from the U.S. Census Bureau, 2004-2005. For entertainment technologies effect on make-believe in general, see Singer & Singer, 2005.

Disciplinary Inclinations: The MacArthur Foundation organizes its appointments in five groups: Arts, Humanities, Public Issues, Social Sciences and Sciences. As one might expect, the arts include choreography, music, visual and performing arts, and creative writing. The humanities include the scholarly study of history, musicology and the philosophy of science as well as the writing of biography or translation. The social sciences cover disciplinary work as far afield as economics and linguistics, archeology and psychology. The sciences cover some twenty fields, from biology, chemistry and physics to agriculture, medicine and computer science. The public issues category includes diverse work in the areas of community affairs, education, human rights, international security and arms control, journalism, labor, public health and public policy.

Intended professions among students were substituted for actual profession and fit within the categories established by the MacArthur Foundation. This meant adding careers in landscape design or theater management to the arts, assigning careers as translators or ministers to the humanities, and placing careers in various technologies, medicine and nursing in the sciences. Students who indicated criminology or social work or business as a career choice were placed in the social sciences as practical applications of scholarly fields in this category. Students who planned to become lawyers, teachers, journalists, and politicians were placed for similar reasons in the public issues category.

Perceptions of Connection: All MacArthur Fellow and MSU Student quotations are taken from Worldplay Project queries and interviews (most of which are cited anonymously as a condition of research), unless otherwise noted. For Mortmere, see Isherwood, 1947. On links between daydreams and originality, see Singer, 1975, 67, 163; on "creativity does not spring to life," see Sawyer, et al, 2003, 224. Galway Kinnell on 'Little Men' play, in telephone interview, July 3, 2003. Rivlin on barge bed story, in Alice Rivlin, telephone interview, March 14, 2003. Berry on war game and link between worldplay and science, in telephone interview, March 18, 2004.

Note for Figure 3.3: Compared to a control population of students at Michigan State University, the incidence of worldplay among MacArthur Fellows, in whole or by professional part, proves for the most part to be greater than one might expect in a general population. Moreover, most of the differences in worldplay incidence between the two populations turned out to be significant using chi-squared analysis, a measure of the discrepancy of observed results from expected figures.

In the graph comparing the students with the MacArthur Fellows a single asterisk indicates a p-value of .05, two asterisks a p-value of .001 and three asterisks a p-value of .0001. P-value, in this instance, reflects the probability that there is real difference between the two populations. P-values of .05 indicate a minimal probability (1 in 20 that the result is by chance), with p-values of .001 and .0001 (1 in 1000 or 1 in 10,000 that the result is due to chance) routinely considered optimal.

This means we can accept with confidence that the greater rate of worldplay among MacArthur Fellow scientists (.001) and social scientists (.0001) than among the student population is a real phenomenon. It is less certain that observed differences between MacArthur Fellows and students when it comes to worldplay and the arts (.05) did not occur by chance. Nevertheless, an increased incidence of worldplay in the arts is more plausible for MacArthur Fellows than it is in public issues professions or the humanities, both of which failed to show statistical significance at all. When totals of all professions are compared, the incidence of worldplay amongst MacArthur Fellows has a p-value of .001; thus the difference between the two groups *as a whole* can be accepted as valid.

For further analysis of the statistical differences between MacArthur Fellows and MSU students, see M. Root-Bernstein & R. Root-Bernstein, 2006.

PART II: EXPLORING THE GARDENS OF MAKE-BELIEVE

Chapter 4: Pretense and Place: The Poetics of Play in Middle Childhood

The Playful Mind. Play as "simulated actions. . . ." Mitchell, 2002, 23. We know play when we see it and ironic stance, discussed in de Waal, 2003, 16, 20; see also Fagen, 1995, 24, 40. Play as "galumphing:" Miller, 1973, 89-93. Play as hunt practice: Tinbergen, 1975. Play developing individual/group welfare: Fagen, 1995; Fagen & Fagen, 2004; Held & Spinka, 2011. Play as sign of flexible intelligence: Fagen, 1988 and Mitchell, 2002. Play as suspension of objective truth: Harris, 2000, 10; dual existence of actual/simulated worlds: Harris, 2000, ix-x; Mitchell, 2002, 113. Like bi-pedal gait, make-believe play distinguishing characteristic of man: Gomez & Martin-Andrade, 2005, 169. Imaginative games of chimpanzees: Savage-Rumbaugh & Lewin, 1994, 276-277; "use language to pretend": Savage-Rumbaugh & Lewin, 1994, 278. Note: Gomez & Martin-Andrade, 2005, survey the literature on fantasy play in apes and conclude that make-believe is not typical of wild apes.

The Development of Make-Believe: Singer on study of "the most ephemeral phenomena:" telephone interview, February 18, 2004. Early scholarship on pretend play: Rochat, 2013. Psychological studies of play: Cohen, 1987, 14-35. Play not mere diversion: Groos, 1901/1899; Piaget & Inhelder, 1969, 60. Make-believe becomes superfluous: Harris, 2000, 1-7; Cohen, 1987, 7 & passim. Play as therapeutic mastery of realities: Erikson, 1963/1950, 222. Play involves challenge, novelty, incongruity: Singer & Singer, 1990, 40; positive emotional response: Singer & Singer, 1990, 24-28, 40; growing sense of autonomy: Singer & Singer, 1990, 29. "Childhood fantasies . . . a reflection of our common humanity:" Singer & Singer, 1990, viii. Children turn to rule-bound games: Piaget & Inhelder, 1969, 59n; desire to organize physical world: Singer & Singer, 1990, 235. Unstructured play time replaced: Singer & Singer, 1990, 88; make-believe in hiding: Singer & Singer, 1990, 32. Singer on miniature stadium and "little metal baseball characters:" Jerome Singer, telephone interview, February 18, 2004; Singer also discusses his childhood play in Singer, 1975, 17-32; his internalized baseball fantasy: Singer, 1975, 19, 21-22 and telephone interview, February 18, 2004. Pretend play emerging with facility for speech: Singer & Singer, 1990, 72; internalized reading/playing: Singer & Singer, 1990, 41; "ongoing fantasy activity": Singer & Singer, 1990, 32. Pretend play persisting internally: Singer & Singer, 1990, 34.

The Poetics of Place-Making. "every corner in a house. . . ." Bachelard, 1964, 136. All MacArthur Fellow and MSU Student quotations are taken from Worldplay Project queries and interviews (most of which are cited anonymously as a condition of research), unless otherwise noted. The child's discovery of secrecy: van Manen, 1996. Benefits of secrecy/privacy: van Manen, 1996, 8 and passim. Child's love of secret places/" "forts:" Sobel, 1993, 52, 64, 73-74; Hart, 1979. Place-making involves organizing things material and immaterial: Hart, 1979; Sobel, 1993, 95-96; van Manen, 1996, 31-33. Art and craft fabrications as daydream structures: Singer, 1975, 28.

Chapter 5. Imaginary Countries and Gifted Play: First Investigations of "Creative IQ"

Terman and the Child Genius. Terman's work on IQ: Minton, 1988; Seagoe, 1975. Child D's "all-round intellectual ability:" Terman, 1919, 251-253. Distasteful qualities of giftedness: Terman, 1954/1925, 634 & 637; 1915, 534; reversal of stigmas: Hollingworth, 1929/1926, 229. D's worldplay, "of the text so far:" Terman, 1919, 257. In the presence of "real genius": Terman, 1919, 251; "A child of four . . .": Terman, 1917, 214. "Considering [D's] fine balance of . . . traits . . . :" Terman, 1919, 259-260.

Locating Creative Giftedness. Creative capacity among children: Getzels & Jackson, 1962, 3-7; Milgram, 1990, 217. Stravinsky on creativity: Stravinsky, 1970, 60-70.

Hollingworth Picks Up the Baton of "Creative IQ". Hollingworth's sense of giftedness: Klein, A. G., 2002, 2; talent requires nurture: Klein, A.G., 2002, 155 & passim. Yoder on imaginative capacity in childhood: Yoder, 1894, 151. "Reading, calculation . . . among the recreational interests" of high IQ subjects: Hollingworth, 1929/1926, 262. Child A's imaginary land: Hollingworth, 1942, 88; Child's E's: Hollingworth, 1929/1926, 239. D spending hours "laying out roads. . . :" Hollingworth, 1942, 123; counting parts of speech: Hollingworth, 1929/1926, 245; inventing words: Hollingworth, 1942, 126; experimenting with tack: Hollingworth, 1942, 129-132. Highly complex play aligned with precocity: Hollingworth, 1929/1926, 135.

Terman's Turn with 1000 Smart Children—and Worldplay. Terman's IQ criteria: Terman, 1954/1925, 45. Worldplay in Terman's questionnaire: Terman, 1954/1925, 435. "A good many gifted children have . . . imaginary countries:" Terman, 1954/1925, 439. Fifteen test subjects above 180 IQ: Hollingworth, 1929/1926, 223; her argument, as described above: Hollingworth, 1929/1926, 135. Rates of play with imaginary companions: Taylor, 1999; Singer, 1975, 135; Harris, 2000, 32;

Singer & Singer, 1990, 97-100. Creative qualities distinct from IQ: Ochse, 1990, 204. Definitions of eminence: Terman, 1954/1925, 640; Burks, Jensen, & Terman, 1930, 4; Galton, 1925/1869. Terman's hopes for his study subjects: Terman, 1954/1925, 640. *Who's Who* expectations: Terman, 1954/1925, 640; appearances in *Who's Who*: Terman & Oden, 1959, 145-146, 150; successful careers: Terman & Oden, 1959, 43-152; setbacks: Shurkin, 1992, 158; no outstanding eminence: Subotnik, et al., 1993, 117. Terman's subjects selected for "superior intellectuality . . . :" Terman, 1954-1925, 631.

NOTE for figure 5.1: Terman focused his study on 643 children ranging in age from 2 to 13, most of whom were 8 to 12 years of age at time of study (mode is at 10). It is not known what percentage of home reports for these children answered Terman's questions on imaginary companions or countries. Return rates for other questions ranged from 91%-98% of the gifted group as a whole or, when broken down by sex, from 86-89% of boys and from 89-92% of girls. If we assume a 100% return rate, then reported numbers represented ALL children in the gifted group with imaginary companions and/or countries and percentages reflect an absolute incidence in this population. If we assume an 85% return rate, however, then reported numbers may represent most but not all children in the gifted group with those play behaviors, suggesting higher percentages and a higher incidence of imaginary companions and countries. Actual rates presumably lay within these two parameters.

Hollingworth Distinguishes Between the Intellectual and the Creative. "Are their distinctive achievements . . . signs of originality . . . :" Hollingworth, 1942, 235-236. Child E as case study: Garrison, Burke & Hollingworth, 1917; Hollingworth, 1922; Hollingworth, 1927. E as "famed prodigy:" Anonymous, 1934. Hollingworth on "the problem of the correlation of originality with intelligence scores . . . :" Hollingworth, 1942, 241. Attempts to trace Hollingworth's study subjects: Montour, 1976; Feldman, 1984, 519; Klein, A.G., 2002, viii. Development of tests for original thinking: Ochse, 1990, 205.

What We Know Now: Creativity Predicts Creativity. Giftedness does not segregate: Pritchard, 1951, 83; efforts to identify giftedness disappointing: Terman, 1954/1925; Terman & Oden, 1959; Subotnik, et al, 1993. Critique of creative thinking tests: Ochse, 1990, 45; Tannenbaum, 1992, 13. Prodigious behavior as *"openly masterful now . . . :"* Tannenbaum, 1992, 13. Prodigies' near-adult talent: Feldman, 1986, 16; prodigies not necessarily creative: Feldman, 1986, 13, 15; Sternberg & Lubart, 1992, 34; creative potential/behaviors particular to childhood: M. Root-Bernstein, 2009. "Fantasy . . . an important aspect of . . . genius:" McCurdy, 1960, 38; McCurdy, 1957. The Brontës' "learning laboratory:" McGreevy, 1995, 146-147. Creative potential and leisure activities: Milgram, 1990, 217, 222, 228-229; Subotnik, et al., 1993, 38; Klein, P. S., 1992, 248; Gross, 2004, 130-133; Kearney, 2000. Gifted play joining "complex clusters of diverse concepts . . . into consistent conceptual structures:" Morelock, 1997, 2. "Since gifted children . . . a stable and rational group . . . :" Hollingworth, 1942, 275. Prodigies as specialists in learning and talent: Feldman, 1986, 9-11. No single measure consistently predicts mature achievement: Terman, 1954/1925, 640.

Chapter 6: A Learning Laboratory in Creative Practice: Plumbing the Plausible Imagination

A Child's Mind. Hall to Folsom, "the childhood you describe . . . :" CUA: Hall Collection, Box B1-6-5, letter dated Feb 12, 1915, italics mine. Folsom to Hall, "do or create something of . . . value . . . to the world:" CUA: Box B1-6-5, letter dated April 16, 1914. Folsom's paper "an addition of real value to . . . autobiographies . . . :" CUA: B1-6-5, March 10, 1915; Folsom as "gifted . . .": CUA, B1-6-5, March 27, 1916; May 18, 1915. Folsom on his "mental grasp . . . " and solitary play: Folsom, 1915, 181, 162; on "network of currents" and other aspects of "concrete play:" 1915, 177; on his paracosm "with New York . . . fairly well located . . . :" and "railroad wrecks . . . and crime:" 1915, 179; on "I truly lived . . . my being:" 1915, 163; on giving up "childish things:" 1915, 178; on a "full account," "carefully divided into chapters . . . and foot-note references:" 1915, 162; on "still mapping the cities . . . through that mysterious country:"1915, 180.

Play Practice Analyzed. Folsom on "the general process . . .a consistent play-world:" Folsom, 1915, 178.

Ideas taken from experience. Folsom on "material content . . . taken from my real environment:" 1915, 163. Thinking as interior flow of sense impressions: R. Root-Bernstein & M. Root-Bernstein, 1999. Folsom on "a universe of objective facts" and "mysterious elements:" 1915, 164.

Associations of Ideas and Feelings. Turner on "blending" in "childhood thought:" Turner, 1996, 114. Nachmanovitch on "bricolage" and incorporating "information . . . picked up at breakfast:" Nachmanovitch, 1990, 86. Folsom on "certain rather striking . . . elements . . . and curiosity:" 1915, 164. On notice of make-believe chimeras: Turner, 1996, 89. Foslom on "an original imaginary creation . . . :" 1915, 181.

Elaboration by Play Creation. Folsom on "my interest in objects . . . of comparison and classification . . ." and "orderly series . . . of phenomena:" 1915, 165-166; on "unheard of number:" 1915, 176 and "the most terrible of all. . . . Volcanoes . . . :" 1915, 177; on "fiercity," "a sort of paper machine . . ." and temperature readings: 1915, 172; on fiercity of Volcanoes: 1915, 177; on narrative play with his sister, "using several . . . tones of voice:" 1915, 168; on laying "plans" with sister's "sympathy of cooperation:" 1915, 173. Narrative exploration of experience: Bruner, 2002, 16, 28 & passim: Harris, 2000, xi-xii, 195; Turner, 1996. Children infusing props, informing entities and linking events: Harris, 2000. Narrative as "basic principle" and "mental instrument:" Turner, 1996, preface, 4, 7 & passim. Personal knowledge: Polanyi, 1958. Folsom on "possibility of inflicting death by fright . . . :" 1915, 174.

The Synthesis of a Consistent Play-World. Folsom on "my mind . . . realistic and logical:" 1915, 163; play "narrated so as to be consistent . . . :" 1915, 180; on creatures "with their tongues half out:" 1915, 173; on his play "like a system of geometry:" 1915, 167. Leonora on frequent interruptions: Cohen & MacKeith, 1991, 40; Ambrose on regularities and reasons: Cohen & MacKeith, 1991, 88-89; Jeremy on constructed rules: Cohen & MacKeith, 1991, 94. Play as rule-governed behavior: Mitchell, 2002, 31; Bruner, 1990, 94; Paley, 2004, 33. Dan on amending elements: Cohen & MacKeith, 1991, 75-75; Brenda on plausible pattern: Cohen & MacKeith, 1991, 98.

Cohen and MacKeith on "this kind of systematic imagination . . . more like work than play:" Cohen & MacKeith, 1991, 53. Piaget on Siwimbal: Piaget, 1962, 140-142; on that make-believe "halfway between play and . . . work:" 1962, 113; on its imitative reproduction: 1962, 142. "Imagination on a half-grand scale:" Cohen & MacKeith, 1991, 54. Folsom on "the real world modified . . . :" 1915, 179. Imagination depends on constraints: Stokes, 2006. Stravinsky on "abyss of freedom:" Stravinsky, 1970, 85, 87. Borel on vocabulary and syntax of Ladahi: Borel, 1968, 64. Auden on "certain principles [of] . . . fabrication:" Auden, 1970,14, 424-425.

Modeling and Mnemonic Invention. New Hentian States as "models in Meccano:" Silvey cited in Cohen & MacKeith, 71. Analogon "to the world of fact:" D.Coleridge, 1851, xliii. Bruner on what "embodies our thoughts" and "thought and its product . . . interwoven:" Bruner, 1996, 23. Readers interested in a closer analysis of worldplay artifacts and the manner in which they structure narrative are referred to M. Root-Bernstein, 2013a. Lewis on "solitary memory": cited in Hooper, 1985, 197; on tracing "the process" and "oral tradition": cited in Hooper, 1985, 196-197; Kilby & Mead, 1982, 6 fn13; on "conviction . . . of reality": cited in Hooper, 1985, 19. Oldenburg on "first serious drawings": Lee, 2002, 17; on "an imaginary universe": Lee, 2002, 23; on his originality: cited in Rose, 1970, 19; "I always begin": cited in Rose, 1970, 143. Lewis on "reverie/invention": Lewis, 1955, 15; "mood of systematizer:" 1955, 12, 15.

The Creating Self. "Unusual features" of Folsom's play: Folsom, 1915, 161. Hall on sand pile play: Hall, 1907, 143; "My Country": Hunt, 1914, also mentioned in Hall, 1914 and in Mergen, 1995, 261-262. Folsom's introduction to Day: CUA: Hall, B1-6-5, February 12, 1915 & March 10, 1915; Day also mentioned in Hall, 1914. Hunt on "the known and the unknown": Hunt, 1914, vii; on "wishes come true": 1914, 67. Day on Exlose according to his desires: Day, 1917, 184; on himself as "first Cause": Day, 1914a, 309. Folsom on "rulers of universe": Folsom, 1915, 168; on sister's passive play: Folsom, 1915, 165; on "truth more wonderful . . . my own fiction . . . better still": Folsom, 1915, 181. Andrea on ultimate pleasure of worldplay: cited in Cohen & MacKeith, 1991, 49; Erica on "chance to be creative": cited in C&M, 1991, 51; Rosalind on "creation": cited in C&M, 1991, 84; Ambrose on "earth-sized moon . . . how the imagination works": cited in C&M, 1991, 88-89. The creative practice in organizing and synthesizing: Witty, 1940, 504. Dan "ravished by my world . . . :" cited in C&M, 1991, 76.

Worldplay and Synesthesia—A Connection? Cytowic on perception "experienced directly . . . transcendent:" Cytowic, 1993, 78. 4 in 100 adults synesthetic: Simner, et al, 2006. Synesthesia in children: R. Root-Bernstein & M. Root-Bernstein, 1999, 300-301; Cytowic, R. 2002, 8, 81; Domino, 1989, 18; Hornik, 2001, 56; Simner, et al, 2009. Hunt on "nearly everything had color . . . :" Hunt, 1914, 200, 241. Day on alphabet personalities: Day, 1914b, 325-326. Folsom on "green..the most dignified . . . color:" citing his childhood ms, in Folsom, 1915, 171. Hunt on "tawny orange zigzag" in rug "like the sound of the word:" Hunt, 1914, 70. Folsom on "each system . . . had a flag . . . :" Folsom, 1915, 171. Lionni's synesthesia: Lionni, 1997, 54; Lem's: Lem, 1995, 23-24.

Transitions to Adult Endeavor. Social psychology to "make human life more worth living:" Folsom, 1931, 663. *Plan for Marriage* censored: *PUA*. Folsom valued for "creative . . . outlook:" Koempel, 1960, 960. Folsom on "We do not wholly lose our childhood. . . . " Folsom, 1915, 180. The creative adult channels skills into valued endeavors: Ochse, 1990, 31.

PART III: GRAFTING WORLDPLAY TO ADULT WORK

Chapter 7. The Maturation of Creative Imagination: Robert Louis Stevenson as Mentor

In Praise of the Playbox. Stevenson on boy "remarkably fond of toys . . . among my playthings until the day I die:" Stevenson, *Works*, v. 25, 47. Hall on "fictitious nature" of child's play: Hall, 1907, 153. Cultural canalization: Mitchell, 2002, 13; tapering of imagination/creativity: Sternberg, 2003, 98. "Farewell to Angria": Alexander, 1983, 199, 288. Godfrey's farewell to Dobid: cited in Cohen & MacKeith, 1991, 83-84. Folsom on transforming "pressing interests:" Folsom, 1915, 180.

A Lifelong Passion for Make-Believe. Stevenson as "one of the few . . . who do not forget their childhood:" cited in Terry, 1996, 24 fn5.
The Playful Child. Stevenson's "brilliant episodes:" RL Stevenson, *Works*, v. 22, xix; "myself so hotly . . . almost a vision": RLS, *Works*, v. 29, 151. Play with cousins: Terry, 1996, 15; they "lived . . . in visionary state:" RLS, *Works*, v. 29, 156. "Game[s] of play": RLS, *Works*, v. 25, 114-115; "porridge of a morning . . . seasoned it with dreams": RLS, *Works*, v. 25, 113. Pasteboard theatre one of Stevenson's "dearest pleasures": RLS, *Works*, v. 29, 156; Skelt's "gallery of scenes": RLS, *Works*, v. 29, 108.
The Playful Man. Stevenson "excessively . . . silly": cited in Terry, 1996, 55. His "literary horse-play": cited in Terry, 1996, 94; also Hart, 1996, 11; RLS, *Works*, v. 22, 175. On his "abiding spirit": Osbourne, 1923-24, 191; his helping to "slide the actors . . . ": Osbourne, 1924, 36. The kriegspiel's "rules innumerable": Osbourne, 1923-24, 191; modeling "real conditions": Obsourne, 1923-24, 191; and "miasma": Osbourne, 1923-24, 193. Inviting cousin Bob into the war game: Harman, 2005, 216, 317. Stevenson's embarrassment, "crimsoned to the ears:" Osbourne, 1924, 27; relinquishing embarrassment, "a very conscious pride:" cited in Terry, 1996, 120. Stevenson on play filling "vacant and idle seasons:" RLS, *Works*, v. 30, 188. James on "capacity . . . for successful make-believe:" cited in Hart, 1966, 23.

From Child's Play to Literary Craft. Stevenson's "respects to Wordsworth:" RLS, *Works*, v. 29, 151, 157. Wordsworth and unitary imagination: Plotz, 2001, 18, passim; and natural creative genius: Plotz, 2001, 17-18; on "child is father": Wordsworth, *Poems*, 522. "To H.C., Six Years Old": Wordsworth, *Poems*, 522-23. Celebrated child-men and children's literature: Plotz, 2001.Gombroon: de Quincey, 1853, 97-98. Stevenson "never again . . . happy in the same way:" RLS, *Works*, v. 29, 151; the child's "gaping wonderment:" RLS, *Works*, v. 25, 107; the child's "pedestrian fancy:"

RLS, *Works*, v. 25, 110. Stevenson on "playability:" RLS, *Works*, v. 25, 115; on "dank gardens. . . . for shipwreck:" RLS, *Works*, v. 29, 121. Skelt dramas "stamped:" RLS, *Works*, v. 29, 108; the child's "weakness to create:" [Stevenson], 1888/1920, 155; children "preserve the text": RLS, *Works*, v. 25, 110.

Literary Make-Believe. Stevenson a "master of psychology:" McLynn, 1993, 22. His nurse on "long before he could write . . . :" cited in Terry, 1996, 13. On "History of Moses": McLynn, 1993, 20. Stevenson's appetite to write: Stevenson, 1947, ix; "whenever I read a book . . ." [Stevenson], 1888/1920, 2; also Terry, 1996, 21; a clothesbasket of drafts: Terry, 1996, 79. Stevenson on "daydreams:" RLS, *Works*, v. 29, 122-123; readers "push the hero aside:" RLS, *Works*, v. 29, 128-129; "fiction . . . is play:" RLS, *Works*, v. 29, 129. James on "perfect . . . boys game:" cited in Anonymous, 2007. *Treasure Island's* "list of chapters:" cited in Harman, 2005, 225; Stevenson unable to write, "he chose play . . . :" in Stevenson, 1912, preface.

Stevenson Plus Osbourne: Some Factors in Play. Lloyd as ne'er-do-well: McLynn, 1993, 345; Terry, 1996, 81; Harman, 2005, 460. Collaboration rekindling imagination's "intoxicating pleasures": RLS, *Works*, v. 30, 187; its "high spirits:" Osbourne, 1924, 107-108; discussions described: Osbourne, 1924, 108. The two spent "five days weighing money . . . :" cited in Terry, 1996, 188; Stevenson on "the ground ploughed:" cited in McLynn, 1993, 362. *The Wrecker* a "measly yarn:" Booth & Mehew, v. 7, 178; Stevenson's "bother": Booth & Mehew, v. 7, 178; his "old cure. . . . " [Stevenson], 1888/1920, 107. Osbourne's career: Baise, 2000, 131. The "simple pathos" of his fiction: Advertisement 111, 1903; also cited in Baise, 2000, 133; his critical failure "in spite of talent:" Clark, 1909; his "post-collaboration career . . . expressed mathematically": Harman, 2005, 460. Stevenson correcting for "shallowness:" cited in Swearingen, 1980, 131. Propriety and politics motivating critical dislike: Jolly, 1966, xii, xxx; Menikoff, 1984, 4, 59.

A Brief Look at "Outsider Play". Originality of private activity: Ames, 1997, 78. Outsider art defined: *Raw Vision*, 2011. On Darger: Anonymous, 2011; MacGregor, 2002. On Kuhler: Strausbaugh, 2009; Ingram & Manley, 2009. On 'Mingering Mike': Strauss, 2004; Lynskey, 2007; Cherkis, 2008; Bisceglio, 2013. On Wyatt and Chris James: Chris James, personal communication, April 2006. Wyatt on imaginary castles combining the "mental skills of architecture and . . . research:" Shortling, n.d. On home-grown sci-fi languages: Okrent, 2009, 98, 262. For Tréhin's cityscapes, Tréhin, 2011.

Chapter 8. Worldplay At Work:
MacArthur Fellows Straddle a Creative Divide

An Imaginary Beast in Real Gardens. On world invention: Gardner, 1991/1983; Lionni, 1997, 20; Mahler, cited in Jacobi, 2001, 6; Hrdy, cited in Zimmer, 1996, 78; Jacob, 1988, 8-9. Descriptions of Globbershnuckle and Zarf: Laura Otis, juvenilia. Otis on "the ability to concentrate . . . important as an historian of science . . . :" Laura Otis, query communication, April 3, 2002; on research/worldplay connection, "because to write a book . . . ." and "planning things [on Zarf]" similar: Laura Otis, telephone interview, March 6, 2003. For peer-reviewed study of worldplay at work supporting much of this chapter, see M. Root-Bernstein & R. Root-Bernstein, 2006, 415.

Worldplay Across the Professions. *The Arts: Fabricating Truths.* In this and following discussion, all Fellow comments, quoted or paraphrased, are taken from the Worldplay Project Survey, 2002, unless otherwise noted. Paul Taylor exploring "places" and "paths . . . :" P. Taylor, 1987, 18, 360. Galway Kinnell on "inner world": Kinnell, 1978, 6; on game of 'Little Men' and poetic "capacity to concentrate . . . :" Kinnell, telephone interview, July 3, 2003. Kinnell on "the best poems . . ." Kinnell, 1978, 23, 56. Artists lie to tell the truth: e.g. Le Guin, 1976, introduction. Wallace Stevens on transcendent vision: Stevens, 1954/1997, 684, 689.

The Humanities: Documenting Imagination. In this and following discussion, all Fellow comments, quoted or paraphrased, are taken from the Worldplay Project Survey, 2002, unless otherwise noted. Jeffery on study of Gregorian chant and historical imagination: Peter Jeffery, personal interview, February 21, 2003. Ulrich on historical imagination, study of 18th century midwife, 'deep play' of her research: Laurel Ulrich, telephone interview, March 6, 2003. 'Deep play' defined: Geertz, 1973, 431-432; Harkin, 2001, 58.

The Public Issues Professions: Engaging the Plausible Pragmatic. In this and following discussion, all Fellow comments, quoted or paraphrased, are taken from the Worldplay Project Survey, 2002, unless otherwise noted. Levine on creating "utopian worlds," infusing public policy with personal stories in imagined scenarios: Carol Levine, telephone interview, February 19, 2003.

The Social Sciences: Constructing Probable Possibles. In this and following discussion, all Fellow comments, quoted or paraphrased, are taken from the Worldplay Project Survey, 2002, unless otherwise noted. Robert Kates on "alternate hypotheses": Kates, 2001, 3/Table 2; on "conceptual insight": Kates, 2001, 22/Table 5. Scenario as "a summary of a play;" essay as "story . . . about how the future might play out:" Raskin, et al, 2002, 14. A 'history of future' giving "voice to . . . values . . . ;" telling "plausible and interesting stories . . . ;" offering balance of modeling and narrative "texture . . . :" Raskin, et al, 2002, 14 and passim. Robert Axelrod on art of computer simulation and its game-like qualities: Axelrod, telephone interview, March 5, 2004, unless otherwise noted. Simulation as "thought experiment:" Axelrod, 1997/2005, 5/website copy. Simulation as "third way of doing science:" Axelrod, 1997/2005, 5/website copy. Simulation combining inductive/deductive reasons, starting with a "set of explicit assumptions:" Axelrod, 1997/2005, 5/website copy. Simulation differs from mid-range theorizing: Axelrod, 1997/2005, 4/website copy.

The Sciences: Imagining the Provisionally Real. In this and following discussion, all Fellow comments, quoted or paraphrased, are taken from the Worldplay Project Survey, 2002, unless otherwise noted. Paul Adams on story-telling aspects of science in personal practice: Adams, email interview, April 4, 2003. R. Stephen Berry on worlplay in early stage of theory conception, afterwards "the work comes when you try to carry it beyond . . . :" Berry, telephone interview, March 18, 2004.

Creative Divide in Intellectual Culture. "ArtsSmarts" study: Lamore, R., et al, 2013; Root-Bernstein, R., et al, 2013. Scientists' imaginative thinking styles: R. Root-Bernstein, 1989a; R. Root-Bernstein, 1989b; R. Root-Bernstein et al, 1995; R. Root-Bernstein & M. Root-Bernstein, 2004. Informal study of science textbooks: M. Root-Bernstein & R. Root-Bernstein, 2005, 192; and unpublished study by Root-Bernstein, Root-Bernstein and Norm Lounds, Michigan State University.

Chapter 9: The Worldplay Avocation-Vocation: Some Case Studies in Creative Polymathy

Encoded Monoliths and Imaginary Museums. On the *Encoded Monolith* and its metaphorm of brain and universe: Siler, 1990, 292-301; Siler, 1995, 33-34; as "physical embodiment of worldplay:" Todd Siler, telephone interview, November 24, 2004. Shur's song-singing ants: Barry Shur, telephone interview, July 5, 2011. Versatile patterns of creative development: R. & M. Root-Bernstein, 2011; Cassandro & Simonton, 2010, 9-10. Study covering 1000 years of eminence: Gray, December 1966; Lubart & Guignard, 2004, 48. Study of 2012 eminent individuals: Cassandro, 1998, 815. Investigation of robust polymathy: R. & M. Root-Bernstein, 2004; R. Root-Bernstein, et al, 2008; R. Root-Bernstein, 2009; R. Root-Bernstein, et al, 2013. On hobbies among Nobels: van't Hoff, 1878/1967; R. Root-Bernstein, 2009, 858; R. Root-Bernstein, 1989b, 316-327. Geniuses broadly talented: R. Root-Bernstein, 2009, 853-4, citing Cox, 1926; White, 1931; Terman as cited in Seagoe, 1975; Hutchinson, 1959. Hobbies predict success: Milgram & Hong, 1994. Arts/crafts avocations in science: Eiduson, 1962, 258; R. Root-Bernstein et al, 2008; R. Root-Bernstein & M. Root-Bernstein, 2004; R. Root-Bernstein et al, 1995.

J.R.R. Tolkien: Faery Tongue and Asterisk World. Explosion of fantasy: Lobdell, 2005, 141-165. Unconstrained imagination and Middle-earth: Cohen & MacKeith, 1991, 2, 70. Tolkien and "private lang." passion: Garth, 2003, 15. Philology and asterisk-words, -language: Shippey, 2003, 20-22. Tolkien's "brightest of angels": cited in Shippey, 2003, 246-247. His asterisk-myth: Garth, 2003, 45; title of myth/poem: *The Voyage of Earendel the Evening Star* as cited in Garth, 2003, 46. Tolkien's imaginary landscapes: Hammond & Scull, 1995, 45. Material in legendarium: Garth, 2003, 279. Tolkien on "home-made languages" and "making instinct:" Tolkien, 1983, n3; on inventing "skillful bits of . . . languages:" Tolkien, 1983, 212; on "the making of language and mythology:" Tolkien, 1983, 210; on the philology of 'hobbit': Tolkien, 1965, v. 3, Appendix F, 416; Shippey, 2003, 66; on "stories . . . late in coming": cited in Carpenter, 1981, 214; on "attempt to give a background . . . :" cited in Carpenter, 1981, 214. Tolkien to Naomi Mitchison on "clash between" technique/elaborating: cited in Carpenter, 1981, 174; on her understanding "the *game* of inventing a country": cited in Carpenter, 1981, 196. Tolkien a better artist than understood: Hammond & Scull, 1995; C. Tolkien, 1992. Inability to transpose with fidelity: Hammond & Scull, 1995, 9 & 164. Clear pictorial vision: Hammond & Scull, 1995, 91 & 164-167. Tolkien to Mitchison on Middle-earth as "an imaginary historical moment:" cited in Carpenter, 1981, 239. Mitchison on Middle-earth as "a bigger bit of creation . . . a mythology:" Mitchison, 1954, 331. Tolkien on fantasy's "ideal creations": Tolkien, 1983, 138; on its "sudden glimpse of the underlying reality:" Tolkien, 1983, 155.

Gregory Benford, Ursula Le Guin, Leo Lionni, Stanislaw Lem, and Some Others: Science Fiction and Fictional Science. In this discussion: Gregory Benford, personal interview, April 4, 2007, unless otherwise noted. Benford on yen for "the changing lens of science:" Benford, 1985. Freeman Dyson on science fiction providing "more insight . . . than any statistical analysis . . . :" Dyson, 1997, 9. Ursula Le Guin on "Outer space"/"Inner Lands": Le Guin, 1973, 21, 24; on a "country called Thorn": Le Guin, 1976, 74-75; on "archaeology of the future:" Le Guin, 1985, 'A First Note'; and reference to 'secret vice': Le Guin, 1985, 509. Leo Lionni citing Marianne Moore: Lionni, 1977. His childhood play with terrariums: Lionni, 1997, 20; 1977. Beauvais Lyons on "archeological fiction" in art: Lyons, 1985; Norman Daly as director of "Llhuroscian Studies": Daly, 1972. On Stanislaw Lem's body of sci-fi, wide recognition, and output: Swirski, winter 2003. Lem models knowledge-building: Swirski, 1997, 16; Suvin, 1970. Lem on writing strategy, "I started to produce . . . the 'world' to be created by me . . . :" Lem, 1984, 23. Lem's ideas "too bold to claim scientific accuracy:" cited in Swirski, 1997, 6.

Desmond Morris: Experimental Inquiry and the Secret Kingdom of Biomorphs. Versatility and meta-craft concerns: Lubart & Guignard, 2004, 48 reworking Gray, 1966; Gray, 1966, 1395. Tolkien's music collaborations: Tolkien & Swann, 1967, vi. Morris hosting shows on "everything from sex . . . :" R. Root-Bernstein, 2005, 319. Morris on self as "extremely shy": cited in Remy, 1991, 10; on his "secret kingdom" in childhood: Morris, 1980, 15. The appeal of surrealism: Levy, 2001, 10. Scientific papers, compiled in Morris, 1970. Morris on his "private world": Morris, 1987, 12; on the artist's "personal world": cited in Levy, 2001, 14; on *Entry to a Landscape*, "I slipped through this crack . . . :" Morris, 1987, 17; into an "inner, personal world": Morris, 1987, 17. Biomorph world as "fantasy . . . lake": Morris, personal interview, July 17, 2007; biomorph "relationships and interactions": Morris cited in Levy, 2001, 13; on biomorph "evolution": Morris, 1987, 7. Dream scenario, as described in *Animal Days*: Morris, 1980, 58. Morris on "irrational, intuitive leaps" in scientific thinking: Morris, 1974, 205; on artists/scientists alike: as cited in Remy, 1991, 13. Morris on "playfulness of childhood": Morris, 1974, 204; on "explorers or non-explorers": Morris, 1974, 204; on "myself as a zoologist . . . or as a painter": Morris, 1987, 9. Morris's "parallel world . . . [as] mythmaking . . . :" cited in Morris, 1987, 7-9.

Todd Siler and the ArtScience Enterprise. On "integrated activity sets:" Dewey, 1934; on "networks of enterprise:" Gruber, 1988; on "correlative talents:" R. Root-Bernstein, 1989b, 314. Siler on "amazing source of power," and other citations in the following discussion: Todd Siler, telephone interviews, November 19 and 24, 2004, unless otherwise noted. Siler on "sunspots of the brain:" Siler, 2007. Siler on metaphorming: Siler, 1996. Siler on integration of his interests; self as "tiny wavicle . . . :" Siler, February 2001.

Synergies: Worldplay and Polymathy. The creative explosions of disparate ideas and interdisciplinary combinations: Bronowski, 1956, 19, 27. Fractal reactor as prod: Siler, 2003; Overbeck, October/November 2006. It is his artwork relevant to the science on exhibit: Siler, 2007. Siler on "worldplay . . . central to . . . creative syntheses . . . :" Siler, personal communication, 13 October, 2008. Tolkien on worldplay as a "new Art . . . :" Tolkien, 1983, 198.

PART IV: SOWING THE SEEDS OF WORLDPLAY

Chapter 10. Imaginary World Invention Goes to School: An Argument for Playful Learning

Project Notes: Educating for Creativity. Mitchel Resnick on need for creative education: Resnick, 2007-08, 18; also, e.g. Pink, 2005; Robinson, 2011; Hirsh-Pasek, et al, 2009, 62-64. Survey of superintendants/business executives: Lichtenberg, et al, 2008.

Deborah Meier and the Case for Classroom Make-Believe. In following discussion material quoting Meier from Deborah Meier, telephone interview, April 20, 2004, unless otherwise noted. On CPE schools and graduation rate: Meier, 1995, 16. Meier as "original thinker:" Winerip, 2003. Meier on curriculum at CPE school as "full of powerful ideas . . . :" Meier, 1995, 16. Worldplay in Meier's classroom practice: Shekerjian, 1990; Meier, 1995; Meier, 2002. Ignore play/shortchange creative readiness: Hirsh-Pasek, et al, 2009, 5-10; Fisher, et al, 2011. Meier on "the pleasure of imaginative play . . . not a luxury . . . :" Meier, 1995, 48.

A Brief History of Classroom Worldplay. Guided worlplay as umbrella term: M. Root-Bernstein, 2013b.
Imaginary Cities/Imagined Civilizations. Description of CPE's 3rd/4th grade imaginary city: Shekerjian, 1990, 22. School-wide themes at Mission Hill: Snyder et al, August 1992, 7. "Nile River" at Mission Hill: Winerip, 2003. Meier's elements of critical thinking: Meier, 1995.
Improbable Geographies and Other Utopias. Murphy on classroom worldplay, the Land of Withershins and geography class as vision: Murphy, 1974. Alice McLerran on mother's "History of Roxaboxen": McLerran, 1998. Classroom construction of Roxaboxen: Magik Theatre, 2008. On Bloom's taxonomy and question types: Overbaugh & Schultz, n.d.
Vision Quests. The following discussion and citation of Stacey Coates based on Coates, telephone and personal interviews, November 6, 2007 and March 9, 2009.
Games of Village and Globe. Game of Village at Prairie Creek Community School: Michelle Martin, telephone interview, May 5, 2011; Game of Village in general: Amy Shuffleton, The Village Project, Inc, telephone interview, May 2, 2011; see also Sobel, 1993, 140-153. On *State of Emergency*: Seith, 2010; Joan Parr, Scottish Arts Council, personal interview and communication May 2010 and June 8, 2010.

Gaming Imaginary Worlds. John Black on 'imaginary worlds' construction as "very productive model of education:" Black, 2007, 20 (web copy). On REAL Planet, in which "students teach an alien:" *Current ILT Projects;* additional material on REAL Planet: Xin Bai (ILT team), personal communication, 23 April 2009.

Game-Based Classrooms. On Quest to Learn Elementary generally and Katie Salen comparing game construction to "building a mini world:" Corbett, 2010, 57. On Creepytown: Chaplin, 2010. On Q2L practice in English/social studies class: Ross Flatt, conference communication, May 26, 2011 and personal communication June 14, 2011.

Building Mental Models in Cyberspace. On TLG modeling: Siler & Psi-Phi Technology Corp., 2008; Siler, 2009.

Worldplay and Embodied Education. Siler on non-linguistic representations: Siler, 2009; Black on "grounded/embodied cognition": Black, 2007. Classroom practice of non-linguistic representation assessed: Marzano, et al, 2000, 86. On embodied cognition: Barsalou, 2008, 618, 623-630; Marzano et al, 2000. On materializing the immaterial in embodied thinking: Wilson, 2002; Barsalou, 2008, 621, 626-627. On imaginative thinking skills: R. Root-Bernstein & M. Root-Bernstein, 1999; for an example of their deliberate exercise in classroom practice: Overby, Post & Newman, 2005; on assessment of thinking tool use: M. Root-Bernstein & Overby, 2012. On multiple "intelligences": Gardner, 1983. Problem solving in learning/playing: Kass & MacDonald, 1999; Dewey, 1902/1990, 118; also Smilansky, 1968, especially 25, n. 117. On worldplay in college classroom: Ren Hullender, personal interview and communication, May 26-28, 2011.

Creative Schooling: Caveats and Callings. Educational punch/effective learning: Najjar, 1996a, 1996b; Barsalou, 2008, 625; Griggs, 2008. Learning falsely pitted against playing: Hirsh-Pasek, et al, 2009, x.

Chapter 11: Worldplay the Computer Way: Children and Youth Reveal Their Lived Experience

Imaginary Worlds at the Crossroads. Discussion of Nate's play based on personal interview, March 28, 2010. Overall access and school access to computers: *Computer and Internet Use,* 2005, 7; in the hands of 90% of children: Children and Technology Project, introductory video. Percent of boys/girls playing computer games: Pew Internet & American Life Project, 2008, 8-9; also *Computer and Internet Use*, 2005, 9, for corroborating data. Teens play "with relative frequency:" Pew, 2008, 8. Percent of children playing every day: Lewin, 2010, 2011. Computer games as "major cultural activity:" Gee cited in Leland, 2005. To place sea change in historical context, see Chudacoff, 2007 and Cross, 1990. For some major voices in the debate, see in the con camp: Elkind, 2007; Singer & Singer, 2005; Anderson et al, 2007; Carr, 2010; Norman, 1993; Linn, 2004, 2008. In the pro camp: Gee, 2003, 2007/2008; Jackson et al, 2008; Turkle, 1995; Pesce, 2000; Steinkuehler, 2006. Bavelier & Davidson, 2013, call for greater collaboration between game designers and neuroscientists to determine and foster beneficial game effects. On the Media altering "how children think:" Singer & Singer, 2005, 5, 63. Computer play in a positive light: Turkle, 1995, 11; Gee, 2003, 2007/2008; Pesce, 2000; Bower, 2010, 12; Steinkuehler, 2006. Virtual play as "new kind of creativity": Pesce, 2000, 6. Media as message: McLuhan, 1964. Value of play in attitude: L'Abate, 2009, 26.

Exploring Computer Simulated Worlds. On privileging lived experience: Van Manen, 1990.

The Lived Experience of Simulated Worlds. Discussion of Lee's play based on personal interview/observation, May 15, 2010. The "vivid present:" cited in Greene, 2001, 15; "presence": Biocca, 2002, 101. Discussion of Andrew's play based on personal interview/observation, May 21, 2010. Discussion of Ian's play based on personal interview/observation, May 21, 2010. Discussion of Thom's play based on personal interview, March 28, 2010. Discussion of Molly's play based on personal interview, March 31, 2010. Discussion of Aaron's play based on personal interview/ observation, April 8, 2010. On flow: Csikszentmihalyi, 1996, 110.

Digging Deeper: Agency in Game Play. Discussion of Ellie's play based on personal interview, March 28, 2010. Percentage of user-generated content on Second Life: Herold, 2007.

Imaginative Literacies Compared. On the reading experience: Stevenson, 1923-24, v. 29, 128-129; Dewey, 1934, 54; Green & Brock, 2002, 321-322, 327. Co-creation of the narrative: Bronowski, 1978, 14; Iser, 1978, ix-x. Dominating (a.k.a. aggressive) image stream: Norman, 1993, 245; Singer & Singer, 2005, 63.

The Doing of "Untaught" Things. Dewey on the self in "formation": cited in Greene, 2001, 99. Green on conforming self and "untaught things": Greene, 2001, 137.

Towards Creative Computer Literacy. The MIT Media Lab is preparing for the release of Scratch Jr. for children in kindergarten through second grade in 2014, as a means of boosting computer literacy from the get-go. On programming initiatives for the young: Resnick, 2007-08; Peppler & Kafai, 2005; Shapiro, 2013a, 2013b, 2013c; Corbett, 2010, Singer & Singer, 2005, 132-135. For more on Scratch programming, see Resnick's website: <http://www.media.mit.edu/research/groups/lifelong-kindergarten>. Discussion of Kyla Gorman's play based on Kyla Gorman, personal communication, June 9, 2011 and personal interview June 18, 2011.

Chapter 12. The Creative Capital of Make-Believe: How to Support Children Playing at Their Best

On the Lookout for Worldplay. Discussion of anonymous, chance paracosmists based on personal communications, except for the web designer/Tollo: Crook, 2003. This discussion of Megan's play is based on Megan Root, personal interview, September 15, 2007.

A Question of Nature and Nurture. On families sharing "a communality of . . . experiences:" Feldman, 1986, 189. Personal reasons for worldplay: Alan Garner in Cooper, 1999, 63; Jane in Cohen & MacKeith, 1991, 53-55; Peter Ustinov in Ustinov,

1998, 278. For a look at how paracosms may, in some cases, help individuals cope with early grief, see Morrison & Morrison, 2006. Worldplay shared with siblings: Winkworth sisters in Winkworth, 1908, 9; Friedrich Nietzsche and sister in Forster-Nietzsche, 1912, 46-47; Leo Tolstoy and siblings, Gertrude Stein and brother, Vera Brittain and brother in Goertzel & Goertzel, 1962, 117n; C.S. Lewis and brother in Lewis, 1955, 6, 79, passim and in Hooper, 1985, 21; Dutch family in Langeveld, 1983, 13; Fairfield Porter, brother and friends in Cummings, 1968, as well as Spring, 2000, 14, and Lawrence Porter (Fairfield's son), personal communication March 20, 2008. On Islandia/Cravay of the Wright brothers, see: Wright, 1958/1966, ix; on her mother's "college town": Wright, 1958/1966, vi. Examples of generational transfer: Stevenson in Stevenson, *Works*, v. 30, 45; Ambrose in Cohen & MacKeith, 1991, 88; Oldenburg in Rose, 1970, 33n1.

Adult Modeling of Make-Believe. All play is learned: L'Abate, 2009, 40. Adult modeling of play: Dansky, 1980; Singer & Singer, 2001; Singer & Singer, 2005, 143-147; Singer & Singer, 2005-2006, 106-108; Russ, 2006; Moore & Russ, 2008. On aesthetic understanding not necessarily natural: Greene, 2001, 59. On moments of wonder: Dewey, 1934, 18; Clark, 1981, 2; Cobb, 1959, 538; Cobb, 1977/1993, 27-30; R. Root-Bernstein & M. Root-Bernstein, 1999, 114, 301. Maxine Green, "it is still necessary to empower children:" Greene, 2001, 59. Adult modeling of worldplay: Allan's father in Cohen & MacKeith, 1991, 81; Brontës' father, as "greatest single influence" in Alexander, 1987, xix.

Encouraging Worldplay. Adult participation in children's play controversial: Spitz, 2006, 41; it is "difficult" to model/parent at the same time: Spitz, 2006, 45. On adult expectation causing child frustration, see: Amabile, 1983, vii. Interference in play suppresses creativity: Batcha, 2005, 94; M. Taylor, 1999, 158. Adults "keep out": Cohen & MacKeith, 1991, 23. Rules of thumb for supporting pretend play: Shmukler, 1988; Singer & Singer, 2005, 33-34; and for supporting a creative climate, see: Fasko, 2000-2001, 319.

Five Rules of Thumb for Pretend Play in Early Childhood. Singers on "sacred place:" Singer & Singer, 2005, 34. Boredom as creative stimulant: Batcha, 2005. Importance of unique play objects and "one-ofs:" Spitz, 2006, 158.

Five More Rules of Thumb for Cultivating Worldplay in Middle and Late Childhood. Bachelard on "images that are too clear . . . :" cited in Spitz, 2006, 38. Bachelard on aloneness: also cited by Spitz, 2006, 158. Creative individuals alone long hours in childhood: Toth, March/April 1994, 82-83. L'Abate on "interdependence" of solitary play: L'Abate, 2009, 215-216. On rehearsing pretend interactions in solitary play: Cowie, 1984, 63. Gorman getting support from mother to play, "the longer creativity muscles stay flexed:" Kyla Gorman, personal interview, June 18, 2011.

But What If It Isn't Worldplay? Modeling imaginary world invention doesn't work for Ambrose's sister: Cohen & MacKeith, 1991, 88; for Silvey's children: Cohen & MacKeith, 1991, 71. Play as "psychological attitude:" Dewey, 1902/1915/1990, 118.

Playing Complexly, Playing At Their Best. Dewey on "the free play" of child's powers: Dewey,1915/1990, 118-119; Dewey's three questions: Dewey, 1915/1990, 120, emphasis mine. Note that this passage has also been updated to include girls as well as boys. The list of ten implicit understandings generated in complex make-believe play is indebted to a similar list of understandings students and teachers may cultivate in arts classrooms, as drawn up by Hope, 2010, 43.

Higher Planes of Action: A Check-In. Discussion of Megan's play, three years later, is based on Megan Root, personal interview, September 18, 2010. On Megan's interest in science as "the result of her imaginary explorations:" Anne Root, personal communication, July 7, 2010.

Conclusion. Wither the Worldplay Impulse?

"Enlightened cherishing" is a phrase used by Greene, 2001, 58. Lewis on "self-sufficient reality:" cited in Hooper, 1985, 19, 196. For researchers on development of moral and social understanding in worldplay, see e.g.: Levernier, et al, 2013. Play in virtual worlds "not simply a childish fad:" Bainbridge, 2007, 472. Professional applications of virtual worldplay, in business: Newitz, 2007; in science and social science: Markoff, 2010; Johnson, 2006; Coppola, 2007; Bainbridge, 2007, 472; Giles, 2007, 19. Virtual worlds as a "future chalkboard of science": Johnson, 2006. Padgett's poem is reprinted in Koch & Farrell, 1985, 67. Play critical, to education: Tinbergen, 1975, 19; to adulthood: Morris in Levy, 1997, 204-205; to art and science: Morris in Schneider, 2008. Chamberlain on "rather the parent strive to be like the babe:" Chamberlain, 1900, 445-446. For a brief and modern essay on the evolutionary trajectory of fantasy play, see Donald, 2013. Stevenson on "a generation that does not know how to play:" cited in *Works*, xix.

Appendix: A Childhood Worldplay List

Goertzel on writers over-represented: Goertzel & Goertzel, 2004, 320. Ludwig on professions acknowledging private experience: Ludwig, 1995, 7. Additional examples of childhood worldplay will "trickle in:" Silvey & MacKeith, 1988, 194.

Works Cited

MANUSCRIPT SOURCES

Clark University Archives and Special Collections (CUA):
  Dr. G. Stanley Hall Collection. Subseries 6, Graduate Student Correspondence:
  Box B1-6-4: Day, L. C.
  Box B1-6-5: Folsom, Joseph K.
Princeton University Archives (PUA):
  Harper & Bros. Collection, Author Files, Box 12.

PUBLISHED SOURCES

Advertisement 111. (December 1903). *The Critic,* 43, 6 (APS Online p. 604).

Alexander, Christine. (1983). *The Early Writings of Charlotte Brontë*. Oxford: Basil Blackwell.

———— (Ed.). (1987). *An Edition of the Early Writings of Charlotte Brontë*, vol. 1. Oxford: Basil Blackwell.

Amabile, Theresa. (1983). *The Social Psychology of Creativity*. New York: Springer-Verlag.

Ames, Joan Evelyn. (1997). *Mastery: Interviews with Thirty Remarkable People*. Portland, OR: Rudra Press.

Anderson, Craig A.; Gentile, Douglas A. & Buckley, Katherine E. (2007). *Violent Video Game Effects on Children and Adolescents. Theory, Research and Public Policy.* New York: Oxford University Press.

Anonymous. (June 4, 1934). A.B., M.A., Th.B., Ph.D., S.T.M. *Time*. Retrieved January 23, 2007, from Time Archives: http://www.time.com/time/magazine/article/0,9171,754233,00.html.

Anonymous. (2007.) *Treasure Island*. Wikipedia. Retrieved May 7, 2007, from http://en.wikipedia.org/wiki/Treasure_Island.

Anonymous. (2011). Henry Darger. Wikipedia. Retrieved April 8, 2011, from http://en.wikipedia.org/wiki/Henry_Darger.

Auden, W. H. (1970). *A Certain World: A Commonplace Book*. New York: A William Cole book, Viking Press.

Axelrod, Robert. (2005). Advancing the Art of Simulation in the Social Sciences. Forthcoming in *Handbook of Research on Nature Inspired Computing for Economy and Management*, Jean-Philippe Rennard (Ed.). Hershey, PA: Idea Group. Retrieved August 26, 2008, from http://www-personal.umich.edu/~axe/ (revised; originally published in Rosario Conte, Rainer Hegselmann, and Pietro Terna (Eds.). 1997. *Simulating Social Phenomena* (pp. 21–40). Berlin: Springer-Verlag).

Bachelard, Gaston. (1964). *The Poetics of Space*. (Maria Jolas, Trans.). New York: Orion Press.

Bainbridge, William Sims. (July 27, 2007). The Scientific Research Potential of Virtual Worlds. *Nature* 317: 472–76.

Baise, Jennifer (Ed.). (2000). Lloyd Osbourne, 1868–1947. *Twentieth-Century Literary Criticism*, vol. 93, New York: Gale Group.

Baring, Maurice. (1922). *The Puppet Show of Memory*. Boston: Little, Brown & Co.

Barker, Juliet. (1994). *The Brontës*. New York: St. Martin's Press.

———. (1997). *The Brontës: A Life in Letters*. New York: Overlook Press.

Barsalou, Lawrence. (2008). Grounded Cognition. *Annual Review of Psychology* 59: 618–45.

Batcha, Becky. (February 2005). The Benefits of Boredom. *Child*, 93–96.

Bavelier, Daphne & Davidson, Richard J. (February 28, 2013). Games to Do You Good. *Nature* 494: 425–26.

Benford, Gregory. (1985). Why Does a Scientist Write Science Fiction? Speech, UC San Diego class reunion, 1985. Retrieved March 31, 2007, from http://www.benford-rose.com/scientistwrite.php.

Bentley, Phyllis. (1969). *The Brontës and Their World*. London: Thames and Hudson.

Biocca, Frank. (2002). The Evolution of Interactive Media: Toward "Being There" in Nonlinear Narrative Worlds. In M. C. Green, J. J. Strange & T. C. Brock. *Narrative Impact: Social and Cognitive Foundations* (pp. 97–130). Mahwah, NJ: L. Erlbaum Associates.

Bisceglio, Paul. (April 2013). This Just In, Urban Legend Found. *Smithsonian*, 92.

Black, John B. (2007.) Imaginary Worlds. In M. A. Gluck, J. R. Anderson & S. M. Kosslyn (Eds.). *Memory and Mind: A Festschrift for Gordon H. Bower*. Hoboken, NJ: Lawrence Erlbaum Associates. Web copy retrievable at http://www.ilt.columbia.edu/publicAtions/index.html.

Booth, Bradford A. & Mehew, Ernest. (Eds.). (1994–1995). *The Letters of Robert Louis Stevenson*. New Haven, CT: Yale University Press, 8 vols.

Borel, Jacques. (1968). *The Bond*. (Norman Denny, Trans.). London: Collins (Originally published in 1965).

Bower, Bruce. (October 9, 2010). Action Games Cut Reaction Times. *Science News*, 12.

Bridgman, P. W. (Winter, 1958). Quo Vadis. In G. Levine & T. Owen (Eds.).1963. *The Scientist vs. the Humanist* (pp. 167–76). New York: W. W. Norton & Company. (Originally published in *Daedalus* (The Journal of the American Academy of Arts and Sciences) 87: 85–93.)

Bronowski, J. (1956). *Science and Human Values*. New York: Harper & Row.

———. (1978). *The Visionary Eye: Essays in the Arts, Literature, and Science*. Cambridge, MA: MIT Press.

Bruner, Jerome. (1990). *Acts of Meaning*. Boston: Harvard University Press.

———. (1996). *The Culture of Education*. Cambridge, MA: Harvard University Press.

———. (2002). *Making Stories: Law, Literature and Life*. New York: Farrar, Straus and Giroux.

Burks, B. X.; Jensen, D. W. & Terman, L. M. (1930). *The Promise of Youth, vol. 3. Genetic Studies of Genius*. Stanford, CA: Stanford University Press.

Carpenter, Humphrey (Ed.). (1981). *The Letters of J.R.R. Tolkien*. Boston: Houghton Mifflin.

Carr, Nicolas. (2010). *The Shallows: What the Internet Is Doing to Our Brains.* New York: W. W. Norton and Co.

Cassandro, Vincent J. (1998). Explaining Premature Mortality Across Fields of Creative Endeavor. *Journal of Personality* 66 (5): 805–33.

Cassandro, Vincent J. & Simonton, Dean Keith. (2010). Versatility, Openness to Experience, and Topical Diversity in Creative Products: An Exploratory Historiometric Analysis of Scientists, Philosophers, and Writers. *Journal of Creative Behavior* 44 (1): 9–26.

Chamberlain, Alexander Francis. (1900). *The Child; A Study in the Evolution of Man*, 3rd edition. New York: Charles Scribner's Sons. (Digitized 2007, Center for Research Libraries.)

Chaplin, H. (June 28, 2010). School Uses Video Games to Teach Thinking Skills, *National Public Radio*, available at http://www.npr.org/templates/story/story.php?storyId=128081896.

Cherkis, Jason. (October 24, 2008). The Return of the Magnificent Mingering. *Washington City Paper*. Retrieved April 9, 2011, from http://www.washingtoncitypaper.com/articles/36388/the-return-of-the-magnificent-mingering.

Children and Technology Project. (n.d.) Funded by the National Science Foundation, at https://www.msu.edu/user/jackso67/CT/children/. Introductory video retrieved September 13, 2010, from https://www.msu.edu/user/jackso67/CT/children/intro.htm

Chudacoff, Howard P. (2007). *Children at Play: An American History.* New York: New York University Press.

Clark, Kenneth. (1981). *Moments of Vision.* London: John Murray.

Clark, Ward. (June 1909). Mr. Osbourne's "Infatuation." *The Bookman, A Review of Books and Life* 29, 4 (APS Online, p. 406).

Cobb, Edith. (1959). The Ecology of Imagination in Childhood: Work in Progress. *Daedalus* 88 (3): 537–48.

———. (1993). *The Ecology of Imagination in Childhood.* Republication. Dallas: Spring Publications. (Originally published in 1977)

Cohen, David. (1987). *The Development of Play.* New York: New York University Press.

———. (December 22/29, 1990). Private Worlds of Childhood. *New Scientist,* 28–30.

Cohen, David & MacKeith, Stephen A. (1991). *The Development of Imagination: The Private Worlds of Childhood.* London: Routledge.

Coleridge, Hartley. (1851a). *Essays and Marginalia* (Derwent Coleridge, Ed.). London: Edward Moxon, 2 vols.

———. (1851b). *Poems by Hartley Coleridge, with a Memoir of His Life by His Brother.* (2nd ed.) London: Edward Moxon, 2 vols.

Computer and Internet Use in the United States: 2003. (October 2005). Special Studies, U.S. Census Bureau, Retrieved September 13, 2010, from http://www.census.gov/prod/2005pubs/p23-208.pdf.

Cooper, Susan. (1999). Worlds Apart. In Barbara Harrison & Gregory Maquire (Eds.). *Origins of Story: On Writing for Children.* New York: McElderry Books.

Coppola, Kim. (February 24, 2007). Virtual Outbreak. *New Scientist,* 39–41.

Corbett, Sara. (September 19, 2010). Games Theory. *New York Times Magazine*, p. 54–61, 66–70.

Cowie, Helen (Ed.). (1984). *The Development of Children's Imaginative Writing.* New York: St. Martin's Press.

Cox, Catherine. (1926). *The Early Mental Traits of Three Hundred Geniuses.* Genetic Studies of Genius, vol. II, Stanford, CA: Stanford University Press.

Crook, Mike. (2003). The History of My Imagined World. Retrieved August 26, 2003, from http://www.mikecrook.com/docs/paracosm/tollo.htm.

Cropley, David H., Cropley, Arthur J., Kaufman, James C. & Runco, Mark A. (Eds.). (2010). *The Dark Side of Creativity*. New York: Cambridge University Press.

Cross, Gary S. (1990). *A Social History of Leisure since 1600*. State College, PA: Venture Publishing.

Csikszentmihalyi, M. (1996). *Creativity: Flow and the Psychology of Discovery and Invention*. New York: Harper Perennial.

Cummings, Paul. (June 6, 1968). Interview with Fairfield Porter at Southhampton, New York. Archives of American Art, Smithsonian Institution.

Current ILT Projects (n.d.). Reflective Agent Learning Environment Project (REAL). Project Director: John Black. Retrieved January 7, 2009, from http://www.ilt.columbia.edu/projects/projects_current.html.

Cytowic, Richard. (1993). *The Man Who Tasted Shapes*. New York: G. P. Putnam's Sons.

———. (2002). Touching Tastes, Seeing Smells—And Shaking up Brain Science. *Cerebrum, the Dana Forum On Brain Science* 4 (3): 7–26.

Daly, Norman. (1972). *The Civilization of Llhuros*. Ithaca, NY: Office of University Publications, Cornell University.

Daniels, Elizabeth A. (1994). The Disappointing First Thrust of Euthenics. In Elizabeth Daniels. *Bridges to the World: Henry Noble MacCracken and Vassar College* (Clinton Corners, NY: College Avenue Press). Retrieved February 5, 2007, from http://vcencyclopedia.vassar.edu/index.php/The_Disappointing_First_Thrust_of_Euthenics.

Dansky, Jeffrey L. (1980). Make-Believe: A Mediator of the Relationship Between Play and Associative Fluency. *Child Development* 51 (2): 576–79.

Day, Lorey C. (1914a). The Child God. *Pedagogical Seminary* 21 (3): 309–20.

———. (1914b). Alphabet Friendships. *Pedagogical Seminary* 21 (3): 321–28.

———. (1917). A Small Boy's Newspapers and the Evolution of a Social Conscience. *Pedagogical Seminary* 24 (2): 180–203.

de la Roche, Mazo. (1957). *Ringing the Changes: An Autobiography*. Toronto: Little, Brown & Co.

de Quincey, Thomas. (1853). *Autobiographical Sketches*. Boston: Ticknor, Reed & Fields.

de Waal, F. (2003). *My Family Album: Thirty Years of Primate Photography*. (Los Angeles: University of California Press.

Dewey, John. (1934). *Art as Experience*. New York: Minton, Balch & Company.

———. (1990). *The School and Society and The Child and the Curriculum* (Philip Jackson, Ed.). Chicago: University of Chicago Press. (Originally published in 1902)

Domino, G. (1989). Synesthesia and Creativity in Fine Arts Students: An Empirical Look. *Creativity Research Journal* 2: 17–29.

Donald, Merlin. (2013). Implications for Developing a Creative Mindset. Essay commissioned by the Lego Foundation, for David Gauntlett & Bo Stjerne Thomsen, *Cultures of Creativity: Nurturing Creative Mindsets across Cultures*. Retrieved October 1, 2013, from http://www.legofoundation.com/en-us/research-and-learning/foundation-research/cultures-of-creativity/.

Du Maurier, Daphne. (1961). *The Infernal World of Branwell Brontë*. Garden City, NY: Doubleday.

Dyson, Freeman. (1997). *Imagined Worlds*. Cambridge, MA: Harvard University Press.

Eiduson, Bernice. (1962). *Scientists: Their Psychological World*. New York: Basic Books.

Elkind, David. (2007). *The Power of Play: How Spontaneous, Imaginative Activities Lead to Happier, Healthier Children*. Cambridge, MA: Da Capo Press.

Erikson, E. (1963). *Childhood and Society*. (2nd ed.). New York: W. W. Norton & Co. (Originally published in 1950)

Evans, Barbara & Evans, Gareth Lloyd. (1982). *The Scribner Companion to the Brontës*. New York: Charles Scribner's Sons.

Fagen, Robert. (1988). Animal Play and Phylogenetic Diversity of Creative Minds. *Journal of Social and Biological Structures* 11 (1): 79–82.

———. (1995). Animal Play, Games of Angels, Biology, and Brian. In A. D. Pellegrini (Ed.). *The Future of Play Theory: A Multidisciplinary Inquiry into the Contributions of Brian Sutton-Smith*, pp. 23–44. Albany, NY: State University of New York Press.

Fagen, Robert & Fagen, J. (2004). Juvenile Survival and Benefits of Play Behaviour in Brown Bears, Ursus Arctos. *Evolutionary Ecology Research* 6 (1): 89–102.

Fasko, Jr., Daniel. (2000–2001). Education and Creativity. *Creativity Research Journal* 13 (3&4): 317–27.

Feldman, D. H. (1984). A Follow-up of Subjects Scoring above 180 IQ in Terman's "Genetic Studies of Genius." *Exceptional Children* 50 (6): 518–23.

———. (1986). *Nature's Gambit: Child Prodigies and the Development of Human Potential*. New York: Basic Books.

Fisher, Kelly; Hirsh-Pasek, Kathy; Golinkoff, Roberta M.; Singer, Dorothy G. & Berk, Laura. (2011). Playing Around in School: Implications for Learning and Educational Policy. In Anthony D. Pellegrini (Ed.). *The Oxford Handbook of the Development of Play* (pp. 341–60). Oxford: Oxford University Press.

Folsom, Joseph K. (1915). The Scientific Play World of a Child. *The Pedagogical Seminary* 22 (2): 161–82.

———. (1931). *Social Psychology*. New York: Harper & Bros.

——— (Ed.). (1938). *Plan for Marriage: An Intelligent Approach to Marriage and Parenthood*. New York: Harper & Bros.

Forster-Nietzsche, Elisabeth. (1912). *The Life of Nietzsche*. Anthony M. Ludovici (Trans.). New York, Sturgis & Walton, 2 vols. (Vol. 1, *The Young Nietzsche*)

Galton, Francis. (1925). *Hereditary Genius: An Inquiry into Its Laws and Consequences*. London: MacMillan and Co. (Originally published in 1869)

Gardner, Howard. (1983). *Frames of Mind: The Theory of Multiple Intelligences*. New York: Basic Books.

Gardner, John. (1991). *The Art of Fiction: Notes on Craft for Young Writers*. New York: Vintage Books/Random House. (Original published 1983)

Garrison, Charlotte G; Burke, Agnes & Hollingworth, Leta S. (1917). The Psychology of a Prodigious Child. *Journal of Applied Psychology* 1 (2): 101–10.

Garth, John. (2003). *Tolkien and the Great War: The Threshold of Middle-Earth*. Boston: Houghton Mifflin

Gee, James P. (2003). *What Video Games Have to Teach Us About Learning and Literacy*. Gordonsville, VA: Palgrave Macmillan.

———. (2007/2008). *Good Video Games + Good Learning: Collected Essays on Video Games, Learning, and Literacy*. New York: P. Lang.

Geertz, Clifford. (1973). *The Interpretation of Cultures: Selected Essays*. New York: Basic Books.

Getzels, J. W. & Jackson, P. W. (1962). *Creativity and Intelligence: Explorations with Gifted Students*. New York: John Wiley & Sons.

Giles, Jim. (January 4, 2007). Life's a Game. *Nature* 445: 19.

Goertzel, Victor & Goertzel, Mildred George. (1962). *Cradles of Eminence*. London: Constable and Co.

———. (2004). *Cradles of Eminence, Second Edition: Childhoods of More Than 700 Famous Men and Women* (Updated by Ted George Goertzel & Arile Hanson). Scottsdale, AZ: Great Potential Press. (Originally published in1962)

Gómez, Juan-Carlos & Martín-Andrade, Beatriz. (2005). Fantasy Play in Apes. In A. D. Pellegrini & P. K. Smith (Eds.). *The Nature of Play: Great Apes and Humans* (pp. 139–72). New York: The Guilford Press.

Gopnik, Alison. (July/August 2012). Why Play Is Serious. *Smithsonian.*

Grahame, Kenneth. (1895). The Roman Road. Reprinted in *The Golden Age*. London: John Lane.

Gray, Charles Edward. (December 1966). A Measurement of Creativity in Western Civilization. *American Anthropologist* 68 (6): 1384–1417.

Green, Melanie C. & Brock, Timothy, C. (2002). In the Mind's Eye, Transportation-Imagery Model of Narrative Persuasion. In M. C. Green, J. J. Strange & T. C. Brock. *Narrative Impact: Social and Cognitive Foundations* (pp. 315–41). Mahwah, NJ: L. Erlbaum Associates.

Green, Peter. (1982). *Beyond the Wild Wood: The World of Kenneth Grahame*. Exeter: Webb & Bower. (Edited and abridged version of *Kenneth Grahame: A Biography*, 1959)

Greenberg, Joanne (Hannah Green). (1964). *I Never Promised You a Rose Garden*. New York: Penguin Books.

Greene, Maxine. (2001). *Variations on a Blue Guitar: The Lincoln Center Institute Lectures on Aesthetic Education*. New York: Teachers College Press.

Griggs, Richard A. (2008). *Psychology: A Concise Introduction*. New York: Worth Publishers.

Groos, Karl. (1901). *The Play of Man*. (E. L. Baldwin, Trans.). New York: Appleton. (Originally published in 1899)

Gross, M. U. M. (2004). *Exceptionally Gifted Children* (2nd ed.). New York: RoutledgeFalmer.

Gruber, H. (1988). The Evolving Systems Approach to Creative Work. *Creativity Research Journal* 1: 27–51.

Hall, G. Stanley (Ed.). (1907). *Aspects of Child Life and Education, by G. Stanley Hall and Some of His Pupils*. Theodate L. Smith (Ed.). Boston: Ginn & Company/Athenaeum Press.

———. (February 1914). An Expert's Opinion (Endorsement of *Una Mary*, by Una Hunt). *Book Buyer: A Monthly Review of American and Foreign Literature*, 39 (1).

Hambleton, Ronald. (1966). *Mazo de la Roche of Jalna*. New York: Hawthorn Books.

Hammond, Wayne G. & Scull, Christina. (1995). *J.R.R. Tolkien Artist & Illustrator*. Boston: Houghton Mifflin.

Harkin, Michael. (2001). Ethnographic Deep Play: Boas, McIlwraith and Fictive Adoption on the Northwest Coast. In Sergei Kan (Ed.). *Strangers to Relatives: The Adoption and Naming of Anthropologists in Native North America* (pp. 57–79). Lincoln, NE: University of Nebraska Press.

Harman, Claire. (2005). *Myself and the Other Fellow: A Life of Robert Louis Stevenson*. New York: HarperCollins.

Harris, Paul. (2000). *The Work of the Imagination*. Oxford: Blackwell Publishers.

Hart, James D. (1966). *The Private Press Ventures of Samuel Lloyd Osbourne and R.L.S.* (limited edition). San Francisco: The Book Club of California.

Hart, Roger. (1979). *Children's Experience of Place*. New York: Irvington Publishers.

Hartmann, Herbert. (1931). *Hartley Coleridge: Poet's Son and Poet*. Oxford: Oxford University Press.

Held, Suzanne D. E. and Spinka, Marek. (2011). Animal Play and Animal Welfare. *Animal Behaviour* 81: 891–99.

Herold, Charles. (September 21–23, 2007). Customize Your Game Worlds. *USA Weekend*, 14.

Hirsh-Pasek, Kathy; Golinkoff, Roberta Michnick; Berk, Laura E. & Singer, Dorothy G. (2009). *A Mandate for Playful Learning in Preschool*. Oxford: Oxford University Press.

Hollingworth, Leta S. (1922). Subsequent History of E—; Five Years After the Initial Report. *Journal of Applied Psychology* 6: 205–10.

———. (1927). Subsequent History of E—; Ten Years After the Initial Report. *Journal of Applied Psychology* 11: 385–90.

———. (1929). *Gifted Children: Their Nature and Nurture*. New York: MacMillan. (Originally published in1926)

———. (1942). *Children above 180 IQ: Origin and Development*. Yonkers-on-Hudson, NY: World Book Company.

Hooper, Walter (Ed.). (1985). *Boxen: The Imaginary World of the Young C.S. Lewis*. London: Collins.

Hope, Samuel. (2010). Creativity, Content, and Policy. *Arts Education Policy Review* 111: 39–47.

Hornik, S. (2001). For Some, Pain Is Orange. *Smithsonian*, 31 (11): 48–56.

Hunt, Una. (1914). *Una Mary: The Inner Life of a Child*. New York: Charles Scribner's Sons.

Hutchinson, Eliot Dole. (1959). *How to Think Creatively*. New York: Abington-Cokesbury Press.

Ingram, Brett & Manley, Roger. (Autumn 2009). Welcome To Rocaterrania. *Raw Vision* 67.

Iser, Wolfgang. (1978). *The Act of Reading: A Theory of Aesthetic Response*. Baltimore, MD: Johns Hopkins University Press.

Isherwood, Christopher. (1947*). Lions and Shadows: An Education in the Twenties*. Norfolk, CT: New Directions.

Jackson, Linda A.; Fitzgerald, Hiram E.; Zhao, Yong; Kolenic, Anthony; von Eye, Alexander & Harold, Rena. (2008). Information Technology (IT) Use and Children's Psychological Well-Being. *CyberPsychology & Behavior* 11 (6): 755–57.

Jacob, François. (1988). *The Statue Within: An Autobiography*. New York: Basic Books.

Jacobi, Peter. (2001). A Music Lesson for Writers, *Writing for Children: The Report of the 2001 Highlights Foundation Writers Workshop at Chautauqua, New York*. Honesdale, PA: Highlights Foundation.

Johnson, Kirk. (February 28, 2006). Theoretical Physics, in Video: A Thrill Ride to "the Other Side of Infinity." *New York Times*, D1.

Jolly, Roslyn. (1966). Introduction. In Robert Louis Stevenson, *South Sea Tales*. Oxford: Oxford University Press.

Jung, C. G. (1961). *Memories, Dreams, Reflections*. Aniela Jaffé (Ed.). Richard & Clara Winston (Trans.). New York: Vintage Books/Random House.

Kass, Heidi & MacDonald, A. Leo. (1999). The Learning Contribution of Student Self-directed Building Activity in Science. *Science Education* 83: 449–71.

Kates, Robert W. (November, 2001). Queries on the Human Use of the Earth. *Annual Review of Energy and the Environment*, vol. 26: 1–26.

Kaye-Smith, Sheila. (1956). *All the Books of My Life*. New York: Harper & Bros.

Kearney, K. (2000.) Frequently Asked Questions about Extreme Intelligence in Very Young Children. What about Play? Do Highly and Profoundly Gifted Preschoolers Play Differently From Other Children? Paragraph 7. Retrieved August 22, 2006, from Davidson Institute for Talent Development: www.davidsoninstitute.org.

Kerouac, Jack. (1960/1995). Introduction to Lonesome Traveler. Reprinted in Ann Charters (Ed.). *The Portable Jack Kerouac* (1995). New York: Viking.

Kilby, Clyde S. & Mead, Majorie Lamp. (1982). *Brothers and Friends: The Diaries of Major Warren Hamilton Lewis*. New York: Harper & Row.

Kinnell, Galway. (1978). *Walking Down Stairs: Selections from Interviews*. (Ann Arbor: University of Michigan Press).

Klein, Ann G. (2002). *A Forgotten Voice: A Biography of Leta Stetter Hollingworth* (Scottsdale, AZ: Great Potential Press).

Klein, P. S. (1992). Mediating the Cognitive, Social and Aesthetic Development of Precocious Young Children. In P. S. Klein & A. J. Tannenbaum (Eds.), *To Be Young and Gifted* (pp. 245–77). Norwood, NJ: Ablex Publishing.

Koch, Kenneth & Farrell, Kate (Eds.). (1985). *Talking to the Sun: An Illustrated Anthology of Poems for Young People.* New York: Henry Holt & Company.

Koempel, Leslie Alice. (1960). Folsom, Joseph Kirk 1893–1960. *American Sociological Review* 25 (6): 959–60.

L'Abate, Luciano. (2009). *The Praeger Handbook of Play Across the Life Cycle: Fun from Infancy to Old Age.* Santa Barbara, CA: ABC Clio.

Lamore, R.; Root-Bernstein, R. S.; Lawton, J.; Schweitzer, J.; Root-Bernstein, M. M.; Roraback, E.; Peruski, A.; Van Dyke, M. & Fernandez, L. (2013). Arts and Crafts: Critical to Economic Innovation, *Econonic Development Quarterly,* 27 (3): 221–229. See also ArtSmarts and Innovators in Science, Technology, Engineering and Mathematics (STEM) [White paper]. Lansing, MI: Center for Community Economic Development, Michigan State University, 2011, http://www.ced.msu.edu/reports/ARTSMART%20Report-FINAL.pdf.

Lane, Margaret. (1980). *The Drug-Like Brontë Dream.* London: John Murray. (Originally published in 1952)

Langeveld, M. J. 1983. The Stillness of the Secret Place. *Phenomenology & Pedagogy* 1 (1): 12–13.

Lee, David M. (2000–2001). *Nobel Voices Video Project, 2000–2001.* The Smithsonian Institution, Interview. Retrieved October 19, 2011 from http://invention.smithsonian.org/downloads/fa_nobel_lee.pdf.

Lee, J. C. (2002). Interview with Claes Oldenburg. In *Claes Oldenburg drawings (1959–1977) in the Whitney Museum of American Art.* Exhibit Catalogue. New York: Harry N. Abrams, Inc.

Le Guin, Ursula. (July 1973). A Citizen of Mondath. *Foundation, The Review of Science Fiction,* 4: 20–24.

———. (1976). *The Left Hand of Darkness.* New York: Ace Books.

———. (1985). *Always Coming Home.* New York: Harper and Row.

Leland, John. (December 4, 2005). The Gamer as Artiste. *New York Times, Week in Review,* p. 1.

Lem, Stanislaw. (1984). *Microworlds: Writings on Science Fiction and Fantasy.* (Franz Rottensteiner, Ed.) New York: Harcourt Brace Jovanovich.

———. (1995). *Highcastle: A Remembrance* (M. Kandel, Trans.). New York: Harcourt Brace.

Levernier, Jacob G.; Mottweiler, Candice M.; and Taylor, Marjorie. (July 2013). The Creation of Imaginary Worlds in Middle Childhood. Conference paper presented at *Making Sense of Play,* Mansfield College, University of Oxford.

Levy, Silvano. (1997). *Desmond Morris: 50 Years of Surrealism.* London: Barrie & Jenkins Limited/Random House.

——— (2001). *Desmond Morris: Analytical Catalogue Raisonné, 1944–2000.* Antwerp: Pandora.

Lewin, Tamar. (January 20, 2010). Children Awake? Then They're Probably Online. *New York Times,* p. A1.

———. (October 25, 2011). Children Watching More Than Ever. *New York Times,* p. A16.

Lewis, C. S. (1955). *Surprised By Joy: The Shape of My Early Life.* New York: Harcourt, Brace & World.

Lichtenberg, James; Woock, Chris & Wright, Mary. (2008). *Ready to Innovate, Key Findings.* New York: The Conference Board, Inc. Retrieved April 30, 2013, from http://www.artsusa.org/pdf/information_services/research/policy_roundtable/ready_to_innovate.pdf.

———. (2008). *Reading to Innovate: Are Educators and Executives Aligned on the Creative Readiness of the U.S. Workforce?* The Conference Board, Research Report 1424.

Lindner, Robert. (1955). *The Fifty-Minute Hour: A Collection of Psychoanalytic Tales.* New York: Rinehart & Co.

Linn, Susan. (2004). *Consuming Kids: The Hostile Takeover of Childhood.* New York: The New Press.

———. (2008). *The Case for Make Believe: Saving Play in a Commercialized World.* New York: The New Press.

Lionni, Leo. (1997). *Between Worlds: The Autobiography of Leo Lionni.* New York: Alfred A. Knopf.

———. (1977). *Parallel Botany.* New York: Alfred A. Knopf.

Lobdell, Jared. (2005). *The Rise of Tolkienian Fantasy.* Peru, IL: Carus Publishing Company.

Louv, Richard. (2006). *Last Child in the Woods: Saving Our Children from Nature-Deficit Disorder.* Chapel Hill, NC: Algonquin Books of Chapel Hill.

Lubart, Todd & J. -H. Guignard. (2004). The Generality-Specificity of Creativity: A Multivariate Approach. In Robert Sternberg, E. Grigorenko & J. Singer (Eds.). *Creativity: From Potential to Realization* (pp. 43–56).Washington, DC: American Psychological Association.

Ludwig, Arnold M. (1995). *The Price of Greatness: Resolving the Creativity and Madness Controversy.* New York: The Guilford Press.

Lynskey, Dorian. (May 11, 2007). A Legend in His Own Mind. *The Guardian.* Retrieved April 9, 2011, from http://www.guardian.co.uk/music/2007/may/11/urban.popandrock.

Lyons, Beauvais. (1985). The Excavation of the Apasht: Artifacts from an Imaginary Past. *Leonardo: Journal of the International Society for the Arts, Sciences and Technology,* 18(2): 81–89. See also: Lyons, Beauvais. Issues Raised by Folk Art Parody. *Hokes Archives.* Essay retrieved April 2, 2008, from http://web.utk.edu/~blyons/.

MacGregor, John M. (2002). *Henry Darger: In the Realms of the Unreal.* New York: Delano Greenidge Editions.

MacKeith, Stephen A. (1982–1983). Paracosms and the Development of Fantasy in Childhood. *Imagination, Cognition and Personality,* vol. 2 (3): 261–67.

MacPherson, Karen. (October 1, 2002). Development Experts Say Children Suffer Due to Lack of Unstructured Fun. Post-Gazette Now (*Pittsburgh Post-Gazette*). Retrieved May 20, 2009, from http://www.post-gazette.com.

———. (August 15, 2004). Experts Concerned about Children's Creative Thinking. Post Gazette Now (*Pittsburgh Post-Gazette*). Retrieved February 17, 2009, from www.post-gazette. com/pg/04228/361969.stm.

Magik Theatre. (2008). *Roxaboxen by Alice McLerran* Study Guide. Retrieved May 18, 2009, from http://www.magiktheatre.org/study_guides/Roxaboxen_Study_Guide.pdf.

Malkin, Benjamin Heath. (1997). *A Father's Memoirs of His Child.* Washington, DC: Woodstock Books. (Originally published in 1806)

Markoff, John. (August 10, 2010). In a Video Game, Tackling the Complexities of Protein Folding. *New York Times,* D3.

Marzano, R.; Gaddy; B. & Dean, C. (2000). *What Works in Classroom Instruction.* Aurora, CO: Mid-continent Research for Education and Learning (McREL).

McBride, James. (1996). *The Color of Water: A Black Man's Tribute to His White Mother.* New York: Riverhead Books.

McCurdy, Harold G. (1957). The Childhood Pattern of Genius. *Journal of the Elisha Mitchell Scientific Society,* 73: 448–62.

———. (1960). The Childhood Pattern of Genius. *Horizon,* 11(5): 32–38.

———. (1966). *Barbara: The Unconscious Autobiography of a Child Genius*. In collaboration with Helen Follett. Chapel Hill: University of North Carolina Press.

McGreevy, A. L. (1995). The Parsonage Children: An Analysis of the Creative Early Years of the Brontës at Haworth. *Gifted Child Quarterly*, 19(3): 146–53.

McLerran, Alice. (1998). *The Legacy of Roxaboxen: A Collection of Voices*. Spring, TX: Absey & Company.

McLuhan, Marshall. (1964). *Understanding Media: The Extensions of Man*. New York: Mc-Graw Hill.

McLynn, Frank. (1993). *Robert Louis Stevenson: A Biography*. London: Hutchinson.

———. (1996). *Carl Gustav Jung*. New York: St. Martin's Press.

Mechling, Lauren. (July 23, 2006). Drawing on Life's Experiences, However Few. *New York Times,* p. AR 29.

Meier, Deborah. (1995). *The Power of Their Ideas: Lessons for America from a Small School in Harlem.* Boston: Beacon Press.

———. (2002). *In Schools We Trust*. Boston: Beacon Press.

———. (November/December 2006). What Happened to Play? Retrieved February 16, 2009, from http://www.deborahmeier.com/Columns/column06-11.htm.

Meier, Deborah. & Oschshorn, Susan. (2006). Mission statement: In Defense of Childhood, New York Voices of Childhood. Retrieved February 16, 2009 from http://www.deborah-meier.com/Columns/column06-11.htm.

Menikoff, Barry. (1984). *Robert Louis Stevenson and "The Beach of Falesá": A Study in Victorian Publishing.* Stanford, CA: Stanford University Press.

Mergen, Bernard. (1995). Past Play: Relics, Memory, and History. In A. D. Pellegrini (Ed.), *The Future of Play Theory: A Multidisciplinary Inquiry into the Contributions of Brian Sutton-Smith* (pp. 257–74). Albany, NY: State University of New York Press.

Milgram, R. M. (1990). Creativity: An Idea Whose Time Has Come and Gone? In M. A. Runco and R. S. Alberts (Eds.). *Theories of Creativity* (pp. 215–33). Newbury Park, CA: Sage.

Milgram, Roberta & Hong, Eunsook. (1994). Creative Thinking and Creative Performance in Adolescents as Predictors of Creative Attainments in Adults: A Follow-Up Study after 18 Years. In R. Subotnik & K. Arnold (Eds.). *Beyond Terman: Longitudinal Studies in Contemporary Gifted Education*, pp. 212–28. Norwood, NJ: Ablex Publishing.

Miller, S. (1973). "Ends, Means, and Galumphing: Some Leitmotifs of Play." *American Anthropologist* 75: 87–98.

Milne, Jonathan. (2008). *Go! The Art of Change*. Wellington, NZ: Steele Roberts Publishers.

Minton, Henry L. (1988). *Lewis M. Terman: Pioneer in Psychological Testing.* New York: New York University Press.

Mitchell, Robert W. (Ed.). (2002). *Pretending and Imagination in Animals and Children*. Cambridge: Cambridge University Press.

Mitchison, Naomi. (September 18, 1954). One Ring to Bind Them: *The New Statesman and Nation,* p. 331.

Montour, Kathleen. (1976). Three Precocious Boys: What Happened to Them. *The Gifted Child Quarterly* 20(2): 173–79.

Moore, Melissa & Russ, Sandra W. (2008). Follow-up of a Pretend Play Intervention: Effects on Play, Creativity, and Emotional Processes in Children. *Creativity Research Journal*, 20(4): 427–36.

Morelock, M. (1997). Imagination, Logic and the Exceptionally Gifted. *Roeper Review* 19 (3): 1–4.

Morris, Desmond. (1970). *Patterns of Reproductive Behaviour: Collected Papers by Desmond Morris*. London: Jonathan Cape, Ltd.

————. (1974). Biomorphia. Reprinted in S. Levy. (1997). *Desmond Morris: 50 Years of Surrealism.* London: Barrie & Jenkins.

————. (1980). *Animal Days.* New York: William Morrow and Company. (Originally published in 1979)

————. (1987). *The Secret Surrealist: The Paintings of Desmond Morris.* Oxford: Phaidon Press Limited.

Morrison, Delmont & Morrison, Shirley Linden.(2006). *Memories of Loss and Dreams of Perfection: Unsuccessful Childhood Grieving and Adult Creativity.* Amityville, NY: Baywood Publishing Company.

Murphy, Richard. (1974). *Imaginary Worlds: Notes on a New Curriculum.* New York: Teachers & Writers Collaborative.

Najjar, Lawrence J. (1996a). *The Effects of Multimedia and Elaborative Encoding on Learning.* Technical Report, School of Psychology and Graphics, Visualization, and Usability Laboratory, Georgia Institute of Technology. Retrieved June 3, 2009, from ftp://ftp.cc.gatech.edu/pub/gvu/tr/1996/96-05.pdf.

————. (1996b). Multimedia Information and Learning. *Journal of Educational Multimedia and Hypermedia* 5(2): 129–50.

Newitz, Annalee. (September 8, 2007). You Can't Beat Reality. *New Scientist,* 30–31.

Norman, Donald. (1993). *Things That Make Us Smart: Defending Human Attributes in the Age of the Machine.* New York: Addison-Wesley.

Ochse, R. (1990). *Before the Gates of Excellence: The Determinants of Creative Genius.* Cambridge: Cambridge University Press.

Okrent, Arika. (2009). *In the Land of Invented Languages.* New York: Spiegel & Grau.

Osbourne, Lloyd. (1924). *An Intimate Portrait of R.L.S.* New York: Charles Scribner's Sons.

————. (1923–1924). Stevenson at Play, War Correspondence from Stevenson's Note-Book. In Robert Louis Stevenson, *The Works of Robert Louis Stevenson.* (Tusitala Edition, vol. 30, pp. 191– 19X). London: William Heinemann.

Overbaugh, Richard C. & Schultz, Lynn. Bloom's Taxonomy. Retrieved May 19, 2009, from http://ww2.odu.edu/educ/roverbau/Bloom/blooms_taxonomy.htm.

Overbeck, Joy. (October/November 2006). Todd Siler. *Colorado Expression* 15(5): 72–74.

Overby, Lynnett Young; Post, Beth C. & Newman, Diane. (2005). *Interdisciplinary Learning Through Dance: 101 Moventures.* Champaign, IL: Human Kinetics.

Paley, Vivian Gussin. (2004). *A Child's Work: The Importance of Fantasy Play.* Chicago: The University of Chicago Press.

Peppler, Kylie A. & Kafai, Yasmini B. (2005). Creative Coding: Programming for Personal Expression. Available at http://download.scratch.mit.edu/CreativeCoding.pdf.

Pesce, Mark. (2000). *The Playful World: How Technology Is Transforming Our Imagination.* New York: Ballantine Books.

Pew Internet and American Life Project. (September 16, 2008). Teens, Video Games, and Civics. Retrieved April 10, 2014 from http://www.pewinternet.org/2008/09/16/teens-video-games-and-civics/.

Piaget, Jean. (1962). *Play, Dreams and Imitation in Childhood.* C. Gattegno and F. M. Hodgson (Trans.). New York: W. W. Norton & Company. (Originally published in French, 1946)

Piaget, J. & B. Inhelder. (1969). *The Psychology of the Child.* New York: Basic Books. Trans. H. Weaver. (Originally published in1966)

Pink, Daniel. (2005). *A Whole New Mind: Why Right-Brainers Will Rule the Future.* New York: Riverhead Boos/Penguin Books.

Plotz, Judith. (2001). *Romanticism and the Vocation of Childhood.* New York: Palgrave.

Polanyi, M. (1958). *Personal Knowledge: Towards a Post-Critical Philosophy.* Chicago: University of Chicago Press.

Pope-Hennessy, James. (1971). *Anthony Trollope*. London: Phoenix Press.

Prairie Creek Community School, Village Game (n.d.). Available at http://prairiecreek.type-pad.com/the_game_of_village.

Pritchard, Miriam C. (1951). The Contributions of Leta S. Hollingworth to the Study of Gifted Children. In Paul Witty (Ed.). *The Gifted Child* (pp. 47–85). Boston: D. C. Heath and Co.

Raskin, Paul; Banuri, Tariz; Gallopin, Gilberto; Gutman, Pablo; Hammond, Al; Kates, Robert & Swart, Rob. (2002). *Great Transition: The Promise and Lure of the Times Ahead*. Boston: Stockholm Environment Institute.

Ratchford, Fannie Elizabeth. (1949). *The Brontës Web of Childhood*. New York: Columbia University Press.

Raw Vision, quarterly journal, website page retrieved April 11, 2011, from http://www.rawvision.com/rawvision/whatisrv.html.

Remy, Michel. (1991). *The Surrealist World of Desmond Morris*. (Léon Sagaru, Trans.). London: Jonathan Cape.

Resnick, Mitchel. (December/January 2007–2008). Sowing the Seeds for a More Creative Society. *Learning & Leading with Technology*, pp. 18–22. (International Society for Technology in Education at www.iste.org).

Richards, Ellen H. (1910). *Euthenics: The Science of Controllable Environment*. Boston: Whitcomb & Barrows.

Robinson, Ken. (2011). *Out of Our Minds: Learning to Be Creative* (revised edition). Chichester: Wiley. (Originally published in 2001)

Rochat, Philippe. (2013). The Meaning of Play in Relation to Creativity. Essay commissioned by the Lego Foundation, for David Gauntlett & Bo Stjerne Thomsen, *Cultures of Creativity: Nurturing Creative Mindsets across Cultures*. Retrieved October 1, 2013, from http://www.legofoundation.com/en-us/research-and-learning/foundation-research/cultures-of-creativity/.

Root-Bernstein, Michele. (2009). Imaginary Worldplay as an Indicator of Creative Giftedness. In L. Shavinina (Ed.). *The International Handbook on Giftedness* (pp. 599–616). London: Springer Science.

———. (2013a). The Creation of Imaginary Worlds. In M. Taylor (Ed.). *Oxford Handbook of the Development of Imagination* (pp. 417–37). Oxford: Oxford University Press.

———. (2013b).Worldplay as Creative Practice and Educational Strategy. In L. Book & D. P. Phillips (Eds.). *Creativity and Entrepreneurship: Changing Currents in Education and Public Life* (pp.55–65). Northampton, MA: Edward Elgar Publishing.

Root-Bernstein, Michele & Overby, Lynnette. (2012). Thinking Tools and the Multi-Disciplinary Imagination: Exploring Abstraction in Dance and Creative Writing. Workshop packet, developed in association with the John F. Kennedy Center for the Performing Arts. Unpublished; available from the authors.

Root-Bernstein, Michele & Root-Bernstein, Robert. (2005). Body Thinking Beyond Dance. In Lynnette Young Overby & Billie Lepczyk (Eds.). *Dance: Current Selected Research* (vol. 5, pp. 173–201). New York: AMS Press.

———. (2006). Imaginary Worldplay in Childhood and Maturity and Its Impact on Adult Creativity, *Creativity Research Journal* 18 (4): 405–25.

Root-Bernstein, Robert. (1983). Mendel and Methodology. *History of Science*, xxi, 275–95.

———. (1989a). How Do Scientists Really Think? *Perspectives in Biology and Medicine* 32: 472–88.

———. (1989b). *Discovering: Inventing and Solving Problems at the Frontiers of Scientific Knowledge*. Cambridge, MA: Harvard University Press.

———. (2005). ArtScience: The Essential Connection. *Leonardo* 38 (4): 318–21.

———. (2009). Multiple Giftedness in Adults: The Case of Polymaths. In L. V. Shavinina (Eds), *International Handbook on Giftedness* (pp. 853–70). London: Springer Science.

Root-Bernstein, R.; Allen, L.; Beach; L.; Bhadula, R.; Fast, J.; Hosey, C.; Dremkow, B.; Lapp, J.; Lonc, K.; Pawelec, K.; Podufaly, A.; Russ, C.; Tennant, L.; Vrtis E. & Weinlander, S. (2008). Arts Foster Success: Comparison of Nobel Prizewinners, Royal Society, National Academy, and Sigma Xi members. *Journal of the Psychology of Science and Technology* 1 (2): 51–63.

Root-Bernstein, R.; Bernstein, M. & Garnier H. (1995). Correlations between Avocations, Scientific Style, Work Habits, and Professional Impact of Scientists. *Creativity Research Journal* 8: 115–37.

Root-Bernstein, R.; Lamore, R.; Lawton, J.; Schweitzer, J.; Root-Bernstein, M. M.; Roraback, E.; Peruski, A. & Van Dyke, M. (2013). Arts, Crafts and STEM Innovation: A Network Approach to Understanding the Creative Knowledge Economy. In Michael Rush (Ed.). *Creative Communitics: Art Works in Economic. Development* (pp. 97–117). Washington D C: National Endowment for the Arts and The Brookings Institution.

Root-Bernstein, Robert & Root-Bernstein, Michele. (1999). *Sparks of Genius: The Thirteen Thinking Tools of the World's Most Creative People.* New York: Houghton Mifflin.

———. (2004). Artistic Scientists and Scientific Artists: The Link between Polymathy and Creativity. In R. Sternberg, E. Grigorenko, & J. Singer (Eds.). *Creativity: From Potential to Realization* (pp. 127–51). Washington, DC: American Psychological Association.

———. (2011). Life Stages of Creativity. In M. Runco & S. Pritzker (Eds.), *The Encyclopedia of Creativity* (2nd ed., pp. 47–55). Oxford: Elsevier.

Rose, Barbara. (1970). *Claes Oldenburg.* New York: The Museum of Modern Art.

Runco, Mark. (2007). *Creativity, Theories and Themes: Research, Development, and Practice.* New York: Elsevier.

Russ, Sandra W. (2006). Pretend Play, Affect, and Creativity. *New Directions in Aesthetics, Creativity, and the Arts,* 1: 239–50.

Sacks, Oliver. (2001). *Uncle Tungsten: Memories of a Chemical Boyhood.* New York: Alfred A. Knopf.

Savage-Rumbaugh, S. & Lewin, R.. (1994). *Kanzi: The Ape at the Brink of the Human Mind.* New York: John Wiley & Sons.

Sawyer, R. K.; John-Stein, V.; Moran, S.; Sternberg, R. J.; Feldman, D. H.; Nakamura; J., Csikszentmihalyi, M. (2003). *Creativity and Development.* New York: Oxford University Press.

Schneider, Dan. (February 16, 2008). The Dan Schneider Interview 8: Desmond Morris. Retrieved September 29, 2008 from www.cosmoetica.com/DSI8.htm.

Seagoe, May V. (1975). *Terman and the Gifted.* Los Altos, CA: William Kaufmann.

Seith, E. (October 29, 2010), State of Emergency Allows Pupils to Experience and Judge a National Crisis, *Times Educational Supplement Scotland.* Available at http://www.tes.co.uk/article.aspx?storycode=6061845 (accessed April 21, 2011).

Shaler, Nathaniel Southgate. (1909). *The Autobiography of Nathaniel Southgate Shaler.* Boston: Houghton Mifflin.

Shapiro, Jordan. (February 18, 2013). How Game-Based Learning Can Save the Humanities, *Forbes.com.* Retrieved August 27, 2013, from http://www.forbes.com/sites/jordanshapiro/2013/02/18/how-game-based-learning-can-save-the-humanities/.

———. (February 27, 2013). Sesame Workshop Wants Your Kid to Design Video Games, *Forbes.com.* Retrieved August 27, 2013, from http://www.forbes.com/sites/jordanshapiro/2013/02/27/sesame-workshop-wants-your-kid-to-design-video-games/.

———. (April 1, 2013). Microsoft Launches "Kodu" Game Design Challenge for Younger Kids, *Forbes.com*. Retrieved August 27, 2013, from http://www.forbes.com/sites/jordanshapiro/2013/04/01/microsoft-launches-kodu-game-design-challenge-for-younger-kids/.

Shekerjian, Denise. (1990). *Uncommon Genius: How Great Ideas Are Born*. New York: Viking.

Shippey. Tom. (2003). *The Road to Middle-Earth*. Boston: Houghton Mifflin.

Shmukler, Diana. (1988). Imagination and Creativity in Childhood: The Influence of the Family. In *Organizing Early Experience: Imagination and Cognition in Childhood*. (Demont C. Morrison, Ed). pp. 77–91. New York: Baywood Publishing Co.

Shortling, Grobius.(n.d.). *Imaginary Places*. Retrieved April 9, 2011, from www.estalia.net/imaginary/.

Shurkin, Joel N. (1992). *Terman's Kids: The Groundbreaking Study of How the Gifted Grow Up*. Boston: Little, Brown & Co.

Siler, Todd. (1990). *Breaking the Mind Barrier: The Artscience of Neurocosmology*. New York: Simon and Schuster.

———. (April 10, 1995). ArtScience: Integrating the Arts and Sciences to Connect Our World and Improve Communication. Keynote Address, NAEA, Houston, TX.

———. (1996). *Think Like A Genius*. New York: Bantam Books.

———. (February 2001). Questions and Answers: Todd Siler PhD '86. *openDOOR* (MIT Alumni Association). Retrieved September 9, 2011, from http://www.feldmangallery.com/media/siler/general%20press/2001_siler_mit%20opendoor.pdf.

———. (2003). Fractal Reactor: A New Geometry for Plasma Fusion. *Proceedings of the Third Symposium on Current Trends in International Fusion*. Ottawa: NRC Research Press.

———. (2007). Todd Siler, Adventures in ArtScience July 11–November 9, 2007. Exhibit, National Science Foundation, Arlington, VA.

———. (March 2009). A Wake-Up Call for Cultivating a World of Creative-Critical Thinkers, Problem Solvers & Innovators. Unpublished paper. Creativity: Worlds in the Making Symposium. Wake Forest University.

Siler, Todd & Psi-Phi Technology Corporation. (2008). *Think Like a Genius*, software and website: http://www.thinklikeagenius.com/.

Silvey, Robert. (1974). *Who's Listening? The Story of BBC Audience Research*. London: George Allen & Unwin.

———. (May 13, 1977). But That Was In Another Country. . . . *Times Educational Supplement*, 18.

Silvey, Robert & Stephen MacKeith. (1988). The Paracosm: A Special Form of Fantasy. In Delmont C. Morrison (Ed.). *Organizing Early Experience: Imagination and Cognition in Childhood* (pp. 173–97). Amityville, NY: Baywood Publishing Company.

Simner, J.; Mulvenna, C; Sagiv, N; Tsakanikos, E; Witherby, S. A.; Fraser, C; Scott, K; & Ward, J. (2006). Synaesthesia: The Prevalence of Typical Cross-modal Experiences. *Perception* 35 (8): 1024–33.

Simner, J.; Harrold, J; Creed, H; Monro, L. & Foulkes, L. (2009). Early Detection of Markers for Synaesthesia in Childhood Populations. *Brain* 132: 57–64.

Simonton, Dean Keith. (2010). So You Want to Become a Creative Genius? You *Must* Be Crazy! In D. H. Cropley, A. J. Cropley, J. C. Kaufman, & M. Runco (Eds.), *The Dark Side of Creativity* (pp. 218–34). New York: Cambridge University Press.

Singer, D. G. & Singer, J. L. (1990). *The House of Make-Believe: Play and the Developing Imagination*. Cambridge: Harvard University Press.

———. (2001). *Make-Believe: Games and Activities for Imaginative Play*, APA Books/Magination Press.

———. (2005). *Imagination and Play in the Electronic Age.* Cambridge, MA: Harvard University Press.

Singer, J. L. (1975). *The Inner World of Daydreaming.* New York: Harper & Row.

Singer, Jerome & Singer, Dorothy G. (2005–2006). Preschoolers' Imaginative Play as Precursor of Narrative Consciousness. *Imagination, Cognition and Personality* 25 (2): 97–117.

Smilansky, S. (1968). *The Effects of Sociodramatic Play on Disadvantaged Preschool Children.* New York: Wiley.

Smith, Dinitia. (October 7, 2003). Finding a Middle Earth in Montana. *New York Times,* B1.

Snyder, Jon; Lieberman, Ann; Macdonald, Maritza B. & Goodwin, A. Lin. (August 1992). Makers of Meaning in a Learning-Centered School: A Case Study of Central Park East 1 Elementary School. Research Report. Retrieved February 24, 2009, from http://www.eric.ed.gov/ERICDocs/data/ericdocs2sql/contant_storage_01/0000019b/80/13/91/a9.pdf.

Sobel, David. (1993). *Children's Special Places: Exploring the Role of Forts, Dens, and Bush Houses in Middle Childhood.* Tucson, AZ: Zephyr Press.

Solomon, Maynard. (1995). *Mozart: A Life.* New York: HarperCollins.

Spitz, Ellen Handler. (2006). *The Brightening Glance: Imagination and Childhood.* New York: Pantheon Books.

Spring, Justin. (2000). *Fairfield Porter: A Life in Art.* New Haven: Yale University Press.

Steinkuehler, Constance. (November 17, 2006). Virtual Worlds, Learning, & the New Pop Cosmopolitanism. *Teachers College Record.* Retrieved November 18, 2006, from http://www.tcrecord.org, ID Number: 12843.

Sternberg, Robert J. (2003). The Development of Creativity as a Decision-Making Process. In R. K. Sawyer, V. John-Steiner, S. Moran, R. J. Sternberg, D. H. Feldman, J. Nakamura & M. Csikszentmihalyi (Eds.), *Creativity and Development* (pp. 91–138). Oxford: Oxford University Press.

Sternberg, Robert J. & Lubart, T. (1992). Creative Giftedness in Children. In P. S. Klein & A. J. Tannenbaum, (Eds.). *To Be Young and Gifted* (pp. 33–51). Norwood, NJ: Ablex Publishing.

Stevens, Wallace. (1997). The Necessary Angel. In *Wallace Stevens Collected Poetry and Prose.* New York: Literary Classics of the United States. (Originally published in 1954)

[Stevenson, Robert Louis.] (1888/1920). *Learning to Write: Suggestions and Counsel from Robert Louis Stevenson.* J. W. Rogers, Jr., (Ed.). New York: Charles Scribner's Sons.

Stevenson, Robert Louis. (1912). *Treasure Island: With a Preface by Mrs. Stevenson.* New York: Charles Scribner's Sons. (Originally published in 1894)

———. (1923–1924). *The Works of Robert Louis Stevenson.* Tusitala Edition. London: William Heinemann, 35 vols.

———. (1947). *Selected Writings of Robert Louis Stevenson.* Saxe Commins (Ed.). New York: The Modern Library.

Stokes, Patricia. (2006). *Creativity From Constraints: The Psychology of Breakthrough.* New York: Springer Publishing Co.

Stout, Hilary. (January 6, 2011). Play's the Thing . . . *The New York Times,* D1.

Strausbaugh, John. (February 22, 2009). His Secret World, Opening to Tourists. *New York Times,* AR 30.

Strauss, Neil. (February 2, 2004). A Well-Imagined Star, Unearthing a Trove of Albums That Never Existed. *New York Times,* B1.

Stravinsky, Igor. (1970). *Poetics of Music in the Form of Six Lessons.* (Arthur Knodel & Ingolf Dahl, Trans.). Cambridge, MA: Harvard University Press. (Originally published in 1942)

Subotnik, R.; Kassan, L.; Summers, E. & Wasser, A. (1993). *Genius Revisited: High IQ Children Grown Up.* Norwood, NJ: Ablex Publishing.

Suvin, Darko. (1970). The Open-Ended Parables of Stanislaw Lem and "Solaris." Afterword in Stanislaw Lem, *Solaris* (1961/1970). New York: Walker and Company.

Swearingen, Roger G. (1980). *The Prose Writings of Robert Louis Stevenson: A Guide*. Archon Books.

Swirski, Peter. (1997). *A Stanislaw Lem Reader*. Evanston, IL: Northwestern University Press.

———. (Winter 2003). Solaris Author Commands a Cult Following. *Ideas* (Faculty of Arts, University of Alberta). Retrieved November 5, 2008, from http://www.uofaweb.ualberta.ca/arts_new//pdfs/Ideas_Winter_2003.pdf.

Tannenbaum, A. J. (1992). Early Signs of Giftedness: Research and Commentary. In P. S. Klein and A. J. Tannenbaum, (Eds.) *To Be Young and Gifted* (pp. 3–32). Norwood, NJ: Ablex Publishing.

Taylor, Marjorie. (1999). *Imaginary Companions and the Children Who Create Them*. New York: Oxford University Press.

Taylor, Paul. (1987). *Private Domain*. New York: Alfred A. Knopf.

Terman, Lewis. (1915). The Mental Hygiene of Exceptional Children. *Pedagogical Seminary* 22: 529–37.

———. (1917). The Intelligence Quotient of Francis Galton in Childhood. *American Journal of Psychology* 28: 209–15.

———. (1919). *The Intelligence of School Children*. New York: Houghton Mifflin.

Terman, L. M., assisted by B. T. Baldwin, E. Bronson, J. C. DeVoss, F. Fuller, F. L. Goodenough, T. L. Kelley, M. Lima, H. Marshall, A. H. Moore, A. S. Raubenhaimner, G. M. Ruch, R. L. Willoughby, J. B. Wyman, & D. H.Yates. (1954). *Mental and Physical Traits of a Thousand Gifted Children, vol. 1. Genetic Studies of Genius* (2nd ed.). Stanford, CA: Stanford University Press. (Originally published in 1925)

Terman, L. M. & Oden, M. H. (1959). *The Gifted Group at Mid-Life, vol. 5. Genetic Studies of Genius*. Stanford, CA: Stanford University Press.

Terry, R. C. (Ed.). (1996). *Robert Louis Stevenson: Interview and Recollections*. London: MacMillan.

Tinbergen, N. (October 1, 1975). The Importance of Being Playful, *Times Educational Supplement*, 19–21.

Tolkien, Christopher (Ed.). (1992). *Pictures by J.R.R. Tolkien*. Boston: Houghton Mifflin Co.

Tolkien, J. R. R. (1965). *The Lord of the Rings* (vols. 1–3). Boston: Houghton Mifflin.

———. (1983). *The Monsters and the Critics and Other Essays*. (Christopher Tolkien, Ed.). London: George Allen & Unwin.

Tolkien, J. R. R. & Swann, Donald. (1967). *The Road Goes Ever On: A Song Cycle*. Boston: Houghton Mifflin.

Toth, Susan Allen. (March/April 1994). The Importance of Time Alone. *Family Life*, 81–85.

Tréhin, Gilles. Artwork at http://urville.com/. Further information at http://www.wisconsin-medicalsociety.org/savant_syndrome/savant_profiles/gilles_trehin.

Turkle, Sherry. (1995). *Life on the Screen: Identity in the Age of the Internet*. New York: Simon & Schuster.

Turner, Mark. (1996). *The Literary Mind*. New York: Oxford University Press.

U.S. Census Bureau. (2004–2005). Table 1232. Attendance Rates for Various Arts Activities: 2002 and Table 1238. Adult Participation in Selected Leisure Activities by Frequency: 2003. *Statistical Abstract of the United States: 2004–2005*, 768, 771. Arts, Entertainment and Recreation. Retrieved October 7, 2006, from http://www.census.gov/prod/2004pubs/094statab/arts.pdf.

Ustinov, Peter. (1998). *Dear Me*. London: Arrow Books. (Originally published in 1976)

VanderMeer, Jeff. (October 2007). Dangerous Offspring: An Interview with Steph Swainston. *Clarkesworld* Magazine, http://clarkesworldmagazine.com/swainston_interview/.

Van Manen, Max. (1990). *Researching Lived Experience: Human Science for an Action Sensitive Pedagogy.* London, Ontario, Canada: The University of Western Ontario/The State University of New York.

Van Manen, M. & B. Levering. (1996). *Childhood's Secrets: Intimacy, Privacy, and the Self Reconsidered.* New York: Teachers College Press.

Van't Hoff, J. H. (1967). Imagination in Science (G. F. Springer, Trans.). *Molecular Biology, Biochemistry, and Biophysics, 1*, 1–18. (Original work published in 1878)

The Village Project. (n.d.). Available at http://www.villageproject.org/moreinformation.htm (accessed April 21, 2011). See also The Game of Village, available at http://www.thegameofvillage.com/about.html (accessed May 2, 2011).

Watts, Alan. (1973*). In My Own Way: An Autobiography 1915–1965.* New York: Vintage Books.

Webster's Third New International Dictionary of the English Language Unabridged. (1964). Springfield, MA: G. & C. Merriam Co.

Wenner, Melinda. (February/March 2009). The Serious Need for Play. *Scientific American Mind*, 29.

Who's Who in America (vol. 28). (1953–1954). Chicago, IL: A. N. Marquis. (Continuously published since 1899)

White, R. K. (1931). The Versatility of Genius. *Journal of Social Psychology, 2*: 482.

Whitebread, David & Basilio, Marisol. (2013). Play, Culture and Creativity. Essay commissioned by the Lego Foundation, for David Gauntlett & Bo Stjerne Thomsen, *Cultures of Creativity: Nurturing Creative Mindsets across Cultures.* Retrieved October 1, 2013, from http://www.legofoundation.com/en-us/research-and-learning/foundation-research/cultures-of-creativity/.

Wilson, M. (2002). Six Views of Embodied Cognition. *Psychonomic Bulletin and Review, 9* (4): 625–36.

Winerip, Michael. (June 11, 2003). Going for Depth Instead of Prep. *New York Times.* Retrieved April 13, 2004 from http://www.ccebos.org/timesmissionhill6.11.03.html.

Winkworth, Susanna & Winkworth, Catherine. (1908). *Memorials of Two Sisters.* Margaret J. Shaen (Ed.). London: Longmans, Green and Co.

Witty, Paul. (1940). Contributions to the IQ Controversy from the Study of Superior Deviates. *School and Society*, 51 (1321): 503–8.

Wordsworth, William. (1977). *Poems. Volume I.* John O. Hayden (Ed.). New York: Penguin Books.

Wright, Austin Tappan. (1966). *Islandia.* New York: New American Library. (Originally published in 1942; introduction by Sylvia Wright originally published in 1958)

Yoder, A.H. (1894). The study of the Boyhood of Great Men. *Pedagogical Seminary*, 3 :134–56.

Ziegfeld, Richard E. (1985). *Stanislaw Lem.* New York: F. Ungar.

Zimmer, Carl. (September 1996). First, Kill the Babies. *Discover* 17 (9): 72–78.

Index

About the Author

Michele Root-Bernstein is a historian, a haiku poet, an independent scholar in creativity studies affiliated with Michigan State University, and a teaching artist associated with the John F. Kennedy Center. Co-author of the book *Sparks of Genius: The Thirteen Thinking Tools of the World's Most Creative People*, she researches, writes and workshops on the practices and processes of creative imagination in all walks of life.